Gospel Workers

GOSPEL WORKERS

Instruction for All Who Are "Laborers Together With God"

Compiled From the Complete Published
Writings of the Author, and From
Unpublished Manuscripts

———

By Mrs. E. G. White

———

Revised and Enlarged Edition

1948
REVIEW & HERALD PUBLISHING ASSN.
WASHINGTON, D. C.

PREFACE

THIS revised and enlarged edition of "Gospel Workers" needs but few words of introduction. The first edition, issued in 1892, found a place in nearly every Seventh-day Adventist home. It has become a highly prized handbook of counsel and instruction to ministers and to all other missionary workers connected with this movement.

Since the publication of the first edition the ever-active pen of the author has produced much of vital interest to this people. The work on this book was completed after the author had closed her active life work as a writer and speaker. It represents, therefore, a compilation from her complete writings. It is the ripened fruit of the life of one whom God has greatly blessed as His "messenger," to the glory of His name and the upbuilding of this movement from its beginning. The value and importance of this book will therefore be appreciated.

It is our earnest prayer that the Holy Spirit who indited these messages of counsel may be present to impress the instruction upon the hearts of all who read it. THE PUBLISHERS.

CONTENTS

[9]

Contents

Section XI. IN RELATION WITH ONE ANOTHER

Section XII. CLOSING WORDS

Called With a Holy Calling

*" Ye shall be named the Priests
of the Lord: men shall call you
the Ministers of our God."*

IN CHRIST'S STEAD

In every period of this earth's history, God has had
His men of opportunity, to whom He has said, "Ye
are My witnesses." In every age there have been de-
vout men, who gathered up the rays of light as they
flashed upon their pathway, and who spoke to the people the words of God. Enoch, Noah, Moses, Daniel,
and the long roll of patriarchs and prophets,— these
were ministers of righteousness. They were not infal-
lible; they were weak, erring men; but the Lord wrought
through them as they gave themselves to His service.

Since His ascension, Christ the great Head of the
church, has carried forward His work in the world by
chosen ambassadors, through whom He speaks to the
children of men, and ministers to their needs. The
position of those who have been called of God to labor
in word and doctrine for the upbuilding of His church,
is one of grave responsibility. In Christ's stead they
are to beseech men and women to be reconciled to
God; and they can fulfil their mission only as they
receive wisdom and power from above.

God's ministers are symbolized by the seven stars,
which He who is the first and the last has under His
special care and protection. The sweet influences that

[13]

are to be abundant in the church are bound up with these ministers of God, who are to represent the love of Christ. The stars of heaven are under God's control. He fills them with light. He guides and directs their movements. If He did not, they would become fallen stars. So with His ministers. They are but instruments in His hands, and all the good they accomplish is done through His power.

It is to the honor of Christ that He makes His ministers a greater blessing to the church, through the working of the Holy Spirit, than are the stars to the world. The Saviour is to be their efficiency. If they will look to Him as He looked to His Father, they will do His works. As they make God their dependence, He will give them His brightness to reflect to the world.

Christ's ministers are the spiritual guardians of the people entrusted to their care. Their work has been likened to that of watchmen. In ancient times, sentinels were often stationed on the walls of cities, where, from points of vantage, they could overlook important points to be guarded, and give warning of the approach of an enemy. Upon their faithfulness depended the safety of all within. At stated intervals they were required to call to one another, to make sure that all were awake, and that no harm had befallen any. The cry of good cheer or of warning was borne from one to another, each repeating the call till it echoed round the city.

To every minister the Lord declares: "O son of man, I have set thee a watchman unto the house of Israel; therefore thou shalt hear the word at My mouth, and warn them from Me. When I say unto the wicked, O wicked man, thou shalt surely die; if thou dost not speak to warn the wicked from his way, that wicked man shall die in his iniquity; but his blood will I require at thine hand. Nevertheless, if thou warn the wicked of his way to turn from it, . . . thou hast delivered thy soul." [1]

These words of the prophet declare the solemn responsibility resting upon those who are appointed as guardians of the church, stewards of the mysteries of God. They are to stand as watchmen on the walls of Zion, to sound the note of alarm at the approach of the enemy. If for any reason their spiritual senses become so benumbed that they are unable to discern danger, and through their failure to give warning the people perish, God will require at their hands the blood of those who are lost.

It is the privilege of the watchmen on the walls of Zion to live so near to God, and to be so susceptible to the impressions of His Spirit, that He can work through them to tell sinners of their peril, and point them to the place of safety. Chosen of God, sealed with the blood of consecration, they are to rescue men and women from impending destruction. Faithfully are they to warn their fellow-men of the sure result of transgression, and faithfully are they to safeguard the interests of the church. At no time may they relax their vigilance. Theirs is a work requiring the exercise of every faculty of the being. In trumpet tones their voices are to be lifted, and never should they sound one wavering, uncertain note. Not for wages are they to labor, but because they cannot do otherwise, because they realize that there is a woe upon them if they fail to preach the gospel.

[1] Eze. 33 : 7-9.

FAITHFULNESS IN SERVICE

The minister who is a co-worker with Christ will have a deep sense of the sacredness of his work, and of the toil and sacrifice required to perform it successfully. He does not study his own ease or convenience. He is forgetful of self. In his search for the lost sheep, he does not realize that he himself is weary, cold, and hungry. He has but one object in view,— the saving of the lost.

He who serves under the blood-stained banner of Emmanuel often has that to do which calls for heroic effort and patient endurance. But the soldier of the cross stands unshrinkingly in the forefront of the battle. As the enemy presses the attack against him, he turns to the Stronghold for aid; and as he brings to the Lord the promises of the Word, he is strengthened for the duties of the hour. He realizes his need of strength from above. The victories that he gains do not lead to self-exaltation, but cause him to lean more and more heavily on the Mighty One. Relying upon that power, he is enabled to present the message of salvation so forcibly that it awakens an answering chord in other minds.

The Lord sends His ministers to hold forth the word of life, to preach, not "philosophy and vain deceit," nor "science falsely so called," but the gospel, "the power of God unto salvation." [2] "I charge thee therefore," Paul wrote to Timothy, "before God, and the Lord Jesus Christ, who shall judge the quick and the dead at His appearing and His kingdom: Preach the word; be instant in season, out of season; reprove, rebuke, exhort with all long-suffering and doctrine. For the time will come when they will not endure

[2] Col. 2 : 8 ; 1 Tim. 6 : 20 ; Rom. 1 : 16.

sound doctrine; but after their own lusts shall they heap to themselves teachers, having itching ears; and they shall turn away their ears from the truth, and shall be turned unto fables. But watch thou in all things, endure afflictions, do the work of an evangelist, make full proof of thy ministry." [3] In this charge every minister has his work outlined,— a work that he can do only through the fulfilment of the promise that Jesus gave to His disciples, "Lo, I am with you alway, even unto the end." [4]

Ministers of the gospel, God's messengers to their fellow-men, should never lose sight of their mission and their responsibilities. If they lose their connection with heaven, they are in greater danger than others, and can exert a stronger influence for wrong. Satan watches them continually, waiting for some weakness to develop, through which he may make a successful attack upon them. And how he triumphs when he succeeds! for an ambassador for Christ, off his guard, allows the great adversary to secure many souls to himself.

The true minister will do nothing that would belittle his sacred office. He will be circumspect in deportment, and wise in his course of action. He will work as Christ worked; he will do as Christ did. He will use all his powers in carrying the tidings of salvation to those who know it not. A deep hunger for the righteousness of Christ will fill his heart. Feeling his need, he will seek earnestly for the power that must come to him before he can present in simplicity, truthfulness, and humility the truth as it is in Jesus.

[3] 2 Tim. 4 : 1-5.　　　　[4] Matt. 28 : 20.

EXAMPLES OF HUMAN STEADFASTNESS

God's servants receive no honor or recognition from the world. Stephen was stoned because he preached Christ and Him crucified. Paul was imprisoned, beaten, stoned, and finally put to death, because he was a faithful messenger of God to the Gentiles. The apostle John was banished to the Isle of Patmos, "for the word of God, and for the testimony of Jesus Christ." [5] These examples of human steadfastness in the might of divine power, are a witness to the world of the faithfulness of God's promises, of His abiding presence and sustaining grace.

No hope of glorious immortality lights up the future of the enemies of God. The great military commander conquers nations, and shakes the armies of half the world; but he dies of disappointment, and in exile. The philosopher who ranges in thought through the universe, everywhere tracing the manifestations of God's power and delighting in their harmony, often fails to behold in these marvelous wonders the Hand that formed them all. "Man that is in honor, and understandeth not, is like the beasts that perish." [6] But God's heroes of faith are heirs to an inheritance of greater value than any earthly riches,— an inheritance that will satisfy the longings of the soul. By the world they may be unknown and unacknowledged, but in the record books above they are enrolled as citizens of heaven, and an exalted greatness, an eternal weight of glory, will be theirs.

The greatest work, the noblest effort, in which men can engage, is to point sinners to the Lamb of God. True ministers are co-laborers with the Lord in the accomplishment of His purposes. God says to them, Go,

[5] Rev. 1 : 9.   [6] Ps. 49 : 20.

teach and preach Christ. Instruct and educate all who know not of His grace, His goodness, and His mercy. Teach the people. "How then shall they call on Him in whom they have not believed? and how shall they believe in Him of whom they have not heard? and how shall they hear without a preacher?" [7]

"How beautiful upon the mountains are the feet of him that bringeth good tidings, that publisheth peace; that bringeth good tidings of good, that publisheth salvation; that saith unto Zion, Thy God reigneth!" "Break forth into joy, sing together, ye waste places of Jerusalem: for the Lord hath comforted His people, He hath redeemed Jerusalem. The Lord hath made bare His holy arm in the eyes of all the nations; and all the ends of the earth shall see the salvation of our God." [8]

———◆———

Workers for Christ are never to think, much less to speak, of failure in their work. The Lord Jesus is our efficiency in all things; His Spirit is to be our inspiration; and as we place ourselves in His hands, to be channels of light, our means of doing good will never be exhausted. We may draw upon His fulness, and receive of that grace which has no limit.

[7] Rom. 10 : 14.   [8] Isa. 52 : 7, 9, 10.

THE SACREDNESS OF THE WORK

The minister stands as God's mouthpiece to the people, and in thought, in word, in act, he is to represent his Lord. When Moses was chosen as the messenger of the covenant, the word given him was, "Be thou for the people to Godward." [1] To-day God chooses men as He chose Moses, to be His messengers, and heavy is the woe resting on the one who dishonors his holy calling, or lowers the standard set for him in the life and labors of the Son of God.

The punishment that fell upon Nadab and Abihu, the sons of Aaron, shows how God regards those ministers who do that which dishonors their sacred office. These men were consecrated to the priesthood, but they had not learned to control themselves. Habits of self-indulgence, long cherished, had obtained a hold upon them which even the responsibility of their office had not power to break.

At the hour of worship, as the prayers and praise of the people were ascending to God, Nadab and Abihu, partially intoxicated, took each his censer, and burned fragrant incense thereon. But they transgressed God's command by using "strange fire," instead of the sacred fire which God himself had kindled, and which He had commanded should be used for this purpose. For this sin, a fire went out from the Lord, and devoured them in the sight of the people. "Then Moses said unto Aaron, This is it that the Lord spake, saying, I will be sanctified in them that come nigh Me, and before all the people I will be glorified." [2]

[1] Ex. 18 : 19.　　　[2] See Lev. 10 : 1-7.

ISAIAH'S COMMISSION

When God was about to send Isaiah with a message to His people, He first permitted the prophet to look in vision into the holy of holies within the sanctuary. Suddenly the gate and the inner veil of the temple seemed to be uplifted or withdrawn, and he was permitted to gaze within, upon the holy of holies, where even the prophet's feet might not enter. There rose before him a vision of Jehovah sitting upon a throne high and lifted up, while the train of His glory filled the temple. Around the throne were seraphim, as guards about the great King, and they reflected the glory that surrounded them. As their songs of praise resounded in deep notes of adoration, the pillars of the gate trembled, as if shaken by an earthquake. With lips unpolluted by sin, these angels poured forth the praises of God. "Holy, holy, holy, is the Lord of hosts," they cried; "the whole earth is full of His glory." [3]

The seraphim around the throne are so filled with reverential awe as they behold the glory of God, that they do not for an instant look upon themselves with admiration. Their praise is for the Lord of hosts. As they look into the future, when the whole earth shall be filled with His glory, the triumphant song is echoed from one to another in melodious chant, "Holy, holy, holy, is the Lord of hosts." They are fully satisfied to glorify God; abiding in His presence, beneath His smile of approbation, they wish for nothing more. In bearing His image, in doing His bidding, in worshiping Him, their highest ambition is reached.

As the prophet listened, the glory, the power, and the majesty of the Lord was opened to his vision; and

[3] See Isa. 6 : 1-8.

in the light of this revelation his own inward defilement appeared with startling clearness. His very words seemed vile to him. In deep humiliation he cried, "Woe is me! for I am undone; because I am a man of unclean lips: . . . for mine eyes have seen the King, the Lord of hosts."

Isaiah's humiliation was genuine. As the contrast between humanity and the divine character was made plain to him, he felt altogether inefficient and unworthy. How could he speak to the people the holy requirements of Jehovah?

"Then flew one of the seraphim unto me," he writes, "having a live coal in his hand, which he had taken with the tongs from off the altar: and he laid it upon my mouth, and said, Lo, this hath touched thy lips; and thine iniquity is taken away, and thy sin purged."

Then Isaiah heard the voice of the Lord, saying, "Whom shall I send, and who will go for us?" and strengthened by the thought of the divine touch, he answered, "Here am I; send me."

As God's ministers look by faith into the holy of holies, and see the work of our great High Priest in the heavenly sanctuary, they realize that they are men of unclean lips, men whose tongues have often spoken vanity. Well may they despair as they contrast their own unworthiness with the perfection of Christ. With contrition of heart, feeling wholly unworthy and unfit for their great work, they cry, "I am undone." But if, like Isaiah, they humble their hearts before God, the work done for the prophet will be performed for them. Their lips will be touched with a live coal from off the altar, and they will lose sight of self in a sense of the greatness and power of God and His readiness to help them. They will realize the sacredness of the work entrusted to them, and will be led to abhor everything that would cause them to dishonor Him who has sent them forth with His message.

The live coal is symbolical of purification, and it also represents the potency of the efforts of God's true servants. To those who make so full a consecration that the Lord can place His touch upon their lips, the word is spoken, Go forth into the harvest-field. I will co-operate with you.

The minister who has received this preparation will be a power for good in the world. His words will be right words, pure and true, fraught with sympathy and love; his actions will be right actions, a help and a blessing to the weak. Christ will be to him an abiding presence, controlling thought, word, and deed. He has pledged himself to overcome pride, covetousness, selfishness. As he seeks to fulfil this pledge, he gains spiritual strength. By daily communion with God he becomes mighty in a knowledge of the Scriptures. His fellowship is with the Father and the Son; and as he constantly obeys the divine will, he becomes daily better fitted to speak words that will guide wandering souls to the fold of Christ.

THE FIELD IS THE WORLD

"Jesus, walking by the Sea of Galilee, saw two brethren, Simon called Peter, and Andrew his brother, casting a net into the sea: for they were fishers. And He saith unto them, Follow Me, and I will make you fishers of men. And they straightway left their nets, and followed Him. And going on from thence, He saw two other brethren, James the son of Zebedee, and John his brother, in a ship with Zebedee their father, mending their nets; and He called them. And they immediately left the ship and their father, and followed Him." [1]

The prompt, unquestioning obedience of these men, with no promise of wages, seems remarkable; but the words of Christ were an invitation that carried with it an impelling power. Christ would make these humble fishermen, in connection with Himself, the means of taking men out of the service of Satan, and placing them in the service of God. In this work they would become his witnesses, bearing to the world His truth unmingled with the traditions and sophistries of men. By practicing His virtues, by walking and working with Him, they were to be qualified to be fishers of men.

Thus were the first disciples appointed to the work of the gospel ministry. For three years they labored in connection with the Saviour, and by His teaching, His works of healing, His example, they were prepared to carry on the work that He began. By the simplicity of faith, by pure, humble service, the disciples were taught to carry responsibilities in God's cause.

[1] Matt. 4 : 18-22.

There are lessons for us to learn from the experience of the apostles. These men were as true as steel to principle. They were men who would not fail nor be discouraged. They were full of reverence and zeal for God, full of noble purposes and aspirations. They were by nature as weak and helpless as any of those now engaged in the work, but they put their whole trust in the Lord. Wealth they had, but it consisted of mind and soul culture; and this every one may have who will make God first and last and best in everything. They toiled long to learn the lessons given them in the school of Christ, and they did not toil in vain. They bound themselves up with the mightiest of all powers, and were ever longing for a deeper, higher, broader comprehension of eternal realities, that they might successfully present the treasures of truth to a needy world.

Workers of this character are needed now, men who will consecrate themselves without reserve to the work of representing the kingdom of God to a world lying in wickedness. The world needs men of thought, men of principle, men who are constantly growing in understanding and discernment. There is great need of men who can use the press to the best advantage, that the truth may be given wings to speed it to every nation, and tongue, and people.

THE GOSPEL TO ALL COUNTRIES

Everywhere the light of truth is to shine forth, that hearts may be awakened and converted. In all countries the gospel is to be proclaimed. God's servants are to labor in places nigh and afar off, enlarging the cultivated portions of the vineyard, and going to the regions beyond. They are to work while the day lasts; for the night cometh, in which no man can work. Sinners are to be pointed to a Saviour uplifted on the cross, and from many voices is to be heard the invitation, "Behold the Lamb of God, which taketh away the sin of the world." [2] Churches are to be organized, and plans laid for work to be done by the members of the newly organized churches. As workers go forth filled with zeal, and with the love of God, the churches at home will be revived; for the success of the workers will be regarded as a subject of deep personal concern by every member of the church.

Earnest, self-sacrificing men and women are needed, who will go to God and with strong crying and tears plead for the souls that are on the brink of ruin. There can be no harvest without seed-sowing, no result without effort. Abraham was called to go forth from his home, a light-bearer to the heathen. And without questioning, he obeyed. "He went out, not knowing whither he went." [3] So to-day God's servants are to go where He calls, trusting Him to guide them and to give them success in their work.

The terrible condition of the world would seem to indicate that the death of Christ has been almost in vain, and that Satan has triumphed. The great majority of this earth's inhabitants have given their allegiance to the enemy. But we have not been deceived. Notwithstanding the apparent triumph of Satan, Christ is carrying forward His work in the heavenly sanctuary and on the earth. The word of God portrays the wickedness and corruption that would exist in the last days. As we see the fulfilment of prophecy, our faith in the final triumph of Christ's kingdom should

[2] John 1 : 29.   [3] Heb. 11 : 8.

strengthen; and we should go forth with renewed courage to do our appointed work.

The solemn, sacred message of warning must be proclaimed in the most difficult fields and in the most sinful cities, in every place where the light of the great threefold gospel message has not yet dawned. Every one is to hear the last call to the marriage supper of the Lamb. From town to town, from city to city, from country to country, the message of present truth is to be proclaimed, not with outward display, but in the power of the Spirit. As the divine principles that our Saviour came to this world to set forth in word and life, are presented in the simplicity of the gospel, the power of the message will make itself felt. In this age, a new life, coming from the Source of all life, is to take possession of every laborer. O, how little do we comprehend the breadth of our mission! We need a faith that is earnest and determined, and a courage that is unshaken. Our time for work is short, and we are to labor with unflagging zeal.

"The field is the world." [4] We understand better what this saying comprehends than did the apostles who received the commission to preach the gospel. The whole world is a vast missionary field, and we who have long known the gospel message should be encouraged by the thought that fields which were once difficult of access are now easily entered. Countries hitherto closed to the gospel are opening their doors, and are pleading for the word of God to be explained to them. Kings and princes are opening their long-closed gates, inviting the heralds of the cross to enter. The harvest truly is great. Eternity alone will reveal the results of well-directed efforts put forth now.

[4] Matt. 13 : 38.

Providence is going before us, and Infinite Power is working with human effort. Blind indeed must be the eyes that do not see the working of the Lord, and deaf the ears that do not hear the call of the True Shepherd to His sheep.

Christ longs to extend His sway over every human mind. He longs to stamp His image and character upon every soul. When He was on this earth, He hungered for sympathy and co-operation, that His kingdom might extend and embrace the whole world. This earth is His purchased possession, and He would have men free and pure and holy. "For the joy that was set before Him," He "endured the cross, despising the shame." [5] His earthly pilgrimage was cheered by the thought that He would not have all this travail for naught, but would win man back to loyalty to God. And there are triumphs yet to be accomplished through the blood shed for the world, that will bring everlasting glory to God and to the Lamb. The heathen will be given for His inheritance, and the uttermost parts of the earth for His possession. Christ will see of the travail of His soul, and be satisfied. [6]

"Arise, shine; for thy light is come, and the glory of the Lord is risen upon thee. For, behold, the darkness shall cover the earth, and gross darkness the people: but the Lord shall arise upon thee, and His glory shall be seen upon thee. And the Gentiles shall come to thy light, and kings to the brightness of thy rising. Lift up thine eyes round about, and see: all they gather themselves together, they come to thee: thy sons shall come from far, and thy daughters shall be nursed at thy side. Then thou shalt see, and flow together, and thine heart shall fear, and be enlarged; because the

[5] Heb. 12 : 2.   [6] See Isa. 53 : 11.

abundance of the sea shall be converted unto thee."
"For as the earth bringeth forth her bud, and as the
garden causeth the things that are sown in it to spring
forth; so the Lord God will cause righteousness and
praise to spring forth before all the nations." [7]

———◆———

The commission given to the disciples is given
also to us. To-day, as then, a crucified and risen
Saviour is to be uplifted before those who are without
God and without hope in the world. The Lord calls
for pastors, teachers, and evangelists. From door to
door His servants are to proclaim the message of
salvation. To every nation, kindred, tongue, and people the tidings of pardon through Christ are to be
carried. Not with tame, lifeless utterances is the
message to be given, but with clear, decided, stirring
utterances. Hundreds are waiting for the warning to
escape for their lives. The world needs to see in
Christians an evidence of the power of Christianity.
Not merely in a few places, but throughout the world,
messages of mercy are needed.

———◆———

He who beholds the Saviour's matchless love will
be elevated in thought, purified in heart, transformed
in character. He will go forth to be a light to the
world, to reflect in some degree this mysterious love.
The more we contemplate the cross of Christ, the more
fully shall we adopt the language of the apostle when
he said, "God forbid that I should glory, save in the
cross of our Lord Jesus Christ.[8]

[7] Isa. 60 : 1-5 ; 61 : 11.　　　　　　　[8] Gal. 6 : 14.

THE MINISTER'S RESPONSIBILITY

"I charge thee therefore," Paul wrote to Timothy, "before God, and the Lord Jesus Christ, who shall judge the quick and the dead at His appearing and His kingdom: Preach the word; be instant in season, out of season; reprove, rebuke, exhort with all long-suffering and doctrine." [1]

This solemn charge to one so zealous and faithful as was Timothy, is a strong testimony to the importance and responsibility of the work of the gospel minister. Summoning Timothy before the bar of God, Paul bids him preach the word, not the sayings and customs of men; to be ready to witness for God whenever opportunity should present itself,— before large congregations and private circles, by the way and at the fireside, to friends and to enemies, whether in safety or exposed to hardship and peril, reproach and loss.

Fearing that Timothy's mild, yielding disposition might lead him to shun an essential part of his work, Paul exhorted him to be faithful in reproving sin, and even to rebuke with sharpness those who were guilty of gross evils. Yet he was to do this "with all long-suffering and doctrine." He was to reveal the patience and love of Christ, explaining and enforcing his reproofs by the truths of the Word.

To hate and reprove sin, and at the same time to show pity and tenderness for the sinner, is a difficult achievement. The more earnest our own efforts to attain to holiness of heart and life, the more acute will be our perception of sin, and the more decided our

[1] 2 Tim. 4 : 1, 2.

[30]

disapproval of it. We must guard against undue severity toward the wrong-doer; but we must also be careful not to lose sight of the exceeding sinfulness of sin. There is need of showing Christlike patience and love for the erring one, but there is also danger of showing so great toleration for his error that he will look upon himself as undeserving of reproof, and will reject it as uncalled for and unjust.

A BURDEN FOR SOULS

God's ministers must come into close companionship with Christ, and follow His example in all things — in purity of life, in self-denial, in benevolence, in diligence, in perseverance. To win souls to the kingdom of God must be their first consideration. With sorrow for sin and with patient love, they must work as Christ worked, putting forth determined, unceasing effort.

John Welch, a minister of the gospel, felt so great a burden for souls that he often rose in the night to send up to God his supplication for their salvation. On one occasion his wife pleaded with him to regard his health, and not venture on such exposure. His answer was, "O woman, I have the souls of three thousand to answer for, and I know not how it is with them."

In a town in New England a well was being dug. When the work was nearly finished, while one man was still at the bottom, the earth caved in and buried him. Instantly the alarm was sent out, and mechanics, farmers, merchants, lawyers, hurried breathlessly to the rescue. Ropes, ladders, spades, and shovels were brought by eager, willing hands. "Save him, O save him!" was the cry.

Men worked with desperate energy, till the sweat stood in beads upon their brows and their arms trembled with the exertion. At length a pipe was thrust down, through which they shouted to the man to answer if he were still alive. The response came, "Alive, but make haste. It is fearful in here." With a shout of joy they renewed their efforts, and at last he was reached and saved, and the cheer that went up seemed to pierce the very heavens. "He is saved!" echoed through every street in the town.

Was this too great zeal and interest, too great enthusiasm, to save one man? It surely was not; but what is the loss of temporal life in comparison with the loss of a soul? If the threatened loss of a life will arouse in human hearts a feeling so intense, should not the loss of a soul arouse even deeper solicitude in men who claim to realize the danger of those apart from Christ? Shall not the servants of God show as great zeal in laboring for the salvation of souls as was shown for the life of that one man buried in a well?

STARVING FOR THE BREAD OF LIFE

A godly woman once made the remark, "O that we could hear the pure gospel as it used to be preached from the pulpit! Our minister is a good man, but he does not realize the spiritual needs of the people. He clothes the cross of Calvary with beautiful flowers, which hide all the shame, conceal all the reproach. My soul is starving for the bread of life. How refreshing it would be to hundreds of poor souls like me, to listen to something simple, plain, and scriptural, that would nourish our hearts!"

There is need of men of faith, who will not only preach, but will minister to the people. Men are needed who walk daily with God, who have a living connection with heaven, whose words have power to bring conviction to hearts. Not that they may make a display of their talents and intelligence, are ministers to labor, but that the truth may cut its way to the soul as an arrow from the Almighty.

A minister, after preaching a Bible discourse which brought deep conviction to one of his hearers, was accosted with the question, "Do you really believe what you have preached?"

"Certainly," he answered.

"But is it really so?" asked the anxious questioner.

"Certainly," said the minister, as he reached for his Bible.

Then the man broke out, "O, if this is the truth, what shall *we* do?"

"What shall *we* do?" thought the minister — "we"? What could the man mean? But the question forced its way to his soul. He went away to plead with God to tell him what to do. And as he prayed there came to him with overwhelming force the thought that he had the solemn realities of eternity to present to a dying world. For three weeks his place in the desk was vacant. He was seeking an answer to the question, "What shall we do?"

The minister returned to his charge with an in-tion from the Holy One. He realized that his preaching had made little impression on his hea Now he felt upon him the terrible weight of souls he came to his desk, he was not alone. There great work to be done, but he knew that God

2

not fail him. Before his hearers he exalted the Saviour and His matchless love. There was a revelation of the Son of God, and a revival began that spread through the churches of the surrounding districts.

THE URGENCY OF CHRIST'S WORK

If our ministers realized how soon the inhabitants of the world are to be arraigned before the judgment-seat of God, they would work more earnestly to lead men and women to Christ. Soon the last test is to come to all. Only a little longer will the voice of mercy be heard; only a little longer can the gracious invitation be given, "If any man thirst, let him come unto Me, and drink." [2] God sends the gospel invitation to people everywhere. Let the messengers He sends work so harmoniously, so untiringly, that all will take knowledge of them that they have been with Jesus, and learned of Him.

Of Aaron, the high priest of Israel, it is written, He "shall bear the names of the children of Israel in the breastplate of judgment upon his heart, when he goeth in unto the holy place, for a memorial before the Lord continually." [3] What a beautiful and expressive figure this is of the unchanging love of Christ for His church! Our great High Priest, of whom Aaron was a type, bears His people upon His heart. And should not His earthly ministers share His love and sympathy and solicitude?

Divine power alone will melt the sinner's heart and bring him, a penitent, to Christ. No great reformer or teacher, not Luther, Melanchthon, Wesley, or Whitefield, could of himself have gained access to hearts, or

[2] John 7 : 37.   [3] Ex. 28 : 29.

have accomplished the results that these men achieved. But God spoke through them. Men felt the influence of a superior power, and involuntarily yielded to it. To-day those who forget self and rely on God for success in the work of soul-saving, will have the divine co-operation, and their efforts will tell gloriously in the salvation of souls.

I feel constrained to say that the labors of many of our ministers lack power. God is waiting to bestow His grace upon them, but they pass on from day to day, possessing only a cold, nominal faith, presenting the theory of the truth, but presenting it without that vital force which comes from a connection with heaven, and which sends the spoken words home to the hearts of men. They are half asleep, while all around them are souls perishing in darkness and error.

Ministers of God, with hearts aglow with love for Christ and your fellow-men, seek to arouse those who are dead in trespasses and sins. Let your earnest entreaties and warnings pierce their consciences. Let your fervent prayers melt their hearts, and lead them in penitence to the Saviour. You are ambassadors for Christ, to proclaim His message of salvation. Remember that a lack of consecration and wisdom in you may turn the balance for a soul, and send it to eternal death. You cannot afford to be careless and indifferent. You need power, and this power God is willing to give you without stint. He asks only a humble, contrite heart, that is willing to believe and receive His promises. You have only to use the means that God has placed within your reach, and you will obtain the blessing.

THE OUTLOOK

We are nearing the close of this earth's history. We have before us a great work,— the closing work of giving the last warning message to a sinful world. There are men who will be taken from the plow, from the vineyard, from various other branches of work, and sent forth by the Lord to give this message to the world.

The world is out of joint. As we look at the picture, the outlook seems discouraging. But Christ greets with hopeful assurance the very men and women who cause us discouragement. In them He sees qualifications that will enable them to take a place in His vineyard. If they will constantly be learners, through His providence He will make them men and women fitted to do a work that is not beyond their capabilities; through the impartation of the Holy Spirit, He will give them power of utterance.

Many of the barren, unworked fields must be entered by beginners. The brightness of the Saviour's view of the world will inspire confidence in many workers, who, if they begin in humility and put their hearts into the work, will be found to be the right men for the time and place. Christ sees all the misery and despair of the world, the sight of which would bow down some of our workers of large capabilities with a weight of discouragement so great that they would not know how even to begin the work of leading men and women to the first round of the ladder. Their precise methods are of little value. They would stand above the lower rounds of the ladder, saying, "Come up where we are." But the poor souls do not know where to put their feet.

Christ's heart is cheered by the sight of those who are poor in every sense of the term; cheered by His view of the ill-used ones who are meek; cheered by the seemingly unsatisfied hungering after righteousness, by the inability of many to begin. He welcomes, as it were, the very condition of things that would discourage many ministers. He corrects our erring piety, giving the burden of the work for the poor and needy in the rough places of the earth, to men and women who have hearts that can feel for the ignorant and for those that are out of the way.

The Lord teaches these workers how to meet those whom He wishes them to help. They will be encouraged as they see doors opening for them to enter places where they can do medical missionary work. Having little self-confidence, they give God all the glory. Their hands may be rough and unskilled, but their hearts are susceptible to pity; they are filled with an earnest desire to do something to relieve the woe so abundant; and Christ is present to help them. He works through those who discern mercy in misery, gain in the loss of all things. When the Light of the world passes by, privileges appear in all hardships, order in confusion, the success and wisdom of God in that which has seemed to be failure.

My brethren and sisters, in your ministry come close to the people. Uplift those who are cast down. Treat of calamities as disguised blessings, of woes as mercies. Work in a way that will cause hope to spring up in the place of despair.

The common people are to take their place as work-- ers. Sharing the sorrows of their fellow-men as the Saviour shared the sorrows of humanity, they will by faith see Him working with them.

"The great day of the Lord is near, it is near, and hasteth greatly." [1] To every worker I would say: Go forth in humble faith, and the Lord will go with you. But watch unto prayer. This is the science of your labor. The power is of God. Work in dependence upon Him, remembering that you are laborers together with Him. He is your Helper. Your strength is from Him. He will be your wisdom, your righteousness, your sanctification, your redemption. Wear the yoke of Christ, daily learning of Him His meekness and lowliness. He will be your comfort, your rest.—*"Testimonies for the Church," Vol. VII, pages 270-272.*

The Saviour knows the depths of the world's misery and despair, knows by what means to bring relief. He sees on every hand souls in darkness, bowed down with sin and sorrow and pain. But He sees also their possibilities. He sees the height to which they may attain. Although human beings have abused their mercies, wasted their talents, and lost the dignity of godlike manhood, the Creator is to be glorified in their redemption.

Christ rejoiced that He could do more for His followers than they could ask or think. He knew that the truth, armed with the omnipotence of the Holy Spirit, would conquer in the contest with evil; and

[1] Zeph. 1 : 14.

that the blood-stained banner would wave trium-
phantly over His followers. He knew that the life
of His trusting disciples would be like His,— a series
of uninterrupted victories, not seen to be such here,
but recognized as such in the great hereafter.

"These things I have spoken unto you," He said,
"that in Me ye might have peace. In the world ye
shall have tribulation: but be of good cheer; I have
overcome the world." [2] Christ did not fail, neither
was He discouraged; and His followers are to manifest a faith of the same enduring nature. They are
to live as He lived, and work as He worked, because
they depend on Him as the great Master-worker.

Courage, energy, and perseverance they must possess. Though apparent impossibilities obstruct their
way, by His grace they are to go forward. Instead of
deploring difficulties, they are called upon to sur-
mount them. They are to despair of nothing, and to
hope for everything. With the golden chain of His
matchless love, Christ had bound them to the throne
of God. It is His purpose that the highest influence
in the universe, emanating from the Source of all
power, shall be theirs. They are to have power to
resist evil, power that neither earth, nor death, nor
hell can master, power that will enable them to overcome as Christ overcame.

[2] John 16 : 33,

FOR FURTHER STUDY

In Christ's Stead

Test. Vol. VIII, pp. 14-18.
Desire, pp. 349-358.

The Sacredness of the Work

Acts, pp. 498-508.

The Field Is the World

Test. Vol. VIII, pp. 14-18.
Desire, pp. 244-251, 818-828.
C. O. L., pp. 219-237.

The Minister's Responsibility

Test. Vol. I, pp. 248, 249.
Test. Vol. II, pp. 336-341, 506, 650.
Test. Vol. III, pp. 242, 243, 358, 359.
Test. Vol. IV, p. 185.
Acts, pp. 206, 207, 326-329, 394, 395.
Desire, pp. 493, 640, 641.

Ministers of Righteousness

"Our sufficiency is of God, who also hath made us able ministers."

CHRIST OUR EXAMPLE

Our Lord Jesus Christ came to this world as the unwearied servant of man's necessity. He "took our infirmities, and bare our sicknesses," [1] that He might minister to every need of humanity. The burden of disease and wretchedness and sin He came to remove. It was His mission to bring to men complete restoration; He came to give them health and peace and perfection of character.

Varied were the circumstances and needs of those who besought His aid, and none who came to Him went away unhelped. From Him flowed a stream of healing power, and in body and mind and soul men were made whole.

The Saviour's work was not restricted to any time or place. His compassion knew no limit. On so large a scale did He conduct His work of healing and teaching that there was no building in Palestine large enough to receive the multitudes that thronged to Him. On the green hillslopes of Galilee, in the thoroughfares of travel, by the seashore, in the synagogues, and in every place where the sick could be brought to Him, was to be found His hospital. In every city, every town, every village through which He passed, He laid His

[1] Matt. 8 : 17.

hands upon the afflicted ones, and healed them. Wherever there were hearts ready to receive His message, He comforted them with the assurance of their heavenly Father's love. All day He ministered to those who came to Him; in the evening He gave attention to such as through the day must toil to earn a pittance for the support of their families.

Jesus carried the awful weight of responsibility for the salvation of men. He knew that unless there was a decided change in the principles and purposes of the human race, all would be lost. This was the burden of His soul, and none could appreciate the weight that rested upon Him. Through childhood, youth, and manhood, He walked alone. Yet it was heaven to be in His presence. Day by day He met trials and temptations; day by day He was brought into contact with evil, and witnessed its power upon those whom He was seeking to bless and save. Yet He did not fail nor become discouraged.

In all things He brought His wishes into strict abeyance to His mission. He glorified His life by making everything in it subordinate to the will of His Father. When in His youth, His mother, finding Him in the school of the rabbis, said, "Son, why hast Thou thus dealt with us?" He answered,— and His answer is the key-note of His life-work,—"How is it that ye sought Me? wist ye not that I must be about My Father's business?" [2]

His life was one of constant self-sacrifice. He had no home in this world, except as the kindness of friends provided for Him as a wayfarer. He came to live in our behalf the life of the poorest, and to walk and work among the needy and the suffering. Unrecognized and

[2] Luke 2 : 48, 49.

unhonored, He walked in and out among the people for whom He had done so much.

He was always patient and cheerful, and the afflicted hailed Him as a messenger of life and peace. He saw the needs of men and women, children and youth, and to all He gave the invitation, "Come unto Me."

During His ministry, Jesus devoted more time to healing the sick than to preaching. His miracles testified to the truth of His words, that He came not to destroy, but to save. Wherever He went, the tidings of His mercy preceded Him. Where He had passed, the objects of His compassion were rejoicing in health, and making trial of their new-found powers. Crowds were collecting around them to hear from their lips the works that the Lord had wrought. His voice was the first sound that many had ever heard, His name the first word they had ever spoken, His face the first they had ever looked upon. Why should they not love Jesus, and sound His praise? As He passed through the towns and cities, He was like a vital current, diffusing life and joy. . . .

The Saviour made each work of healing an occasion of implanting divine principles in the mind and soul. This was the purpose of His work. He imparted earthly blessings, that He might incline the hearts of men to receive the gospel of His grace.

Christ might have occupied the highest place among the teachers of the Jewish nation, but He preferred rather to take the gospel to the poor. He went from place to place, that those in the highways and byways might hear the words of truth. By the sea, on the mountainside, in the streets of the city, in the synagogue, His voice was heard explaining the Scriptures.

Often He taught in the outer court of the temple, that the Gentiles might hear His words.

So unlike the explanations of Scripture given by the scribes and Pharisees was Christ's teaching, that the attention of the people was arrested. The rabbis dwelt upon tradition, upon human theory and speculation. Often that which men had taught and written about the Scripture was put in place of the Scripture itself. The subject of Christ's teaching was the word of God. He met questioners with a plain, "It is written," "What saith the Scripture?" "How readest thou?" At every opportunity, when an interest was awakened by either friend or foe, He presented the Word. With clearness and power He proclaimed the gospel message. His words shed a flood of light on the teachings of patriarchs and prophets, and the Scriptures came to men as a new revelation. Never before had His hearers perceived in the word of God such depth of meaning.

SIMPLICITY OF CHRIST'S TEACHING

Never was there such an evangelist as Christ. He was the Majesty of heaven, but He humbled Himself to take our nature, that He might meet men where they were. To all people, rich and poor, free and bond, Christ, the Messenger of the covenant, brought the tidings of salvation. His fame as the great Healer spread throughout Palestine. The sick came to the places through which He would pass, that they might call on Him for help. Hither, too, came many anxious to hear His words and to receive a touch of His hand. Thus He went from city to city, from town to town, preaching the gospel and healing the sick,— the King of glory in the lowly garb of humanity.

He attended the great yearly festivals of the nation, and to the multitude absorbed in outward ceremony He spoke of heavenly things, bringing eternity within their view. To all He brought treasures from the storehouse of wisdom. He spoke to them in language so simple that they could not fail of understanding. By methods peculiarly His own, He helped all who were in sorrow and affliction. With tender, courteous grace, He ministered to the sin-sick soul, bringing healing and strength.

The Prince of teachers, He sought access to the people by the pathway of their most familiar associations. He presented the truth in such a way that ever after it was to His hearers intertwined with their most hallowed recollections and sympathies. He taught in a way that made them feel the completeness of His identification with their interests and happiness. His instruction was so direct, His illustrations were so appropriate, His words so sympathetic and cheerful, that His hearers were charmed. The simplicity and earnestness with which He addressed the needy, hallowed every word.

TO RICH AND POOR ALIKE

What a busy life He led! Day by day He might have been seen entering the humble abodes of want and sorrow, speaking hope to the downcast and peace to the distressed. Gracious, tender-hearted, pitiful, He went about lifting up the bowed-down and comforting the sorrowful. Wherever He went, He carried blessing.

While He ministered to the poor, Jesus studied also to find ways of reaching the rich. He sought the acquaintance of the wealthy and cultured Pharisee, the Jewish nobleman, and the Roman ruler. He accepted their invitations, attended their feasts, made Himself familiar with their interests and occupations, that He might gain access to their hearts, and reveal to them the imperishable riches.

Christ came to this world to show that by receiving power from on high, man can live an unsullied life. With unwearying patience and sympathetic helpfulness, He met men in their necessities. By the gentle touch of grace, He banished from the soul unrest and doubt, changing enmity to love, and unbelief to confidence. . . .

Christ recognized no distinction of nationality or rank or creed. The scribes and Pharisees desired to make a local and a national benefit of the gifts of heaven, and to exclude the rest of God's family in the world. But Christ came to break down every wall of partition. He came to show that His gift of mercy and love is as unconfined as the air, the light, or the showers of rain that refresh the earth.

The life of Christ established a religion in which there is no caste, a religion by which Jew and Gentile, free and bond, are linked in a common brotherhood, equal before God. No question of policy influenced His movements. He made no difference between neighbors and strangers, friends and enemies. That which appealed to His heart was a soul thirsting for the waters of life.

He passed by no human being as worthless, but sought to apply the healing remedy to every soul. In whatever company He found Himself, He presented a lesson appropriate to the time and the circumstances. Every neglect or insult shown by men to their fellow-men, only made Him more conscious of their need of His divine-human sympathy. He sought to inspire with hope the roughest and most unpromising, setting before them the assurance that they might become blameless and harmless, attaining such a character as would make them manifest as the children of God.

Often He met those who had drifted under Satan's control, and who had no power to break from his snare. To such a one, discouraged, sick, tempted, fallen, Jesus would speak words of tenderest pity, words that were needed and could be understood. Others He met who were fighting a hand-to-hand battle with the adversary of souls. These He encouraged to persevere, assuring them that they would win; for angels of God were on their side, and would give them the victory.

At the table of the publicans He sat as an honored guest, by His sympathy and social kindliness showing that He recognized the dignity of humanity; and men longed to become worthy of His confidence. Upon their thirsty hearts His words fell with blessed, life-giving power. New impulses were awakened, and to these outcasts of society there opened the possibility of a new life.

Though He was a Jew, Jesus mingled freely with the Samaritans, setting at naught the Pharisaic customs of His nation. In face of their prejudices He accepted the hospitality of this despised people. He slept with them under their roofs, ate with them at their tables, — partaking of the food prepared and served by their hands,— taught in their streets, and treated them with the utmost kindness and courtesy. And while He drew their hearts to Him by the tie of human sympathy, His divine grace brought to them the salvation which the Jews rejected.—*"Ministry of Healing," pages 17-26.*

CHRIST AS A TEACHER

The world's Redeemer went about doing good. When before the people, speaking to them the words of eternal truth, with what earnestness He watched the changing countenances of His hearers! The faces that expressed deep interest and pleasure as they listened to His words, gave Him great satisfaction. And when the truth, plainly uttered, touched some cherished sin or idol, He marked the change of countenance, the cold, stern, forbidding look, which told that the truth was unwelcome. Jesus knew that the plain reproof of sin was the very thing that His hearers needed; and the light He shed into the darkened chambers of their minds would have been the greatest blessing to them, had they accepted it.

Christ's work was to lay down in simple lines, yet so as to be clearly understood, truths that, if obeyed, would bring peace and happiness to the soul. He could look beneath the surface, and see the cherished sins that were ruining the life and character, and shutting souls away from God. He pointed out these sins, that all might see them in the true light, and put them away. In some who presented the most hardened exterior, He discerned hopeful subjects. He knew that they would respond to the light, and that they would become His true followers.

As the arrows of truth pierced the hearts of Christ's hearers, breaking through the barriers of selfishness and bringing humiliation, contrition, and finally gratitude, the Saviour's heart was made glad. When His eyes swept over the throng of listeners about Him, and

He recognized among them the same faces that He had seen on former occasions, joy was expressed in His countenance, that here were hopeful subjects of His kingdom.

The messengers of Christ, those whom He sends in His stead, will have the same feelings, the same earnest interest. And those who are tempted to think that their labor is not appreciated, and are inclined to be discouraged, should remember that Jesus had just as hard hearts to deal with, and had a more trying experience than they have had or ever can have. He taught the people with patient love. His deep, searching wisdom knew the wants of every soul among His listeners; and when He saw them refuse the message of peace and love that He came to give them, His heart felt anguish to the very depths.

The world's Redeemer did not come with outward display, or a show of worldly wisdom. Men could not see, beneath the guise of humanity, the glory of the Son of God. He was "despised and rejected of men; a man of sorrows, and acquainted with grief." He was to them as "a root out of a dry ground," with "no form nor comeliness," [1] that they should desire Him. But He declared, "The Spirit of the Lord God is upon Me; because the Lord hath anointed Me to preach good tidings unto the meek; He hath sent Me to bind up the broken-hearted, to proclaim liberty to the captives, and the opening of the prison to them that are bound." [2]

Christ reached the people where they were. He presented the plain truth to their minds in the most

[1] Isa. 53 : 3, 2.   [2] Isa. 61 : 1.

forcible, simple language. The humble poor, the most
unlearned, could comprehend, through faith in Him,
the most exalted truths. No one needed to consult
the learned doctors as to His meaning. He did not
perplex the ignorant with mysterious inferences, or use
unaccustomed and learned words, of which they had
no knowledge. The greatest Teacher the world has
ever known, was the most definite, simple, and practical in His instruction.

———◆———

"That was the true Light, which lighteth every
man that cometh into the world." [3] The world has
had its great teachers, men of giant intellect and
wonderful research, men whose utterances have stimulated thought and opened to view vast fields of knowledge; and these men have been honored as guides
and benefactors of their race. But there is One who
stands higher than they. "As many as received Him,
to them gave He power to become the sons of God."
"No man hath seen God at any time; the only begotten Son, which is in the bosom of the Father, He
hath declared Him." [3]

We can trace the line of the world's great teachers
as far back as human records extend; but the Light
was before them. As the moon and the stars of the
solar system shine by the reflected light of the sun, so,
as far as their teaching is true, do the world's great
thinkers reflect the rays of the Sun of Righteousness.
Every gem of thought, every flash of the intellect, is
from the Light of the world.

[3] John 1 : 9, 12, 18..

A LESSON FOR OUR TIME

The experience of Enoch and of John the Baptist represents what ours should be. Far more than we do, we need to study the lives of these men,— he who was translated to heaven without seeing death; and he who, before Christ's first advent, was called to prepare the way of the Lord, to make His paths straight.

THE EXPERIENCE OF ENOCH

Of Enoch it is written that he lived sixty-five years and begat a son; after that he walked with God three hundred years. During those earlier years, Enoch had loved and feared God, and had kept His commandments. After the birth of his first son, he reached a higher experience; he was drawn into closer relationship with God. As he saw the child's love for its father, its simple trust in his protection; as he felt the deep yearning tenderness of his own heart for that first-born son, he learned a precious lesson of the wonderful love of God to man in the gift of His Son, and the confidence which the children of God may repose in their heavenly Father. The infinite, unfathomable love of God through Christ, became the subject of his meditations day and night. With all the fervor of his soul he sought to reveal that love to the people among whom he dwelt.

Enoch's walk with God was not in a trance or a vision, but in all the duties of his daily life. He did not become a hermit, shutting himself entirely from the world; for he had, in the world, a work to do for God.

In the family and in his intercourse with men, as a husband and father, a friend, a citizen, he was the steadfast, unwavering servant of God.

In the midst of a life of active labor, Enoch steadfastly maintained his communion with God. The greater and more pressing his labors, the more constant and earnest were his prayers. He continued to exclude himself at certain periods from all society. After remaining for a time among the people, laboring to benefit them by instruction and example, he would withdraw, to spend a season in solitude, hungering and thirsting for that divine knowledge which God alone can impart.

Communing thus with God, Enoch came more and more to reflect the divine image. His face was radiant with a holy light, even the light that shineth in the face of Jesus. As he came forth from these divine communings, even the ungodly beheld with awe the impress of heaven upon his countenance.

His faith waxed stronger, his love became more ardent, with the lapse of centuries. To him prayer was as the breath of the soul. He lived in the atmosphere of heaven.

As the scenes of the future were opened to his view, Enoch became a preacher of righteousness, bearing God's message to all who would hear the words of warning. In the land where Cain had sought to flee from the divine presence, the prophet of God made known the wonderful scenes that had passed before his vision. "Behold," he declared, "the Lord cometh with ten thousands of His saints, to execute judgment upon all, and to convince all that are ungodly among them of all their ungodly deeds." [1]

[1] Jude 14, 15.

The power of God that wrought with His servant was felt by those who heard. Some gave heed to the warning and renounced their sins; but the multitudes mocked at the solemn message. The servants of God are to bear a similar message to the world in the last days, and it also will be received by the majority with unbelief and mockery.

As year after year passed, deeper and deeper grew the tide of human guilt, darker and darker gathered the clouds of divine judgment. Yet Enoch, the witness of faith, held on his way, warning, pleading, and teaching, striving to turn back the tide of guilt and to stay the bolts of vengeance.

The men of that generation mocked the folly of him who sought not to gather gold or silver, or to build up possessions here. But Enoch's heart was upon eternal treasures. He had looked upon the celestial city. He had seen the King in His glory in the midst of Zion. The greater the existing iniquity, the more earnest was his longing for the home of God. While still on earth, he dwelt by faith in the realms of light.

"Blessed are the pure in heart: for they shall see God." [2] For three hundred years Enoch had been seeking purity of heart, that he might be in harmony with heaven. For three centuries he had walked with God. Day by day he had longed for a closer union; nearer and nearer had grown the communion, until God took him to Himself. He had stood at the threshold of the eternal world, only a step between him and the land of the blest; and now the portals opened, the walk with God, so long pursued on earth, continued, and he passed through the gates of the holy city,— the first from among men to enter there.

[2] Matt. 5 : 8.

"By faith Enoch was translated that he should not see death; . . . for before his translation he had this testimony, that he pleased God." [3]

To such communion God is calling us. As was Enoch's, so must be their holiness of character who shall be redeemed from among men at the Lord's second coming.

THE EXPERIENCE OF JOHN THE BAPTIST

John the Baptist in his desert life was taught of God. He studied the revelations of God in nature. Under the guiding of the divine Spirit, he studied the scrolls of the prophets. By day and by night, Christ was his study, his meditation, until mind and heart and soul were filled with the glorious vision.

He looked upon the King in His beauty, and self was lost sight of. He beheld the majesty of holiness, and knew himself to be inefficient and unworthy. It was God's message that he was to declare. It was in God's power and His righteousness that he was to stand. He was ready to go forth as Heaven's messenger, unawed by the human, because he had looked upon the Divine. He could stand fearless in the presence of earthly monarchs, because with trembling he had bowed before the King of kings.

With no elaborate arguments or fine-spun theories did John declare his message. Startling and stern, yet full of hope, his voice was heard from the wilderness, "Repent ye: for the kingdom of heaven is at hand." [4] With a new, strange power it moved the people. The whole nation was stirred. Multitudes flocked to the wilderness.

[3] Heb. 11 : 5.　　　　[4] Matt. 3 : 2.

Unlearned peasants and fishermen from the surrounding country; the Roman soldiers from the barracks of Herod; chieftains with their swords at their sides, ready to put down anything that might savor of rebellion; the avaricious tax-gatherers from their toll-booths; and from the Sanhedrim the phylactered priests,— all listened as if spellbound; and all, even the Pharisee and the Sadducee, the cold, unimpressible scoffer, went away with the sneer silenced, and cut to the heart with a sense of their sins. Herod in his palace heard the message, and the proud, sin-hardened ruler trembled at the call to repentance.

In this age, just prior to the second coming of Christ in the clouds of heaven, such a work as that of John is to be done. God calls for men who will prepare a people to stand in the great day of the Lord. The message preceding the public ministry of Christ was, Repent, publicans and sinners; repent, Pharisees and Sadducees; "repent ye: for the kingdom of heaven is at hand." As a people who believe in Christ's soon coming, we have a message to bear,—"Prepare to meet thy God." [5]

Our message must be as direct as was the message of John. He rebuked kings for their iniquity. Notwithstanding that his life was imperiled, he did not hesitate to declare God's word. And our work in this age must be done as faithfully.

In order to give such a message as John gave, we must have a spiritual experience like his. The same work must be wrought in us. We must behold God, and in beholding Him, lose sight of self.

John had by nature the faults and weaknesses common to humanity; but the touch of divine love had

[5] Amos 4 : 12.

transformed him. When, after Christ's ministry began, the disciples of John came to him with the complaint that all men were following the new Teacher, John showed how clearly he understood his relation to the Messiah, and how gladly he welcomed the One for whom he had prepared the way.

"A man can receive nothing," he said, "except it be given him from heaven. Ye yourselves bear me witness, that I said, I am not the Christ, but that I am sent before Him. He that hath the bride is the bridegroom: but the friend of the bridegroom, which standeth and heareth him, rejoiceth greatly because of the bridegroom's voice: this my joy therefore is fulfilled. He must increase, but I must decrease." [6]

Looking in faith to the Redeemer, John had risen to the height of self-abnegation. He sought not to attract men to himself, but to lift their thoughts higher and still higher, until they should rest upon the Lamb of God. He himself had been only a voice, a cry in the wilderness. Now with joy he accepted silence and obscurity, that the eyes of all might be turned to the Light of life.

Those who are true to their calling as messengers of God, will not seek honor for themselves. Love for self will be swallowed up in love for Christ. They will recognize that it is their work to proclaim, as did John the Baptist, "Behold the Lamb of God, which taketh away the sin of the world." [7]

The soul of the prophet, emptied of self, was filled with the light of the Divine. In words that were almost a counterpart of the words of Christ Himself, he bore witness to the Saviour's glory. "He that cometh

[6] John 3 : 27-30.　　　　　　　　[7] John 1 : 29.

from above," he said, "is above all: he that is of the earth is earthly, and speaketh of the earth: He that cometh from heaven is above all." "For He whom God hath sent speaketh the words of God." [8]

In this glory of Christ all His followers are to share. The Saviour could say, "I seek not Mine own will, but the will of the Father which hath sent Me." [9] And John declared, "God giveth not the Spirit by measure unto Him." So with the followers of Christ. We can receive of heaven's light only as we are willing to be emptied of self. We can discern the character of God, and accept Christ by faith, only as we consent to the bringing into captivity of every thought to the obedience of Christ. And to all who do this, the Holy Spirit is given without measure. In Christ "dwelleth all the fulness of the Godhead bodily. And ye are complete in Him." [10]

———◆———

The life of John was not spent in idleness, in ascetic gloom, or in selfish isolation. From time to time he went forth to mingle with men; and he was ever an interested observer of what was passing in the world. From his quiet retreat he watched the unfolding of events. With vision illuminated by the Divine Spirit he studied the character of men, that he might understand how to reach their hearts with the message of heaven. The burden of his mission was upon him. In solitude, by meditation and prayer, he sought to gird up his soul for the life-work before him.

[8] John 3 : 31, 34.   [9] John 5 : 30.   [10] Col. 2 : 9, 10.

PAUL, THE APOSTLE TO THE GENTILES

Foremost among those called to preach the gospel of Christ stands the apostle Paul, to every minister an example of loyalty, devotion, and untiring effort. His experiences and his instruction regarding the sacredness of the minister's work, are a source of help and inspiration to those engaged in the gospel ministry.

Before his conversion, Paul was a bitter persecutor of the followers of Christ. But at the gate of Damascus a voice spoke to him, light from heaven shone into his soul, and in the revelation that there came to him, of the Crucified One, he beheld that which changed the whole current of his life. Henceforth love for the Lord of glory, whom he had so relentlessly persecuted in the person of His saints, came before all else. To him had been given the ministry of making known "the mystery" which had been "kept secret since the world began." [1] "He is a chosen vessel unto Me," declared the Angel who appeared to Ananias, "to bear My name before the Gentiles, and kings, and the children of Israel." [2]

And throughout his long term of service, Paul never faltered in his allegiance to his Saviour. "I count not myself to have apprehended," he wrote to the Philippians; "but this one thing I do, forgetting those things which are behind, and reaching forth unto those things which are before, I press toward the mark for the prize of the high calling of God in Christ." [3]

Paul's was a life of intense and varied activities. From city to city, from country to country, he jour-

[1] Rom. 16 : 25. [2] Acts 9 : 15. [3] Phil. 3 : 13, 14.

neyed, telling the story of the cross, winning converts to the gospel, and establishing churches. For these churches he had a constant care, and he wrote many letters of instruction to them. At times he worked at his trade to earn his daily bread. But in all the busy activity of his life, he never lost sight of the one great purpose,— to press toward the mark of his high calling.

Paul carried with him the atmosphere of heaven. All who associated with him felt the influence of his union with Christ. The fact that his own life exemplified the truth he proclaimed, gave convincing power to his preaching. Here lies the power of the truth. The unstudied, unconscious influence of a holy life is the most convincing sermon that can be given in favor of Christianity. Argument, even when unanswerable, may provoke only opposition; but a godly example has a power that it is impossible wholly to resist.

The apostle's heart burned with love for sinners, and he put all his energies into the work of soul-winning. There never lived a more self-denying, persevering worker. The blessings he received he prized as so many advantages to be used in blessing others. He lost no opportunity of speaking of the Saviour or of helping those in trouble. Wherever he could find a hearing, he sought to counteract wrong and to turn the feet of men and women into the path of righteousness.

Paul never forgot the responsibility resting on him as a minister of Christ; or that if souls were lost through unfaithfulness on his part, God would hold him accountable. "I take you to record this day," he declared, "that I am pure from the blood of all men." [4] "Whereof I am made a minister," he said of the gospel, "according to the dispensation of God which is given

[4] Acts 20 : 26.

to me for you, to fulfil the word of God; even the mystery which hath been hid from ages and from generations, but now is made manifest to His saints: to whom God would make known what is the riches of the glory of this mystery among the Gentiles; which is Christ in you, the hope of glory: whom we preach, warning every man, and teaching every man in all wisdom; that we may present every man perfect in Christ Jesus: whereunto I also labor, striving according to His working, which worketh in me mightily." [5]

These words present before the worker for Christ a high standard of attainment, yet this standard all can reach who, putting themselves under the control of the great Teacher, learn daily in the school of Christ. The power at God's command is limitless; and the minister who in his great need shuts himself in with the Lord, may be assured that he will receive that which will be to his hearers a savor of life unto life.

Paul's writings show that the gospel minister should be an example of the truths that he teaches, "giving no offense in anything, that the ministry be not blamed." [6] To Titus he wrote, "Young men likewise exhort to be sober-minded. In all things showing thyself a pattern of good works: in doctrine showing uncorruptness, gravity, sincerity, sound speech, that cannot be condemned; that he that is of the contrary part may be ashamed, having no evil thing to say of you." [7]

Of his own work he has left us a picture in his letter to the Corinthian believers: "In all things approving ourselves as the ministers of God, in much patience, in afflictions, in necessities, in distresses, in stripes, in imprisonments, in tumults, in labors, in watchings, in

[5] Col. 1 : 25-29.   [6] 2 Cor. 6 : 3.   [7] Titus 2 : 6-8.

fastings; by pureness, by knowledge, by long-suffering, by kindness, by the Holy Ghost, by love unfeigned, by the word of truth, by the power of God, by the armor of righteousness on the right hand and on the left, by honor and dishonor, by evil report and good report: as deceivers, and yet true; as unknown, and yet well known; as dying, and, behold, we live; as chastened, and not killed; as sorrowful, yet alway rejoicing; as poor, yet making many rich." [8]

Paul's heart was filled with a deep, abiding sense of his responsibility; and he labored in close communion with Him who is the fountain of justice, mercy, and truth. He clung to the cross of Christ as his only guaranty of success. The love of the Saviour was the undying motive that upheld him in his conflicts with self and in his struggle against evil, as in the service of Christ he pressed forward against the unfriendliness of the world and the opposition of his enemies.

What the church needs in these days of peril, is an army of workers who, like Paul, have educated themselves for usefulness, who have a deep experience in the things of God, and who are filled with earnestness and zeal. Sanctified, self-sacrificing men are needed; men who are brave and true; men in whose hearts Christ is formed, "the hope of glory," [9] and who with lips touched with holy fire will "preach the word." [10] For the want of such workers the cause of God languishes, and fatal errors, like a deadly poison, taint the morals and blight the hopes of a large part of the human race.

As the faithful, toil-worn standard-bearers are offering up their lives for the truth's sake, who will come forward to take their place? Will our young men ac-

---

[8] 2 Cor. 6 : 4-10.   [9] Col. 1 : 27.   [10] 2 Tim. 4 : 2.

cept the holy trust at the hand of their fathers? **Are** they preparing to fill the vacancies made by the death of the faithful? Will the apostle's charge be heeded, the call to duty be heard, amid the incitements to self-ishness and ambition that allure the youth?

————◆————

FOR FURTHER STUDY

CHRIST OUR EXAMPLE	Test. Vol. II, p. 628. Test. Vol. III, pp. 421-423. Test. Vol. IV, pp. 263, 268, **373.** Desire, pp. 253-255. M. of H., pp. 503, 504.
CHRIST AS A TEACHER	Ed., pp. 73-83. Desire, pp. 168-177, 183-**195,** 298-314, 365-371. M. of H., pp. 52-54. Counsels, pp. 28, 29, 49-52, **178-** 180, 259-263, 381, 385, **386.**
A LESSON FOR OUR (Enoch) TIME	Test. Vol. II, pp. 121, **122.** Test. Vol. VI, p. 392. P. and P., pp. 84-89. C. O. L., p. 332.
(John)	Test. Vol. V, pp. 224-227. Test. Vol. VIII, pp. 221, **222.** Desire, pp. 100-108, 178-182, 214-225. C. O. L., pp. 277, 278. Acts, pp. 269, 270. Counsels, pp. 445-447.
PAUL, THE APOSTLE TO THE GENTILES	See "Acts of the Apostles." M. of H., pp. 154, 166, **167,** 214, 215.

The Needed Preparation

"Study to show thyself approved unto God, a workman that needeth not to be ashamed, rightly dividing the word of truth."

YOUNG MEN IN THE MINISTRY

There must be no belittling of the gospel ministry. No enterprise should be so conducted as to cause the ministry of the word to be looked upon as an inferior matter. It is not so. Those who belittle the ministry are belittling Christ. The highest of all work is ministry in its various lines, and it should be kept before the youth that there is no work more blessed of God than that of the gospel minister.

Let not our young men be deterred from entering the ministry. There is danger that through glowing representations some will be drawn away from the path where God bids them walk. Some have been encouraged to take a course of study in medical lines who ought to be preparing themselves to enter the ministry. The Lord calls for more ministers to labor in His vineyard. The words were spoken, "Strengthen the outposts; have faithful sentinels in every part of the world." God calls for you, young men. He calls for whole armies of young men who are large-hearted and large-minded, and who have a deep love for Christ and the truth.

The measure of capacity or learning is of far less consequence than is the spirit with which you engage in the work. It is not great and learned men that the ministry needs; it is not eloquent sermonizers. God calls for men who will give themselves to Him to be imbued with His Spirit. The cause of Christ and humanity demands sanctified, self-sacrificing men, those who can go forth without the camp, bearing the reproach. Let them be strong, valiant men, fit for worthy enterprises, and let them make a covenant with God by sacrifice.

The ministry is no place for idlers. God's servants are to make full proof of their ministry. They will not be sluggards, but as expositors of His word they will put forth their utmost energies to be faithful. They should never cease to be learners. They are to keep their own souls alive to the sacredness of the work and to the great responsibilities of their calling, that they may at no time or place bring to God a maimed sacrifice, an offering which has cost them neither study nor prayer.

The Lord has need of men of intense spiritual life. Every worker may receive an endowment of strength from on high, and may go forward with faith and hope in the path where God bids him walk. The word of God abides in the young, consecrated laborer. He is quick, earnest, powerful, having in the counsel of God an unfailing source of supply.

God has called this people to give to the world the message of Christ's soon coming. We are to give to men the last call to the gospel feast, the last invitation to the marriage supper of the Lamb. Thousands of places that have not heard the call are yet to hear it. Many who have not given the message are yet to proclaim it. Again I appeal to our young men:

Has not God called upon you to sound this message?

How many of our young men will enter the service of God, not to be served, but to serve? In times past there were those who fastened their minds upon one soul after another, saying, "Lord, help me to save this soul." But now such instances are rare. How many act as if they realized the peril of sinners? How many take those whom they know to be in peril, presenting them to God in prayer, and supplicating Him to save them?

The apostle Paul could say of the early church, "They glorified God in me." [1] Shall we not strive to live so that the same words can be said of us? The Lord will provide ways and means for those who will seek Him with the whole heart. He desires us to acknowledge the divine superintendence shown in preparing fields of labor and in preparing the way for these fields to be occupied successfully.

Let ministers and evangelists have more seasons of earnest prayer with those who are convicted by the truth. Remember that Christ is always with you. The Lord has in readiness the most precious exhibitions of His grace to strengthen and encourage the sincere, humble worker. Then reflect to others the light which God has caused to shine upon you. Those who do this bring to the Lord the most precious offering. The hearts of those who bear the good tidings of salvation are aglow with the spirit of praise. . . .

The number of workers in the ministry is not to be lessened, but greatly increased. Where there is now

[1] Gal. 1 : 24.

one minister in the field, twenty are to be added; and if the Spirit of God controls them, these twenty will so present the truth that twenty more will be added.

———◆———

Christ's dignity and office-work are in imposing such conditions as He pleases. His followers are to become more and more a power in the proclamation of the truth as they draw nearer to the perfection of faith and of love for their brethren. God has provided divine assistance for all the emergencies to which our human resources are unequal. He gives the Holy Spirit to help in every strait, to strengthen our hope and assurance, to illuminate our minds and purify our hearts. He means that sufficient facilities shall be provided for the working out of His plans. I bid you seek counsel from God. Seek Him with the whole heart, and "whatsoever He saith unto you, do." [2] —*"Testimonies for the Church," Vol. VI, pages 414, 415.*

———◆———

With such an army of workers as our youth, rightly trained, might furnish, how soon the message of a crucified, risen, and soon-coming Saviour might be carried to the whole world! How soon might the end come,— the end of suffering and sorrow and sin! How soon, in place of a possession here, with its blight of sin and pain, our children might receive their inheritance where "the righteous shall inherit the land, and dwell therein forever;" where "the inhabitant shall not say, I am sick," and "the voice of weeping shall be no more heard!" [3] —*"Education," page 271.*

[2] John 2 : 5.   [3] Ps. 37 : 29 ; Isa. 33 : 24 ; 65 : 19.

THE YOUTH TO BE BURDEN-BEARERS

"I have written unto you, young men, because ye are strong, and the word of God abideth in you, and ye have overcome the wicked one." [1]

In order that the work may go forward in all its branches, God calls for youthful vigor, zeal, and courage. He has chosen the youth to aid in the advancement of His cause. To plan with clear mind and execute with courageous hand demands fresh, uncrippled energies. Young men and women are invited to give God the strength of their youth, that through the exercise of their powers, through keen thought and vigorous action, they may bring glory to Him and salvation to their fellow-men.

In view of their high calling, the youth among us should not seek for amusement or live for selfish gratification. The salvation of souls is to be the motive that inspires them to action. In their God-given strength they are to rise above every enslaving, debasing habit. They are to ponder well the paths of their feet, remembering that where they lead the way, others will follow.

No one lives to himself; all exert an influence for good or for evil. Because of this, the apostle exhorts young men to be sober-minded. How can they be otherwise when they remember that they are to be co-workers with Christ, partakers with Him of His self-denial and sacrifice, His forbearance and gracious benevolence?

To the youth of to-day, as surely as to Timothy, are spoken the words, "Study to show thyself approved

[1] 1 John 2:14.

unto God, a workman that needeth not to be ashamed, rightly dividing the word of truth." "Flee also youthful lusts: but follow righteousness, faith, charity, peace." "Be thou an example of the believers, in word, in conversation, in charity, in spirit, in faith, in purity." [2]

The burden-bearers among us are falling in death. Many of those who have been foremost in carrying out the reforms instituted by us as a people, are now past the meridian of life, and are declining in physical and mental strength. With the deepest concern the question may be asked, Who will fill their places? To whom are to be committed the vital interests of the church when the present standard-bearers fall? We cannot but look anxiously upon the youth of to-day as those who must take these burdens, and upon whom responsibilities must fall. These must take up the work where others leave it, and their course will determine whether morality, religion, and vital godliness shall prevail, or whether immorality and infidelity shall corrupt and blight all that is valuable.

Those who are older must educate the youth, by precept and example, to discharge the claims that society and their Maker have upon them. Upon these youth must be laid grave responsibilities. The question is, Are they capable of governing themselves, and standing forth in the purity of their God-given manhood, abhorring everything that savors of wickedness?

Never before was there so much at stake; never were there results so mighty depending upon a generation as upon these now coming upon the stage of action. Not for one moment should the youth think that

[2] 2 Tim. 2 : 15, 22 ; 1 Tim. 4 : 12.

they can acceptably fill any position of trust without possessing a good character. Just as well might they expect to gather grapes of thorns, or figs of thistles.

A good character must be built up brick by brick. Those characteristics which will enable the youth to labor successfully in God's cause must be obtained by the diligent exercise of their faculties, by improving every advantage Providence gives them, and by connecting with the Source of all wisdom. They must be satisfied with no low standard. The characters of Joseph and Daniel are good models for them to follow, and in the life of the Saviour they have a perfect pattern.

All are given an opportunity to develop character. All may fill their appointed places in God's great plan. The Lord accepted Samuel from his very childhood, because his heart was pure. He was given to God, a consecrated offering, and the Lord made him a channel of light. If the youth of to-day will consecrate themselves as did Samuel, the Lord will accept them and use them in His work. Of their life they may be able to say with the psalmist, "O God, Thou hast taught me from my youth: and hitherto have I declared Thy wondrous works." [3]

THE NEED OF TRAINING WORKERS

The youth must soon bear the burdens that older workers are now carrying. We have lost time in neglecting to give young men a solid, practical education. The cause of God is constantly progressing, and we must obey the command, Go forward. There is need of young men and women who will not be swayed by

[3] Ps. 71 : 17.

circumstances, who walk with God, who pray much, and who put forth earnest efforts to gather all the light they can.

The worker for God should put forth the highest mental and moral energies with which nature, cultivation, and the grace of God have endowed him; but his success will be proportionate to the degree of consecration and self-sacrifice in which his work is done, rather than to either natural or acquired endowments. Earnest, continuous endeavor to acquire qualifications for usefulness is necessary; but unless God works with humanity, nothing good can be accomplished. Divine grace is the great element of saving power; without it all human effort is unavailing.

Whenever the Lord has a work to be done, He calls not only for the commanding officers, but for all the workers. To-day He is calling for young men and women who are strong and active in mind and body. He desires them to bring into the conflict against principalities and powers and spiritual wickedness in high places, their fresh, healthy powers of brain, bone, and muscle. But they must have the needed preparation. Some young men are urging their way into the work who have no real fitness for it. They do not understand that they need to be taught before they can teach. They point to men who, with little preparation, have labored with a measure of success. But if these men were successful, it was because they put heart and soul into the work. And how much more effective their labors might have been if at the first they had received suitable training!

The cause of God needs efficient men. Education and training are rightly regarded as an essential preparation for business life; and how much more essential is thorough preparation for the work of presenting the last message of mercy to the world. This training cannot be gained by merely listening to preaching. In our schools our youth are to bear burdens for God. They are to receive a thorough training under experienced teachers. They should make the best possible use of their time in study, and put into practice the knowledge acquired. Hard study and hard work are required to make a successful minister or a successful worker in any branch of God's cause. Nothing less than constant cultivation will develop the value of the gifts that God has bestowed for wise improvement.

A great injury is often done our young men by permitting them to begin to preach when they have not sufficient knowledge of the Scriptures to present our faith in an intelligent manner. Some who enter the field are novices in the Scriptures. In other things also they are incompetent and inefficient. They cannot read the Scriptures without hesitating, mispronouncing words, and jumbling them together in such a manner that the word of God is abused. Those who cannot read correctly should learn to do so, and should become apt to teach, before they attempt to stand before the public.

The teachers in our schools are obliged to apply themselves closely to study, that they may be prepared to instruct others. These teachers are not accepted until they have passed a critical examination, and their capabilities to teach have been tested by competent judges. No less caution should be used in the examination of ministers; those who are about to enter upon the sacred work of teaching Bible truth to the world, should be carefully examined by faithful, experienced men.

The teaching in our schools is not to be the same as in other colleges and seminaries. It is not to be of an inferior order; the knowledge essential to prepare a people to stand in the great day of God is to be made the all-important theme. The students are to be fitted to serve God, not only in this life, but in the future life. The Lord requires that our schools shall fit students for the kingdom to which they are bound. Thus they will be prepared to blend in the holy, happy harmony of the redeemed. . . .

Let those who have been trained for service now take their places quickly in the Lord's work. House-to-house laborers are needed. The Lord calls for decided efforts to be put forth in places where the people know nothing of Bible truth. Singing and praying and Bible-readings are needed in the homes of the people. Now, just now, is the time to obey the commission, "Teaching them to observe all things whatsoever I have commanded you." [4] Those who do this work must have a ready knowledge of the Scriptures. "It is written" is to be their weapon of defense. God has given us light on His word, that we may give this light to our fellow-men. The truth spoken by Christ will reach hearts. A "Thus saith the Lord" will fall upon the ear with power, and fruit will appear wherever honest service is done.—*"Counsels to Teachers," pages 535-540.*

[4] Matt. 28 : 20.

EDUCATION FOR MISSIONARY WORK *

"We are laborers together with God: ye are God's husbandry, ye are God's building." [1]

The work of the Christian laborer is not light or unimportant. He has a high vocation, from which his whole future life must take its mould and coloring. He who gives himself to so sacred a work should bend all his energies to its accomplishment. He should aim high; he will never reach a higher standard than that which he seeks to attain. He cannot diffuse light until he has first received it. He must be a learner before he can have sufficient wisdom and experience to become a teacher, able to open the Scriptures to those who are in darkness. If God has called men to be laborers together with Him, it is equally certain that He has called them to make the best possible preparation rightly to represent the sacred, elevating truths of His word.

Those who desire to give themselves to the work of God should receive an education and training for this work, that they may be prepared to engage in it intelligently. They should not feel that they can step at once upon the higher rounds of the ladder; those who would succeed must begin at the first round, and climb upward step by step. Opportunities and privileges are granted them for improvement, and they should make every effort in their power to learn how to do the work of God acceptably.

* First published in "Historical Sketches of S. D. A. Foreign Missions," 1886.
[1] 1 Cor. 3 : 9.

Wherever our ministers labor, in Europe or in America, they should seek to arouse the youth to prepare for active service in God's great field of battle. All who claim to be the servants of Christ have a work to do for Him. The very name of servant conveys the idea of hire, work, responsibility. To every one God has entrusted powers to be employed in His service. He has given to each his work, and He requires that every faculty shall be improved to His glory.

THE TRAINING OF SOLDIERS

Just in front of our printing-office in Basel, Switzerland, is a large park of many acres, reserved by the government for military drill. Here, day after day, at certain seasons of the year, we see the soldiers training. They are drilled in all the duties of the army, so that in case of war they may be ready at the call of the government to engage in actual service.

One day a fine tent was brought upon the ground. Then came the discipline of pitching it and taking it down. Instruction was given as to setting it up in proper order, every man having his specific work to do. Several times the tent was pitched and taken down.

By another company many small cannon were brought upon the ground, and lessons were given by the officers in the matter of moving these quickly from place to place, in taking apart the cannon wagon, and setting the gun ready for use, and in quickly attaching again the fore wheels, so as to be ready at the call to set them in motion in an instant.

Ambulances were brought to the ground, and the sanitary corps were taught to take care of the wounded.

Men were laid upon stretchers, and their heads and limbs were bandaged as are those of the wounded on the field of battle. Then they were laid in the ambulance and drawn from the ground.

For hours, soldiers are drilled to disencumber themselves of their knapsacks, and place them quickly in position again upon the person. They are taught how to stack their arms, and how to seize them quickly. They are drilled in making a charge against the enemy, and are trained in all kinds of maneuvers.

Thus the drill goes on, preparing men for any emergency. And should those who are fighting the battle for Prince Emmanuel be less earnest and painstaking in their preparation for the spiritual warfare? Those who engage in this great work must take part in the necessary drill. They must learn to obey before they are fitted to command.

FACILITIES FOR TRAINING

There should be decided advancement in the matter of special preparatory work. In all our conferences there should be well-organized plans for the instruction and training of those who desire to give themselves to the work of God. Our city missions afford favorable opportunities for education in missionary labor; but these are not enough. There ought to be connected with our schools the best possible facilities for the preparation of laborers for both home and foreign fields. There should also be in our larger churches special training-schools for young men and women, to fit them to become workers for God. And far more attention should be given by our ministers to the matter of assisting and educating younger laborers.

When an effort is made to introduce the truth in an important place, our ministers should give special attention to the instruction and training of those who are to co-operate with them. Colporteurs and canvassers are needed, and those who are fitted to give Bible-readings in families, so that while the ministers are laboring in word and doctrine, these can also be calling minds to the truth.

Our ministers who have gone to important places to hold tent-meetings, have often made a serious mistake in devoting all their time to sermonizing. There should be less preaching and more teaching,— teaching the people, and also teaching young men how to labor successfully. Ministers should become efficient in teaching others how to study the Bible, and in training the minds and manners of those who would become workers in the cause of God. And they should be ready to counsel and instruct those who have newly come to the faith, and who give promise of possessing ability to work for the Master. . . .

All who would be efficient workers must give much time to prayer. The communication between God and the soul must be kept open, that the workers may recognize the voice of their Captain. The Bible should be diligently studied. The truth of God, like gold, is not always lying right on the surface; it is to be obtained only by earnest thought and study. This study will not only store the mind with most valuable knowledge, but will strengthen and expand the mental powers, and will give a true estimate of eternal things. Let the divine precepts be brought into the daily life; let the life be fashioned after God's great standard of righteousness, and the whole character will be strengthened and ennobled.

He who is seeking to qualify himself for the sacred work of God should be careful not to place himself on the enemy's ground, but should choose the society of those who will help him to obtain divine knowledge. God suffered John, the beloved disciple, to be exiled to Patmos, where he was separated from the world's bustle and strife, shut away from every outside influence, and even from the work that he loved. Then the Lord could commune with him, opening before him the closing scenes of this world's history. John the Baptist made his home in the wilderness, there to receive from God the message that he was to bear,— a message that was to prepare the way for the Coming One.

So far as consistent, we should shun every influence that would tend to divert the mind from the work of God. And those especially who are young in faith and experience should beware that they do not in self-confidence place themselves in the way of temptation.

Those who take hold of the work aright, will feel the necessity of having Jesus with them at every step, and they will feel that the cultivation of the mind and the manners is a duty due to themselves and required by God,— a duty which is essential to the success of the work.

SELF-SUFFICIENCY

Some who contemplate becoming missionary workers may think themselves so far advanced that they do not need all this particular drill; but those who feel thus are the very ones who stand in the greatest need of thorough training. When they know much more in regard to the truth and the importance of the work, they will realize their ignorance and inefficiency.

When they closely examine their own hearts, they will see themselves in such contrast to the pure character of Christ that they will cry out, "Who is sufficient for these things?" Then they will in deep humility strive daily to place themselves in close connection with Christ. While overcoming the selfish inclinations of the natural heart, they are placing their feet in the path where Christ leads the way. "The entrance of Thy words giveth light; it giveth understanding unto the simple." [2] But those who have a high estimate of their own ability and acquisitions, are so full of self-importance that there is no opportunity for the entrance of the word of God to instruct and enlighten them.

Many feel that they are fitted for a work that they know scarcely anything about; and if they start to labor in a self-important manner, they will fail to receive that knowledge which they must obtain in the school of Christ. These will be doomed to struggle with many difficulties, for which they are wholly unprepared. They will ever lack experience and wisdom until they learn their great inefficiency.

Very much has been lost to the cause by the defective labors of men who possess ability, but who have not had proper training. They have engaged in a work which they knew not how to manage, and as the result have accomplished but little. They have not done a tithe of what they could have done had they received the right discipline at the start. They seized upon a few ideas, managed to get a runway of a few discourses, and here their progress ended. They felt competent to be teachers, when they had scarcely mastered their *a b c* in the knowledge of the truth. They have been stumbling along ever since, not do-

[2] Ps. 119 : 130.

ing justice to themselves or to the work. They do not seem to have sufficient interest to arouse their dormant energies, or to tax their powers to become efficient workers. They have not taken pains to form thorough and well-devised plans, and their work shows deficiency in every part.

Some have given up in discouragement, and have engaged in other employment. Had these patiently and humbly placed their feet on the lowest round of the ladder, and then with persevering energy climbed step by step, diligently improving the privileges and opportunities within their reach, they might have become able, useful workmen, who could give full proof of their ministry, and of whom the Master would not be ashamed.

If those who propose to work for the salvation of souls depend on their own finite wisdom, they will certainly fail. If they entertain humble views of self, and rely fully upon the promises of God, He will never fail them. "Trust in the Lord with all thine heart; and lean not unto thine own understanding. In all thy ways acknowledge Him, and He shall direct thy paths." [3] We have the privilege of being directed by a wise Counselor.

God can make humble men mighty in His service. Those who obediently respond to the call of duty, improving their abilities to the very utmost, may be sure of receiving divine assistance. Angels will come as messengers of light to the help of those who will do all that they can on their part, and then trust in God to co-operate with their efforts.

It should be impressed on all who have decided to become workers for God, that they must give evidence

[3] Prov. 3 : 5, 6.

that they are converted men. A young man without a sound, virtuous character will be no honor to the truth. Every worker should be pure in heart; in his mouth should be found no guile. He should bear in mind that, to be successful, he must have Christ by his side, and that every sinful practice, however secret, is open to the view of Him with whom we have to do.

Sin has marred the divine image in man. Through Christ this may be restored, but it is only through earnest prayer and the conquest of self that we can become partakers of the divine nature. . . .

The true toilers in the Lord's vineyard will be men of prayer, of faith, of self-denial,— men who hold in restraint the natural appetites and passions. These will in their own lives give evidence of the power of the truth which they present to others; and their labors will not be without effect.

———◆———

The worker for God should be prepared to put forth the highest mental and moral energies with which nature, cultivation, and the grace of God have endowed him; but his success will be proportionate to the degree of consecration and self-sacrifice in which the work is done, rather than to either natural or acquired endowments. The most earnest and continued efforts to acquire qualifications for usefulness are necessary; but unless God works with the human effort, nothing can be accomplished. Christ says, "Without Me ye can do nothing." [4] Divine grace is the great element of saving power; without it all human efforts are unavailing.—"*Testimonies for the Church,*" *Vol. V, page 583.*

[4] John 15 : 5.

YOUNG MEN AS MISSIONARIES

Young men who desire to enter the field as ministers, colporteurs, or canvassers, should first receive a suitable degree of mental training, as well as a special preparation for their calling. Those who are uneducated, untrained, and unrefined, are not prepared to enter a field in which the powerful influences of talent and education combat the truths of God's word. Neither can they successfully meet the strange forms of error, religious and philosophical combined, to expose which requires a knowledge of scientific as well as Scriptural truth.

Those especially who have the ministry in view, should feel the importance of the Scriptural method of ministerial training. They should enter heartily into the work, and while they study in the schools, they should learn of the great Teacher the meekness and humility of Christ. A covenant-keeping God has promised that in answer to prayer His Spirit shall be poured out upon these learners in the school of Christ, that they may become ministers of righteousness.

There is hard work to be done in dislodging error and false doctrine from the head, that Bible truth and Bible religion may find a place in the heart. It was as a means ordained of God to educate young men and women for the various departments of missionary labor, that colleges were established among us. It is God's will that they send forth not merely a few, but many laborers. But Satan, determined to overthrow this purpose, has often secured the very ones whom God would qualify for places of usefulness in His work.

There are many who would work if urged into service, and who would save their souls by thus working. The church should feel her great responsibility in shutting up the light of truth, and restraining the grace of God within her own narrow limits, when money and influence should be freely employed in bringing competent persons into the missionary field.

Hundreds of young men should have been preparing to act a part in the work of scattering the seeds of truth beside all waters. We want men who will push the triumphs of the cross; men who will persevere under discouragements and privations; who will have the zeal and resolution and faith that are indispensable in the missionary field. . . .

FOREIGN LANGUAGES

There are among us those who, without the toil and delay of learning a foreign language, might qualify themselves to proclaim the truth to other nations. In the primitive church, missionaries were miraculously endowed with a knowledge of the languages in which they were called to preach the unsearchable riches of Christ. And if God was willing thus to help His servants then, can we doubt that His blessing will rest upon our efforts to qualify those who naturally possess a knowledge of foreign tongues, and who, with proper encouragement, would bear to their own countrymen the message of truth? We might have had more laborers in foreign missionary fields, had those who entered these fields availed themselves of every talent within their reach. . . .

It may in some cases be necessary that young men learn foreign languages. This they can do with most success by associating with the people, and at the same time devoting a portion of each day to studying the language. This should be done, however, only as a necessary step preparatory to educating such as are found in the missionary fields themselves, and who, with proper training, can become workers. It is essential that those be urged into the service who can speak in their mother tongue to the people of different nations.

It is a great undertaking for a man of middle age to learn a foreign language; and with all his efforts, it will be next to impossible for him to speak it so readily and correctly as to render him an efficient laborer. We cannot afford to deprive our home missions of the influence of middle-aged and aged ministers, to send them into distant fields to engage in a work for which they are not qualified, and to which no amount of training will enable them to adapt themselves. The men thus sent out leave vacancies which inexperienced laborers cannot supply.

YOUNG MEN WANTED FOR HARD PLACES

The church may inquire whether young men can be entrusted with the grave responsibilities involved in the establishing and superintending of a foreign mission. I answer, God designed that they should be so trained in our colleges and by association in labor with men of experience, that they would be prepared for places of usefulness in this cause.

We must manifest confidence in our young men. They should be pioneers in every enterprise involving toil and sacrifice, while the overtaxed servants of Christ should be cherished as counselors, to encourage and bless those who strike the heaviest blows for God. Providence thrust these experienced fathers into trying, responsible positions at an early age, when neither physical nor intellectual powers were fully developed. The magnitude of the trust committed to them aroused their energies, and their active labor in the work aided both physical and mental development.

Young men are wanted. God calls them to missionary fields. Being comparatively free from care and responsibilities, they are more favorably situated to engage in the work than are those who must provide for the training and support of a large family. Furthermore, young men can more readily adapt themselves to new climates and new society, and can better endure inconveniences and hardships. By tact and perseverance, they can reach the people where they are.

Strength comes by exercise. All who put to use the ability which God has given them, will have increased ability to devote to His service. Those who do nothing in the cause of God, will fail to grow in grace and in the knowledge of the truth. A man who would lie down and refuse to exercise his limbs, would soon lose all power to use them. Thus the Christian who will not exercise his God-given powers, not only fails to grow up into Christ, but he loses the strength which he already had; he becomes a spiritual paralytic.

It is those who, with love for God and their fellow-men, are striving to help others, that become established, strengthened, settled, in the truth. The true Christian works for God, not from impulse, but from principle; not for a day or a month, but during the entire life. . . .

The Master calls for gospel workers. Who will respond? Not all who enter the army are to be generals, captains, sergeants, or even corporals. Not all have the care and responsibility of leaders. There is hard work of other kinds to be done. Some must dig trenches and build fortifications; some are to stand as sentinels, some to carry messages. While there are but few officers, it requires many soldiers to form the rank and file of the army; yet its success depends upon the fidelity of every soldier. One man's cowardice or treachery may bring disaster upon the entire army. . . .

He who has appointed "to every man his work," [1] according to his ability, will never let the faithful performance of duty go unrewarded. Every act of loyalty and faith will be crowned with special tokens of God's favor and approbation. To every worker is given the promise, "He that goeth forth and weepeth, bearing precious seed, shall doubtless come again with rejoicing, bringing his sheaves with him." [2] —*"Testimonies for the Church," Vol. V, pages 390-395.*

———◆———

Many a lad of to-day, growing up as did Daniel in his Judean home, studying God's word and His works, and learning the lessons of faithful service, will yet stand in legislative assemblies, in halls of justice, or in royal courts, as a witness for the King of kings. Multitudes will be called to a wider ministry. The whole world is opening to the gospel. Ethiopia is stretching out her hands unto God. From Japan and China and India, from the still darkened lands of our own continent, from every quarter of this world of ours, comes the cry of sin-stricken hearts for a knowledge of the God of love.—*"Education," page 262.*

[1] Mark 13 : 34.   [2] Ps. 126 : 6.

VOICE TRAINING FOR WORKERS

In all our ministerial work, more attention should be given to the culture of the voice. We may have knowledge, but unless we know how to use the voice correctly, our work will be a failure. Unless we can clothe our ideas in appropriate language, of what avail is our education? Knowledge will be of little advantage to us unless we cultivate the talent of speech; but it is a wonderful power when combined with the ability to speak wise, helpful words, and to speak them in a way that will command attention.

Students who expect to become workers in the cause of God should be trained to speak in a clear, straightforward manner, else they will be shorn of half their influence for good. The ability to speak plainly and clearly, in full, round tones, is invaluable in any line of work. This qualification is indispensable in those who desire to become ministers, evangelists, Bible-workers, or canvassers. Those who are planning to enter these lines of work should be taught to use the voice in such a way that when they speak to people about the truth, a decided impression for good will be made. The truth must not be marred by being communicated through defective utterance.

The canvasser who can speak clearly and distinctly about the merits of the book he wishes to sell, will find this a great help in his work. He may have an opportunity to read a chapter of the book, and by the music of his voice and the emphasis placed on the words, he can make the scene presented stand out as clearly before the mind of the listener as if it could actually be seen.

The one who gives Bible-readings in the congregation or in the family should be able to read with a soft, musical cadence which will charm the hearers.

Ministers of the gospel should know how to speak with power and expression, making the words of eternal life so expressive and impressive that the hearers cannot but feel their weight. I am pained as I hear the defective voices of many of our ministers. Such ministers rob God of the glory He might have if they had trained themselves to speak the word with power.

OVERCOMING DEFECTS

No man should regard himself as qualified to enter the ministry until by persevering effort he has overcome every defect in his utterance. If he attempts to speak to the people without knowing how to use the talent of speech, half his influence is lost, for he has little power to hold the attention of a congregation.

Whatever his calling, every person should learn to control the voice, so that when something goes wrong, he will not speak in tones that stir the worst passions of the heart. Too often the speaker and the one addressed speak sharply and harshly. Sharp, dictatorial words, uttered in hard, rasping tones, have separated friends and resulted in the loss of souls. . . .

In the social meeting there is special need of clear, distinct utterance, that all may hear the testimonies borne and be benefited by them. Difficulties are removed and help is given as in social meeting God's people relate their experiences. But too often the testimonies are borne with faulty, indistinct utterance, and it is impossible to gain a correct idea of what is said. Thus the blessing is often lost.

Let those who pray and those who speak pronounce their words properly, and speak in clear, distinct, even tones. Prayer, if properly offered, is a power for good. It is one of the means used by the Lord to communicate to the people the precious treasures of truth. But prayer is not what it should be, because of the defective voices of those who utter it. Satan rejoices when the prayers offered to God are almost inaudible.

Let God's people learn how to speak and pray in a way that will properly represent the great truths they possess. Let the testimonies borne and the prayers offered be clear and distinct. Thus God will be glorified. Let all make the most of the talent of speech.

God calls for a higher, more perfect ministry. He is dishonored by the imperfect utterance of the one who by painstaking effort could become an acceptable mouthpiece for Him. The truth is too often marred by the channel through which it passes.

The Lord calls upon all who are connected with His service to give attention to the cultivation of the voice, that they may utter in an acceptable manner the great and solemn truths He has entrusted to them. Let none mar the truth by defective utterance. Let not those who have neglected to cultivate the talent of speech suppose that they are qualified to minister; for they have yet to obtain the power to communicate.

DISTINCT ENUNCIATION

When you speak, let every word be full and well rounded, every sentence clear and distinct, to the very last word. Many as they approach the end of a sentence lower the tone of the voice, speaking so indistinctly that the force of the thought is destroyed. Words that are worth speaking at all are worth speaking in a clear, distinct voice, with emphasis and expression. But never search for words that will give the impression that you are learned. The greater your simplicity, the better will your words be understood.

Young men and women, has God placed in your hearts a desire to do service for Him? Then by all means cultivate the voice to the utmost of your ability, so that you can make plain the precious truth to others. Do not fall into the habit of praying so indistinctly and in so low a tone that your prayers need an interpreter. Pray simply, but clearly and distinctly. To let the voice sink so low that it cannot be heard, is no evidence of humility.

To those who are planning to enter God's service as ministers, I would say, Strive with determination to be perfect in speech. Ask God to help you to accomplish this great object. When in the congregation you offer prayer, remember that you are addressing God, and that He desires you to speak so that all who are present can hear and can blend their supplications with yours. A prayer uttered so hurriedly that the words are jumbled together, is no honor to God and does the hearers no good. Let ministers and all who offer public prayer learn to pray in such a way that God will be glorified and the hearers will be blessed. Let them speak slowly and distinctly, and in tones loud enough to be heard by all, so that the people may unite in saying **Amen.**—*"Testimonies for the Church,"* *Vol. VI, pages 380-383.*

Some of our most talented ministers are doing themselves great injury by their defective manner of speaking. While teaching the people their duty to obey God's moral law, they should not be found violating the laws of God in regard to health and life. Ministers should stand erect, and speak slowly, firmly, and distinctly, taking a full inspiration of air at every sentence, and throwing out the words by exercising the abdominal muscles. If they will observe this simple rule, giving attention to the laws of health in other respects, they may preserve their life and usefulness much longer than men in any other profession. The chest will become broader, and . . . the speaker need seldom become hoarse, even by constant speaking. Instead of becoming consumptives, ministers may, by exercising care, overcome all tendency to consumption.

Unless ministers educate themselves to speak in accordance with physical law, they will sacrifice life, and many will mourn the loss of "those martyrs to the cause of truth;" when the facts in the case are, that by indulging in wrong habits, they did injustice to themselves and to the truth which they represented, and robbed God and the world of the service they might have rendered. God would have been pleased to have them live, but they slowly committed suicide.

The manner in which the truth is presented often has much to do in determining whether it will be accepted or rejected. All who labor in the great cause of reform should study to become efficient workmen, that they may accomplish the greatest possible amount of good, and not detract from the force of the truth by their own deficiencies.

Ministers and teachers should discipline themselves to articulate clearly and distinctly, allowing the full sound to every word. Those who talk rapidly, from the throat, jumbling the words together, and raising the voice to an unnaturally high pitch, soon become hoarse, and the words spoken lose half the force which they would have if spoken slowly, distinctly, and not so loud. The sympathies of the hearers are awakened for the speaker; for they know that he is doing violence to himself, and they fear that he will break down at any moment. It is no evidence that a man has zeal for God because he works himself up into a frenzy of excitement and gesticulation. "Bodily exercise," says the apostle, "profiteth little." [1]

The Saviour of the world would have His co-laborers represent Him; and the more closely a man walks with God, the more faultless will be his manner of address, his deportment, his attitude, and his gestures. Coarse and uncouth manners were never seen in our pattern, Christ Jesus. He was a representative of heaven, and His followers must be like Him.

Some reason that the Lord will by His Holy Spirit qualify a man to speak as He would have him; but the Lord does not propose to do the work that He has given man to do. He has given us reasoning powers, and opportunities to educate the mind and manners. And after we have done all we can for ourselves, making the best use of the advantages within our reach, then we may look to God with earnest prayer to do by His Spirit that which we cannot do for ourselves.—*"Testimonies for the Church," Vol. IV, pages 404, 405.*

[1] 1 Tim. 4 : 8.

"STUDY TO SHOW THYSELF APPROVED"

The cause of God needs efficient men; it needs men who are trained to do service as teachers and preachers. Men have labored with a measure of success who have had little training in school or college; but these might have attained a greater measure of success, and might have been more efficient laborers, if at the very start they had acquired mental discipline.

To Timothy, a youthful minister, the apostle Paul wrote, "Study to show thyself approved unto God, a workman that needeth not to be ashamed, rightly dividing the word of truth." [1] The work of winning souls to Christ demands careful preparation. Men cannot enter the Lord's service without the needed training, and expect the highest success. Mechanics, lawyers, merchants, men of all trades and professions, are educated for the line of business they hope to enter. It is their policy to make themselves as efficient as possible. Go to the milliner or the dressmaker, and she will tell you how long she toiled before she had a thorough knowledge of her business. The architect will tell you how long it took him to understand how to plan a tasteful, commodious building. And so it is in all the callings that men follow.

Should the servants of Christ show less diligence in preparing for a work infinitely more important? Should they be ignorant of the ways and means to be employed in winning souls? It requires a knowledge of human nature, close study, careful thought, and earnest prayer, to know how to approach men and women on the great subjects that concern their eternal welfare.

[1] 2 Tim. 2:15.

Not a few of those called to be co-laborers with the Master have failed to learn their trade. They have dishonored their Redeemer by entering His work without the needed preparation. There are some who, becoming wearied by the superficial gloss that the world calls refinement, have gone to the other extreme, and one fully as harmful. They refuse to receive the polish and refinement that Christ desires His children to possess. The minister should remember that he is an educator, and that if in manner and speech he is coarse and unrefined, those who have less knowledge and experience will follow in his steps.

SUPERFICIAL KNOWLEDGE

Never should a young minister rest satisfied with a superficial knowledge of the truth, for he knows not where he may be required to bear witness for God. Many will have to stand before kings and before the learned of the earth, to answer for their faith. Those who have only a superficial understanding of the truth have failed to become workmen that need not be ashamed. They will be confused, and will not be able clearly to expound the Scriptures.

It is a lamentable fact that the advancement of the cause is hindered by the dearth of educated laborers. Many are wanting in moral and intellectual qualifications. They do not tax the mind, they do not dig for the hidden treasure. Because they only skim the surface, they gain only that knowledge which is to be found upon the surface.

Do men think that they will be able, under pressure of circumstances, to step into an important position, when they have neglected to train and discipline themselves for the work? Do they imagine that they can be polished instruments in the hands of God for the salvation of souls, if they have not used the opportunities placed at their command for obtaining a fitness for the work? The cause of God calls for all-round men, who can devise, plan, build up, and organize. And those who appreciate the probabilities and possibilities of the work for this time, will seek by earnest study to obtain all the knowledge they can from the Word, to use in ministering to needy, sin-sick souls.

A minister should never think that he has learned enough, and may now relax his efforts. His education should continue throughout his lifetime; every day he should be learning, and putting to use the knowledge gained.

Let those who are in training for the ministry never forget that the preparation of the heart is of all the most important. No amount of mental culture or theological training can take the place of this. The bright beams of the Sun of Righteousness must shine into the heart of the worker and purify his life, before light from the throne of God can shine through him to those in darkness.

During the night many scenes passed before me, and many points in reference to the work that we are to do for our Master, the Lord Jesus Christ, were made plain and clear. Words were spoken by One of authority, and I will try to repeat in finite words the instruction given regarding the work to be done. The heavenly Messenger said:

The ministry is becoming enfeebled because men are assuming the responsibility of preaching without gaining the needed preparation for this work. Many have made a mistake in receiving credentials. They will have to take up work to which they are better adapted than the preaching of the word. They are being paid from the tithe, but their efforts are feeble, and they should not continue to be paid from this fund. In many ways the ministry is losing its sacred character.

Those who are called to the ministry of the word are to be true, self-sacrificing laborers. God calls for men who realize that they must put forth earnest effort, men who bring thought, zeal, prudence, capability, and the attributes of Christ's character into their labors. The saving of souls is a vast work, which calls for the employment of every talent, every gift of grace. Those engaged in it should constantly increase in efficiency. They should have an earnest desire to strengthen their powers, knowing that they will be weak without a constantly increasing supply of grace. They should seek to attain larger and still larger results in their work. When this is the experience of our workers, fruit will be seen. Many souls will be won to the truth.

————◆————

Higher than the highest human thought can reach is God's ideal for His children. Godliness — Godlikeness — is the goal to be reached. Before the student here is opened a path of continual progress. He has an object to achieve, a standard to attain, that includes everything good, and pure, and noble. He will advance as fast and as far as possible in every branch of true knowledge.—*"Education," page 18.*

CANVASSING AS AN EDUCATION FOR THE MINISTRY

One of the very best ways in which young men can obtain a fitness for the ministry is by entering the canvassing field. Let them go into towns and cities to canvass for the books which contain the truth for this time. In this work they will find opportunity to speak the words of life, and the seeds of truth they sow will spring up to bear fruit. By meeting the people and presenting to them our publications, they will gain an experience that they could not gain by preaching.

When young men enter the canvassing field filled with an intense longing to save their fellow-men, a harvest for the Lord will be reaped as a result of their efforts. Then let them go forth as missionaries, to proclaim present truth, praying constantly for increased light, and for the guidance of the Spirit, that they may know how to speak words in season to those who are weary. Let them improve every opportunity for performing deeds of kindness, remembering that they are doing errands for the Lord.

All who desire an opportunity for true ministry, and who will give themselves unreservedly to God, will find in the canvassing work opportunity to speak upon many things pertaining to the future immortal life. The experience thus gained will be of the greatest value to those who are fitting themselves for the ministry.

It is the accompaniment of the Holy Spirit of God that prepares workers, both men and women, to become pastors to the flock of God. As they cherish the thought that Christ is their companion, a holy awe, a sacred joy, will be felt by them amid all their trying experiences and all their tests. They will learn to pray as they work. They will be educated in patience, kindness, affability, and helpfulness. They will practice true Christian courtesy, bearing in mind that Christ, their companion, cannot approve of harsh, unkind words or feelings. Their words will be purified. The power of speech will be regarded as a precious talent, lent them to do a high and holy work.

The human agent will learn how to represent the divine Companion with whom he is associated. To that unseen Holy One he will show respect and reverence, because he is wearing His yoke and is learning His pure, holy ways. Those who have faith in this divine Attendant will develop. They will be gifted with power to clothe the message of truth with a sacred beauty.—*"Testimonies for the Church," Vol. VI, p. 322.*

Follow on, young men, to know the Lord, and you will know that "His going forth is prepared as the morning." [1] Seek constantly to improve. Strive earnestly for close fellowship with the Redeemer. Live by faith in Christ. Do the work He did. Live for the saving of the souls for whom He laid down His life. Try in every way to help those with whom you come in contact. . . . Talk with your Elder Brother, who will complete your education line upon line, precept upon precept, here a little and there a little. A close connection with Him who offered Himself as a sacrifice to save a perishing world, will make you acceptable workers.—*"Testimonies for the Church," Vol. VI, page 416.*

[1] Hosea 6 : 3.

BIBLE STUDY NECESSARY TO EFFICIENCY

Those young men who desire to give themselves to the ministry, or who have already done so, should become familiar with every line of prophetic history and every lesson given by Christ. The mind gains in strength, breadth, and acuteness by active use. It must work, or it will become weak. It must be trained to think, to think habitually, or it will in a great measure lose the power of thought. Let the young minister wrestle with the difficult problems found in the word of God, and his intellect will be thoroughly awakened. As he gives diligent study to the great truths found in the Scriptures, he will be enabled to preach sermons which will contain a direct, definite message, and which will help his hearers to choose the right way.

The minister who ventures to teach the truth when he has only a smattering knowledge of the word of God, grieves the Holy Spirit. But he who begins with a little knowledge, and tells what he knows, at the same time seeking for more knowledge, will become qualified to do a larger work. The more light he gathers to his own soul, the more of heavenly illumination will he be able to impart to others.

There is no need for weakness in the ministry. The message of truth that we bear is all-powerful. But many ministers do not put their minds to the task of studying the deep things of God. If these would have power in their service, obtaining an experience that will enable them to help others, they must overcome their indolent habits of thought. Let ministers put the whole heart into the task of searching the Scriptures, and a new power will come to them. A divine element unites with human effort when the soul reaches out after God; and the yearning heart may say, "My soul, wait thou only upon God; for my expectation is from Him." [1]

Ministers who would labor effectively for the salvation of souls must be Bible students and men of prayer. It is a sin to be neglectful of the study of the Word while attempting to teach it to others. Those who feel the worth of souls realize that too much is at stake for them to dare to be careless in regard to their advancement in divine knowledge, and they flee to the stronghold of truth, whence they may obtain wisdom, knowledge, and strength to work the works of God. They will not rest without an unction from on high.

As the worker makes a constant companion of the word of God, he gains an increased ability to labor. Continually advancing in knowledge, he becomes constantly better able to represent Christ. He is strengthened in faith, and can present to unbelievers a proof of the fulness of the grace and love that is in Christ. His mind is a treasure-house, from which he can draw to supply the needs of others. By the work of the Holy Spirit the truth is graven on his mind, and those to whom he communicates truth, and for whom he must one day give account, are greatly blessed. He who in this way obtains a preparation for the ministry, is entitled to the reward promised to those who turn many to righteousness.

The perusal of works upon our faith, the reading of arguments from the pens of others, is an excellent and important aid, but this will not give the mind the great-

[1] Ps. 62 : 5.

est strength. The Bible is the best book in the world for giving intellectual culture. Its study taxes the mind, strengthens the memory, and sharpens the intellect more than the study of all the subjects that human philosophy embraces. The great themes which it presents, the dignified simplicity with which these themes are handled, the light which is shed upon the great problems of life, bring strength and vigor to the understanding.

In the great conflict before us, he who would keep true to Christ must penetrate deeper than the opinions and doctrines of men. My message to ministers, young and old, is this: Guard jealously your hours for prayer, Bible study, and self-examination. Set aside a portion of each day for a study of the Scriptures and communion with God. Thus you will obtain spiritual strength, and will grow in favor with God. He alone can give you noble aspirations; He alone can fashion the character after the divine similitude. Draw near to Him in earnest prayer, and He will fill your hearts with high and holy purposes, and with deep, earnest longings for purity and clearness of thought.

———◆———

A true knowledge of the Bible can be gained only through the aid of that Spirit by whom the Word was given. And in order to gain this knowledge, we must live by it. All that God's word commands, we are to obey. All that it promises, we may claim. The life which it enjoins is the life that, through its power, we are to live. Only as the Bible is thus held, can it be studied effectively.—*"Education," page 189.*

YOUNG MINISTERS TO LABOR WITH
OLDER MINISTERS

In gaining a preparation for the ministry, young men should be associated with older ministers. Those who have gained an experience in active service are to take young, inexperienced workers with them into the harvest-field, teaching them how to labor successfully for the conversion of souls. Kindly and affectionately these older workers are to help the younger ones to prepare for the work to which the Lord may call them. And the young men in training should respect the counsel of their instructors, honoring their devotion, and remembering that their years of labor have given them wisdom.

Wise counsel for church and conference officers is given by Peter in the following words: "Feed the flock of God which is among you, taking the oversight thereof, not by constraint, but willingly; not for filthy lucre, but of a ready mind; neither as being lords over God's heritage, but being ensamples to the flock. And when the Chief Shepherd shall appear, ye shall receive a crown of glory that fadeth not away. Likewise, ye younger, submit yourselves unto the elder. Yea, all of you be subject one to another, and be clothed with humility: for God resisteth the proud, and giveth grace to the humble." [1]

Let the older workers be educators, keeping themselves under the discipline of God. Let the young men feel it a privilege to study under older workers, and let them carry every burden that their youth and experi-

[1] 1 Peter 5 : 2-5.

ence will allow. Thus Elijah educated the youth of Israel in the schools of the prophets; and young men to-day are to have a similar training. It is not possible to advise in every particular the part that the youth should act; but they should be faithfully instructed by the older workers, and taught to look ever to Him who is the author and finisher of our faith.

The apostle Paul saw the importance of training younger workers. After making a missionary tour, he and Barnabas retraced their steps, and visited the churches they had raised up, choosing men whom they could unite with them, to train for the work of proclaiming the gospel.

Paul made it a part of his work to educate young men for the gospel ministry. He took them with him on his missionary journeys, and thus they gained an experience that later enabled them to fill positions of responsibility. When separated from them, he still kept in touch with their work, and his letters to Timothy and Titus are an evidence of how deep was his desire for their success. "The things that thou hast heard," he wrote, "commit thou to faithful men, who shall be able to teach others also." [2]

This feature of Paul's work teaches an important lesson to ministers to-day. Experienced laborers do a noble work when, instead of trying to carry all the burdens themselves, they train younger men, and place burdens on their shoulders. It is God's desire that those who have gained an experience in His cause, shall train young men for His service.

The younger worker must not become so wrapped up in the ideas and opinions of the one in whose charge he is placed, that he will forfeit his individuality. He

[2] 2 Tim. 2:2.

must not lose his identity in the one who is instructing him, so that he dare not exercise his own judgment, but does what he is told, irrespective of his own understanding of what is right and wrong. It is his privilege to learn for himself of the great Teacher. If the one with whom he is working pursues a course which is not in harmony with a "Thus saith the Lord," let him not go to some outside party, but let him go to his superior in office, and lay the matter before him, freely expressing his mind. Thus the learner may be a blessing to the teacher. He must faithfully discharge his duty. God will not hold him guiltless if he connives at a wrong course of action, however great may be the influence or responsibility of the one taking the wrong course.

Young men will be bidden to link up with the aged standard-bearers, that they may be strengthened and taught by these faithful ones, who have passed through so many conflicts, and to whom, through the testimonies of His Spirit, God has so often spoken, pointing out the right way and condemning the wrong. When perils arise which try the faith of God's people, these pioneer workers are to recount the experiences of the past, when in just such crises the truth was questioned, and strange sentiments, proceeding not from God, were brought in. To-day Satan is seeking opportunities to tear down the waymarks of truth,— the monuments that have been raised up along the way; and we need the experience of the aged workers who have built their house upon the solid rock, who through evil report as well as good report have been steadfast to the truth.

THE YOUNG MINISTER

Young men are to enter the ministry as co-workers with Jesus, sharing His life of self-denial and sacrifice, voicing the words of the Master, "I sanctify Myself, that they also might be sanctified." [1] If they will yield themselves to God, He will use them in helping to carry out His plan for the salvation of souls. Let the young man who has entered the ministry look his calling fairly in the face, and determine to devote his time, his strength, his influence, to the work, well aware of the conditions under which he serves the Redeemer.

The standard-bearers are falling, and young men must be prepared to take the places left vacant, that the message may still be proclaimed. The aggressive warfare is to be extended. Those who have youth and strength are to go into the dark places of the earth, to call perishing souls to repentance. But they must first cleanse the soul-temple of all impurity, and enthrone Christ in the heart.

"TAKE HEED"

To every young man who enters the ministry, Paul's words to Timothy are spoken, "Take heed unto thyself, and unto the doctrine." [2] "Thyself" needs the first attention. First give yourself to the Lord for purification and sanctification. A godly example will tell more for the truth than the greatest eloquence, unaccompanied by a well-ordered life. Trim the lamp of the soul, and replenish it with the oil of the Spirit.

[1] John 17:19.　　[2] 1 Tim. 4:16.

Seek from Christ that grace, that clearness of comprehension, which will enable you to do successful work. Learn from Him what it means to work for those for whom He gave His life.

"Take heed," first to yourself, and then to the doctrine. Do not let your heart become hardened by sin. Closely examine your manners and habits. Compare them with the word of God, and then cut away from the life every wrong habit and indulgence. Kneel before God, and plead with Him for an understanding of His word. Be sure that you know the real principles of the truth; and then when you meet opponents, it will not be in your own strength; an angel of God will stand by your side, to help in answering every question that may be asked. Day by day you are to be shut in, as it were, with Jesus; and then your words and example will have a strong influence for good.

NO EXCUSE FOR IGNORANCE

Some who enter the ministry do not feel the burden of the work. They have false ideas of the qualifications of a minister. They think that it requires little close study of the sciences or of the word of God in order to gain a fitness for the ministry. Some who are teaching present truth are so deficient in Bible knowledge that it is difficult for them to quote a text of Scripture correctly from memory. By blundering along in the awkward manner that they do, they sin against God. They wrest the Scriptures, and make the Bible say things that are not written therein.

Some think that an education or a thorough knowledge of the Scriptures is of little consequence if only a man has the Spirit. But God never sends His Spirit to sanction ignorance. He may and does pity and bless those who are so situated that it is impossible for them to obtain an education; and sometimes He condescends to make His strength perfect in their weakness. But it is the duty of such to study His word. A lack of knowledge in the sciences is no excuse for a neglect of Bible study; for the words of inspiration are so plain that the unlearned may understand them.

Young ministers should make themselves useful wherever they are. When visiting people in their homes, they should not be idle, making no effort to help those whose hospitality they share. Obligations are mutual; if the minister shares the hospitality of his friends, it is his duty to respond to their kindness by thoughtfulness and consideration in his conduct toward them. The entertainer may be a man of care and hard labor. By manifesting a disposition, not only to wait upon himself, but to render timely assistance to others, the minister may often find access to the heart, and open the way for the reception of truth.

The love of ease, and, I may say, physical laziness, unfits a man to be a minister. Those who are preparing to enter the ministry should train themselves to do hard physical work; then they will be better able to do hard thinking.

Let young men set up well-defined landmarks, by which they may be governed in emergencies. When a crisis comes that demands active, well-developed physical powers and a clear, strong, practical mind; when difficult work is to be done, where every stroke must tell; when perplexities arise which can be met only by wisdom from on high, then the youth who have learned to overcome difficulties by earnest labor can respond to the call for workers.

THE NECESSITY FOR STEADFASTNESS

In Paul's letter to Timothy there are many lessons for the young minister to learn. The aged apostle urged upon the younger worker the necessity of steadfastness in the faith. "I put thee in remembrance," he wrote, "that thou stir up the gift of God, which is in thee by the putting on of my hands. For God hath not given us the spirit of fear; but of power, and of love, and of a sound mind. Be not thou therefore ashamed of the testimony of our Lord, nor of me His prisoner: but be thou partaker of the afflictions of the gospel according to the power of God."

Paul entreated Timothy to remember that he had been called "with a holy calling" to proclaim the power of Him who had "brought life and immortality to light through the gospel: whereunto," he declared, "I am appointed a preacher, and an apostle, and a teacher of the Gentiles. For the which cause I also suffer these things: nevertheless I am not ashamed: for I know whom I have believed, and am persuaded that He is able to keep that which I have committed unto Him against that day." [3]

Wherever Paul was,— whether before scowling Pharisees, or Roman authorities; before the furious mob at Lystra, or the convicted sinners in the Macedonian dungeon; whether reasoning with the panic-stricken

[3] 2 Tim. 1 : 6-12.

sailors on the shipwrecked vessel, or standing alone before Nero to plead for his life,— he had never been ashamed of the cause he was advocating. The one great purpose of his Christian life had been to serve Him whose name had once filled him with contempt; and from this purpose no opposition or persecution had been able to turn him aside. His faith, made strong by effort and pure by sacrifice, upheld and strengthened him.

"Thou therefore, my son," Paul continued, "be strong in the grace that is in Christ Jesus. And the things that thou hast heard of me among many witnesses, the same commit thou to faithful men, who shall be able to teach others also. Thou therefore endure hardness, as a good soldier of Jesus Christ." [4]

The true minister of God will not shun hardship or responsibility. From the Source that never fails those who sincerely seek for divine power, he draws strength that enables him to meet and overcome temptation, and to perform the duties that God places upon him. The nature of the grace that he receives, enlarges his capacity to know God and His Son. His soul goes out in longing desire to do acceptable service for the Master. And as he advances in the Christian pathway, he becomes "strong in the grace that is in Christ Jesus." This grace enables him to be a faithful witness of the things that he has heard. He does not despise or neglect the knowledge that he has received from God, but commits this knowledge to faithful men, who in their turn teach others.

In this his last letter to Timothy, Paul held up before the younger worker a high ideal, pointing out the duties devolving on him as a minister of Christ.

[4] 2 Tim. 2 : 1-3.

"Study to show thyself approved unto God," the apostle wrote, "a workman that needeth not to be ashamed, rightly dividing the word of truth." "Flee also youthful lusts: but follow righteousness, faith, charity, peace, with them that call on the Lord out of a pure heart. But foolish and unlearned questions avoid, knowing that they do gender strifes. And the servant of the Lord must not strive; but be gentle unto all men, apt to teach, patient, in meekness instructing those that oppose themselves; if God peradventure will give them repentance to the acknowledging of the truth." [5] —"*The Acts of the Apostles*," *pages 499-502.*

FOR FURTHER STUDY

Young Men in the Ministry	Test. Vol. VI, p. 135.
The Youth to be Burden-Bearers	Test. Vol. II, p. 128. Test. Vol. III, pp. 362-367. Test. Vol. V, pp. 580-586. Test. Vol. VI, pp. 133-136. Test. Vol. VII, pp. 280-282. Test. Vol. VIII, pp. 28, 29. Acts, pp. 572-577.
Education for Missionary Work	Test. Vol. II, p. 556. Test. Vol. III, p. 551.
Young Men as Missionaries	Test. Vol. IV, pp. 437-449, 603-607. Test. Vol. V, pp. 580-586.
Voice Training for Workers	Test. Vol. II, p. 672. Ed., p. 199. C. O. L., pp. 335, 336. Counsels, pp. 237-247.
"Study to Show Thyself Approved"	Test. Vol. V, pp. 528, 529. M. of H., pp. 497-502.

[5] 2 Tim. 2 : 15, 22-25.

Qualifications

"In all things approving ourselves as the ministers of God."

CONSECRATION

In order for a man to be a successful minister, something more than book knowledge is essential. The laborer for souls needs consecration, integrity, intelligence, industry, energy, and tact. Possessing these qualifications, no man can be inferior; instead, he will have a commanding influence for good.

Christ brought His desires and wishes into strict abeyance to His mission,— the mission that bore the insignia of Heaven. He made everything subordinate to the work that He came to this world to accomplish. When in His youth His mother found Him in the school of the rabbis, and said to Him, "Son, why hast Thou thus dealt with us? behold, Thy father and I have sought Thee sorrowing," He answered,— and His answer is the key-note of His life-work,—"How is it that ye sought Me? wist ye not that I must be about My Father's business?" [1]

The same devotion, the same consecration, the same subjection to the claims of the word of God, that were manifest in Christ, must be seen in His servants. He left His home of security and peace, left the glory that He had with the Father before the world was, left His

[1] Luke 2 : 48, 49.

position upon the throne of the universe, and went forth, a suffering, tempted man; went forth in solitude, to sow in tears, to water with His blood the seed of life for a lost world.

His servants in like manner must go forth to sow. When called to become a sower of the seed of truth, Abraham was bidden, "Get thee out of thy country, and from thy kindred, and from thy father's house, unto a land that I will show thee." [2] "And he went out, not knowing whither he went," [3] as God's light-bearer, to keep His name alive in the earth. He forsook his country, his home, his relatives, and all the pleasant associations connected with his earthly life, to become a pilgrim and a stranger.

So to the apostle Paul, praying in the temple at Jerusalem, came the message, "Depart: for I will send thee far hence unto the Gentiles." [4] So those who are called to unite with Christ must leave all in order to follow Him. Old associations must be broken up, plans of life relinquished, earthly hopes surrendered. In toil and tears, in solitude and through sacrifice, must the seed be sown.

Those who consecrate body, soul, and spirit to God, will constantly receive a new endowment of physical, mental, and spiritual power. The inexhaustible supplies of heaven are at their command. Christ gives them the breath of His own Spirit, the life of His own life. The Holy Spirit puts forth His highest energies to work in heart and mind. The grace of God enlarges and multiplies their faculties, and every perfection of the divine nature comes to their assistance in the work of saving souls. Through co-operation with Christ,

[2] Gen. 12 : 1.   [3] Heb. 11 : 8.   [4] Acts 22 : 21.

they are made complete in Him, and in their human weakness they are enabled to do the deeds of Omnipotence.

The Redeemer will not accept divided service. Daily the worker for God must learn the meaning of self-surrender. He must study the word of God, learning its meaning and obeying its precepts. Thus he may reach the standard of Christian excellence. Day by day God works with him, perfecting the character that is to stand in the time of final test. And day by day the believer is working out before men and angels a sublime experiment, showing what the gospel can do for fallen human beings.

When Christ called His disciples to follow Him, He offered them no flattering prospects in this life. He gave them no promise of gain or worldly honor, nor did they make any stipulation as to what they should receive. To Matthew as he sat at the receipt of custom, the Saviour said, "Follow Me. And he arose, and followed Him." [5] Matthew did not, before rendering service, wait to demand a certain salary, equal to the amount received in his former occupation. Without question or hesitation he followed Jesus. It was enough for him that he was to be with the Saviour, that he might hear His words and unite with Him in His work.

So it was with the disciples previously called. When Jesus bade Peter and his companions follow Him, they immediately left their boats and nets. Some of these disciples had friends dependent on them for support; but when they received the Saviour's invitation, they did not hesitate, inquiring, How shall I live, and sustain my family? They were obedient to the call;

[5] Matt. 9 : 9.

and when afterward Jesus asked them, "When I sent you without purse, and scrip, and shoes, lacked ye anything?" they could answer, "Nothing." [6]

To-day the Saviour calls us, as He called Matthew and John and Peter, to His work. If our hearts are touched by His love, the question of compensation will not be uppermost in our minds. We shall rejoice to be co-workers with Christ, and we shall not fear to trust His care. If we make God our strength, we shall have clear perceptions of duty, and unselfish aspirations; our life will be actuated by a noble purpose, which will raise us above sordid motives.

Many whom the Lord could use will not hear and obey His voice above all others. Kindred and friends, former habits and associations, have so strong an influence upon them that God can give them but little instruction, can communicate to them but little knowledge of His purposes. The Lord would do much more for His servants if they were wholly consecrated to Him, placing His service above the ties of kindred and all other earthly associations.

DEEPER CONSECRATION NEEDED

The time demands greater efficiency and deeper consecration. I cry to God, Raise up and send forth messengers filled with a sense of their responsibility, men in whose hearts self-idolatry, which lies at the foundation of all sin, has been crucified; who are willing to consecrate themselves without reserve to God's service; whose souls are alive to the sacredness of the work and the responsibility of their calling; who are determined not to bring to God a maimed sacrifice, which costs them neither effort nor prayer.

[6] Luke 22 : 35.

The Duke of Wellington was once present where a party of Christian men were discussing the possibility of success in missionary effort among the heathen. They appealed to the duke to say whether in his judgment such efforts were likely to prove a success commensurate to the cost. The old soldier replied:

"Gentlemen, what are your marching orders? Success is not the question for you to discuss. If I read your orders aright, they run thus, 'Go ye into all the world, and preach the gospel to every creature.' Gentlemen, obey your marching orders."

My brethren, the Lord is coming, and we need to bend every energy to the accomplishment of the work before us. I appeal to you to give yourselves wholly to the work. Christ gave His time, His soul, His strength, to labor for the benefit and blessing of humanity. Entire days were devoted to labor, and entire nights were spent in prayer, that He might be braced to meet the foe and fortified to help those who came to Him for relief. As we trace a stream of living water by the line of green that it produces, so Christ may be seen in the deeds of mercy that marked His path at every step. Wherever He went, health sprang up, and happiness followed where He passed. So simply did He present the words of life that a child could understand them. The youth caught His spirit of ministry, and sought to pattern after His gracious ways by assisting those who needed help. The blind and deaf rejoiced in His presence. His words to the ignorant and sinful opened to them a fountain of life. He dispensed His blessings abundantly and continuously; they were the garnered riches of eternity, given in Christ, the Father's gift to man.

Workers for God should as surely feel that they are not their own as if the very stamp and seal of identification were placed upon their persons. They are to be sprinkled with the blood of Christ's sacrifice, and in the spirit of entire consecration they should resolve that by the grace of Christ they will be a living sacrifice. But how few of us regard the salvation of sinners in the light in which it is viewed by the heavenly universe,— as a plan devised from eternity in the mind of God! How few of us are heart to heart with the Redeemer in this solemn, closing work! There is scarcely a tithe of the compassion that there should be for souls unsaved. There are so many to be warned, and yet how few sympathize with God sufficiently to be anything or nothing if only they can see souls won to Christ!

When Elijah was about to leave Elisha, he said to him, "Ask what I shall do for thee, before I be taken away from thee. And Elisha said, I pray thee, let a double portion of thy spirit be upon me." [7] Elisha did not ask for worldly honor, for a place among the great men of the earth. That which he craved was a large portion of the spirit given to the one whom God was about to honor with translation. He knew that nothing else could fit him for the work that would be required of him.

Ministers of the gospel, had this question been asked you, what would you have answered? What is the greatest desire of your heart, as you engage in the service of God?

[7] 2 Kings 2:9.

TACTFULNESS

In the work of soul-winning, great tact and wisdom are needed. The Saviour never suppressed the truth, but He uttered it always in love. In His intercourse with others, He exercised the greatest tact, and He was always kind and thoughtful. He was never rude, never needlessly spoke a severe word, never gave unnecessary pain to a sensitive soul. He did not censure human weakness. He fearlessly denounced hypocrisy, unbelief, and iniquity, but tears were in His voice as He uttered His scathing rebukes. He never made truth cruel, but ever manifested a deep tenderness for humanity. Every soul was precious in His sight. He bore Himself with divine dignity; yet He bowed with the tenderest compassion and regard to every member of the family of God. He saw in all, souls whom it was His mission to save.

PAUL'S DISCRETION

The minister must not feel that the whole truth is to be spoken to unbelievers on any and every occasion. He should study carefully when to speak, what to say, and what to leave unsaid. This is not practicing deception; it is working as Paul worked. "Though I be free from all men," he wrote to the Corinthians, "yet have I made myself servant unto all, that I might gain the more. And unto the Jews I became as a Jew, that I might gain the Jews; to them that are under the law, as under the law, that I might gain them that are under the law; to them that are without law, as without law, (being not without law to God, but under the law to Christ,) that I might gain them that are without law. To the weak became I as weak, that I might gain the weak: I am made all things to all men, that I might by all means save some." [1]

Paul did not approach the Jews in such a way as to arouse their prejudices. He did not at first tell them that they must believe in Jesus of Nazareth; but dwelt upon the prophecies that spoke of Christ, His mission and His work. Step by step he led his hearers on, showing the importance of honoring the law of God. He gave due honor to the ceremonial law, showing that it was Christ who instituted the Jewish economy and the sacrificial service. Then he brought them down to the first advent of the Redeemer, and showed that in the life and death of Christ every specification of the sacrificial service had been fulfilled.

The Gentiles, Paul approached by exalting Christ, and then presenting the binding claims of the law. He showed how the light reflected by the cross of Calvary gave significance and glory to the whole Jewish economy.

Thus the apostle varied his manner of labor, shaping his message to the circumstances under which he was placed. After patient labor he was successful to a large degree; yet there were many who would not be convinced. Some there are to-day who will not be convinced by any method of presenting the truth; and the laborer for God is to study carefully the best methods, that he may not arouse prejudice or combativeness. This is where some have failed. By following their natural inclinations, they have closed doors through which they might, by a different method of

[1] 1 Cor. 9 : 19-22.

labor, have found access to hearts, and through them to other hearts.

God's workmen must be many-sided men; that is, they must have breadth of character. They are not to be one-idea men, stereotyped in their manner of working, unable to see that their advocacy of truth must vary with the class of people among whom they work and the circumstances they have to meet.

There is delicate work for the minister to do as he meets with alienation, bitterness, and opposition. More than others, he needs that wisdom which "is first pure, then peaceable, gentle, and easy to be entreated, full of mercy and good fruits, without partiality, and without hypocrisy." [2] As the dew and the still showers fall gently upon withering plants, so his words are to fall gently when he proclaims the truth. He is to win souls, not to repulse them. He is to study to be skilful when there are no rules to meet the case.

Many souls have been turned in the wrong direction, and thus lost to the cause of God, by a lack of skill and wisdom on the part of the worker. Tact and good judgment increase the usefulness of the laborer a hundred-fold. If he will speak the right words at the right time, and show the right spirit, this will exert a melting power on the heart of the one he is trying to help.

IN NEW FIELDS

In laboring in a new field, do not think it your duty to say at once to the people, We are Seventh-day Adventists; we believe that the seventh day is the Sabbath; we believe in the non-immortality of the soul. This would often erect a formidable barrier between

[2] James 3 : 17.

you and those you wish to reach. Speak to them, as you have opportunity, upon points of doctrine on which you can agree. Dwell on the necessity of practical godliness. Give them evidence that you are a Christian, desiring peace, and that you love their souls. Let them see that you are conscientious. Thus you will gain their confidence; and there will be time enough for doctrines. Let the heart be won, the soil prepared, and then sow the seed, presenting in love the truth as it is in Jesus.

God will surely help those who seek Him for wisdom. We are not to wait until opportunities come to us; we are to seek for opportunities, and we are to be ready always to give a reason for the hope that is in us. If the worker keeps his heart uplifted in prayer, God will help him to speak the right word at the right time.

———————◆———————

In seeking to correct or reform others, we should be careful of our words. They will be a savor of life unto life, or of death unto death. In giving reproof or counsel, many indulge in sharp, severe speech, words not adapted to heal the wounded soul. By these ill-advised expressions the spirit is chafed, and often the erring ones are stirred to rebellion.

All who would advocate the principles of truth need to receive the heavenly oil of love. Under all circumstances reproof should be spoken in love. Then our words will reform, but not exasperate. Christ by His Holy Spirit will supply the force and the power. This is His work.

THE GRACE OF COURTESY

Those who work for Christ are to be upright and trustworthy, firm as a rock to principle, and at the same time kind and courteous. Courtesy is one of the graces of the Spirit. To deal with human minds is the greatest work ever given to man; and he who would find access to hearts must heed the injunction, "Be pitiful, be courteous." [1] Love will do that which argument will fail to accomplish. But a moment's petulance, a single gruff answer, a lack of Christian politeness and courtesy in some small matter, may result in the loss of both friends and influence.

What Christ was on this earth, the Christain worker should strive to be. He is our example, not only in His spotless purity, but in His patience, gentleness, and winsomeness of disposition. His life is an illustration of true courtesy. He had ever a kind look and a word of comfort for the needy and the oppressed. His presence brought a purer atmosphere into the home. His life was as leaven working amid the elements of society. Pure and undefiled, He walked among the thoughtless, the rude, the uncourteous; among unjust publicans, unrighteous Samaritans, heathen soldiers, rough peasants, and the mixed multitude. He spoke a word of sympathy here and a word there. As He saw men weary, and compelled to bear heavy burdens, He shared their burdens, and repeated to them the lessons He had learned from nature, of the love, the kindness, the goodness of God. He sought to inspire with hope the most rough and unpromising, setting before them the assur-

[1] 1 Peter 3 : 8.

ance that they might attain such a character as would make them manifest as children of God.

The religion of Jesus softens whatever is hard and rough in the temper, and smooths whatever is rugged and sharp in the manners. It makes the words gentle and the demeanor winning. Let us learn from Christ how to combine a high sense of purity and integrity with sunniness of disposition. A kind, courteous Christian is the most powerful argument that can be produced in favor of Christianity.

Kind words are as dew and gentle showers to the soul. The Scripture says of Christ, that grace was poured into His lips, that He might "know how to speak a word in season to him that is weary." [2] And the Lord bids us, "Let your speech be alway with grace" "that it may minister grace unto the hearers." [3]

Some with whom you are brought in contact may be rough and uncourteous, but do not, because of this, be less courteous yourself. He who wishes to preserve his own self-respect must be careful not to wound needlessly the self-respect of others. This rule should be sacredly observed toward the dullest, the most blundering. What God intends to do with these apparently unpromising ones, you do not know. He has in the past accepted persons no more promising or attractive to do a great work for Him. His Spirit, moving upon the heart, has roused every faculty to vigorous action. The Lord saw in these rough, unhewn stones precious material, which would stand the test of storm and heat and pressure. God does not

[2] Isa. 50 : 4.   [3] Col. 4 : 6; Eph. 4 : 29.

see as man sees. He does not judge from appearances, but searches the heart and judges righteously.

The Lord Jesus demands our acknowledgment of the rights of every man. Men's social rights, and their rights as Christians, are to be taken into consideration. All are to be treated with refinement and delicacy, as the sons and daughters of God.

Christianity will make a man a gentleman. Christ was courteous, even to His persecutors; and His true followers will manifest the same spirit. Look at Paul when brought before rulers. His speech before Agrippa is an illustration of true courtesy as well as persuasive eloquence. The gospel does not encourage the formal politeness current with the world, but the courtesy that springs from real kindness of heart.

The most careful attention to the outward proprieties of life is not sufficient to shut out all fretfulness, harsh judgment, and unbecoming speech. True refinement will never be revealed so long as self is considered as the supreme object. Love must dwell in the heart. A thoroughgoing Christian draws his motives of action from his deep heart-love for his Master. Up through the roots of his affection for Christ springs an unselfish interest in his brethren. Love imparts to its possessor grace, propriety, and comeliness of deportment. It illuminates the countenance and subdues the voice; it refines and elevates the entire being.

To those who handle sacred things comes the solemn injunction, "Be ye clean, that bear the vessels of the Lord." [1] Of all men, those who have been trusted and honored by the Lord, those who have been given special service to perform, should be circumspect in word and deed. They should be men of devotion, who, by works of righteousness and pure, true words, can lift their fellow-men to a higher level; men who are not unsettled by every passing temptation; men of firm, earnest purpose, whose highest aim is to gather souls to Christ.

Satan's special temptations are directed against the ministry. He knows that ministers are but human, possessing no grace or holiness of their own; that the treasures of the gospel have been placed in earthen vessels, which divine power alone can make vessels unto honor. He knows that God has ordained ministers to be a powerful means for the salvation of souls, and that they can be successful in their work only as they allow the eternal Father to rule their lives. Therefore he tries with all his ingenuity to lead them into sin, knowing that their office makes sin in them more exceeding sinful; for in committing sin, they make themselves ministers of evil.

Those whom God has called to the ministry are to give evidence that they are fit to minister in the sacred desk. The Lord has commanded, "Be ye holy in all manner of conversation." [2] "Be thou an example of the believers," Paul writes. "Take heed unto thyself,

[1] Isa. 52 : 11.　　　　　　　　　[2] 1 Peter 1 : 15.

and unto the doctrine; continue in them: for in doing this thou shalt both save thyself, and them that hear thee." [3] "The end of all things is at hand: be ye therefore sober, and watch unto prayer." [4]

The subject of purity and propriety of deportment is one to which we must give heed. We must guard against the sins of this degenerate age. Let not Christ's ambassadors descend to trifling conversation, to familiarity with women, married or single. Let them keep their proper place with becoming dignity; yet at the same time they may be sociable, kind, and courteous to all. They must stand aloof from everything that savors of commonness and familiarity. This is forbidden ground, upon which it is unsafe to set the feet. Every word, every act, should tend to elevate, to refine, to ennoble. There is sin in thoughtlessness about such matters.

Paul urged Timothy to meditate upon those things that are pure and excellent, that his profiting might appear unto all. The same counsel is greatly needed by men of the present age. I urge upon our workers the necessity of purity in every thought, every act. We have an individual accountability to God, an individual work which no one else can do for us. It is to strive to make the world better. While we should cultivate sociability, let it not be merely for amusement, but for a higher purpose.

Is there not enough taking place around us to show the need for this caution? Everywhere are seen wrecks of humanity, broken-down family altars, ruined homes. There is a strange abandonment of principle, the standard of morality is lowered, and the earth is

[3] 1 Tim. 4 : 12, 16.   [4] 1 Peter 4 : 7.

fast becoming a Sodom. The practices which brought the judgment of God upon the antediluvian world, and which caused Sodom to be destroyed by fire, are fast increasing. We are nearing the end, when the earth is to be purified by fire.

Let those in whose hands God has placed the light of truth, depart from all iniquity. Let them walk in the paths of rectitude, mastering every passion and habit that would in any way mar the work of God, or leave a spot upon its sacredness. It is the work of the minister to resist the temptations that lie in his pathway, to rise above those debasements that drag the mind down to a low level. By watchfulness and prayer, he may so guard his weakest points that they will become his strongest points. Through the grace of Christ, men may acquire moral stamina, strength of will, and stability of purpose. There is power in this grace to enable them to rise above the alluring, infatuating temptations of Satan, and to become loyal, devoted Christians.

MINISTERS TO SET A WORTHY EXAMPLE

Ministers should set the youth a worthy example, one corresponding to their holy calling. They should help the young to be frank, yet modest and dignified in all their associations. Day by day they are sowing seed that will spring up and bear fruit. They are to put away all coarseness, all trifling, ever remembering that they are educators; that, whether they will or not, their words and acts are to those with whom they come in contact a savor of life or of death.

It is discipline of spirit, cleanness of heart and thought, that is needed. Moral purity depends on right thinking and right acting. Evil thoughts destroy the soul, while a right control of the thoughts prepares the mind to labor harmoniously for the Master. Every thought should be brought into captivity to the obedience of Christ.

The teachers of truth must be wise men, very careful of their words and actions. They must be men who will give meat in due season to the flock of God; men who will not give the least sanction to low standards of living; men who have that faith which works by love, and purifies the soul from all carnal thoughts and desires. Workers of this character will not grovel in earthliness; they will not be in bondage to human beings or to Satan's temptations. They will quit themselves like men, and be strong. They will turn their faces to the Sun of Righteousness, rising above all base things into an atmosphere free from spiritual and moral defilement.

He who lives the principles of Bible religion, will not be found weak in moral power. Under the ennobling influence of the Holy Spirit, the tastes and inclinations become pure and holy. Nothing takes so strong a hold upon the affections, nothing reaches so fully down to the deepest motives of action, nothing exerts so potent an influence upon the life, and gives so great firmness and stability to the character, as the religion of Christ. It leads its possessor ever upward, inspiring him with noble purposes, teaching him propriety of deportment, and imparting a becoming dignity to every action.

By what means shall the young man repress his evil propensities, and develop that which is noble and good in his character? Let him heed the words, "Whether therefore ye eat, or drink, or whatsoever ye do, do all to the glory of God." [5] Here is a principle that is to underlie every motive, thought, and act. Unholy passions must be crucified. They will clamor for indulgence, but God has implanted in the heart high and holy purposes and desires, and these need not be debased. It is only when we refuse to submit to the control of reason and conscience that we are dragged down. Paul declared, "I can do all things through Christ." [6]

———◆———

If you draw close to Jesus, and seek to adorn your profession by a well-ordered life and godly conversation, your feet will be kept from straying into forbidden paths. If you will only watch, continually watch unto prayer, if you will do everything as if you were in the immediate presence of God, you will be saved from yielding to temptation, and may hope to be kept pure, spotless, and undefiled till the last. If you hold the beginning of your confidence firm unto the end, your ways will be established in God, and what grace has begun, glory will crown in the kingdom of our God. The fruits of the Spirit are love, joy, peace, long-suffering, gentleness, goodness, faith, meekness, temperance; against such there is no law. If Christ be within us, we shall crucify the flesh with the affections and lusts.

[5] 1 Cor. 10 : 31. [6] Phil. 4 : 13.

THE SOCIAL RELATIONS

The usefulness of young ministers, married or unmarried, is often destroyed by the attachment shown to them by young women. Such women do not realize that other eyes are upon them, and that the course pursued by them may have a tendency to injure the influence of the minister to whom they give so much attention. If they would strictly regard the rules of propriety, it would be much better for them and much better for the minister. Their failure to do this places him in a disagreeable position, and causes others to look upon him in a wrong light.

But the burden of this matter rests upon the ministers themselves. They should show a distaste for such attention; and if they take the course which God would have them, they will not long be troubled. They should shun every appearance of evil; and when young women are very sociable, it is the ministers' duty to let them know that this is not pleasing. They must repulse forwardness, even if they are thought to be rude, in order to save the cause from reproach. Young women who have been converted to the truth and to God, will listen to reproof, and will be reformed.

Jesting, joking, and worldly conversation belong to the world. Christians who have the peace of God in their hearts, will be cheerful and happy without indulging in lightness or frivolity. While watching unto prayer, they will have a serenity and peace which will elevate them above all superfluities.

5

The mystery of godliness, opened to the mind of the minister of Christ, will raise him above earthly and sensual enjoyments. He will be a partaker of the divine nature, having escaped the corruption that is in the world through lust. The communion opened between God and his soul will make him fruitful in the knowledge of God's will, and open before him treasures of practical subjects that he can present to the people, which will not cause levity or the semblance of a smile, but will solemnize the mind, touch the heart, and arouse the moral sensibilities to the sacred claims that God has upon the affections and life. Those who labor in word and doctrine should be men of God, pure in heart and life.—*"Testimonies for the Church," Vol. III, page 241.*

Young men are arising to engage in the work of God, some of whom have scarcely any sense of the sacredness and responsibility of the work. They have but little experience in exercising faith, and in earnest soul-hunger for the Spirit of God, which ever brings returns. Some men of good capabilities, who might fill important positions, do not know what spirit they are of. They run in a jovial mood as naturally as water flows downhill. They talk nonsense, and sport with young girls, while almost daily listening to the most solemn, soul-stirring truths. These men have a religion of the head, but their hearts are not sanctified by the truths they hear. Such can never lead others to the Fountain of living waters until they have drunk of the stream themselves.

It is no time now for lightness, vanity, or trifling. The scenes of this earth's history are soon to close. Minds that have been left to loose thought, need change. The apostle Peter says, "Gird up the loins of your mind, be sober, and hope to the end for the grace that is to be brought unto you at the revelation of Jesus Christ; as obedient children, not fashioning yourselves according to the former lusts in your ignorance: but as He which hath called you is holy, so be ye holy in all manner of conversation; because it is written, Be ye holy; for I am holy." [1]

Loose thoughts must be gathered up and centered on God. The very thoughts should be in obedience to the will of God. Praise should not be given or expected; for this will have a tendency to foster self-confidence rather than to increase humility, to corrupt rather than to purify. Men who are really qualified, and who feel that they have a part to act in connection with the work of God, will feel pressed beneath a sense of the sacredness of the work, as a cart beneath sheaves. Now is the time to make the most earnest efforts to overcome the natural feelings of the carnal heart.—*"Testimonies for the Church," Vol. III, pages 473, 474.*

When a minister bearing the solemn message of warning to the world, receives the hospitable courtesies of friends and brethren, and neglects the duties of a shepherd of the flock, and is careless in his example and deportment, engaging with the young in trifling conversation, in jesting and joking, and in relating humorous anecdotes to create laughter, he is unworthy of being a

[1] 1 Peter 1 : 13-16.

gospel minister, and needs to be converted before he is entrusted with the care of the sheep and lambs. Ministers who are neglectful of the duties devolving on a faithful pastor, give evidence that they are not sanctified by the truths they present to others, and should not be sustained as laborers in the vineyard of the Lord till they have a high sense of the sacredness of the work of a minister.—"*Testimonies for the Church,*" *Vol. III, page 233.*

The minister of Christ should be a man of prayer, a man of piety; cheerful, but never coarse and rough, jesting or frivolous. A spirit of frivolity may be in keeping with the profession of clowns and theatrical performers, but it is altogether beneath the dignity of a man who is chosen to stand between the living and the dead, and to be a mouthpiece for God.

The mystery of godliness, opened to the mind of the minister of Christ, will raise him above earthly and sensual enjoyments. He will be a partaker of the divine nature, having escaped the corruption that is in the world through lust. The communication opened between God and his soul will make him fruitful in the knowledge of God's will, and open before him treasures of practical subjects that he can present to the people, which will not cause levity or the semblance of a smile, but will solemnize the mind, touch the heart, and arouse the moral sensibilities to the sacred claims that God has upon the affections and life. Those who labor in word and doctrine should be men of God, pure in heart and life.

DECISION AND PROMPTNESS

Independent men of earnest endeavor are needed, not men as impressible as putty. Those who want their work made ready to their hand, who desire a fixed amount to do and a fixed salary, and who wish to prove an exact fit without the trouble of adaptation or training, are not the men whom God calls to work in His cause. A man who cannot adapt his abilities to almost any place, if necessity requires, is not the man for this time. Men whom God will connect with His work are not limp and fiberless, without muscle or moral force of character. . . .

There are men who flatter themselves that they might do something great and good if they were only circumstanced differently, while they make no use of the faculties they already have, by working in the positions where Providence has placed them. . . . Individual independence and individual power are the qualities now needed. Individual character need not be sacrificed, but it should be modulated, refined, elevated. . . .

The cause of God demands men who can see quickly and act instantaneously at the right time and with power. If you wait to measure every difficulty and balance every perplexity you meet, you will do but little. You will have obstacles and difficulties to encounter at every turn, and you must with firm purpose decide to conquer them, or they will conquer you.

Sometimes various ways and purposes, different modes of operation in connection with the work of God, are about evenly balanced in the mind; and it is at this very point that the nicest discrimination is necessary. And if anything is accomplished to the purpose, it must be done at the golden moment. The slightest inclination of the weight in the balance should be seen, and should determine the matter at once. Long delays tire the angels. It is even more excusable to make a wrong decision sometimes than to be continually in a wavering position; to be hesitating, sometimes inclined in one direction, then in another. More perplexity and wretchedness result from thus hesitating and doubting than from sometimes moving too hastily.

I have been shown that the most signal victories and the most fearful defeats have been on the turn of minutes. God requires promptness of action. Delays, doubtings, hesitation, and indecision frequently give the enemy every advantage. . . .

The timing of things may tell much in favor of truth. Victories are frequently lost through delays. There will be crises in this cause. Prompt and decisive action at the right time will gain glorious triumphs, while delay and neglect will result in great failures and positive dishonor to God. Rapid movements at the critical moment often disarm the enemy, and he is disappointed and vanquished, for he had expected time to lay plans and work by artifice. . . .

The greatest promptness is positively necessary in the hour of peril and danger. Every plan may be well laid to accomplish certain results, and yet a delay of a very short time may leave things to assume an entirely different shape, and the great objects which might have been gained are lost through lack of quick foresight and prompt dispatch.

Much may be done in training the mind to overcome indolence. There are times when caution and great deliberation are necessary; rashness would be folly. But even here much has been lost by too great hesitancy. Caution, up to a certain point, is required; but hesitancy and policy on particular occasions have been more disastrous than would have been a failure through rashness.—*"Testimonies for the Church," Vol. III, pages 496-498.*

———◆———

There are those who for a time are successful in the struggle against their selfish desire for pleasure and ease. They are sincere and earnest, but grow weary of protracted effort, of daily death, of ceaseless turmoil. Indolence seems inviting, death to self repulsive; and they close their drowsy eyes, and fall under the power of temptation instead of resisting it.

The directions laid down in the word of God leave no room for compromise with evil. The Son of God was manifested that He might draw all men unto Himself. He came not to lull the world to sleep, but to point out the narrow path in which all must travel who reach at last the gates of the city of God. His children must follow where He has led the way; at whatever sacrifice of ease or selfish indulgence, at whatever cost of labor or suffering, they must maintain a constant battle with self.

GATHERING THE FRUIT — A DREAM

In a dream given me Sept. 29, 1886, I was walking with a large company who were looking for berries. There were many young men and women in the company who were to help in gathering the fruit. We seemed to be in a city, for there was very little vacant ground; but around the city there were open fields, beautiful groves, and cultivated gardens. A large wagon laden with provisions for our company went before us.

Soon the wagon halted, and the party scattered in every direction to look for fruit. All around the wagon were both high and low bushes, bearing large, beautiful whortleberries; but the company were all looking too far away to see them. I began to gather the fruit near by, but very carefully, for fear of picking the green berries, which were so mingled with the ripe fruit that I could pick only one or two berries from a cluster.

Some of the nice large berries had fallen to the ground, and were half consumed by worms and insects. "Oh," thought I, "if this field had only been entered before, all this precious fruit might have been saved! But it is too late now. I will, however, pick these from the ground, and see if there is any good in them. Even if the whole berry is spoiled, I can at least show the brethren what they might have found if they had not been too late."

Just then two or three of the party came sauntering around where I was. They were chatting, and seemed to be much occupied with each other's company. Seeing me, they said, "We have looked everywhere, and can find no fruit." They looked with astonishment at the quantity I had. I said, "There are more to be gathered from these bushes." They began picking, but soon stopped, saying, "It is not fair for us to pick here; you found this spot, and the fruit is yours." But I replied, "That makes no difference. Gather wherever you can find anything. This is God's field, and these are His berries; it is your privilege to pick them."

But soon I seemed to be alone again. Every little while I heard talking and laughing at the wagon. I called out to those who were there, "What are you doing?" They answered, "We could not find any berries, and as we were tired and hungry, we thought we would come to the wagon and take a lunch. After we have rested awhile, we will go out again."

"But," I said, "you have brought in nothing as yet. You are eating up all our supplies, without giving us any more. I cannot eat now; there is too much fruit to be picked. You did not find it because you did not look close enough. It does not hang on the outside of the bushes; you must search for it. True, you cannot pick it by handfuls; but by looking carefully among the green berries, you will find very choice fruit."

My small pail was soon full of berries, and I took them to the wagon. Said I, "This is the nicest fruit that I ever picked, and I gathered it near by, while you have wearied yourselves by searching at a distance without success."

Then all came to see my fruit. They said, "These are high-bush berries, firm and good. We did not think we could find anything on the high bushes, so we hunted for low-bush berries only, and found but few of these."

Then I said, "Will you take care of these berries, and then go with me to look for more fruit on the high bushes?" But they had made no preparation to care for the fruit. There were dishes and sacks in abundance, but they had been used to hold food. I became tired of waiting, and finally asked, "Did you not come to gather fruit? Then why are you not prepared to take care of it?"

One responded, "Sister White, we did not really expect to find any fruit where there were so many houses, and so much going on; but as you seemed so anxious to gather fruit, we decided to come with you. We thought we would bring enough to eat, and would enjoy the recreation, if we did not gather any fruit."

I answered, "I cannot understand this kind of work. I shall go to the bushes again at once. The day is already far spent, soon the night will be here, in which we can gather no fruit." Some went with me, but others remained by the wagon to eat.

In one place a little company had collected, and were busily talking about something in which they seemed much interested. I drew near, and found that a little child in a woman's arms had attracted their attention. I said, "You have but a little time, and might better work while you can."

The attention of many was attracted by a young man and a young woman who were running a race to the wagon. On reaching it, they were so tired that they had to sit down and rest. Others also had thrown themselves down on the grass to rest.

Thus the day wore on, and very little was accomplished. At last I said: "Brethren, you call this an unsuccessful expedition. If this is the way you work,

I do not wonder at your lack of success. Your success or failure depends upon the way you take hold of the work. There are berries here; for I have found them. Some of you have been searching the low bushes in vain; others have found a few berries; but the high bushes have been passed by, simply because you did not *expect* to find fruit on them. You see that the fruit which I have gathered is large and ripe. In a little while other berries will ripen, and we can go over the bushes again. This is the way in which I was taught to gather fruit. If you had searched near the wagon, you might have found fruit as well as I.

"The lesson that you have this day given to those who are just learning how to do this kind of work, will be copied by them. The Lord has placed these fruit-bearing bushes right in the midst of these thickly settled places, and He expects you to find them. But you have been altogether too much engaged in eating, and amusing yourselves. You did not come to the field with an earnest determination to find fruit.

"You must hereafter work with more zeal and earnestness, and with an altogether different object in view, or your labors will never be successful. By working in the right way, you will teach the younger workers that such matters as eating and recreation are of minor importance. It has been hard work to bring the wagon of supplies to the ground, but you have thought more of the supplies than of the fruit you ought to carry home as the result of your labors. You should be diligent, first to pick the berries nearest you, and then to search for those farther away; after that you can return and work near by again, and thus you will be successful."

ESSENTIALS TO SERVICE

SYMPATHY

God desires to unite His workers by a common sympathy, a pure affection. It is the atmosphere of Christlike love surrounding the soul of the believer that makes him a savor of life unto life, and enables God to bless his efforts. Christianity builds no walls of separation between man and his fellow-man, but binds human beings to God and to one another.

Mark how tender and pitiful the Lord is in His dealings with His creatures. He loves His erring child, and entreats him to return. The Father's arm is placed about His repentant son; the Father's garments cover his rags; the ring is placed upon his finger as a token of his royalty. And yet how many there are who look upon the prodigal not only with indifference, but with contempt. Like the Pharisee, they say, "God, I thank Thee, that I am not as other men." [1] But how, think you, does God look upon those who, while claiming to be co-workers with Christ, while the soul is making its struggle against the flood of temptation, stand by like the elder brother in the parable, stubborn, self-willed, selfish?

How little do we enter into sympathy with Christ on that which should be the strongest bond of union between us and Him,— compassion for depraved, guilty, suffering souls, dead in trespasses and sins! The inhumanity of man toward man is our greatest sin.

[1] Luke 18 : 11.

Many think that they are representing the justice of God, while they wholly fail of representing His tenderness and His great love. Often the ones whom they meet with sternness and severity are under the stress of temptation. Satan is wrestling with these souls, and harsh, unsympathetic words discourage them, and cause them to fall a prey to the tempter's power. . . .

We need more of Christlike sympathy; not merely sympathy for those who appear to us to be faultless, but sympathy for poor, suffering, struggling souls, who are often overtaken in fault, sinning and repenting, tempted and discouraged. We are to go to our fellowmen, touched, like our merciful High Priest, with the feeling of their infirmities.—*"Ministry of Healing," pages 163, 164.*

INTEGRITY

Men of tried courage and strong integrity are needed for this time, men who are not afraid to lift their voices for the right. To every laborer I would say, In all your official duties, let integrity characterize each act. All tithes, all moneys entrusted to you for any special purpose, should be promptly placed where they belong. Money given for the cause of God should not be appropriated for personal use, with the thought that it can be replaced later on. This the Lord forbids. It is a temptation from the one who works evil and evil only. The minister who receives funds for the Lord's treasury should give the donor a written receipt for the same, with the date. Then, without waiting to be tempted by financial pressure to use this means for himself, let him deposit it where, when called for, it will be forthcoming.

UNION WITH CHRIST

A vital connection with the Chief Shepherd will make the under-shepherd a living representative of Christ, a light indeed to the world. An understanding of all points of our faith is essential, but it is of still greater importance that the minister be sanctified through the truth he presents.

The worker who knows the meaning of union with Christ, has a constantly increasing desire and capacity to grasp the meaning of service for God. His knowledge enlarges; for to grow in grace means to have an increased ability to understand the Scriptures. Such a one is indeed a laborer together with God. He realizes that he is but an instrument, and that he must be passive in the Master's hands. Trials come to him; for unless thus tested, he would never know his lack of wisdom and experience. But if he seeks the Lord with humility and trust, every trial will work for his good. He may sometimes seem to fail, but his apparent failure may be God's way of bringing him true advancement, and may mean a better knowledge of himself and a firmer trust in Heaven. He may still make mistakes, but he learns not to repeat these mistakes. He becomes stronger to resist evil, and others reap benefit from his example.

HUMILITY

The minister for God should in an eminent degree possess humility. Those who have the deepest experience in the things of God are the farthest removed from pride and self-exaltation. Because they have an exalted conception of the glory of God, they feel that the lowest place in His service is too honorable for them.

When Moses came down from the mount after forty days spent in communion with God, he did not know that his face shone with a brightness that was terrifying to those who beheld.

Paul had a very humble opinion of his advancement in the Christian life. He speaks of himself as the chief of sinners. And again he says, "Not as though I had already attained, either were already perfect." [2] Yet Paul had been highly honored by the Lord.

Our Saviour declared John the Baptist to be the greatest of prophets; yet when asked if he were the Christ, John declared himself unworthy even to unloose his Master's sandals. When his disciples came with the complaint that all men were turning to the new Teacher, John reminded them that he was but the forerunner of the Coming One.

Workers with this spirit are needed to-day. The self-sufficient, satisfied with themselves, can well be spared from the work of God. Our Lord calls for laborers who, feeling their own need of the atoning blood of Christ, enter upon their work, not with boasting or self-sufficiency, but with full assurance of faith, realizing that they will always need the help of Christ in order to know how to deal with minds.

EARNESTNESS

There is need of greater earnestness. Time is fast passing, and men willing to work as Christ worked are needed. It is not enough to live a quiet, prayerful life. Meditation alone will not satisfy the need of the world. Religion is not to be a subjective influence in our lives. We are to be wide-awake, energetic, earnest Christians, filled with a desire to give others the truth.

[2] Phil. 3 : 12.

People need to hear the tidings of salvation through faith in Christ, and by earnest, faithful effort the message is to be given to them. Souls are to be sought for, prayed for, labored for. Earnest appeals are to be made, fervent prayers offered. Our tame, lifeless prayers need to be changed to petitions of intense earnestness.

CONSISTENCY

The characters of many who profess godliness are imperfect and one-sided. These show that as pupils in the school of Christ they have learned their lessons very imperfectly. Some who have learned to imitate Christ in meekness, do not show His diligence in doing good. Others are active and zealous, but they are boastful; they have never learned humility. Still others leave Christ out of their work. They may be pleasing in their manners; they may show sympathy for their fellow-men; but their hearts are not centered on the Saviour, and they have not learned the language of heaven. They do not pray as Christ prayed; they do not place His estimate upon souls; they have not learned to endure hardship in their efforts to save souls. Some, knowing little of the transforming power of grace, become egotistical, critical, harsh. Others are plastic and yielding, bending this way and that to please their fellow-men.

However zealously the truth may be advocated, if the every-day life does not testify to its sanctifying power, the words spoken will avail nothing. An inconsistent course hardens the heart and narrows the mind of the worker, and places stumbling-blocks in the way of those for whom he labors.

THE DAILY LIFE

The minister should be free from every unnecessary temporal perplexity, that he may give himself wholly to his sacred calling. He should be much in prayer, and should bring himself under discipline to God, that his life may reveal the fruits of true self-control. His language should be correct; no slang phrases, no cheap utterances, should fall from his lips. His dress should be in harmony with the character of the work he is doing. Let ministers and teachers strive to reach the standard set forth in the Scriptures. Let them not neglect the little things, which are often looked upon as of no moment. Neglect of little things often leads to neglect of larger responsibilities.

———

Workers in the Lord's vineyard have the example of the good in all ages to encourage them. They have also the love of God, the ministration of angels, the sympathy of Jesus, and the hope of winning souls to the right. "They that be wise shall shine as the brightness of the firmament; and they that turn many to righteousness as the stars forever and ever." [3]

FOR FURTHER STUDY

CONSECRATION

Test. Vol. II, pp. 262, 263, 343-346, 516, 521, 522, 628, 629.
Test. Vol. III, pp. 301, 500.
Test. Vol. IV, pp. 118-125, 144, 145, 213-221, 543, 544.
Test. Vol. V, pp. 573-580.
Test. Vol. VIII, pp. 28, 29, 47.
Desire, pp. 250, 251, 827.
Acts, pp. 469-484, 519-523, 557-567.
Counsels, pp. 522, 523.

[3] Dan. 12 : 3.

The Minister in the Pulpit

"Giving no offense in anything, that the ministry be not blamed."

"PREACH THE WORD"

"I charge thee therefore before God, and the Lord Jesus Christ, who shall judge the quick and the dead at His appearing and His kingdom: Preach the word; be instant in season, out of season; reprove, rebuke, exhort with all long-suffering and doctrine." [1]

In these direct and forcible words is made plain the duty of the minister of Christ. He is to "preach the word," not the opinions and traditions of men, not pleasing fables or sensational stories, to move the fancy and excite the emotions. He is not to exalt himself, but as in the presence of God he is to stand before a dying world and preach the word. There is to be no levity, no trifling, no fanciful interpretation; the minister must speak in sincerity and deep earnestness, as a voice from God expounding the Sacred Scriptures. He is to bring to his hearers those things which most concern their present and eternal good.

My ministering brethren, as you stand before the people, speak of those things that are essential, those things that will instruct. Teach the great practical truths that must be brought into the life. Teach the saving power of Jesus, "in whom we have redemption, . . . even the forgiveness of sins." [2] Strive to

[1] 2 Tim. 4 : 1, 2.   [2] Col. 1 : 14.

make your hearers comprehend the power of truth.

Ministers should present the sure word of prophecy as the foundation of the faith of Seventh-day Adventists. The prophecies of Daniel and the Revelation should be carefully studied, and in connection with them the words, "Behold the Lamb of God, which taketh away the sin of the world." [3]

The twenty-fourth chapter of Matthew is presented to me again and again as something that is to be brought to the attention of all. We are to-day living in the time when the predictions of this chapter are fulfilling. Let our ministers and teachers explain these prophecies to those whom they instruct. Let them leave out of their discourses matters of minor consequence, and present the truths that will decide the destiny of souls.

The time in which we are living calls for constant vigilance, and God's ministers are to present the light on the Sabbath question. They should warn the inhabitants of the world that Christ is soon to come with power and great glory. The last message of warning to the world is to lead men to see the importance that God attaches to his law. So plainly is the truth to be presented that no transgressor, hearing it, shall be excusable in failing to discern the importance of obedience to God's commands.

I am instructed to say, Gather from the Scriptures the proofs that God has sanctified the seventh day, and let these proofs be read before the congregation. Let those who have not heard the truth be shown that all who turn aside from a plain "Thus saith the Lord," must suffer the result of their course. In all ages the Sabbath has been the test of loyalty to God. "It is a

[3] John 1 : 29.

sign between Me and the children of Israel forever," the Lord declares.[4]

POLICY IN SACRED THINGS

The gospel is now opposed on every side. Never was the confederacy of evil stronger than at the present time. Spirits of evil are combining with human agencies to war against the commandments of God. Tradition and falsehood are exalted above the Scriptures; reason and science above revelation; human talent above the teaching of the Spirit; forms and ceremonies above the vital power of godliness. Grievous sins have separated the people from God. Infidelity is fast becoming fashionable. "We will not have this man to reign over us," is the language of thousands. God's ministers must lift up the voice like a trumpet, and show the people their transgressions. The smooth sermons so often preached make no lasting impression. Men are not cut to the heart, because the plain, sharp truths of the word of God are not spoken to them.

Many of those who profess to believe the truth would say, if they expressed their real sentiments, What need is there of speaking so plainly? They might as well ask, Why need John the Baptist have said to the Pharisees, "O generation of vipers, who hath warned you to flee from the wrath to come?" [5] Why need he have provoked the anger of Herodias by telling Herod that it was unlawful for him to live with his brother's wife? He lost his life by speaking so plainly. Why could he not have moved along without incurring the anger of Herodias?

[4] Ex. 31 : 17.   [5] Matt. 3 : 7.

So men have argued, till policy has taken the place of faithfulness. Sin is allowed to go unrebuked. When will be heard once more in the church the voice of faithful rebuke, "Thou art the man"? [6] If these words were not so rare, we should see more of the power of God. The Lord's messengers should not complain of their efforts' being fruitless until they repent of their love of approbation, their desire to please men, which leads them to suppress the truth, and to cry, Peace, when God has not spoken peace.

Would that every minister of God realized the holiness of his work and the sacredness of his calling. As divinely appointed messengers, ministers are in a position of awful responsibility. In Christ's stead they are to labor as stewards of the mysteries of heaven, encouraging the obedient and warning the disobedient. Worldly policy is to have no weight with them. Never are they to swerve from the path in which Jesus has bidden them walk. They are to go forward in faith, remembering that they are surrounded by a cloud of witnesses. They are not to speak their own words, but the words that One greater than the potentates of earth has bidden them speak. Their message is to be, "Thus saith the Lord."

God calls for men who, like Nathan, Elijah, and John, will bear His message with fearlessness, regardless of consequences; who will speak the truth, though to do this calls for the sacrifice of all they have.

AS SHARP ARROWS

The words of Christ were as sharp arrows, which went to the mark and wounded the hearts of His hearers. Every time He addressed the people, whether

[6] See 2 Sam. 12: 7.

His audience was large or small, His words took saving effect upon the soul of some one. No message that fell from His lips was lost. Every word He spoke placed a new responsibility upon those who heard. And to-day the ministers who in sincerity are giving the last message of mercy to the world, relying on God for strength, need not fear that their efforts will be in vain. Although no human eye can see the path of the arrow of truth, who can say that the arrow has not sped to the mark, and pierced the souls of those who listened? Although no human ear has heard the cry of the wounded soul, yet the truth has silently cut its way to the heart. God has spoken to the soul; and in the day of final account, His faithful ministers will stand with the trophies of redeeming grace, to give honor to Christ.

No one can tell what is lost by attempting to preach without the unction of the Holy Spirit. In every congregation there are souls who are hesitating, almost decided to be wholly for God. Decisions are being made; but too often the minister has not the spirit and power of the message, and no direct appeals are made to those who are trembling in the balance.

In this age of moral darkness, it will take something more than dry theory to move souls. Ministers must have a living connection with God. They must preach as if they believe what they say. Living truths, falling from the lips of the man of God, will cause sinners to tremble, and the convicted to cry out, Jehovah is my God; I am resolved to be wholly on the Lord's side.

Never should the messenger of God cease his strivings for greater light and power. He should toil on, pray on, hope on, amid discouragement and darkness, determined to gain a thorough knowledge of the Scriptures and to come behind in no gift. As long as there is one soul to be benefited, he should press forward with new courage at every effort. So long as Jesus has said, "I will never leave thee, nor forsake thee," [7] so long as the crown of righteousness is offered to the overcomer, so long as our Advocate pleads in the sinner's behalf, ministers of Christ should labor with hopeful, tireless energy and persevering faith.

Men who assume the responsibility of giving to the people the word from the mouth of God, make themselves accountable for the influence they exert on their hearers. If they are true men of God, they will know that the object of preaching is not to entertain. It is not merely to convey information. nor to convince the intellect.

The preaching of the word should appeal to the intellect and should impart knowledge, but it should do more than this. The minister's utterances, to be effectual, must reach the hearts of his hearers. He should not bring amusing stories into his preaching. He must strive to understand the soul's great need and longing. As he stands before his congregation, let him remember that there are among his hearers those who are wrestling with doubt, almost in despair, well-nigh hopeless; those who, constantly harassed by temptation, are fighting a hard battle with the adversary of souls. Let him ask the Saviour to give him words to speak that will strengthen these souls for the conflict with evil.

[7] Heb. 13 : 5.

BREAKING THE BREAD OF LIFE
TO SOULS

Many of those for whom our ministers labor are ignorant of the truths of the Bible and the requirements of God, and the simplest lessons on practical godliness come to them as a new revelation. These need to know what is truth, and in laboring for them the minister should not take up lines of thought that will simply please the fancy or gratify curiosity. Let him instead break the bread of life to these starving souls. Never should he preach a sermon that does not help his hearers to see more plainly what they must do to be saved.

The immediate requirements, the present trials — for these, men and women need present help. The minister may take a high range into the heavens by poetical descriptions and fanciful presentations, which please the senses and feed the imagination, but which do not touch the life experience, the daily necessities. He may think that by his fanciful eloquence he has fed the flock of God; his hearers may think that they never before saw the truth clothed in language so beautiful. But trace, from cause to effect, the ecstasy of feeling caused by these fanciful representations, and it will be seen that although some truths may have been presented, such sermons do not fortify the hearers for the daily battles of life.

He who in his preaching makes eloquence his highest aim, causes the people to forget the truth that is mingled with his oratory. When the emotion has passed away, it will be found that the word of God has not been fastened upon the mind, nor have the hearers gained in understanding. They may speak in terms of admiration of the minister's eloquence, but they are not brought any nearer to the point of decision. They speak of the sermon as they would of a play, and of the minister as they would of an actor. They may come again to listen to the same kind of discourse, but they will go away unimpressed and unfed.

It is not flowery discourses that are needed, not a flood of words without meaning. Our ministers are to preach in a way that will help people to grasp vital truth. My brethren, do not soar where the common people cannot follow you, and if they could, would be neither benefited nor blessed. Teach the simple lessons given by Christ. Tell the story of His life of self-denial and sacrifice, His humiliation and death, His resurrection and ascension, His intercession for sinners in the courts above. In every congregation there are souls upon whom the Spirit of the Lord is moving. Help them to understand what is truth; break the bread of life to them; call their attention to vital questions.

Many voices are advocating error; let your voice advocate truth. Present subjects that will be as green pastures to the sheep of God's fold. Do not lead your hearers into waste tracts, where they will be no nearer the fountain of living water than they were before hearing you. Present the truth as it is in Jesus, making plain the requirements of the law and the gospel. Present Christ, the way, the truth, and the life, and tell of His power to save all who come to Him. The Captain of our salvation is interceding for His people, not as a petitioner to move the Father to compassion, but as a conqueror, who claims the trophies of His victory.

He is able to save to the uttermost all who come to God by Him. Make this fact very plain

Unless ministers are guarded, they will hide the truth under human ornamentation. Let no minister suppose that he can convert souls by eloquent sermons. Those who teach others should plead with God to imbue them with His Spirit, and enable them to lift up Christ as the sinner's only hope. Flowery speeches, pleasing tales, or inappropriate anecdotes do not convict the sinner. Men listen to such words as they would to a pleasant song. The message that the sinner should hear is, "God so loved the world, that He gave His only begotten Son, that whosoever believeth in Him should not perish, but have everlasting life." [1] The reception of the gospel does not depend on learned testimonies, eloquent speeches, or deep arguments, but upon its simplicity, and its adaptation to those who are hungering for the bread of life

It is the efficiency of the Holy Spirit that makes the ministry of the word effective. When Christ speaks through the minister, the Holy Spirit prepares the hearts of the listeners to receive the word. The Holy Spirit is not a servant, but a controlling power. He causes the truth to shine into minds, and speaks through every discourse where the minister surrenders himself to the divine working. It is the Spirit that surrounds the soul with a holy atmosphere, and speaks to the impenitent through words of warning, pointing them to Him who takes away the sin of the world.

[1] John 3 : 16.

PREACHING CHRIST

Many remarks have been made to the effect that in their discourses our speakers have dwelt upon the law, and not upon Jesus. This statement is not strictly true, but is there not some reason for it? Have there not stood in the desk men who have not had a genuine experience in the things of God, men who have not received the righteousness of Christ? Many of our ministers have merely sermonized, presenting subjects in an argumentative way, and scarcely mentioning the saving power of the Redeemer. Their testimony was destitute of the saving blood of Christ. Their offering resembled the offering of Cain. He brought to the Lord the fruit of the ground, which in itself was acceptable in God's sight. Very good indeed was the fruit; but the virtue of the offering — the blood of the slain lamb, representing the blood of Christ — was lacking. So it is with Christless sermons. By them men are not pricked to the heart; they are not led to inquire, What must I do to be saved?

Of all professing Christians, Seventh-day Adventists should be foremost in uplifting Christ before the world. The proclamation of the third angel's message calls for the presentation of the Sabbath truth. This truth, with others included in the message, is to be proclaimed; but the great center of attraction, Christ Jesus, must not be left out. It is at the cross of Christ that mercy and truth meet together, and righteousness and peace kiss each other. The sinner must be led to look to Calvary; with the simple faith of a little child he must trust in the merits of the Saviour, accepting His righteousness, believing in His mercy.

THE LOVE OF GOD

Through the love of God the treasures of the grace of Christ have been laid open before the church and the world. "God so loved the world, that He gave His only begotten Son, that whosoever believeth in Him should not perish, but have everlasting life." [1] What marvelous, unfathomable love, which led Christ to die for us while we were yet sinners! And what a loss the soul suffers who, understanding the strong claims of the law, fails to acknowledge that where sin abounds, the grace of Christ does much more abound!

When the law is presented as it should be, it reveals the love of God. But it is no wonder that hearts are not melted even by truth when it is presented in a cold, lifeless manner; no wonder that faith staggers at the promises of God, when ministers and workers fail to present Jesus in His relation to the law.

Some workers in the cause of God have been too ready to hurl denunciations against the sinner; the love of the Father in giving His Son to die for the race, has been kept in the background. Let the teacher of truth make known to the sinner what God really is,— a Father waiting with yearning love to receive the returning prodigal, not hurling at him accusations of wrath, but preparing a feast to welcome his return. O that we might all learn the way of the Lord in winning souls!

God would draw minds from the conviction of logic to a conviction deeper, higher, purer, and more glorious. Often human logic has nearly quenched the light

[1] John 3 : 16.

that God would have shine forth in clear rays to convince men that the Lord of nature is worthy of all praise and glory, because He is the Creator of all things.

Some ministers err in making their sermons wholly argumentative. There are those who listen to the theory of the truth, and are impressed with the evidences brought out; then, if Christ is presented as the Saviour of the world, the seed sown may spring up and bear fruit to the glory of God. But often the cross of Calvary is not presented before the people. Some may be listening to the last sermon they will ever hear, and the golden opportunity, lost, is lost forever. If in connection with the theory of the truth, Christ and His redeeming love had been proclaimed, these might have been won to His side.

THE WAY TO CHRIST

More people than we think are longing to find the way to Christ. Those who preach the last message of mercy should bear in mind that Christ is to be exalted as the sinner's refuge. Some ministers think that it is not necessary to preach repentance and faith; they take it for granted that their hearers are acquainted with the gospel, and that matters of a different nature must be presented in order to hold their attention. But many people are sadly ignorant in regard to the plan of salvation; they need more instruction upon this all-important subject than upon any other.

Theoretical discourses are essential, that people may see the chain of truth, link after link, uniting in a perfect whole; but no discourse should ever be preached without presenting Christ and Him crucified as the foundation of the gospel. Ministers would reach more hearts if they would dwell more upon practical godliness. Frequently, when efforts are made to present the truth in new fields, the discourses given are largely theoretical. The people are unsettled by what they hear. Many see the force of the truth, and are anxious to place their feet upon a sure foundation. Then is the time, above all others, to urge home upon the conscience the religion of Christ. If the meetings are allowed to close without this practical work, there is great loss.

Sometimes men and women decide in favor of the truth because of the weight of evidence presented, without being converted. The minister's work is not done until he has urged upon his hearers the necessity of a change of heart. In every discourse fervent appeals should be made to the people to forsake their sins and turn to Christ. The popular sins and indulgences of our day should be condemned, and practical godliness enjoined. Feeling from the heart the importance of the words he utters, the true minister is unable to repress his concern for the souls of those for whom he labors.

O that I could command language of sufficient force to make the impression that I wish to make upon my fellow-laborers in the gospel. My brethren, you are handling the words of life; you are dealing with minds that are capable of the highest development. Christ crucified, Christ risen, Christ ascended into the heavens, Christ coming again, should so soften, gladden, and fill the mind of the minister that he will present these truths to the people in love and deep earnestness. The minister will then be lost sight of and Jesus will be made manifest.

Lift up Jesus, you that teach the people, lift Him up in sermon, in song, in prayer. Let all your powers be directed to pointing souls, confused, bewildered, lost, to "the Lamb of God." Lift Him up, the risen Saviour, and say to all who hear, Come to Him who "hath loved us, and hath given Himself for us." [2] Let the science of salvation be the burden of every sermon, the theme of every song. Let it be poured forth in every supplication. Bring nothing into your preaching to supplement Christ, the wisdom and power of God. Hold forth the word of life, presenting Jesus as the hope of the penitent and the stronghold of every believer. Reveal the way of peace to the troubled and the despondent, and show forth the grace and completeness of the Saviour.

———◆———

There is only one path that leads from darkness upward to the light until it touches the throne of God, — the path of faith. This path is not dark and uncertain; it is not the way of finite minds, not a path made by human hands, in which toll is exacted from every traveler. Entrance to it cannot be gained by works of penance.

The way that God has provided is so complete, so perfect, that man cannot, by any works that he can do, add to its perfection. It is broad enough to receive the most hardened sinner, if he truly repents, and yet so narrow that in it sin can find no place. This is the path cast up for the ransomed of the Lord to walk in.

[2] Eph. 5 : 2.

RIGHTEOUSNESS BY FAITH

The thought that the righteousness of Christ is imputed to us, not because of any merit on our part, but as a free gift from God, is a precious thought. The enemy of God and man is not willing that this truth should be clearly presented; for he knows that if the people receive it fully, his power will be broken. If he can control minds so that doubt and unbelief and darkness shall compose the experience of those who claim to be the children of God, he can overcome them with temptation.

That simple faith which takes God at His word should be encouraged. God's people must have that faith which will lay hold of divine power; "for by grace are ye saved through faith; and that not of yourselves: it is the gift of God." [1] Those who believe that God for Christ's sake has forgiven their sins, should not, through temptation, fail to press on to fight the good fight of faith. Their faith should grow stronger until their Christian life, as well as their words, shall declare, "The blood of Jesus Christ . . . cleanseth us from all sin." [2]

If we would have the spirit and power of the third angel's message, we must present the law and the gospel together, for they go hand in hand. As a power from beneath is stirring up the children of disobedience to make void the law of God, and to trample upon the truth that Christ is our righteousness, a power from above is moving upon the hearts of those who are loyal, to exalt the law, and to lift up Jesus as a complete

[1] Eph. 2:8. [2] 1 John 1:7.

6

Saviour. Unless divine power is brought into the experience of the people of God, false theories and ideas will take minds captive, Christ and His righteousness will be dropped out of the experience of many, and their faith will be without power or life.

Ministers are to present Christ in His fulness both in the churches and in new fields, that the hearers may have an intelligent faith. The people must be instructed that Christ is unto them salvation and righteousness. It is Satan's studied purpose to keep souls from believing in Christ as their only hope; for the blood of Christ that cleanseth from all sin is efficacious in behalf of those only who believe in its merit, and who present it before the Father as did Abel in his offering.

The offering of Cain was an offense to God, because it was a Christless offering. The burden of our message is not only the commandments of God, but the faith of Jesus. A bright light shines upon our pathway to-day, and it leads to increased faith in Jesus. We must receive every ray of light, and walk in it, that it may not be our condemnation in the judgment. Our duties and obligations become more important as we obtain more distinct views of truth. Light makes manifest and reproves the errors that were concealed in darkness; and as light comes, the life and character of men must change correspondingly, to be in harmony with it. Sins that were once sins of ignorance, because of the blindness of the mind, can no more be indulged in without incurring guilt. As increased light is given, men must be reformed, elevated, and refined by it, or they will be more perverse and stubborn than before the light came.

COUNSEL TO AN EVANGELIST

Dear Brother:

. . . I have this message for you from the Lord: Be kind in speech, gentle in action. Guard yourself carefully, for you are inclined to be severe and dictatorial, and to say rash things. The Lord speaks to you, saying, Watch and pray, lest ye enter into temptation. Harsh expressions grieve the Lord; unwise words do harm. I am charged to say to you, Be gentle in your speech; watch well your words; let no harshness come into your utterances or into your gestures. Bring into all you do and say the fragrance of Christlikeness. Let not natural traits of character mar and spoil your work. You are to help and strengthen the tempted. Let not self appear in rash words. Christ has given His life for the flock, and for all for whom you labor. Let no word of yours balance souls in the wrong direction. In the minister of Christ there must be revealed Christlikeness of character.

Rash, overbearing expressions do not harmonize with the sacred work that Christ has given His ministers to do. When the daily experience is one of looking unto Jesus and learning of Him, you will reveal a wholesome, harmonious character. Soften your representations, and let not condemnatory words be spoken. Learn of the great Teacher. Words of kindness and sympathy will do good as a medicine, and will heal souls that are in despair. The knowledge of the word of God brought into the practical life will have a healing, soothing power. Harshness of speech will never bring blessing to yourself or to any other soul.

My brother, you are to be a representative of the mildness and patience and goodness of Christ. In your talks before the public, let your representations be after Christ's order. "The wisdom that is from above is first pure, then peaceable, gentle, and easy to be entreated, full of mercy and good fruits." [1] Watch and pray, and subdue the harshness which at times breaks out in you. By the grace of Christ dwelling in you, your words may become sanctified. If your brethren do not act just as you think they should, do not meet them with harshness. The Lord has been grieved at times by your severe expressions.

Your will is to be yielded to the Lord's will. You need the help of the Lord Jesus. Let only words that are clean and pure and sanctified come from your lips; for as a minister of the gospel, your spirit and example will be followed by others. Be kind and tender to children at all times. . . .

You may reach God's ideal if you will resolve that self shall not be woven into your work. To know that you are striving in spirit and in works to be Christlike, will give you strength and comfort and courage. It is your privilege to become meek and lowly in heart; then angels of God will co-operate with you in your revival efforts. Christ died that His life might be lived in you, and in all who make Him their example. In the strength of your Redeemer you can reveal the character of Christ, and you can work in wisdom and in power to make the crooked places straight.

Los Angeles, Cal., Aug. 22, 1908.

[1] James 3 : 17.

PRACTICAL SUGGESTIONS

Formal Discourses.— Some ministers, in the preparation of their discourses, arrange every detail with such exactness that they give the Lord no room to lead their minds. Every point is fixed, stereotyped, as it were, and they seem unable to depart from the plan marked out. This is a grave error, and if followed, will cause ministers to become narrow-minded, and will leave them as destitute of spiritual life and energy as were the hills of Gilboa of dew and rain.

When a minister feels that he cannot vary from a set discourse, the effect is little better than that produced by reading a sermon. Tame, formal discourses have in them very little of the vitalizing power of the Holy Spirit; and the habit of preaching such discourses will effectually destroy a minister's usefulness and ability.

God would have His workmen wholly dependent upon Him. They must listen to hear what saith the Lord, asking, What is Thy word for the people? Their hearts should be open, so that God may impress their minds, and then they will be able to give the people truth fresh from heaven. The Holy Spirit will give them ideas adapted to meet the needs of those present.

Reverence.— I have heard some ministers talk of Christ's life and teachings in a commonplace manner, as if recounting incidents in the life of some great man of the world. Indeed, it is not unusual for ministers to speak of Christ as if He were a man like themselves.

When I hear this sacred subject treated in such a manner, I feel a grief that I cannot express; for I know that although these men are teachers of truth, they have never had exalted views of Christ; they have never become acquainted with Him. They have not that elevation of thought which would give them a clear conception of the character of the world's Redeemer.

Those who have a correct view of the character and work of Christ, will not become self-sufficient or self-exalted. The weakness and inefficiency of their own efforts, in contrast with those of the Son of God, will keep them humble, distrustful of self, and will lead them to rely on Christ for strength to do their work. Habitually dwelling upon Christ and His all-sufficient merits, increases faith, quickens the power of spiritual discernment, strengthens the desire to be like Him, and brings an earnestness into prayer that makes it efficacious.

Irrelevant Anecdotes.— Ministers should not make a practice of relating irrelevant anecdotes in connection with their sermons; for this detracts from the force of the truth presented. The relation of anecdotes or incidents that create a laugh or a light thought in the minds of the hearers is severely censurable. The truth should be clothed in chaste, dignified language; and the illustrations used should be of a like character.

How to Overcome Inattention.— Often a minister is obliged to preach in a crowded, overheated room. The listeners become drowsy, their senses are benumbed, and it is almost impossible for them to grasp the truths presented.

If, instead of preaching to them, the speaker would try to teach them, speaking in a conversational tone and asking them questions, their minds would be aroused to activity, and they would be able more clearly to comprehend the words spoken.

Small Congregations.— Do not become discouraged when there are only a few present to listen to a discourse. Even if you have but two or three hearers, who knows whether there may not be one with whom the Spirit of the Lord is striving? The Lord may give you a message for that one soul, and he, if converted, may be the means of reaching others. All unknown to you, the results of your labor may be multiplied a thousand-fold.

Do not look at the empty seats, and let your faith and courage sink; but think of what God is doing to bring His truth before the world. Remember that you are co-operating with divine agencies — agencies that never fail. Speak with as much earnestness, faith, and interest as if there were thousands present to listen to your voice.

A minister went to his church to preach one rainy morning, and found that he had only one man for an audience. But he would not disappoint his hearer, and he preached to him with earnestness and interest. As a result, the man was converted, and became a missionary, and through his efforts thousands heard the good news of salvation.

Short Sermons.— Let the message for this time be presented, not in long, labored discourses, but in short talks, right to the point. Lengthy sermons tax the strength of the speaker and the patience of his hearers. If the speaker is one who feels the importance of his message, he will need to be especially careful lest he overtax his physical powers, and give the people more than they can remember.

Do not think, when you have gone over a subject once, that your hearers will retain in their minds all that you have presented. There is danger of passing too rapidly from point to point. Give short lessons, in plain, simple language, and let them be often repeated. Short sermons will be remembered far better than long ones. Our speakers should remember that the subjects they are presenting may be new to some of their hearers; therefore the principal points should be gone over again and again.

Directness.— Many speakers waste their time and strength in long preliminaries and excuses. Some use nearly half an hour in making apologies; thus time is wasted, and when they reach their subject and try to fasten the points of truth in the minds of their hearers, the people are wearied out and cannot see their force.

Instead of apologizing because he is about to address the people, the minister should begin as if he knew that he was bearing a message from God. He should make the essential points of truth as distinct as mile-posts, so that the people cannot fail to see them.

Time is frequently lost in explaining points which are really unimportant, and which would be taken for granted without producing proofs. But the vital points should be made as plain and forcible as language and proof can make them.

Concentration.— Some have cultivated the habit of too great concentrativeness. The power to fix the mind upon one subject to the exclusion of all others, is good to a limited degree, but those who put the whole strength of the mind into one line of thought are frequently deficient on other points. In conversation these become tedious, and weary the listener. Their writings lack a free, easy style. When they speak in public, the subject before them holds their attention, and they are led on and on, to go deeper and deeper into the matter. They seem to see knowledge and light as they become interested and absorbed, but there are few who can follow them.

There is danger that such men will plant the seed of truth so deep that the tender blade will never find the surface. Even the most essential, manifest truths, those which are of themselves clear and plain, may be so covered up with words as to be made cloudy and indistinct.

Simplicity.— Argument is good in its place, but far more can be accomplished by simple explanations of the word of God. The lessons of Christ were illustrated so clearly that the most ignorant could readily comprehend them. Jesus did not use long and difficult words in His discourses; He used plain language, adapted to the minds of the common people. He went no farther into the subject He was expounding than they were able to follow Him.

Ministers should present the truth in a clear, simple manner. There are among their hearers many who need a plain explanation of the steps requisite in conversion. The great masses of the people are more ignorant on this point than is supposed. Among graduates from college, eloquent orators, able statesmen, men in high positions of trust, there are many who have given their powers to other matters, and have neglected the things of greatest importance. When such men form part of a congregation, the speaker often strains every power to preach an intellectual discourse, and fails to reveal Christ. He does not show that sin is the transgression of the law. He does not make plain the plan of salvation. That which would have touched the hearts of his hearers, would have been to point them to Christ dying to bring redemption within their reach.

Revivals.— When the Lord works through human instrumentalities, when men are moved with power from on high, Satan leads his agents to cry, "Fanaticism!" and to warn people not to go to extremes. Let all be careful how they raise this cry; for though there is counterfeit coin, this does not lower the value of that which is genuine. Because there are spurious revivals and spurious conversions, it does not follow that all revivals are to be held in suspicion. Let us not show the contempt manifested by the Pharisees when they said, "This man receiveth sinners." [1]

There is enough in the life of Christ to teach us not to sneer at His work in the conversion of souls. The manifestation of God's renewing grace on sinful men

[1] Luke 15 : 2.

causes angels to rejoice, but often this work has, through unbelief, been termed fanaticism, and the messenger through whom God has worked has been spoken of as having zeal that is not according to knowledge.

Sabbath Services.— The one appointed to conduct Sabbath services should study how to interest his hearers in the truths of the Word. He should not always give so long a discourse that there will be no opportunity for those present to confess Christ. The sermon should frequently be short, so that the people may express their thanksgiving to God. Gratitude-offerings glorify the name of the Lord. In every assembly of the saints holy angels listen to the praise offered to Jehovah in testimony, song, and prayer.

The prayer and social meeting should be a season of special help and encouragement. All should feel it a privilege to take part. Let every one who bears the name of Christ have something to say in the social meeting. The testimonies should be short, and of a nature to help others. Nothing will so completely kill the spirit of devotion as for one person to take up twenty or thirty minutes in a long testimony. This means death to the spirituality of the meeting.

CAREFULNESS IN MANNERS AND DRESS

The minister must remember that favorable or unfavorable impressions are made upon his hearers by his deportment in the pulpit, his attitude, his manner of speaking, his dress. He should cultivate courtesy and refinement of manner, and should carry himself with a quiet dignity becoming to his high calling. Solemnity and a certain godly authority mingled with meekness, should characterize his demeanor. Coarseness and rudeness are not to be tolerated in the common walks of life, much less should they be permitted in the work of the ministry. The minister's attitude should be in harmony with the holy truths he proclaims. His words should be in every respect earnest and well chosen.

Ministers have no license to behave in the desk like theatrical performers, assuming attitudes and making expressions merely for effect. They are not actors, but teachers of truth. Undignified, boisterous actions lend no force to the truth uttered; on the contrary, they disgust men and women of calm judgment and right views.

The minister who has learned of Christ will ever be conscious that he is a messenger of God, commissioned by Him to do a work the influence of which is to endure throughout eternity. It should not be any part of his object to call attention to himself, his learning, or his ability. His whole aim should be to bring sinners to repentance, pointing them, by both precept and example, to the Lamb of God that taketh away the sin of the world. He should speak as one conscious of possessing power and authority from God. His discourses should have an earnestness, a fervor, a power of persuasion, that will lead sinners to take refuge in Christ.

Carefulness in dress is an important consideration. The minister should be clothed in a manner befitting the dignity of his position. Some ministers have failed in this respect. In some cases not only has there been a lack of taste and of orderly arrangement in the dress, but the clothing has been untidy and slovenly.

The God of heaven, whose arm moves the world, who gives us life and sustains us in health, is honored or dishonored by the apparel of those who officiate in His honor. To Moses He gave special instruction regarding everything connected with the tabernacle service, and He specified the dress that those should wear who were to minister before Him. "Thou shalt make holy garments for Aaron thy brother for glory and for beauty," [1] was the direction given to Moses. Everything connected with the apparel and deportment of the priests was to be such as to impress the beholder with a sense of the holiness of God, the sacredness of His worship, and the purity required of those who came into His presence.

The priests were not allowed to enter the sanctuary with their shoes on their feet; for the particles of dust cleaving to them would desecrate the holy place. They were to leave their shoes in the court before entering the sanctuary, and also to wash their hands and their feet before ministering in the tabernacle or at the altar of burnt-offering. Thus was constantly taught the lesson that all defilement must be put away from those who would come into the presence of God.

[1] Ex. 28: 2.

The influence of the minister who is careless in his dress is displeasing to God, and the impression made upon his hearers is that he looks upon the work in which he is engaged as no more sacred than common labor. And not only this, but instead of showing them the importance of propriety and taste in clothing, he sets them an example of slackness and untidiness, which some are not slow to follow.

God expects His ministers, in their manners and in their dress, to give a fitting representation of the principles of truth and the sacredness of their office. They are to set an example that will help men and women to reach a high standard.

———◆———

Men have the power to quench the Spirit of God; the power of choosing is left with them. They are allowed freedom of action. They may be obedient through the name and grace of our Redeemer, or they may be disobedient, and realize the consequences.

Man is responsible for receiving or rejecting sacred and eternal truth. The Spirit of God is continually convicting, and souls are deciding for or against the truth. How important, then, that every act of life be such that it need not be repented of, especially among the ambassadors of Christ, who are acting in His stead!

PUBLIC PRAYER

The prayers offered in public should be short and to the point. God does not require us to make the season of worship tedious by lengthy petitions. Christ did not enforce upon His disciples wearisome ceremonies and long prayers. "When thou prayest," He said, "thou shalt not be as the hypocrites are: for they love to pray standing in the synagogues and in the corners of the streets, that they may be seen of men." [1]

The Pharisees had stated hours for prayer; and when, as often came to pass, they were abroad at the appointed time, they would pause wherever they might be,— perhaps in the street or in the market-place, amid the hurrying throng of men,— and there in a loud voice rehearse their formal prayers. Such worship, offered merely for self-glorification, called forth unsparing rebuke from Jesus. Yet he did not discountenance public prayer; for He Himself prayed with His disciples and with the multitude. But He impressed upon His disciples the thought that their public prayers should be short.

A few minutes is long enough for any ordinary public petition. There may be instances where supplication is in a special manner indited by the Spirit of God. The yearning soul becomes agonized, and groans after God. The spirit wrestles as did Jacob, and will not be at rest without the special manifestation of the power of God. At such times it may be fitting that the petition be of greater length.

Many tedious prayers are offered, which are more like giving the Lord a lecture than presenting to Him a

[1] Matt. 6 : 5.

request. It would be better if those offering such prayers would confine themselves to the one that Christ taught His disciples to offer. Long prayers are tiring to those who hear, and do not prepare the people to listen to the instruction that is to follow.

It is often because secret prayer is neglected that long, tedious prayers are offered in public. Let not ministers go over in their petitions a week of neglected duties, hoping to atone for their neglect and to pacify conscience. Such prayers frequently result in bringing others down to a low level of spirituality.

Before entering the desk, the minister should seek God in his closet, and come into close connection with Him. There he may lift his thirsty soul to God, and be refreshed with the dew of grace. Then with an unction from the Holy Spirit upon him, giving him a burden for souls, he will not dismiss a congregation without presenting before them Jesus Christ, the sinner's only refuge. Feeling that he may never again meet these hearers, he will make appeals that will reach their hearts. And the Master, who knows the hearts of men, will give him utterance, helping him to speak the words he ought to speak at the right time and with power.

REVERENCE IN PRAYER

Some think it a mark of humility to pray to God in a common manner, as if talking with a human being. They profane His name by needlessly and irreverently mingling with their prayers the words, "God Almighty,"— awful, sacred words, which should never pass the lips except in subdued tones and with a feeling of awe.

High-flown language is inappropriate in prayer, whether the petition be offered in the pulpit, in the family circle, or in secret. Especially should the one offering public prayer use simple language, that others may understand what is said and unite with the petition.

It is the heart-felt prayer of faith that is heard in heaven and answered on earth. God understands the needs of humanity. He knows what we desire before we ask Him. He sees the soul's conflict with doubt and temptation. He marks the sincerity of the suppliant. He will accept the humiliation and affliction of the soul. "To this man will I look," He declares, "even to him that is poor and of a contrite spirit, and trembleth at My word." [2]

It is our privilege to pray with confidence, the Spirit inditing our petitions. With simplicity we should state our needs to the Lord, and claim His promise with such faith that those in the congregation will know that we have learned to prevail with God in prayer. They will be encouraged to believe that the Lord's presence is in the meeting, and will open their hearts to receive His blessing. Their faith in our sincerity will be increased, and they will listen with willing ears to the instruction given.

Our prayers should be full of tenderness and love. When we yearn for a deeper, broader realization of the Saviour's love, we shall cry to God for more wisdom. If ever there was a need of soul-stirring prayers and sermons, it is now. The end of all things is at hand. O that we could see as we should the necessity of seeking the Lord with all the heart! Then we should find Him.

[2] Isa. 66 : 2.

May God teach His people how to pray. Let the teachers in our schools and the ministers in our churches, learn daily in the school of Christ. Then they will pray with earnestness, and their requests will be heard and answered. Then the word will be proclaimed with power.

OUR ATTITUDE IN PRAYER

Both in public and in private worship, it is our privilege to bow on our knees before the Lord when we offer our petitions to Him. Jesus, our example, "kneeled down, and prayed." [3] Of His disciples it is recorded that they, too, "kneeled down, and prayed." [4] Paul declared, "I bow my knees unto the Father of our Lord Jesus Christ." [5] In confessing before God the sins of Israel, Ezra knelt. [6] Daniel "kneeled upon his knees three times a day, and prayed, and gave thanks before his God." [7]

True reverence for God is inspired by a sense of His infinite greatness and a realization of His presence. With this sense of the Unseen, every heart should be deeply impressed. The hour and place of prayer are sacred, because God is there; and as reverence is manifested in attitude and demeanor, the feeling that inspires it will be deepened. "Holy and reverend is His name," [8] the psalmist declares. Angels, when they speak that name, veil their faces. With what reverence, then, should we, who are fallen and sinful, take it upon our lips!

Well would it be for old and young to ponder those words of Scripture that show how the place marked by God's special presence should be regarded. "Put

[3] Luke 22 : 41.   [4] Acts 9 : 40; 20 : 36; 21 : 5.   [5] Eph. 3 : 14.
[6] See Ezra 9 : 5.   [7] Dan. 6 : 10.   [8] Ps. 111 : 9.

off thy shoes from off thy feet," He commanded Moses at the burning bush, "for the place whereon thou standest is holy ground." [9] Jacob, after beholding the vision of the angels, exclaimed, "The Lord is in this place; and I knew it not. . . . This is none other but the house of God, and this is the gate of heaven." [10]

"The Lord is in His holy temple: let all the earth keep silence before Him." [11]

———◆———

Prosy, sermonizing prayers are uncalled for and out of place in public. A short prayer, offered in fervor and faith, will soften the hearts of the hearers; but during long prayers they wait impatiently, as if wishing that every word might end it. Had the minister making such a prayer wrestled with God in his chamber until he felt that his faith could grasp the promise, "Ask, and it shall be given you," he would in his public prayer have come to the point at once, asking with earnestness and faith for grace for himself and his hearers.

[9] Ex. 3 : 5.   [10] Gen. 28 : 16, 17.   [11] Hab. 2 : 20.

FOR FURTHER STUDY

PREACH THE WORD

Test. Vol. III, pp. 252, 257.
Test. Vol. V, pp. 299, 300.
C. O. L., pp. 39-43, 124-134.

BREAKING THE BREAD
OF LIFE

Test. Vol. III, p. 237.
Desire, pp. 366-371.
C. O. L., p. 231.

PREACHING CHRIST

Test. Vol. III, pp. 214-216.
Test. Vol. IV, pp. 313-316, 374,
375.
Test. Vol. V, pp. 158-161, 539,
540.
Acts, pp. 201-220.

RIGHTEOUSNESS BY FAITH

Test. Vol. IV, pp. 294, 295.
Ed., pp. 76, 77.
Desire, pp. 300, 306-314.
C. O. L., pp. 128, 307-318.
Steps, pp. 67-69.
Acts, pp. 505-507.

COUNSEL TO AN EVANGELIST

Test. Vol. III, pp. 507, 508.
Test. Vol. IV, p. 486.
Ed., pp. 291-295.
Desire, pp. 253, 254.
C. O. L., pp. 235, 236.
Acts, pp. 515, 516.

PRACTICAL SUGGESTIONS
  Short Sermons

  Anecdotes
  Simplicity
  Reverence
  Small Congregations
  Sabbath Services

Test. Vol. II, pp. 117, 118, 672.
Test. Vol. III, p. 419.
Test. Vol. III, p. 241.
C. O. L., pp. 231, 232.
Ed., pp. 242-244.
Desire, pp. 183-194.
Test. Vol. V, p. 256.

CAREFULNESS IN MANNERS
AND DRESS

Test. Vol. I, pp. 648, 649.

PUBLIC PRAYER

Test. Vol. II, pp. 616, 617.
Test. Vol. V, pp. 201, 202.
C. O. L., pp. 150-152.

The Under-Shepherd

" Feed the flock of God, . . .
taking the oversight thereof."

THE GOOD SHEPHERD

Christ, the great example for all ministers, likens Himself to a shepherd. "I am the good shepherd," He declares; "the good shepherd giveth his life for the sheep." "I am the good shepherd, and know My sheep, and am known of Mine. As the Father knoweth Me, even so know I the Father: and I lay down My life for the sheep." [1]

As an earthly shepherd knows his sheep, so does the divine Shepherd know His flock that are scattered throughout the world. "Ye My flock, the flock of My pasture, are men, and I am your God, saith the Lord God." [2]

In the parable of the lost sheep, the shepherd goes out to search for one sheep,— the very least that can be numbered. Discovering that one of his sheep is missing, he does not look carelessly upon the flock that is safely housed, and say, I have ninety and nine, and it will cost me too much trouble to go in search of the straying one. Let him come back, and I will open the door of the sheepfold and let him in. No; no sooner does the sheep go astray than the shepherd is filled with grief and anxiety. Leaving the ninety and nine

[1] John 10 : 11, 14, 15. [2] Eze. 34 : 31.

in the fold, he goes in search of the straying one. However dark and tempestuous the night, however perilous and uncertain the way, however long and tedious the search, he does not falter until the lost is found.

With what relief does he hear in the distance its first faint cry! Following the sound, he climbs the steepest heights; he goes to the very edge of the precipice, at the risk of his own life. Thus he searches, while the cry, growing fainter, tells him that his sheep is ready to die.

And when the straying one is found, does he command it to follow him? Does he threaten or beat it, or drive it before him, thinking of the discomfort and anxiety that he has suffered on its account? No; he lays the exhausted sheep on his shoulder, and with cheerful gratitude that his search has not been in vain, he returns to the fold. His gratitude finds expression in songs of rejoicing. And "when he cometh home, he calleth together his friends and neighbors, saying unto them, Rejoice with me; for I have found my sheep which was lost."

So when the lost sinner is found by the Good Shepherd, heaven and earth unite in rejoicing and thanksgiving. For "joy shall be in heaven over one sinner that repenteth, more than over ninety and nine just persons, which need no repentance." [3]

The great Shepherd has under-shepherds, to whom He delegates the care of His sheep and lambs. The first work that Christ entrusted to Peter, on restoring him to the ministry, was to feed the lambs. [4] This was a work in which Peter had had little experience. It

[3] Luke 15 : 6, 7.   [4] See John 21 : 15.

would require great care and tenderness, much patience and perseverance. It called him to minister to the children and youth, and to those young in the faith, to teach the ignorant, to open the Scriptures to them, and to educate them for usefulness in Christ's service. Heretofore Peter had not been fitted to do this, or even to understand its importance.

The question that Christ put to Peter was significant. He mentioned only one condition of discipleship and service. "Lovest thou Me?" He said. This is the essential qualification. Though Peter might possess every other, without the love of Christ he could not be a faithful shepherd over the Lord's flock. Knowledge, benevolence, eloquence, gratitude, and zeal are all aids in the good work; but without the love of Jesus in the heart, the work of the Christian minister will prove a failure.

The lesson which Christ taught him by the Sea of Galilee, Peter carried with him throughout his life. Writing by the Holy Spirit to the churches, he said:

"The elders which are among you I exhort, who am also an elder, and a witness of the sufferings of Christ, and also a partaker of the glory that shall be revealed: Feed the flock of God which is among you, taking the oversight thereof, not by constraint, but willingly; not for filthy lucre, but of a ready mind; neither as being lords over God's heritage, but being ensamples to the flock. And when the Chief Shepherd shall appear, ye shall receive a crown of glory that fadeth not away." [5]

The sheep that has strayed from the fold is the most helpless of all creatures. It must be sought for; for it cannot find its way back. So with the soul that has

[5] 1 Peter 5: 1-4.

wandered away from God; he is as helpless as the lost sheep; and unless divine love comes to his rescue, he can never find his way to God. Then with what compassion, what sorrow, what persistence, should the under-shepherd seek for lost souls! How willingly should he endure self-denial, hardship, privation!

There is need of shepherds who, under the direction of the Chief Shepherd, will seek for the lost and straying. This means the bearing of physical discomfort and the sacrifice of ease. It means a tender solicitude for the erring, a divine compassion and forbearance. It means an ear that can listen with sympathy to heart-breaking recitals of wrong, of degradation, of despair and misery.

The spirit of the true shepherd is one of self-forgetfulness. He loses sight of self in order that he may work the works of God. By the preaching of the word and by personal ministry in the homes of the people, he learns their needs, their sorrows, their trials; and, co-operating with the great Burden-bearer, he shares their afflictions, comforts their distresses, relieves their soul-hunger, and wins their hearts to God. In this work the minister is attended by heavenly angels, and he himself is instructed and enlightened in the truth that maketh wise unto salvation.

———◆———

In our work, individual effort will accomplish much more than can be estimated. It is for the want of this that souls are perishing. One soul is of infinite value; Calvary speaks its worth. One soul won to Christ, will be instrumental in winning others, and there will be an ever-increasing result of blessing and salvation.

PERSONAL MINISTRY

In the work of many ministers there is too much sermonizing and too little real heart-to-heart work. There is need of more personal labor for souls. In Christlike sympathy the minister should come close to men individually, and seek to awaken their interest in the great things of eternal life. Their hearts may be as hard as the beaten highway, and apparently it may be a useless effort to present the Saviour to them; but while logic may fail to move, and argument be powerless to convince, the love of Christ, revealed in personal ministry, may soften the stony heart, so that the seed of truth can take root.

Ministry means much more than sermonizing; it means earnest personal labor. The church on earth is composed of erring men and women, who need patient, painstaking labor, that they may be trained and disciplined to work with acceptance in this life, and in the future life be crowned with glory and immortality. Pastors are needed,— faithful shepherds,— who will not flatter God's people, nor treat them harshly, but who will feed them with the bread of life,— men who in their lives feel daily the converting power of the Holy Spirit, and who cherish a strong, unselfish love for those for whom they labor.

There is tactful work for the under-shepherd to do as he is called to meet alienation, bitterness, envy, and jealousy in the church; and he will need to labor in the spirit of Christ to set things in order. Faithful warnings are to be given, sins rebuked, wrongs made right, both by the minister's work in the pulpit and by personal labor. The wayward heart may take exception to the message, and the servant of God be misjudged and criticized. Let him then remember that "the wisdom that is from above is first pure, then peaceable, gentle, and easy to be entreated, full of mercy and good fruits, without partiality, and without hypocrisy. And the fruit of righteousness is sown in peace of them that make peace." [1]

The work of the gospel minister is "to make all men see what is the fellowship of the mystery, which from the beginning of the world hath been hid in God." [2] If one entering upon this work chooses the least self-sacrificing part, contenting himself with preaching, and leaving the work of personal ministry for some one else to do, his labors will not be acceptable to God. Souls for whom Christ died are perishing for want of well-directed personal labor; and he has mistaken his calling who, having entered the ministry, is unwilling to do the personal work that the care of the flock demands.

The minister must be instant in season and out of season, ready to seize and improve every opportunity to further the work of God. To be "instant in season" is to be alert to the privileges of the house and hour of worship, and to the times when men are conversing on topics of religion. And to be instant "out of season" is to be ready, when at the fireside, in the field, by the wayside, in the market, to turn the minds of men, in a suitable manner, to the great themes of the Bible, with tender, fervent spirit urging upon them the claims of God. Many, many such opportunities are allowed to slip by unimproved, because men are per-

[1] James 3 : 17, 18.   [2] Eph. 3 : 9.

suaded that it is out of season. But who knows what might be the effect of a wise appeal to the conscience? It is written, "In the morning sow thy seed, and in the evening withhold not thine hand: for thou knowest not whether shall prosper, either this or that, or whether they both shall be alike good." [3] He who is sowing the seeds of truth may bear a burdened heart, and at times his efforts may seem to be without result. But if he is faithful, he will see fruit of his labor; for God's word declares, "He that goeth forth and weepeth, bearing precious seed, shall doubtless come again with rejoicing, bringing his sheaves with him." [4]

VISITING HOMES

When a minister has presented the gospel message from the pulpit, his work is only begun. There is personal work for him to do. He should visit the people in their homes, talking and praying with them in earnestness and humility. There are families who will never be reached by the truths of God's word unless the stewards of His grace enter their homes and point them to the higher way. But the hearts of those who do this work must throb in unison with the heart of Christ.

Much is comprehended in the command, "Go out into the highways and hedges, and compel them to come in, that My house may be filled." [5] Let ministers teach the truth in families, drawing close to those for whom they labor; and as they thus co-operate with God, He will clothe them with spiritual power. Christ will guide them in their work, giving them words to speak that will sink deep into the hearts of the listeners.

[3] Eccl. 11 : 6.   [4] Ps. 126 : 6.   [5] Luke 14 : 23.

It is the privilege of every minister to be able to say with Paul, "I have not shunned to declare unto you all the counsel of God." "I kept back nothing that was profitable unto you, but have showed you, and have taught you publicly, and from house to house, . . . repentance toward God, and faith toward our Lord Jesus Christ." [6]

Our Saviour went from house to house, healing the sick, comforting the mourners, soothing the afflicted, speaking peace to the disconsolate. He took the little children in His arms and blessed them and spoke words of hope and comfort to the weary mothers. With unfailing tenderness and gentleness, He met every form of human woe and affliction. Not for Himself, but for others did He labor. He was the servant of all. It was His meat and drink to bring hope and strength to all with whom He came in contact. And as men and women listened to the truths that fell from His lips, so different from the traditions and dogmas taught by the rabbis, hope sprang up in their hearts. In His teaching there was an earnestness that sent His words home with convicting power.

To my ministering brethren I would say, By personal labor reach the people where they are. Become acquainted with them. This work cannot be done by proxy. Money loaned or given cannot accomplish it. Sermons from the pulpit cannot do it. Teaching the Scriptures in families,— this is the work of an evangelist, and this work is to be united with preaching. If it is omitted, the preaching will be, to a great extent, a failure.

Those who are seeking for truth need to have words spoken to them in season; for Satan is speak-

[6] Acts 20 : 27, 20, 21.

ing to them by his temptations. If you meet with repulse when trying to help souls, heed it not. If there seems to be little good resulting from your work, do not become discouraged. Keep working; be discreet; know when to speak, and when to keep silent; watch for souls as they that must give an account; and watch for the devices of Satan, lest you be led aside from duty. Do not allow difficulties to dishearten or intimidate you. With strong faith, with intrepid purpose, meet and overcome these difficulties. Sow the seed in faith, and with an unsparing hand.

Much depends upon the manner in which you meet those whom you visit. You can take hold of a person's hand in greeting in such a way as to gain his confidence at once, or in so cold a manner that he will think you have no interest in him.

We should not act as if it were a condescension to come in contact with the poor. They are as precious in God's sight as we are, and we must act as if we thought them so. Our clothing should be plain and simple, so that when we visit the poor, they will not be embarrassed by the contrast between our appearance and their own. The joy that comes to the poor is often very limited, and why should not God's workers carry rays of light into their homes? We need the tender sympathy of Jesus; then we can win our way to hearts.

THE SHEPHERD'S WORK

A true shepherd will have an interest in all that relates to the welfare of the flock, feeding, guiding, and defending them. He will carry himself with great wisdom, and will manifest a tender consideration for all, especially for the tempted, the afflicted, and the desponding. "Even as the Son of man came not to be ministered unto, but to minister, and to give His life a ransom for many." [1] "Verily, verily, I say unto you, The servant is not greater than his lord; neither he that is sent greater than he that sent him." [2] Christ "made Himself of no reputation, and took upon Him the form of a servant, and was made in the likeness of men." [3] "We then that are strong ought to bear the infirmities of the weak, and not to please ourselves. Let every one of us please his neighbor for his good to edification. For even Christ pleased not Himself; but, as it is written, The reproaches of them that reproached thee fell on Me." [4]

Many a laborer fails in his work because he does not come close to those who most need his help. With the Bible in hand, he should seek in a courteous manner to learn the objections which exist in the minds of those who are beginning to inquire, "What is truth?" Carefully and tenderly should he lead and educate them, as pupils in a school. Many have to unlearn theories which they have long believed to be truth. As they become convinced that they have been in error con-

[1] Matt. 20:28. [2] John 13:16. [3] Phil. 2:7. [4] Rom. 15:1-3.

cerning Bible subjects, they are thrown into perplexity and doubt. They need the tenderest sympathy and the most judicious help; they should be carefully instructed, and should be prayed for and prayed with, watched and guarded with the kindest solicitude.

It is a great privilege to be a co-laborer with Christ in the salvation of souls. With patient, unselfish effort the Saviour sought to reach man in his fallen condition, and to rescue him from the consequences of sin. His disciples, who are the teachers of His word, should closely imitate their great Exemplar.

In new fields, much prayer and wise labor are needed. There are wanted, not merely men who can sermonize, but those who have an experimental knowledge of the mystery of godliness, and who can meet the urgent needs of the people,— those who realize the importance of their position as servants of Jesus, and will cheerfully take up the cross that He has taught them how to bear.

It is highly important that a pastor mingle much with his people, and thus become acquainted with the different phases of human nature. He should study the workings of the mind, that he may adapt his teachings to the intellect of his hearers. He will thus learn that grand charity which is possessed only by those who study closely the nature and needs of men.

BIBLE-READINGS WITH FAMILIES

The plan of holding Bible-readings was a heaven-born idea. There are many, both men and women, who can engage in this branch of missionary labor. Workers may thus be developed who will become mighty men of God. By this means the word of God has been given to thousands; and the workers are brought into personal contact with people of all nations and tongues. The Bible is brought into families, and its sacred truths come home to the conscience. Men are entreated to read, examine, and judge for themselves, and they must abide the responsibility of receiving or rejecting the divine enlightenment. God will not permit this precious work for Him to go unrewarded. He will crown with success every humble effort made in His name.

In every new field, patience and perseverance must be exercised. Be not disheartened at small beginnings. It is often the humblest work that yields the greatest results. The more direct our labor for our fellow-men, the greater good will be accomplished. Personal influence is a power. The minds of those with whom we are closely associated, are impressed through unseen influences. One cannot speak to a multitude, and move them as he could if he were brought into closer relationship with them. Jesus left heaven and came to our world to save souls. You must come close to those for whom you labor, that they may not only hear your voice, but shake your hand, learn your principles, feel your sympathy.

My ministering brethren, do not think that the only work you can do, the only way you can labor for souls, is to give discourses. The best work you can do is to teach, to educate. Whenever you can find an opportunity to do so, sit down with some family, and let them ask questions. Then answer them patiently, humbly. Continue this work in connection with your more public efforts. Preach less, and educate more, by holding Bible-readings, and by praying with families and little companies.

To all who are working with Christ I would say, Wherever you can gain access to the people by the fireside, improve your opportunity. Take your Bible, and open before them its great truths. Your success will not depend so much upon your knowledge and accomplishments, as upon your ability to find your way to the heart. By being social and coming close to the people, you may turn the current of their thoughts more readily than by the most able discourse. The presentation of Christ in the family, by the fireside, and in small gatherings in private houses, is often more successful in winning souls to Jesus than are sermons delivered in the open air, to the moving throng, or even in halls or churches.

All who engage in this personal labor should be just as careful not to become mechanical in their manner of working as should the minister who preaches the word. They should be constantly learning. They should have a conscientious zeal to obtain the highest qualifications, to become men able in the Scriptures. They should cultivate habits of mental activity, especially giving themselves to prayer and to the diligent study of the Scriptures.

7

THE VALUE OF INDIVIDUAL EFFORT

Those who have been most successful in soul-winning were men and women who did not pride themselves on their ability, but who in humility and faith sought to help those about them. Jesus did this very work. He came close to those whom He desired to reach. How often, with a few gathered about Him, He gave His lessons, and one by one the passers-by paused to listen, until a great multitude heard with wonder and awe the words of the heaven-sent Teacher.

THE WOMAN OF SAMARIA

Christ did not wait for congregations to assemble. Some of the grandest truths He uttered were spoken to individuals. Listen to His wonderful words to that one woman of Samaria. He was sitting by Jacob's well as the woman came to draw water. To her surprise He asked a favor of her. "Give Me to drink," He said. He wanted a cool draught, and He wished also to open the way whereby He might give to her the water of life.

"How is it," said the woman, "that Thou, being a Jew, askest drink of me, which am a woman of Samaria? for the Jews have no dealings with the Samaritans."

Jesus answered, "If thou knewest the gift of God, and who it is that saith to thee, Give Me to drink; thou wouldst have asked of Him, and He would have given thee living water. . . . Whosoever drinketh of this water shall thirst again: but whosoever drinketh of the water that I shall give him shall never thirst;

but the water that I shall give him shall be in him a well of water springing up into everlasting life."

How much interest Christ manifested in this one woman! How earnest and eloquent were His words! They stirred the heart of the listener, and forgetting her errand to the well, she went into the city and said to her friends, "Come, see a man, which told me all things that ever I did: is not this the Christ?" [1]

Many left their employment to come to the Stranger at Jacob's well. They plied Him with questions, and eagerly received His explanation of many things that had been dark to their understanding. They were like people tracing a sudden ray of light until they found the day.

The result of the work of Jesus, as He sat, weary and hungry, at the well, was wide-spread in blessing. The one soul whom He sought to help became a means of reaching others and bringing them to the Saviour. This is ever the way that the work of God has made progress on the earth. Let your light shine, and other lights will be kindled.

God's servants are to stand as minutemen, ready for service at a moment's notice. My brethren, from hour to hour opportunities to serve God will open before you. These constantly come and go. Be ever ready to make the most of them. That chance to speak in the hearing of some needy soul the word of life may never again offer itself; therefore let no one venture to say, "I pray thee have me excused." Lose no opportunity to make known to others the unsearchable riches of Christ; for an opportunity once neglected may pass forever beyond recall.

[1] See John 4 : 7-30.

A DIVISION OF LABOR

A serious and perhaps unsuspected hindrance to the success of the truth is to be found in our churches themselves. When an effort is made to present our faith to unbelievers, the members of the church too often stand back, as if they were not an interested party, and let all the burden rest upon the minister. For this reason the labor of our most able ministers has been at times productive of little good. The very best sermons may be preached, the message may be just what the people need, and yet no souls be gained as sheaves to present to Christ.

In laboring where there are already some in the faith, the minister should at first seek not so much to convert unbelievers, as to train the church-members for acceptable co-operation. Let him labor for them individually, endeavoring to arouse them to seek for a deeper experience themselves, and to work for others. When they are prepared to sustain the minister by their prayers and labors, greater success will attend his efforts.

Nothing lasting can be accomplished for churches in different places unless they are aroused to feel that a responsibility rests upon them. Every member of the body should feel that the salvation of his own soul depends upon his own individual effort. Souls cannot be saved without exertion. The minister cannot save the people. He can be a channel through which God will impart light to His people; but after the light is given, it is left with the people to appropriate that light, and in their turn to let it shine forth to others.— *"Testimonies for the Church," Vol. II, page 121.*

EDUCATING CHURCH HELPERS

The minister should not feel that it is his duty to do all the talking and all the laboring and all the praying; he should educate helpers in every church. Let different ones take turns in leading the meetings, and in giving Bible-readings; in so doing they will be calling into use the talents which God has given them, and at the same time be receiving a training as workers.

"In some respects the pastor occupies a position similar to that of the foreman of a gang of laboring men or the captain of a ship's crew. They are expected to see that the men over whom they are set, do the work assigned to them correctly and promptly, and only in case of emergency are they to execute in detail.

"The owner of a large mill once found his superintendent in a wheel-pit, making some simple repairs, while a half-dozen workmen in that line were standing by, idly looking on. The proprietor, after learning the facts, so as to be sure that no injustice was done, called the foreman to his office and handed him his discharge with full pay. In surprise the foreman asked for an explanation. It was given in these words: 'I employed you to keep six men at work. I found the six idle, and you doing the work of but one. Your work could have been done just as well by any one of the six. I cannot afford to pay the wages of seven for you to teach the six how to be idle.'

"This incident may be applicable in some cases, and in others not. But many pastors fail in not knowing how, or in not trying, to get the full membership of the church actively engaged in the various departments of church work. If pastors would give more attention to getting and keeping their flock actively engaged at work, they would accomplish more good, have more time for study and religious visiting, and also avoid many causes of friction."

Some, through inexperience, will make mistakes, but they should be kindly shown how they can do their work better. Thus the pastor can be educating men and women to bear responsibilities in the good work that is suffering so much for want of laborers. We need men who can take responsibilities; and the best way for them to gain the experience they need, is to engage with heart and mind in the work.

SAVED BY EFFORT FOR ANOTHER

A working church is a growing church. The members find a stimulus and a tonic in helping others. I have read of a man who, journeying on a winter's day through deep drifts of snow, became benumbed by the cold, which was almost imperceptibly freezing his vital powers. He was nearly chilled to death, and was about to give up the struggle for life, when he heard the moans of a fellow-traveler, who was also perishing with cold. His sympathy was aroused, and he determined to rescue him. He chafed the ice-cold limbs of the unfortunate man, and after considerable effort raised him to his feet. As the sufferer could not stand, he bore him in sympathizing arms through the very drifts he had thought he could never get through alone.

When he had carried his fellow-traveler to a place of safety, the truth flashed home to him that in saving his neighbor he had also saved himself. His earnest efforts to help another had quickened the blood that was freezing in his own veins, and sent a healthy warmth to the extremities of his body.

The lesson that in helping others we ourselves receive help, must be urged upon young believers continually, by precept and example, that in their Christian experience they may gain the best results. Let the desponding ones, those disposed to think that the way to eternal life is trying and difficult, go to work to help others. Such efforts, united with prayer for divine light, will cause their own hearts to throb with the quickening influence of the grace of God, their own affections to glow with more divine fervor. Their whole Christian life will be more of a reality, more earnest, more prayerful.

Let us remember that we are pilgrims and strangers on this earth, seeking a better country, even a heavenly. Those who have united with the Lord in the covenant of service are under bonds to co-operate with Him in the work of soul-saving.

Let church-members during the week act their part faithfully, and on the Sabbath tell their experiences. The meeting will then be as meat in due season, bringing to all present new life and fresh vigor. When God's people see the great need of working as Christ worked for the conversion of sinners, the testimonies borne by them in the Sabbath services will be filled with power. With joy they will bear witness to the preciousness of the experience they have gained in working for others.

THE CHURCH A SACRED TRUST

When Christ ascended, He left the church and all its interests as a sacred trust to His followers. And the work of the church is not to be left to the minister alone, or to a few leading men. Every member should feel that he has entered into a solemn covenant with the Lord to work for the best interests of His cause at all times and under all circumstances. Each should have some part to act, some burden to bear. If all church-members felt an individual responsibility, greater advancement would be made in spiritual things. The solemn burden of responsibility resting upon them would lead them to seek God often for strength and grace.

The real character of the church is measured, not by the high profession she makes, not by the names enrolled on her books, but by what she is actually doing for the Master, by the number of her persevering, faithful workers. Personal, unselfish effort will accomplish more for the cause of Christ than can be wrought by sermons or creeds.

Let ministers teach church-members that in order to grow in spirituality, they must carry the burden that the Lord has laid upon them,— the burden of leading souls into the truth. Those who are not fulfilling their responsibility should be visited, prayed with, labored for. Do not lead people to depend upon you as ministers; teach them rather that they are to use their talents in giving the truth to those around them. In thus working they will have the co-operation of heavenly angels, and will obtain an experience that will increase their faith, and give them a strong hold on God.

THE MINISTER'S WIFE

In former years the wives of ministers endured want and persecution. When their husbands suffered imprisonment, and sometimes death, those noble, self-sacrificing women suffered with them, and their reward will be equal to that bestowed on the husband. Mrs. Boardman and the Mrs. Judsons suffered for the truth, — suffered with their companions. They sacrificed home and friends in every sense of the word, to aid their companions in the work of enlightening those who sat in darkness; to reveal to them the hidden mysteries of the word of God. Their lives were in constant peril. To save souls was their great object, and for this they could suffer cheerfully. . . .

If a minister's wife accompanies her husband in his travels, she should not go for her own special enjoyment, to visit and to be waited upon, but to labor with him. She should have a united interest with him to do good. She should be willing to accompany her husband, if home cares do not hinder, and she should aid him in his efforts to save souls. With meekness and humility, yet with a noble self-reliance, she should have a leading influence upon minds around her, and should act her part and bear her cross and burden in meeting, and around the family altar, and in conversation at the fireside. The people expect this, and they have a right to expect it. If these expectations are not realized, the husband's influence is more than half destroyed.

The wife of a minister can do much if she will. If she possesses the spirit of self-sacrifice, and has a love for souls, she can with him do almost an equal amount of good. A sister-laborer in the cause of truth can understand and reach some cases, especially among the sisters, that the minister cannot.

A responsibility rests upon the minister's wife which she should not and cannot lightly throw off. God will require the talent lent her, with usury. She should work earnestly, faithfully, and unitedly with her husband to save souls. She should never urge her wishes and desires, or express a lack of interest in her husband's labor, or dwell upon homesick, discontented feelings. All these natural feelings must be overcome. She should have a purpose in life which should be unfalteringly carried out. What if this conflicts with the feelings and pleasures and natural tastes! These should be cheerfully and readily sacrificed, in order to do good and save souls.

The wives of ministers should live devoted, prayerful lives. But some would enjoy a religion in which there are no crosses, and which calls for no self-denial and exertion on their part. Instead of standing nobly for themselves, leaning upon God for strength, and bearing their individual responsibility, they have much of the time been dependent upon others, deriving their spiritual life from them. If they would only lean confidingly, in childlike trust, upon God, and have their affections centered in Jesus, deriving their life from Christ, the living vine, what an amount of good they might do, what a help they might be to others, what a support to their husbands; and what a reward would be theirs in the end! "Well done, good and faithful servant," would fall like sweetest music upon their ears. The words, "Enter thou into the joy of thy Lord," would repay them a thousand times for all the suffering and trials endured to save precious souls.—*"Testimonies for the Church," Vol. I, pages 451-453.*

If married men go into the work, leaving their wives to care for the children at home, the wife and mother is doing fully as great and important a work as is the husband and father. While one is in the missionary field, the other is a home missionary, whose cares and anxieties and burdens frequently far exceed those of the husband and father. The mother's work is a solemn and important one,— to mould the minds and fashion the characters of her children, to train them for usefulness here, and to fit them for the future immortal life.

The husband, in the open missionary field, may receive the honor of men, while the home toiler may receive no earthly credit for her labor; but if she works for the best interests of her family, seeking to fashion their characters after the divine Model, the recording angel writes her name as one of the greatest missionaries in the world.

The minister's wife may be a great help to her husband in seeking to lighten his burden, if she keeps her own soul in the love of God. She can teach the Word to her children. She can manage her own household with economy and discretion. United with her husband, she can educate her children in habits of economy, teaching them to restrict their wants.

THE MINISTER IN HIS HOME

God designs that in his home life the teacher of the Bible shall be an exemplification of the truths that he teaches. What a man is, has greater influence than what he says. Piety in the daily life will give power to the public testimony. Patience, consistency, and love will make an impression on hearts that sermons fail to reach.

The minister's duties lie around him, nigh and afar off; but his first duty is to his children. He should not become so engrossed with his outside duties as to neglect the instruction which his children need. He may look upon his home duties as of lesser importance; but in reality they lie at the very foundation of the well-being of individuals and of society. To a large degree the happiness of men and women and the success of the church depend upon home influence. Eternal interests are involved in the proper discharge of the every-day duties of life. The world is not so much in need of great minds, as of good men, who are a blessing in their homes.

Nothing can excuse the minister for neglecting the inner circle for the larger circle outside. The spiritual welfare of his family comes first. In the day of final reckoning, God will inquire what he did to win to Christ those whom he took the responsibility of bringing into the world. Great good done for others cannot cancel the debt that he owes to God to care for his own children.

There should exist in the minister's family a unity that will preach an effectual sermon on practical godliness. As the minister and his wife faithfully do their duty in the home, restraining, correcting, advising, counseling, guiding, they are becoming better fitted to labor in the church, and are multiplying agencies for the accomplishment of God's work outside the home. The members of the family become members of the family above, and are a power for good, exerting a far-reaching influence.

On the other hand, the minister who allows his children to grow up unruly and disobedient, will find that the influence of his labors in the pulpit is counteracted by the unlovely course of his children. He who cannot control the members of his own family, cannot properly minister to the church of God, or preserve it from strife and controversy.

COURTESY IN THE HOME

There is danger of failing to give due attention to the little things of life. There should be no neglect on the part of the minister to speak kindly, encouraging words in the family circle. My ministering brother, do you, in the home circle, show rudeness, unkindness, impoliteness? If you do, no matter how high your profession, you are breaking the commandments. No matter how earnestly you may preach to others, if you fail to manifest the love of Christ in your home life, you are falling short of the standard set for you. Think not that the man who goes from the sacred desk to indulge in harsh, sarcastic remarks, or in jesting and joking, is a representative of Christ. The love of God is not in him. His heart is filled with self-love, self-importance, and he makes it manifest that he has not a true estimate of sacred things. Christ is not with him, and he does not go weighted with the solemn message of truth for this time.

Ministers' children are in some cases the most neglected children in the world, for the reason that the father is with them but little, and they are left to choose their own employment and amusement. If a minister has a family of boys, he should not leave them wholly to the care of the mother. This is too heavy a burden for her. He should make himself their companion and friend. He should exert himself to keep them from evil associates, and should see that they have useful work to do. It may be hard for the mother to exercise self-control. If the husband sees this, he should take more of the burden upon himself, doing all in his power to lead his boys to God.

Let the minister's wife who has children remember that in her home she has a missionary field in which she should labor with untiring energy and unflagging zeal, knowing that the results of her work will endure throughout eternity. Are not the souls of her children of as much value as the souls of the heathen? then let her tend them with loving care. She is charged with the responsibility of showing to the world the power and excellence of home religion. She is to be controlled by principle, not by impulse, and she is to work with the consciousness that God is her helper. She is to allow nothing to divert her from her mission.

The influence of the mother who has a close connection with Christ is of infinite worth. Her ministry of love makes the home a Bethel. Christ works with her, turning the common water of life into the wine of heaven. Her children will grow up to be a blessing and an honor to her in this life and in the life to come.

"FEED MY LAMBS"

The charge given to Peter by Christ just before His ascension was, "Feed My lambs;" [1] and this charge is given to every minister. When Christ said to His disciples, "Suffer the little children to come unto Me, and forbid them not: for of such is the kingdom of God," [2] He was speaking to His disciples in all ages.

Very much has been lost to the cause of truth by a lack of attention to the spiritual needs of the young. Ministers of the gospel should form a happy acquaintance with the youth of their congregations. Many are reluctant to do this, but their neglect is a sin in the sight of Heaven. There are among us many young men and women who are not ignorant of our faith, yet whose hearts have never been touched by the power of divine grace. How can we who claim to be the servants of God pass on day after day, week after week, indifferent to their condition? If they should die in their sins, unwarned, their blood would be required at the hands of the watchman who failed to give them warning.

Why should not labor for the youth in our borders be regarded as missionary work of the highest kind? It requires the most delicate tact, the most watchful consideration, the most earnest prayer for heavenly wisdom. The youth are the objects of Satan's special attacks; but kindness, courtesy, and the sympathy which flows from a heart filled with love to Jesus, will gain their confidence, and save them from many a snare of the enemy.

[1] John 21 : 15.   [2] Mark 10 : 14.

The youth need more than a casual notice, more than an occasional word of encouragement. They need painstaking, prayerful, careful labor. He only whose heart is filled with love and sympathy will be able to reach those youth who are apparently careless and indifferent. Not all can be helped in the same way. God deals with each according to his temperament and character, and we must co-operate with Him. Often those whom we pass by with indifference, because we judge them from outward appearance, have in them the best material for workers, and will repay all the efforts bestowed on them. There must be more study given to the problem of how to deal with the youth, more earnest prayer for the wisdom that is needed in dealing with minds.

PREACHING FOR CHILDREN

At every suitable opportunity let the story of Jesus' love be repeated to the children. In every sermon let a little corner be left for their benefit. The servant of Christ may make lasting friends of these little ones. Then let him lose no opportunity of helping them to become more intelligent in a knowledge of the Scriptures. This will do more than we realize to bar the way against Satan's devices. If children early become familiar with the truths of God's word, a barrier against ungodliness will be erected, and they will be able to meet the foe with the words, "It is written."

Those who give instruction to children and youth should avoid tedious remarks. Short talks, right to the point, will have a happy influence. If there is much to be said, make up for brevity by frequency. A few interesting remarks, every now and then, will be more helpful than to give all the instruction at once.

Long speeches tire the minds of the young. Too much talk will lead them even to loathe spiritual instruction, just as overeating burdens the stomach and lessens the appetite, leading to a loathing for food. Our instruction to the church, and especially to the youth, should be given line upon line, precept upon precept, here a little and there a little. Children must be drawn toward heaven, not harshly, but very gently.

ENTERING INTO THE FEELINGS OF THE YOUTH

We should seek to enter into the feelings of the youth, sympathizing with them in their joys and sorrows, their conflicts and victories. Jesus did not remain in heaven, away from the sorrowing and sinful; He came down to this world, that He might become acquainted with the weakness, the suffering, and the temptations of the fallen race. He reached us where we were, that He might lift us up. In our work for the youth, we must meet them where they are, if we would help them. When youthful disciples are overcome by temptation, let not those older in experience deal with them harshly, or regard their efforts with indifference. Remember that you yourselves have often shown but little strength to resist the tempter's power. Be as patient with these lambs of the flock as you wish others to be with you. God has so constituted us that even the strongest desire sympathy. How much more, then, do children need it! Even a look of compassion will often soothe and strengthen the tried, tempted child.

Jesus calls to every wanderer, "My son, give Me thine heart." [3] "Return, ye backsliding children, and I will heal your backslidings." [4] The youth cannot be

[3] Prov. 23 : 26.   [4] Jer. 3 : 22.

truly happy without the love of Jesus. He is waiting with pitying tenderness to hear the confessions of the wayward, and to accept their penitence. He watches for some return of gratitude from them, as the mother watches for the smile of recognition from her beloved babe. The great God teaches us to call Him Father. He would have us understand how earnestly and tenderly His heart yearns over us in all our trials and temptations. "Like as a father pitieth his children, so the Lord pitieth them that fear Him." [5] The mother might sooner forget her child than God could forget one soul that trusts Him.

THE YOUTH TO ACT A PART IN CHURCH WORK

When the youth give their hearts to God, our responsibility for them does not cease. They must be interested in the Lord's work, and led to see that He expects them to do something to advance His cause. It is not enough to show how much needs to be done, and to urge the youth to act a part. They must be taught how to labor for the Master. They must be trained, disciplined, drilled, in the best methods of winning souls to Christ. Teach them to try in a quiet, unpretending way to help their young companions. Let different branches of missionary effort be systematically laid out, in which they may take part, and let them be given instruction and help. Thus they will learn to work for God.

Do not imagine that you can arouse the interest of the young by going to the missionary meeting and preaching a long sermon. Plan ways whereby a live interest may be aroused. From week to week the youth should bring in their reports, telling what they

[5] Ps. 103 : 13.

have tried to do for the Saviour, and what success has been theirs. If the missionary meeting were made an occasion for bringing in such reports, it would not be dull, tedious, and uninteresting. It would be full of interest, and there would be no lack of attendance.

Youthful talent, well organized and well trained, is needed in our churches. The youth will do something with their overflowing energies. Unless these energies are directed into right channels, they will be used by the youth in a way that will hurt their own spirituality, and prove an injury to those with whom they associate.

Let the heart of the instructor be linked with the hearts of those under his charge. Let him remember that they have many temptations to meet. We little realize the objectionable traits of character given to the youth as a birthright, and how often temptation comes to them as a result of this birthright.

The guarding care that the under-shepherd will give the lambs of his flock is well illustrated by a picture I have seen representing the Good Shepherd. The shepherd is leading the way, while the flock follow close behind. Carried in his arms is a helpless lamb, while the mother walks trustingly by his side. Of the work of Christ, Isaiah says, "He shall gather the lambs with His arm, and carry them in His bosom." [6] The lambs need more than daily food. They need protection, and must constantly be guarded with tender care. If one goes astray, it must be searched for. The figure is a beautiful one, and well represents the loving service that the under-shepherd of the flock of Christ is to give to those under his protection and care.

[6] Isa. 40 : 11.

My brethren in the ministry, open your doors to young men who are exposed to temptation. Come near to them by personal effort. Evil invites them on every hand. Seek to interest them in that which will help them to live the higher life. Do not hold yourself aloof from them. Bring them to your fireside; invite them to join you around the family altar. Let us remember the claim of God upon us to make the path to heaven bright and attractive.

We should educate the youth to help the youth; and as they seek to do this, they will gain an experience that will qualify them to become consecrated workers in a larger sphere. Thousands of hearts can be reached in the most simple, humble way. The most intellectual, those who are looked upon and praised as the world's most gifted men and women, are often refreshed by the simple words that flow from the heart of one who loves God. . . . The true, honest words of a son or daughter of God, spoken in natural simplicity, will open the door to hearts that have long been locked.— *"Testimonies for the Church," Vol. VI, page 115.*

From a child, Timothy knew the Scriptures; and this knowledge was a safeguard to him against evil influences surrounding him, and the temptation to choose pleasure and selfish gratification before duty. Such a safeguard all our children need; and it should be a part of the work of parents and of Christ's ambassadors to see that the children are properly instructed in the word of God.— *"Testimonies for the Church," Vol. IV, page 398.*

PRAYER FOR THE SICK

The very essence of the gospel is restoration, and the Saviour would have His servants bid the sick, the hopeless, and the afflicted take hold upon His strength. God's servants are the channels of His grace, and through them He desires to exercise His healing power. It is their work to present the sick and suffering to the Saviour in the arms of faith. They should live so near to Him, and so clearly reveal in their lives the working of His truth, that He can make them a means of blessing to those in need of bodily as well as spiritual healing.

It is our privilege to pray with the sick, to help them to grasp the cord of faith. Angels of God are very near to those who thus minister to suffering humanity. The consecrated ambassador of Christ who, when appealed to by the sick, seeks to fasten their attention upon divine realities, is accomplishing a work that will endure throughout eternity. And as he approaches the sick with the comfort of a hope gained through faith in Christ and acceptance of the divine promises, his own experience becomes richer and still richer in spiritual strength.

With awakened conscience many a troubled soul, suffering bodily ailments as the result of continued transgression, cries out, "Lord, be merciful to me a sinner; make me Thy child." It is then that the minister, strong in faith, should be ready to tell the sufferer that there is hope for the penitent, that in Jesus every one who longs for help and acceptance may find deliverance and peace. He who in meekness and love thus brings the gospel to the afflicted soul so much in need of its message of hope, is a mouthpiece for the One who gave Himself for mankind. As he speaks helpful, appropriate words, and as he offers prayer for the one lying on a bed of suffering, Jesus makes the application. God speaks through human lips. The heart is reached. Humanity is brought into touch with divinity.

The minister should understand by experience that the soothing power of the grace of Christ brings health and peace and fulness of joy. He should know Christ as the One who has invited the weary and heavy-laden to come to Him and find rest. Let him never forget that the Saviour's loving presence constantly surrounds every human agent ordained of God for the impartation of spiritual blessing. The remembrance of this will give vitality to his faith and earnestness to his petitions.

Then to those who call upon him for help he can impart the health-giving power of God's truth. He can talk of the works of healing wrought by Christ, and direct the minds of the sick to Him as the great Physician, who is light and life, as well as comfort and peace. He can tell them that they need not despair, that the Saviour loves them, and that if they surrender themselves to Him, they will have His love, His grace, His keeping power. Let him urge them to rest in God's promises, knowing that He who has given these promises is our best and truest Friend. As he endeavors to direct the mind heavenward, he will find that the thought of the tender sympathy of the One who knows just how to apply the healing balm, will give the sick a sense of rest and quietude.

The divine Healer is present in the sick-room; He hears every word of the prayers offered to Him in the simplicity of true faith. His disciples to-day are to pray for the sick, as verily as did the disciples of old. And there will be recoveries; for "the prayer of faith shall save the sick." [1]

In the word of God we have instruction relative to special prayer for the recovery of the sick. But the offering of such prayer is a most solemn act, and should not be entered upon without careful consideration. In many cases of prayer for the healing of the sick, that which is called faith is nothing less than presumption.

Many persons bring disease upon themselves by their self-indulgence. They have not lived in accordance with natural law or the principles of strict purity. Others have disregarded the laws of health in their habits of eating and drinking, dressing or working. Often some form of vice is the cause of feebleness of mind or body. Should these persons gain the blessing of health, many of them would continue to pursue the same course of heedless transgression of God's natural and spiritual laws, reasoning that if God heals them in answer to prayer, they are at liberty to continue their unhealthful practices and to indulge perverted appetite without restraint. If God were to work a miracle in restoring these persons to health, He would be encouraging sin.

It is labor lost to teach people to look to God as a healer of their infirmities, unless they are taught

[1] James 5 : 15.

also to lay aside unhealthful practices. In order to receive His blessing in answer to prayer, they must cease to do evil and learn to do well. Their surroundings must be sanitary, their habits of life correct. They must live in harmony with the law of God, both natural and spiritual.

CONFESSION OF SIN

To those who desire prayer for their restoration to health, it should be made plain that the violation of God's law, either natural or spiritual, is sin, and that in order for them to receive His blessing, sin must be confessed and forsaken.

The Scripture bids us, "Confess your faults one to another, and pray one for another, that ye may be healed." [2] To the one asking for prayer, let thoughts like these be presented, "We cannot read the heart, or know the secrets of your life. These are known only to yourself and to God. If you repent of your sins, it is your duty to make confession of them."

Sin of a private character is to be confessed to Christ, the only mediator between God and man. For "if any man sin, we have an advocate with the Father, Jesus Christ the righteous." [3] Every sin is an offense against God, and is to be confessed to Him through Christ. Every open sin should be as openly confessed. Wrong done to a fellow-being should be made right with the one who has been offended. If any who are seeking health have been guilty of evil-speaking, if they have sowed discord in the home, the neighborhood, or the church, and have stirred up

2 James 5 : 16.   3 1 John 2 : 1.

alienation and dissension, if by any wrong practice they have led others into sin, these things should be confessed before God and before those who have been offended. "If we confess our sins, He is faithful and just to forgive us our sins, and to cleanse us from all unrighteousness." [4]

When wrongs have been righted, we may present the needs of the sick to the Lord in calm faith, as His Spirit may indicate. He knows each individual by name, and cares for each as if there were not another upon the earth for whom He gave His beloved Son. Because God's love is so great and so unfailing, the sick should be encouraged to trust in Him and be cheerful. To be anxious about themselves tends to cause weakness and disease. If they will rise above depression and gloom, their prospect of recovery will be better; for "the eye of the Lord is upon them" "that hope in His mercy." [5]

SUBMISSION TO GOD'S WILL

In praying for the sick, it should be remembered that "we know not what we should pray for as we ought." [6] We do not know whether the blessing we desire will be best or not. Therefore our prayers should include this thought: "Lord, Thou knowest every secret of the soul. Thou art acquainted with these persons. Jesus, their Advocate, gave His life for them. His love for them is greater than ours can possibly be. If, therefore, it is for Thy glory and the good of the afflicted ones, we ask, in the name of Jesus, that they may be restored to health. If it be not Thy will that they may be restored, we ask that

[4] 1 John 1 : 9.   [5] Ps. 33 : 18.   [6] Rom. 8 : 26.

Thy grace may comfort and Thy presence sustain them in their sufferings."

God knows the end from the beginning. He is acquainted with the hearts of all men. He reads every secret of the soul. He knows whether those for whom prayer is offered would or would not be able to endure the trials that would come upon them should they live. He knows whether their lives would be a blessing or a curse to themselves and to the world. This is one reason why, while presenting our petitions with earnestness, we should say, "Nevertheless not my will, but Thine, be done." [7] Jesus added these words of submission to the wisdom and will of God when in the garden of Gethsemane He pleaded, "O My Father, if it be possible, let this cup pass from Me." [8] And if they were appropriate for Him, the Son of God, how much more are they becoming on the lips of finite, erring mortals!

The consistent course is to commit our desires to our all-wise heavenly Father, and then, in perfect confidence, trust all to Him. We know that God hears us if we ask according to His will. But to press our petitions without a submissive spirit is not right; our prayers must take the form, not of command, but of intercession.

There are cases where God works decidedly by His divine power in the restoration of health. But not all the sick are healed. Many are laid away to sleep in Jesus. John on the Isle of Patmos was bidden to write, "Blessed are the dead which die in the Lord from henceforth: Yea, saith the Spirit, that they may rest from their labors; and their works do follow

[7] Luke 22 : 42. [8] Matt. 26 : 39.

them." [9] From this we see that if persons are not raised to health, they should not, on this account, be judged as wanting in faith.

We all desire immediate and direct answers to our prayers, and are tempted to become discouraged when the answer is delayed or comes in an unlooked-for form. But God is too wise and good to answer our prayers always at just the time and in just the manner we desire. He will do more and better for us than to accomplish all our wishes. And because we can trust His wisdom and love, we should not ask Him to concede to our will, but should seek to enter into and accomplish His purpose. Our desires and interests should be lost in His will.

These experiences that test faith are for our benefit. By them it is made manifest whether our faith is true and sincere, resting on the word of God alone, or whether, depending on circumstances, it is uncertain and changeable. Faith is strengthened by exercise. We must let patience have its perfect work, remembering that there are precious promises in the Scriptures for those who wait upon the Lord.

Not all understand these principles. Many who seek the Lord's healing mercy think that they must have a direct and immediate answer to their prayers or their faith is defective. For this reason those who are weakened by disease need to be counseled wisely, that they may act with discretion. They should not disregard their duty to the friends who may survive them, or neglect to employ nature's agencies for the restoration of health.

Often there is danger of error here. Believing that they will be healed in answer to prayer, some fear to

[9] Rev. 14 : 13.

do anything that might seem to indicate a lack of faith. But they should not neglect to set their affairs in order as they would desire to do if they expected to be removed by death. Nor should they fear to utter words of encouragement or counsel which at the parting hour they wish to speak to their loved ones.

REMEDIAL AGENCIES

Those who seek healing by prayer should not neglect to make use of the remedial agencies within their reach. It is not a denial of faith to use such remedies as God has provided to alleviate pain and to aid nature in her work of restoration. It is no denial of faith to co-operate with God, and to place themselves in the condition most favorable to recovery. God has put it in our power to obtain a knowledge of the laws of life. This knowledge has been placed within our reach for use. We should employ every facility for the restoration of health, taking every advantage possible, working in harmony with natural laws. When we have prayed for the recovery of the sick, we can work with all the more energy, thanking God that we have the privilege of co-operating with Him, and asking His blessing on the means which He Himself has provided.

We have the sanction of the word of God for the use of remedial agencies. Hezekiah, king of Israel, was sick, and a prophet of God brought him the message that he should die. He cried unto the Lord, and the Lord heard His servant, and sent him a message that fifteen years should be added to his life. Now one word from God would have healed Hezekiah instantly; but special directions were given, "Let them take a lump of figs, and lay it for a plaster upon the boil, and he shall recover." [10]

On one occasion Christ anointed the eyes of a blind man with clay, and bade him, "Go, wash in the pool of Siloam. . . . He went his way therefore, and washed, and came seeing." [11] The cure could be wrought only by the power of the great Healer, yet Christ made use of the simple agencies of nature. While He did not give countenance to drug medication, He sanctioned the use of simple and natural remedies.

When we have prayed for the recovery of the sick, whatever the outcome of the case, let us not lose faith in God. If we are called upon to meet bereavement, let us accept the bitter cup, remembering that a Father's hand holds it to our lips. But should health be restored, it should not be forgotten that the recipient of healing mercy is placed under renewed obligation to the Creator. When the ten lepers were cleansed, only one returned to find Jesus and give Him glory. Let none of us be like the unthinking nine, whose hearts were untouched by the mercy of God. "Every good gift and every perfect gift is from above, and cometh down from the Father of lights, with whom is no variableness, neither shadow of turning." [12] —*"Ministry of Healing," pages 227-233.*

[10] Isa. 38 : 21.   [11] John 9 : 7.   [12] James 1 : 17.

TEACHING THE PEOPLE TO BE LIBERAL

Never should the laborer who raises up little companies here and there, give the impression to those newly come to the faith, that God does not require them to work systematically in helping to sustain the cause by their personal labors and by their means. Frequently those who receive the truth are among the poor of this world; but they should not make this an excuse for neglecting those duties which devolve upon them in view of the precious light they have received. They should not allow poverty to prevent them from laying up a treasure in heaven. The blessings within reach of the rich are also within their reach. If they are faithful in using what little they do possess, their treasure in heaven will increase according to their fidelity. It is the motive with which they work, not the amount they do, that makes their offering valuable in the sight of Heaven.

All should be taught to do what they can for the Master; to render to Him according as He has prospered them. He claims as His just due a tenth of their income, be it large or small; and those who withhold this, commit robbery toward Him, and cannot expect His prospering hand to be with them. Even if the church is composed mostly of poor brethren, the subject of systematic benevolence should be thoroughly explained, and the plan heartily adopted. God is able to fulfil His promises. His resources are infinite, and He employs them all in accomplishing His will. And when He sees a faithful performance of duty in the payment of the tithe, He often, in His wise providence, opens ways whereby it shall increase. He who follows God's arrangement in the little that has been given him, will receive the same returns as he who bestows of his abundance.

The same is true also of those who cheerfully employ their talents of ability in the cause of God, while those who fail to improve that which has been given them will incur the same loss as if that little had been much. It was the man who had only one talent, but who hid that talent in the earth, that received the condemnation of the Lord.

———◆———

God's plan in the tithing system is beautiful in its simplicity and equality. All may take hold of it in faith and courage, for it is divine in its origin. In it are combined simplicity and utility, and it does not require depth of learning to understand and execute it. All may feel that they can act a part in carrying forward the precious work of salvation. Every man, woman, and youth may become a treasurer for the Lord, and may be an agent to meet the demands upon the treasury. . . .

Great objects are accomplished by this system. If one and all would accept it, each would be made a vigilant and faithful treasurer for God; and there would be no want of means with which to carry forward the great work of sounding the last message of warning to the world.—*"Testimonies for the Church," Vol. III, pages 388, 389.*

THE SUPPORT OF THE GOSPEL

The Lord has made the proclamation of the gospel dependent upon the labors and the voluntary gifts of all His people. The one who proclaims the message of mercy to fallen men has another work also,— to set before the people the duty of sustaining the work of God with their means. He must teach them that a portion of their income belongs to God, and is to be sacredly devoted to His work. This lesson he should present by both precept and example; he should beware that he does not by his own course lessen the force of his teaching.

That which has been set apart according to the Scriptures as belonging to the Lord, constitutes the revenue of the gospel, and is no longer ours. It is no better than sacrilege for a man to take from God's treasury in order to serve himself or to serve others in their secular business. Some have been at fault in diverting from the altar of God that which has been especially dedicated to Him. All should regard this matter in the right light. Let no one, when brought into a strait place, take money consecrated to religious purposes, and use it for his own advantage, soothing his conscience by saying that he will repay it at some future time. Far better cut down the expenses to correspond with the income, to restrict the wants and live within the means, than to use the Lord's money for secular purposes.

THE USE OF THE TITHE

God has given special direction as to the use of the tithe. He does not design that His work shall be crip-

pled for want of means. That there may be no haphazard work and no error, He has made our duty on
these points very plain. The portion that God has
reserved for Himself is not to be diverted to any other
purpose than that which He has specified. Let none
feel at liberty to retain their tithe, to use according
to their own judgment. They are not to use it for
themselves in an emergency, nor to apply it as they
see fit, even in what they may regard as the Lord's
work.

The minister should, by precept and example, teach
the people to regard the tithe as sacred. He should
not feel that he can retain and apply it according to
his own judgment because he is a minister. It is not
his. He is not at liberty to devote to himself whatever he thinks is his due. He should not give his
influence to any plans for diverting from their legitimate use the tithes and offerings dedicated to God.
They are to be placed in His treasury, and held
sacred for His service as He has appointed.

God desires all His stewards to be exact in following divine arrangements. They are not to offset the
Lord's plans by performing some deed of charity, or
giving some gift or some offering, when or how they,
the human agents, shall see fit. It is very poor policy
for men to seek to improve on God's plan, and invent
a makeshift, averaging up their good impulses on this
and that occasion, and offsetting them against God's
requirements. God calls upon all to give their influence to His own arrangement. He has made His plan
known; and all who would co-operate with Him must
carry out this plan, instead of daring to attempt an
improvement on it.

The Lord instructed Moses, for Israel, "Thou shalt command the children of Israel, that they may bring thee pure oil olive beaten for the light, to cause the lamp to burn always." [1]　This was to be a continual offering, that the house of God might be properly supplied with that which was necessary for His service. His people to-day are to remember that the house of worship is the Lord's property, and that it is to be scrupulously cared for.　But the funds for this work are not to come from the tithe.

A very plain, definite message has been given to me for our people.　I am bidden to tell them that they are making a mistake in applying the tithe to various objects, which, though good in themselves, are not the object to which the Lord has said that the tithe should be applied.　Those who make this use of the tithe are departing from the Lord's arrangement.　God will judge for these things.

One reasons that the tithe may be applied to school purposes.　Still others reason that canvassers and colporteurs should be supported from the tithe.　But a great mistake is made when the tithe is drawn from the object for which it is to be used — the support of the ministers.　There should be to-day in the field one hundred well-qualified laborers where now there is but one.

A SOLEMN OBLIGATION

The tithe is sacred, reserved by God for Himself. It is to be brought into His treasury to be used to sustain the gospel laborers in their work.　For a long time the Lord has been robbed because there are those who

[1] Ex. 27 : 20.

do not realize that the tithe is God's reserved portion. Some have been dissatisfied, and have said, "I will not longer pay my tithe; for I have no confidence in the way things are managed at the heart of the work." But will you rob God because you think the management of the work is not right? Make your complaint, plainly and openly, in the right spirit, to the proper ones. Send in your petitions for things to be adjusted and set in order; but do not withdraw from the work of God, and prove unfaithful, because others are not doing right.

Read carefully the third chapter of Malachi, and see what God says about the tithe. If our churches will take their stand upon the Lord's word, and be faithful in paying their tithe into His treasury, more laborers will be encouraged to take up ministerial work. More men would give themselves to the ministry were they not told of the depleted treasury. There should be an abundant supply in the Lord's treasury, and there would be if selfish hearts and hands had not withheld the tithes, or made use of them to support other lines of work.

God's reserved resources are to be used in no such haphazard way. The tithe is the Lord's, and those who meddle with it will be punished with the loss of their heavenly treasure, unless they repent. Let the work no longer be hedged up because the tithe has been diverted into various channels other than the one to which the Lord has said it should go. Provision is to be made for these other lines of work. They are to be sustained, but not from the tithe. God has not changed; the tithe is still to be used for the support of the ministry. The opening of new fields requires more ministerial efficiency than we now have, and there must be means in the treasury.

Those who go forth as ministers have a solemn responsibility devolving upon them, which is strangely neglected. Some enjoy preaching, but they do not give personal labor to the churches. There is great need of instruction concerning obligations and duties to God, especially in regard to paying an honest tithe. Our ministers would feel sadly aggrieved if they were not promptly paid for their labor; but will they consider that there must be meat in the treasure-house of God wherewith to sustain the laborers? If they fail to do their whole duty in educating the people to be faithful in paying to God His own, there will be a shortage of means in the treasury to carry forward the Lord's work.

The overseer of the flock of God should faithfully discharge his duty. If he takes the position that, because this is not pleasant to him, he will leave it for some one else to do, he is not a faithful worker. Let him read in Malachi the words of the Lord charging the people with robbery toward God in withholding the tithes. The mighty God declares, "Ye are cursed with a curse." [2] When the one who ministers in word and doctrine sees the people pursuing a course that will bring this curse upon them, how can he neglect his duty to give them instruction and warning? Every church-member should be taught to be faithful in paying an honest tithe.—"*Testimonies for the Church,*" *Vol. IX, pages 246-251.*

[2] Mal. 3 : 9.

THE INFLUENCE OF DIET UPON HEALTH

Those upon whom rest important responsibilities, those, above all, who are guardians of spiritual interests, should be men of keen feeling and quick perception. More than others, they need to be temperate in eating. Rich and luxurious food should have no place upon their tables.

Every day men in positions of trust have decisions to make upon which depend results of great importance. Often they have to think rapidly, and this can be done successfully by those only who practice strict temperance. The mind strengthens under the correct treatment of the physical and mental powers. If the strain is not too great, new vigor comes with every taxation. But often the work of those who have important plans to consider and important decisions to make is affected for evil by the results of improper diet. A disordered stomach produces a disordered, uncertain state of mind. Often it causes irritability, harshness, or injustice. Many a plan that would have been a blessing to the world has been set aside, many unjust, oppressive, even cruel measures have been carried, as the result of diseased conditions due to wrong habits of eating.

Here is a suggestion for all whose work is sedentary or chiefly mental; let those who have sufficient moral courage and self-control try it. At each meal take only two or three kinds of simple food, and eat no more than is required to satisfy hunger. Take active exercise every day, and see if you do not receive benefit.—*"Ministry of Healing," pages 309, 310.*

Some ministers are not particular enough in regard to their habits of eating. They partake of too large quantities of food, and of too great a variety at one meal. Some are reformers in name only. They have no rules by which to regulate their diet, but indulge in eating fruit or nuts between their meals, and thus impose heavy burdens upon the digestive organs.

Because of imprudence in eating, the senses of some seem to be paralyzed, and they are sluggish and sleepy. These pale-faced ministers who are suffering in consequence of selfish indulgence of the appetite, are no recommendation to health reform.

When suffering from overwork, it would be much better to drop out a meal occasionally, and thus give nature a chance to rally. Our laborers could do more by their example to advocate health reform than by preaching it. When elaborate preparations are made for them by well-meaning friends, they are strongly tempted to disregard principle; but by refusing the dainty dishes, the rich condiments, the tea and coffee, they may prove themselves to be true, practical health reformers.

The indulgence of appetite beclouds and fetters the mind, and blunts the holy emotions of the soul. The mental and moral powers of some of our ministers are enfeebled by improper eating and lack of physical exercise. Those who crave great quantities of food should not indulge the appetite, but should practice self-denial, and retain the blessing of active muscles and unoppressed brain. Overeating stupefies the entire being by diverting the energies from the other organs to do the work of the stomach.

MINISTERS TO TEACH HEALTH REFORM

Our ministers should become intelligent on health reform. . . . They should understand the laws that govern physical life, and their bearing upon the health of mind and soul. Thousands upon thousands know little of the wonderful body God has given them or of the care it should receive; they consider it of more importance to study subjects of far less consequence. The ministers have a work to do here. When they take a right position on this subject, much will be gained. In their own lives and homes they should obey the laws of life, practicing right principles and living healthfully. Then they will be able to speak correctly on this subject, leading the people higher and still higher in the work of reform. Living in the light themselves, they can bear a message of great value to those who are in need of just such testimony.

There are precious blessings and a rich experience to be gained if ministers will combine the presentation of the health question with all their labors in the churches. The people must have the light on health reform. This work has been neglected, and many are ready to die because they need the light which they ought to have and must have before they will give up selfish indulgences.

The presidents of our conferences need to realize that it is high time they were placing themselves on the right side of this question. Ministers and teachers are to give to others the light they have received. Their work in every line is needed. God will help them; He will strengthen His servants who stand firm, and will not be swayed from truth and righteousness in order to accommodate self-indulgence. . . .

The light that the Lord has given on this subject in His word is plain, and men will be tested and tried in many ways to see if they will heed it. Every church, every family, needs to be instructed in regard to Christian temperance. All should know how to eat and drink in order to preserve health. We are amid the closing scenes of this world's history; and there should be harmonious action in the ranks of Sabbath-keepers. Those who stand aloof from the great work of instructing the people upon this question, do not follow where the Great Physician leads the way. . . .

The gospel and the medical missionary work are to advance together. The gospel is to be bound up with the principles of true health reform. Christianity is to be brought into the practical life. Earnest, thorough reformatory work is to be done. True Bible religion is an outflowing of the love of God for fallen man. God's people are to advance in straightforward lines to impress the hearts of those who are seeking for truth, who desire to act their part aright in this intensely earnest age. We are to present the principles of health reform before the people, doing all in our power to lead men and women to see the necessity of these principles, and to practice them.—"*Testimonies for the Church*," *Vol. VI, pages 376-379.*

HOW TO PRESENT THE PRINCIPLES
OF HEALTH REFORM

The Lord desires our ministers, physicians, and church-members to be careful not to urge those who are ignorant of our faith to make sudden changes in diet, thus bringing men to a premature test. Hold up the principles of health reform, and let the Lord lead the honest in heart. They will hear and believe. Nor does the Lord require His messengers to present the beautiful truths of healthful living in a way that will prejudice minds. Let no one put stumbling-blocks before the feet that are walking in the dark paths of ignorance. Even in praising a good thing, it is well not to be too enthusiastic, lest you turn out of the way those who come to hear. Present the principles of temperance in their most attractive form.

We must not move presumptuously. The laborers who enter new territory to raise up churches must not create difficulties by attempting to make prominent the question of diet. They should be careful not to draw the lines too closely, for impediments would thus be thrown in the pathway of others. Do not drive the people; lead them.

Wherever the truth is carried, instruction should be given in regard to the preparation of wholesome foods. God desires that in every place the people shall be taught by skilful teachers how to utilize wisely the products that they can raise or readily obtain in their section of the country. Thus the poor, as well as those in better circumstances, can be taught to live healthfully.

THE MINISTER AND MANUAL WORK

While Paul was careful to set before his converts the plain teaching of Scripture regarding the proper support of the work of God, and while he claimed for himself, as a minister of the gospel, the "power to forbear working" [1] at secular employment as a means of self-support, yet at various times during his ministry in the great centers of civilization, he wrought at a handicraft for his own maintenance. . . .

It is at Thessalonica that we first read of Paul's working with his hands in self-supporting labor while preaching the word. Writing to the church of believers there, he reminded them that he "might have been burdensome" to them, and added: "Ye remember, brethren, our labor and travail: for laboring night and day, because we would not be chargeable unto any of you, we preached unto you the gospel of God." [2] And again, in his second epistle to them, he declared that he and his fellow-laborer while with them had not eaten "any man's bread for naught." Night and day we worked, he wrote, "that we might not be chargeable to any of you: not because we have not power, but to make ourselves an ensample unto you to follow us." [3] . . .

When Paul first visited Corinth, he found himself among a people who were suspicious of the motives of strangers. The Greeks on the seacoast were keen traders. So long had they trained themselves in sharp business practices, that they had come to believe that gain was godliness, and that to make money, whether

[1] 1 Cor: 9 : 6.   [2] 1 Thess. 2 : 6, 9.   [3] 2 Thess. 3 : 8, 9.

by fair means or foul, was commendable. Paul was acquainted with their characteristics, and he would give them no occasion for saying that he preached the gospel in order to enrich himself. He might justly have claimed support from his Corinthian hearers; but this right he was willing to forego, lest his usefulness and success as a minister should be injured by the unjust suspicion that he was preaching the gospel for gain. He would seek to remove all occasion for misrepresentation, that the force of his message might not be lost.

Soon after his arrival at Corinth, Paul found "a certain Jew named Aquila, born in Pontus, lately come from Italy, with his wife Priscilla." These were "of the same craft" with himself. Banished by the decree of Claudius, which commanded all Jews to leave Rome, Aquila and Priscilla had come to Corinth, where they established a business as manufacturers of tents. Paul made inquiry concerning them, and learning that they feared God and were seeking to avoid the contaminating influences with which they were surrounded, "he abode with them, and wrought. . . . And he reasoned in the synagogue every Sabbath, and persuaded the Jews and the Greeks." [4] . . .

During the long period of his ministry in Ephesus, where for three years he carried forward an aggressive evangelistic effort throughout that region, Paul again worked at his trade. In Ephesus, as in Corinth, the apostle was cheered by the presence of Aquila and Priscilla, who had accompanied him on his return to Asia at the close of his second missionary journey.

There were some who objected to Paul's toiling with his hands, declaring that it was inconsistent with

[4] Acts 18 : 2-4.

the work of a gospel minister. Why should Paul, a minister of the highest rank, thus connect mechanical work with the preaching of the word? Was not the laborer worthy of his hire? Why should he spend in making tents time that to all appearance could be put to better account?

But Paul did not regard as lost the time thus spent. As he worked with Aquila, he kept in touch with the great Teacher, losing no opportunity of witnessing for the Saviour, and of helping those who needed help. His mind was ever reaching out for spiritual knowledge. He gave his fellow-workers instruction in spiritual things, and he also set an example of industry and thoroughness. He was a quick, skilful worker, diligent in business, "fervent in spirit, serving the Lord." [5] As he worked at his trade, the apostle had access to a class of people that he could not otherwise have reached. He showed his associates that skill in the common arts is a gift from God, who provides both the gift, and the wisdom to use it aright. He taught that even in every-day toil, God is to be honored. His toil-hardened hands detracted nothing from the force of his pathetic appeals as a Christian minister. . . .

If ministers feel that they are suffering hardship and privation in the cause of Christ, let them in imagination visit the workshop where Paul labored. Let them bear in mind that while this chosen man of God is fashioning the canvas, he is working for bread which he has justly earned by his labors as an apostle.

Work is a blessing, not a curse. A spirit of indolence destroys godliness, and grieves the Spirit of God. A stagnant pool is offensive, but a pure, flowing stream

[5] Rom. 12 : 11.

spreads health and gladness over the land. Paul knew that those who neglect physical work soon become enfeebled. He desired to teach young ministers that by working with their hands, by bringing into exercise their muscles and sinews, they would become strong to endure the toils and privations that awaited them in the gospel field. And he realized that his own teachings would lack vitality and force if he did not keep all parts of the system properly exercised. . . .

Not all who feel that they have been called to preach, should be encouraged to throw themselves and their families at once upon the church for continuous financial support. There is danger that some of limited experience may be spoiled by flattery, and by unwise encouragement to expect full support independent of any serious effort on their part. The means dedicated to the extension of the work of God should not be consumed by men who desire to preach only that they may receive support, and thus gratify a selfish ambition for an easy life.

Young men who desire to exercise their gifts in the work of the ministry will find a helpful lesson in the example of Paul at Thessalonica, Corinth, Ephesus, and other places. Although an eloquent speaker, and chosen by God to do a special work, he was never above labor, nor did he ever weary of sacrificing for the cause he loved. "Even unto this present hour," he wrote to the Corinthians, "we both hunger, and thirst, and are naked, and are buffeted, and have no certain dwelling-place; and labor, working with our own hands: being reviled, we bless; being persecuted, we suffer it." [6]

[6] 1 Cor. 4 : 11, 12.

One of the greatest of human teachers, Paul cheerfully performed the lowliest as well as the highest duties. When in his service for the Master circumstances seemed to require it, he willingly labored at his trade. Nevertheless, he ever held himself ready to lay aside his secular work in order to meet the opposition of the enemies of the gospel, or to improve a special opportunity to win souls to Jesus. His zeal and industry are a rebuke to indolence and a desire for ease.—*"The Acts of the Apostles," pages 346-355.*

The failure of some of our ministers to exercise all the organs of the body proportionately, causes some organs to become worn, while others are weak from inaction. If wear is left to come almost exclusively upon one organ or set of muscles, the one most used must become overwearied and greatly weakened.

Each faculty of the mind and each muscle has its distinctive office, and all must be equally exercised in order to become properly developed and to retain healthful vigor. Each organ has its work to do in the living organism. Every wheel in the machinery must be a living, active, working wheel. All the faculties have a bearing upon one another, and all need to be exercised in order to be properly developed.— *"Testimonies for the Church," Vol. III, page 310.*

OUR DUTY TO PRESERVE HEALTH

I am pained at heart as I see so many feeble ministers, so many on beds of sickness, so many prematurely closing their earthly history,— men who have carried the burden of responsibility in the work of God, and whose whole heart was in their work. The conviction that they must cease their labor in the cause they loved, was far more painful to them than their sufferings from disease, or even the thought of death itself.

Our heavenly Father does not willingly afflict or grieve the children of men. He is not the author of sickness and death; He is the source of life. He would have men live; and He desires them to be obedient to the laws of life and health, that they may live.

Those who accept the present truth and are sanctified through it, have an intense desire to represent the truth in their life and character. They have a deep yearning of soul that others may see the light and rejoice in it. As the true watchman goes forth bearing precious seed, sowing beside all waters, weeping and praying, the burden of labor is very taxing to mind and heart. He cannot keep up the strain continuously, his soul stirred to the very depths, without wearing out prematurely. Strength and efficiency are needed in every discourse. And from time to time, fresh supplies of things new and old need to be brought forth from the storehouse of God's word. This will impart life and power to the hearers. God does not want you to become so exhausted that your efforts have no freshness or life.

Those who are engaged in constant mental labor, whether in studying or preaching, need rest and change. The earnest student is constantly taxing the brain, too often while neglecting physical exercise; and as the result the bodily powers are enfeebled, and mental effort is restricted. Thus the student fails of accomplishing the very work that he might have done, had he labored wisely.

If they worked intelligently, giving both mind and body a due share of exercise, ministers would not so readily succumb to disease. If all our workers were so situated that they could spend a few hours each day in outdoor labor, and felt free to do this, it would be a blessing to them; they would be able to discharge more successfully the duties of their calling. If they have not time for complete relaxation, they could be planning and praying while at work with their hands, and could return to their labor refreshed in body and spirit.

Some of our ministers feel that they must every day perform some labor that they can report to the conference. And as the result of trying to do this, their efforts are too often weak and inefficient. They should have periods of rest, of entire freedom from taxing labor. But these cannot take the place of daily physical exercise.

Brethren, when you take time to cultivate your garden, thus gaining the exercise needed to keep the system in good working order, you are just as much doing the work of God as in holding meetings. God is our Father; He loves us, and He does not require any of His servants to abuse their bodies.

Another cause of ill-health and of inefficiency in labor, is indigestion. It is impossible for the brain to do its best work when the digestive powers are abused. Many eat hurriedly of various kinds of food, which set up a war in the stomach, and thus confuse the brain. The use of unhealthful food, and over-eating of even that which is wholesome, should alike be avoided.

Many eat at all hours, regardless of the laws of health. Then gloom covers the mind. How can men be honored with divine enlightenment, when they are so reckless in their habits, so inattentive to the light which God has given in regard to these things?

Brethren, is it not time for you to be converted on these points of selfish indulgence? "Know ye not that they which run in a race run all, but one receiveth the prize? So run, that ye may obtain. And every man that striveth for the mastery is temperate in all things. Now they do it to obtain a corruptible crown; but we an incorruptible. I therefore so run, not as uncertainly; so fight I, not as one that beateth the air: but I keep under my body, and bring it into subjection: lest that by any means, when I have preached to others, I myself should be a castaway." [1]

INSUFFICIENT DIET

Do not, however, feel it your duty to live on an insufficient diet. Learn for yourselves what you should eat, what kinds of food best nourish the body, and then follow the dictates of reason and conscience. At meal-time cast off care and taxing thought. Do not be hurried, but eat slowly and with cheerfulness, your heart filled with gratitude to God for all His

[1] 1 Cor. 9 : 24-27.

blessings. And do not engage in brain labor immediately after a meal. Exercise moderately, and give a little time for the stomach to begin its work.

These are not matters of trifling importance. We must pay attention to them if healthful vigor and a right tone are to be given to the various branches of the work. The character and efficiency of the work depend largely upon the physical condition of the workers. Many committee meetings and other meetings for counsel have taken an unhappy tone from the dyspeptic condition of those assembled. And many a sermon has received a dark shadow from the minister's indigestion.

Health is an inestimable blessing, and one which is more closely related to conscience and religion than many realize. It has a great deal to do with one's capability. Every minister should feel that if he would be a faithful guardian of the flock, he must preserve all his powers in condition for the best possible service.

Our workers should use their knowledge of the laws of life and health. Read the best authors on these subjects, and obey religiously that which your reason tells you is truth.

———◆———

The Lord has presented before me that many, many will be rescued from physical, mental, and moral degeneracy through the practical influence of health reform. Health talks will be given; publications will be multiplied. The principles of health reform will be received with favor, and many . . . will advance step by step to receive the special truths for this time. —*"Testimonies for the Church," Vol. VI, pages 378, 379.*

DANGER FROM OVERWORK

When the apostles returned from their first missionary journey, the Saviour's command to them was, "Come ye yourselves apart into a desert place, and rest awhile." [1] They had been putting their whole souls into labor for the people, and this was exhausting their physical and mental strength. It was their duty to rest.

Christ's words of compassion are spoken to His workers to-day just as surely as to His disciples. "Come ye yourselves apart, . . . and rest awhile," He says to those who are worn and weary. It is not wise to be always under the strain of work and excitement, even in ministering to men's spiritual needs; for in this way personal piety is neglected, and the powers of mind and soul and body are overtaxed. Self-denial is required of the servants of Christ, and sacrifices must be made; but God would have all study the laws of health, and use reason when working for Him, that the life which He has given may be preserved.

Though Jesus could work miracles, and had empowered His disciples to work miracles, He directed His worn servants to go apart into the country and rest. When He said that the harvest was great and the laborers were few, He did not urge upon His disciples the necessity of ceaseless toil, but said, "Pray ye therefore the Lord of the harvest, that He will send forth laborers into His harvest." [2] God has appointed to every man his work, according to his ability; and

[1] Mark 6 : 31. [2] Matt. 9 : 38.

He would not have a few weighted with responsibilities, while others have no burden, no travail of soul.

The servants of Christ are not to treat their health indifferently. Let no one labor to the point of exhaustion, thereby disqualifying himself for future effort. Do not try to crowd into one day the work of two. At the end, those who work carefully and wisely will be found to have accomplished as much as those who so expend their physical and mental strength that they have no deposit from which to draw in time of need.

God's work is world-wide; it calls for every jot and tittle of the ability and power that we have. There is danger that His workers will abuse their powers as they see that the field is ripe for the harvest; but the Lord does not require this. After His servants have done their best, they may say, The harvest truly is great, and the laborers are few; but God "knoweth our frame; He remembereth that we are dust." [3]

Intemperance in eating and drinking, intemperance in labor, intemperance in almost everything, exists on every hand. Those who make great exertions to accomplish just so much in a given time, and continue to labor when their judgment tells them they ought to rest, are never gainers. They are expending force that they will need at a future time. When the energy which they have so recklessly used is called for, they fail for lack of it. Physical strength is gone, and mental power is unavailable. Their time of need has come, and their resources are exhausted.

Each day brings its responsibilities and duties, but the work of to-morrow must not be crowded into the

[3] Ps. 103 : 14.

hours of to-day. God is merciful, full of compassion, reasonable in His requirements. He does not ask us to pursue a course of action that will result in the loss of physical health or the enfeebling of the mental powers. He would not have us work under a pressure and strain until exhaustion follows, with prostration of the nerves.

There is need that God's chosen workmen should listen to the command to go apart and rest awhile. Many valuable lives have been sacrificed because of a disregard of this command. There are those who might be with us to-day, to help forward the cause both at home and in foreign lands, had they but realized before it was too late that they were in need of rest. These workers saw that the field is large and the need for workers great, and they felt that at any cost they must press on. When nature uttered a protest, they paid no heed, but did double the work they should have done; and God laid them in the grave to rest until the last trump shall sound to call the righteous forth to immortality.

When a laborer has been under a heavy pressure of care and anxiety, and is overworked in both body and mind, he should turn aside and rest awhile, not for selfish gratification, but that he may be better prepared for future duties. We have a vigilant foe, who is ever on our track, ready to take advantage of every weakness that would help to make his temptations effective. When the mind is overstrained and the body enfeebled, he presses upon the soul his fiercest temptations. Let the laborer carefully husband his strength, and when wearied with toil, let him turn aside and commune with Jesus.

I do not say this to those who are constitutionally tired, those who think they are carrying heavier burdens than any one else. Those who do not labor have no need of rest. There are always those who spare themselves, and who come far short of bearing their share of responsibility. They can talk of great and crushing burdens, but they do not know what it means to bear them. Their work yields but meager results.

It was to those worn down in His service, not to those who were always sparing themselves, that Christ addressed His gracious words. And to-day it is to the self-forgetful, those who work to the very extent of their ability, who are distressed because they cannot do more, and who in their zeal go beyond their strength, that the Saviour says, "Come ye yourselves apart, . . . and rest awhile."

———◆———

In all who are under the training of God is to be revealed a life that is not in harmony with the world, its customs or its practices; and every one needs to have a personal experience in obtaining a knowledge of the will of God. . . . He bids us, "Be still, and know that I am God." [4]   Here alone can true rest be found. And this is the effectual preparation for all labor for God. Amid the hurrying throng, and the strain of life's intense activities, the soul that is thus refreshed will be surrounded with an atmosphere of light and peace. The life will breathe out fragrance, and will reveal a divine power that will reach men's hearts.—"*The Desire of Ages*," *page 363*.

[4] Ps. 46 : 10.

FOR FURTHER STUDY

THE GOOD SHEPHERD	Test. Vol. II, pp. 21, 22. Desire, pp. 476-484. C. O. L., pp. 186-192.
PERSONAL MINISTRY	Test. Vol. I, pp. 381, 432, **473.** Test. Vol. II, pp. 338, 618, 619, 705, 706. Test. Vol. III, p. 558. Test. Vol. IX, p. 141. Desire, pp. 139-141, 351, 638- 641. Acts, p. 750.
THE SHEPHERD'S WORK	Test. Vol. II, p. 267. Test. Vol. III, pp. 228, 229 Patriarchs, pp. 191, 192. Acts, pp. 514-528.
BIBLE READINGS WITH FAMILIES	Test. Vol. V, p. 255. Test. Vol. IX, pp. 35, 36, 141.
THE VALUE OF INDIVIDUAL EFFORT	Test. Vol. III, p. 233. Test. Vol. IV, pp. 317, 536. Desire, pp. 183-195.
A DIVISION OF LABOR	Test. Vol. III, p. 210. Test. Vol. V, pp. 256, 302, 308. Test. Vol. VI, pp. 49, 302, 431- 435. Test. Vol. VII, pp. 18-24. Test. Vol. IX, pp. 30-42, 116- 136. Desire, pp. 640, 641, 825. Acts, pp. 158, 159.
THE MINISTER'S WIFE	Test. Vol. I, pp. 137-140, 627, 628. Test. Vol. II, pp. 565-569. Test. Vol. VI, p. 285.
THE MINISTER IN HIS HOME	Test. Vol. II, pp. 253-261, 417- 419, 620-624, 698-702. Test. Vol. III, p. 556. Test. Vol. IV, pp. 125-130, 360- 371, 380-383.

Helps in Gospel Work

"Who is wise, and he shall understand these things? prudent, and
he shall know them?"

BIBLE STUDY

Ministers who would labor effectively for the salvation of souls must be both Bible students and men
of prayer. It is a sin for those who attempt to teach
the Word to others to be themselves neglectful of its
study. Are the truths which they handle mighty?
then they should handle them skilfully. Their ideas
should be clearly and strongly presented. Of all men
upon the face of the earth, those who are proclaiming
the message for this time should understand their
Bible, and be thoroughly acquainted with the evidences of their faith. One who does not possess a
knowledge of the Word of life, has no right to try to
instruct others in the way to heaven.

The Bible is our rule of faith and doctrine. There
is nothing more calculated to energize the mind and
strengthen the intellect than the study of the word of
God. No other book is so potent to elevate the
thoughts or give vigor to the faculties, as the broad,
ennobling truths of the Bible. If God's word were
studied as it should be, men would have a breadth
of mind, a nobility of character, and a stability of
purpose that are rarely seen in these times.

Thousands of men who minister in the pulpit are
lacking in the essential qualities of mind and char-

acter because they do not apply themselves to the study of the Scriptures. They are content with a superficial knowledge of the truths of God's word, and they prefer to go on losing much in every way rather than to search diligently for the hidden treasure.

The psalmist declares, "Thy word have I hid in mine heart, that I might not sin against Thee." [1] And Paul wrote to Timothy, "All Scripture is given by inspiration of God, and is profitable for doctrine, for reproof, for correction, for instruction in righteousness: that the man of God may be perfect, thoroughly furnished unto all good works." [2]

The life of God, which gives life to the world, is in His word. It was by His word that Jesus healed disease and cast out demons. By His word He stilled the sea and raised the dead; and the people bore witness that His word was with power. He spoke the word of God as He had spoken it to all the Old Testament writers. The whole Bible is a manifestation of Christ. It is our only source of power.

This word does not repress activity. It opens before the conscientious searcher channels for activity. It does not leave men in uncertainty, without an object, but places before them the highest of all aims, — the winning of souls to Christ. It puts in the hand a lamp that lights the way to heaven. It tells of unsearchable riches, treasure beyond estimate.

The word of God is the standard of character. In giving us this word, God has put us in possession of every truth essential to salvation. Thousands have drawn water from these wells of life, yet there is no diminishing of the supply. Thousands have set the

[1] Ps. 119 : 11. [2] 2 Tim. 3 : 16, 17.

Lord before them, and by beholding have become changed into the same image. But these searchers have not exhausted these grand and holy themes. Thousands more may engage in the work of searching out the mysteries of salvation.

As the worker studies the life of Christ, and the character of His mission is dwelt upon, each fresh search will reveal something more deeply interesting than has yet been unfolded. The subject is inexhaustible. The study of the incarnation of Christ, His atoning sacrifice and mediatorial work, will employ the mind of the diligent student as long as time shall last; and looking to heaven with its unnumbered years, he will exclaim, "Great is the mystery of godliness!" [3]

We talk about the first angel's message and the second angel's message, and we think we have some understanding of the third angel's message. But as long as we are content with a limited knowledge, we shall be disqualified to obtain clearer views of truth. He who holds forth the word of life must take time to study the Bible and to search his own heart. Neglecting this, he will not know how to minister to needy souls. The diligent, humble student, seeking by earnest prayer and study for the truth as it is in Jesus, will most assuredly be rewarded. He seeks for help, not from ideas of human writers, but from the Fountain of wisdom and knowledge; and under the guidance of holy intelligences he gains a clear understanding of truth.

It is not by the might or power of the human agent that truth is to be impressed upon minds, "but

[3] 1 Tim. 3 : 16.

by My Spirit, saith the Lord of hosts." [4]   It is not the temperament or the eloquence of the one who preaches the word that makes his work successful.   Paul may plant and Apollos water, but God gives the increase. It is a minister's familiarity with God's word and his submission to the divine will, that give success to his efforts.

The heart that receives the word of God is not as a pool that evaporates, nor like a broken cistern that loses its treasure.   It is like the mountain stream fed by unfailing springs, whose cool, sparkling waters leap from rock to rock, refreshing the weary, the thirsty, the heavy-laden.

A familiarity with the truths of the Scripture will give the teacher of truth qualifications that will make him a representative of Christ.   The spirit of the Saviour's teaching will give force and directness to his instruction and to his prayers.   His will not be a narrow, lifeless testimony; he will not preach over and over the same set discourses; for his mind will be open to the constant illumination of the Holy Spirit.

"Whoso eateth My flesh, and drinketh My blood," Christ said, "hath eternal life." "As the living Father hath sent Me, and I live by the Father: so he that eateth Me, even he shall live by Me." "It is the spirit that quickeneth; . . . the words that I speak unto you, they are spirit, and they are life." [5]

When the servants of God know of a truth the meaning of these words, the elements of eternal life will be found in the ministry.   The tame, dull sermonizing will cease.   The foundation truths of the gospel will be presented in a new light.   There will be a fresh

[4] Zech. 4 : 6.   [5] John 6 : 54, 57, 63.

perception of truth, a clearness and power that all will discern. Those who have the privilege of sitting under such a ministry will, if susceptible to the Holy Spirit's influence, feel the energizing power of a new life. The fire of God's love will be kindled within them. Their faculties will be quickened to discern the beauty and majesty of truth.

The minister who makes the word of God his constant companion will continually bring forth truth of new beauty. The Spirit of Christ will come upon him, and God will work through him to help others. The Holy Spirit will fill his mind and heart with hope and courage and Bible imagery, and all this will be communicated to those under his instruction.

———◆———

In the Bible we have the unerring counsel of God. Its teachings, practically carried out, will fit men for any position of duty. It is the voice of God speaking every day to the soul. . . . The work of the Holy Spirit is to enlighten the darkened understanding, to melt the selfish, stony heart, to subdue the rebellious transgressor, and save him from the corrupting influences of the world. The prayer of Christ for His disciples was, "Sanctify them through Thy truth; Thy word is truth." The sword of the Spirit, which is the word of God, pierces the heart of the sinner, and cuts it in pieces. When the theory of the truth is repeated without its sacred influence being felt upon the soul of the speaker, it has no force upon the hearers, but is rejected as error, the speaker making himself responsible for the loss of souls.—
"Testimonies for the Church," Vol. IV, page 441.

SECRET PRAYER

Family prayer and public prayer have their place; but it is secret communion with God that sustains the soul-life. It was in the mount with God that Moses beheld the pattern of that wonderful building which was to be the abiding-place of His glory. It is in the mount with God — the secret place of communion — that we are to contemplate His glorious ideal for humanity. Thus we shall be enabled so to fashion our character-building that to us may be fulfilled the promise, "I will dwell in them, and walk in them; and I will be their God, and they shall be My people." [1]

While engaged in our daily work, we should lift the soul to heaven in prayer. These silent petitions rise like incense before the throne of grace; and the enemy is baffled. The Christian whose heart is thus stayed upon God cannot be overcome. No evil arts can destroy his peace. All the promises of God's word, all the power of divine grace, all the resources of Jehovah, are pledged to secure his deliverance. It was thus that Enoch walked with God. And God was with him, a present help in every time of need.

Christ's ministers must watch unto prayer. They may come with boldness to the throne of grace, lifting up holy hands without wrath or doubting. In faith they may supplicate the Father in heaven for wisdom and grace, that they may know how to work, how to deal with minds.

Prayer is the breath of the soul. It is the secret of spiritual power. No other means of grace can be

[1] 2 Cor. 6:16.

substituted, and the health of the soul be preserved. Prayer brings the heart into immediate contact with the Well-spring of life, and strengthens the sinew and muscle of the religious experience. Neglect the exercise of prayer, or engage in prayer spasmodically, now and then, as seems convenient, and you lose your hold on God. The spiritual faculties lose their vitality, the religious experience lacks health and vigor.

It is only at the altar of God that we can kindle our tapers with divine fire. It is only the divine light that will reveal the littleness, the incompetence, of human ability, and give clear views of the perfection and purity of Christ. It is only as we behold Jesus that we desire to be like Him, only as we view His righteousness that we hunger and thirst to possess it; and it is only as we ask in earnest prayer, that God will grant us our heart's desire.

God's messengers must tarry long with Him, if they would have success in their work. The story is told of an old Lancashire woman who was listening to the reasons that her neighbors gave for their minister's success. They spoke of his gifts, of his style of address, of his manners. "Nay," said the old woman, "I will tell you what it is. Your man is very thick with the Almighty."

When men are as devoted as Elijah was and possess the faith that he had, God will reveal Himself as He did then. When men plead with the Lord as did Jacob, the results that were seen then will again be seen. Power will come from God in answer to the prayer of faith.

Because the life of Jesus was a life of constant trust, sustained by continual communion, His service for heaven was without failure or faltering. Daily beset by temptation, constantly opposed by the leaders of the people, Christ knew that He must strengthen His humanity by prayer. In order to be a blessing to men, He must commune with God, from Him obtaining energy, perseverance, steadfastness.

The Saviour loved the solitude of the mountain in which to hold communion with His Father. Through the day He labored earnestly to save men from destruction. He healed the sick, comforted the mourning, called the dead to life, and brought hope and cheer to the despairing. After His work for the day was finished, He went forth, evening after evening, away from the confusion of the city, and bowed in prayer to His Father. Frequently He continued His petitions through the entire night; but He came from these seasons of communion invigorated and refreshed, braced for duty and for trial.

Are the ministers of Christ tempted and fiercely buffeted by Satan? So also was He who knew no sin. In the hour of distress He turned to His Father. Himself a source of blessing and strength, He could heal the sick and raise the dead; He could command the tempest, and it would obey Him; yet He prayed, often with strong crying and tears. He prayed for His disciples and for Himself, thus identifying Himself with human beings. He was a mighty petitioner. As the Prince of life, He had power with God, and prevailed.

Ministers who are truly Christ's representatives will be men of prayer. With an earnestness and faith that will not be denied, they will plead with God to strengthen and fortify them for service, and to sanctify their lips by a touch of the living coal, that they may know how to speak His words to the people.

Prayer is the opening of the heart to God as to a friend. The eye of faith will discern God very near, and the suppliant may obtain precious evidence of the divine love and care for him. The prayer that Nathanael offered came from a sincere heart, and it was heard and answered by the Master. The Lord reads the hearts of all, and "the prayer of the upright is His delight." [2] He will not be slow to hear those who open their hearts to Him, not exalting self, but sincerely feeling their weakness and unworthiness.

There is need of prayer, earnest, fervent, agonizing prayer, such prayer as David offered when he exclaimed, "As the hart panteth after the water brooks, so panteth my soul after Thee, O God." "I have longed after Thy precepts." "I have longed for Thy salvation." "My soul longeth, yea, even fainteth for the courts of the Lord: my heart and my flesh crieth out for the living God." [3]

Those who teach and preach the most effectively are those who wait humbly upon God, and watch hungrily for His guidance and His grace. Watch, pray, work — this is the Christian's watchword. The life of a true Christian is a life of constant prayer. He knows that the light and strength of one day is not sufficient for the trials and conflicts of the next. Satan is continually changing his temptations. Every day we shall be placed in different circumstances; and in the untried scenes that await us we shall be surrounded by fresh dangers, and constantly assailed by new and unexpected temptations. It is only

[2] Prov. 15 : 8.   [3] Ps. 42 : 1 : 119 : 40, 174 ; 84 : 2.

through the strength and grace gained from heaven that we can hope to meet the temptations and perform the duties before us.

It is a wonderful thing that we can pray effectually; that unworthy, erring mortals possess the power of offering their requests to God. What higher power can man desire than this,— to be linked with the infinite God? Feeble, sinful man has the privilege of speaking to his Maker. We may utter words that reach the throne of the Monarch of the universe. We may speak with Jesus as we walk by the way, and He says, I am at thy right hand.[4]

We may commune with God in our hearts; we may walk in companionship with Christ. When engaged in our daily labor, we may breathe out our heart's desire, inaudible to any human ear; but that word cannot die away into silence, nor can it be lost. Nothing can drown the soul's desire. It rises above the din of the street, above the noise of machinery. It is God to whom we are speaking, and our prayer is heard.

Ask, then; ask, and ye shall receive. Ask for humility, wisdom, courage, increase of faith. To every sincere prayer an answer will come. It may not come just as you desire, or at the time you look for it; but it will come in the way and at the time that will best meet your need. The prayers you offer in loneliness, in weariness, in trial, God answers, not always according to your expectations, but always for your good.

[4] See Ps. 16 : 8.

FAITH

The greatest victories gained for the cause of God are not the result of labored argument, ample facilities, wide influence, or abundance of means; they are gained in the audience chamber with God, when with earnest, agonizing faith men lay hold upon the mighty arm of power.

True faith and true prayer — how strong they are! They are as two arms by which the human suppliant lays hold upon the power of Infinite Love. Faith is trusting in God,— believing that He loves us, and knows what is for our best good. Thus, instead of our own way, it leads us to choose His way. In place of our ignorance, it accepts His wisdom; in place of our weakness, His strength; in place of our sinfulness, His righteousness. Our lives, ourselves, are already His; faith acknowledges His ownership, and accepts its blessing. Truth, uprightness, purity, are pointed out as secrets of life's success. It is faith that puts us in possession of these. Every good impulse or aspiration is the gift of God; faith receives from God the life that alone can produce true growth and efficiency.

"This is the victory that overcometh the world, even our faith." [1] It is faith that enables us to look beyond the present, with its burdens and cares, to the great hereafter, where all that now perplexes us shall be made plain. Faith sees Jesus standing as our Mediator at the right hand of God. Faith beholds the mansions that Christ has gone to prepare for those who love Him. Faith sees the robe and crown pre-

[1] 1 John 5 : 4.

pared for the overcomer, and hears the song of the redeemed.

Perfect faith, the surrender of self to God, simple trust in His pledged word, should be a part of every minister's experience. Only as a minister has this experience can he make the subject of faith plain to the doubting and distrustful.

Faith is not feeling. "Faith is the substance of things hoped for, the evidence of things not seen." [2] True faith is in no sense allied to presumption. Only he who has true faith is secure against presumption, for presumption is Satan's counterfeit of faith.

Faith claims God's promises, and brings forth fruit in obedience. Presumption also claims the promises, but uses them as Satan did, to excuse transgression. Faith would have led our first parents to trust the love of God and to obey His commands. Presumption led them to transgress His law, believing that His great love would save them from the consequences of their sin. It is not faith that claims the favor of Heaven without complying with the conditions on which mercy is to be granted. Genuine faith has its foundation in the promises and provisions of the Scriptures.

To talk of religion in a casual way, to pray without soul-hunger and living faith, avails nothing. A nominal faith in Christ, which accepts Him merely as the Saviour of the world, can never bring healing to the soul. The faith that is unto salvation is not a mere intellectual assent to the truth. He who waits for entire knowledge before he will exercise faith, cannot receive blessing from God.

[2] Heb. 11 : 1.

It is not enough to believe *about* Christ; we must believe *in* Him. The only faith that will benefit us is that which embraces Him as a personal Saviour; which appropriates His merits to ourselves. Many hold faith as an opinion. But saving faith is a transaction, by which those who receive Christ join themselves in covenant relation with God. Genuine faith is life. A living faith means an increase of vigor, a confiding trust, by which the soul becomes a conquering power.

UNBELIEF AND DOUBT

Faith takes God at His word, not asking to understand the meaning of the trying experiences that come. But there are many who have little faith. They are always fearing and borrowing trouble. Every day they are surrounded by the tokens of God's love, every day they enjoy the bounties of His providence; but they overlook these blessings. And the difficulties they encounter, instead of driving them to God, separate them from Him, by arousing unrest and repining.

Do they well to be thus unbelieving? Jesus is their friend. All heaven is interested in their welfare, and their fear and repining grieve the Holy Spirit. Not because we see or feel that God hears us are we to believe. We are to trust His promises. When we come to Him in faith, we should believe that every petition enters into the heart of Christ. When we have asked for His blessing, we should believe that we receive it, and thank Him that we have it. Then we are to go about our duties, assured that the blessing will be sent when we need it most. When we have learned to do this, we shall know that our prayers are answered. God will do for us "exceeding abundantly," "according to the riches of His glory," and "the working of His mighty power." [3]

Often the Christian life is beset with dangers, and duty seems hard to perform. The imagination pictures impending ruin before, and bondage and death behind. Yet the voice of God speaks clearly, Go forward. Let us obey the command, even though our sight cannot penetrate the darkness. The obstacles that hinder our progress will never disappear before a halting, doubting spirit. Those who defer obedience till every uncertainty disappears, and there remains no risk of failure or defeat, will never obey. Faith looks beyond the difficulties, and lays hold of the unseen, even Omnipotence, therefore it cannot be baffled. Faith is the clasping of the hand of Christ in every emergency.

The worker for God needs strong faith. Appearances may seem forbidding; but in the darkest hour there is light beyond. The strength of those who, in faith, love and serve God, will be renewed day by day. The understanding of the Infinite is placed at their service, that in carrying out His purposes they may not err. Let these workers hold the beginning of their confidence firm unto the end, remembering that the light of God's truth is to shine amid the darkness that enshrouds our world.

There is to be no despondency in connection with God's service. The faith of the consecrated worker is to stand every test brought upon it. God is able and willing to bestow upon His servants all the

[3] Eph. 3 : 20, 16 ; 1 : 19.

strength they need, and to give them the wisdom that their varied necessities demand. He will more than fulfil the highest expectations of those who put their trust in Him.

Jesus does not call on us to follow Him, and then forsake us. If we surrender our lives to His service, we can never be placed in a position for which God has not made provision. Whatever may be our situation, we have a Guide to direct our way; whatever our perplexities, we have a sure Counselor; whatever our sorrow, bereavement, or loneliness, we have a sympathizing Friend. If in our ignorance we make missteps, Christ does not leave us. His voice, clear and distinct, is heard, saying, "I am the way, the truth, and the life." [4] "He shall deliver the needy when he crieth; the poor also, and him that hath no helper." [5]

"Thou wilt keep him in perfect peace, whose mind is stayed on Thee: because he trusteth in Thee." [6] The arm of Omnipotence is outstretched to lead us onward and still onward. Go forward, the Lord says; I will send you help. It is for My name's glory that you ask; and you shall receive. Those who are watching for your failure shall yet see My word triumph gloriously. "All things, whatsoever ye shall ask in prayer, believing, ye shall receive." [7]

———◆———

God never leaves the world without men who can discern between good and evil, righteousness and unrighteousness. He has men whom He has appointed to stand in the forefront of the battle in times of emergency.

[4] John 14 · 6.   [5] Ps. 72 : 12.   [6] Isa. 26 : 3.   [7] Matt. 21 : 22.

COURAGE

God's servants are not to be easily discouraged by difficulties or opposition. Those who proclaim the third angel's message must stand bravely at their post, in the face of detraction and falsehood, fighting the good fight of faith, and resisting the enemy with the weapon that Christ used, "It is written." In the great crisis through which they are soon to pass, the servants of God will encounter the same hardness of heart, the same cruel determination, the same unyielding hatred, encountered by Christ and the apostles.

All who in that evil day would faithfully serve God according to the dictates of conscience, will need courage, firmness, and a knowledge of God and His word; for those who are true to God will be persecuted, their motives will be impugned, their best efforts misinterpreted, and their names cast out as evil.

Satan will work with his deceptive power to influence the heart and becloud the understanding, to make evil appear good, and good evil. The stronger and purer the faith of God's people, and the firmer their determination to obey Him, the more fiercely will Satan strive to stir up against them the rage of those who, while claiming to be righteous, trample upon the law of God. It will require the firmest trust, the most heroic purpose, to hold fast the faith once delivered to the saints.

The messengers of the cross must arm themselves with watchfulness and prayer, and move forward in

faith and courage, working always in the name of
Jesus. They must have confidence in their Leader;
for troublous times are before us. The judgments of
God are abroad in the land. Calamities follow one
another in rapid succession. Soon God is to rise out
of His place to shake terribly the earth, and to punish
the wicked for their iniquity. Then He will stand
up in behalf of His people, and will give them His
protecting care. He will throw His everlasting arms
about them, to shield them from all harm.

"COURAGE IN THE LORD"

After the passing of the time in 1844, a number
of brethren and sisters were assembled in a meeting.
All were very sad, for the disappointment had been
sore. Presently a man came in, crying, "Courage in
the Lord, brethren; courage in the Lord!" This he
repeated again and again, till every face was aglow,
and every voice lifted in praise to God.

To-day I say to every worker for the Master,
"Courage in the Lord!" Ever since 1844 I have been
proclaiming present truth, and to-day this truth is
dearer to me than ever before.

Some look always at the objectionable and discouraging features, and therefore discouragement over-
takes them. They forget that the heavenly universe
is waiting to make them agencies of blessing to the
world; and that the Lord Jesus is a never-failing
storehouse from which human beings may draw
strength and courage. There is no need for despondency and apprehension. The time will never come
when the shadow of Satan will not be cast athwart

our pathway. Thus the enemy seeks to hide the light shining from the Sun of Righteousness. But our faith should pierce this shadow.

God calls for cheerful co-workers, who refuse to become discouraged and disheartened by opposing agencies. The Lord is leading us, and we may go forward courageously, assured that He will be with us, as He was in past years, when we labored in feebleness, but under the power of the Holy Spirit.

Angels ministered to Christ, but their presence did not make His life one of ease and freedom from temptation. He "was in all points tempted like as we are, yet without sin." [1] If ministers, while engaged in the work that the Master has appointed them, have trials and perplexities and temptations, should they be discouraged? Should they cast away their confidence because their labors do not always bring the results that they so greatly desire to see? True workers will not despond in view of the work before them, arduous though it may be. Shrinking from hardship, complaining under tribulation, makes the servants of God weak and inefficient.

As those who stand in the forefront of the battle see that the special warfare of Satan is directed against them, they will realize their need of strength from God, and they will labor in His strength. The victories that they gain will not exalt them, but will cause them to lean more securely upon the Mighty One. Deep and fervent gratitude to God will spring up in their hearts, and they will be joyful in the tribulation that comes to them while pressed by the enemy.

[1] Heb. 4 : 15.

A SEASON OF TRUST AND PRIVILEGE

The present is a season of solemn privilege and sacred trust. If the servants of God keep faithfully the trust given to them, great will be their reward when the Master shall say, "Give an account of thy stewardship." [2] The earnest toil, the unselfish work, the patient, persevering effort, will be abundantly rewarded. Jesus will say, Henceforth I call you not servants, but friends. [3] The approval of the Master is not given because of the greatness of the work performed, but because of fidelity in all that has been done. It is not the results we attain, but the motives from which we act, that weigh with God. He prizes goodness and faithfulness above all else.

I entreat the heralds of the gospel of Christ never to become discouraged, never to regard the most hardened sinner as beyond the reach of the grace of God. The one apparently hopeless may accept the truth in the love of it. He who turns the hearts of men as the rivers of water are turned, can bring the most selfish, sin-hardened soul to Christ. Is anything too hard for God to do? "My word," He declares, "shall not return unto Me void, but it shall accomplish that which I please, and it shall prosper in the thing whereto I sent it." [4]

Those who are endeavoring to build up the work in new territory will often find themselves in great need of better facilities. Their work will seem to be hindered for lack of these facilities; but let them not lose their faith and courage. Often they are obliged to go to the limit of their resources. At times it may seem

[2] Luke 16:2.   [3] See John 15:15.   [4] Isa. 55:11.

as if they could advance no farther. But if they pray and work in faith, God will answer their petitions, sending them means for the advancement of the work. Difficulties will arise; they will wonder how they are going to accomplish what must be done. At times the future will look very dark. But let the workers bring to God the promises He has made, and thank Him for what He has done. Then the way will open before them, and they will be strengthened for the duty of the hour.

———————◆———————

Few realize the significance of the words of Luke, that when Paul saw his brethren, "he thanked God, and took courage."[5] In the midst of the weeping, sympathizing company of believers, who were not ashamed of his bonds, the apostle praised God aloud. The cloud of sadness that had rested upon his spirit was swept away. His Christian life had been a succession of trials, sufferings, and disappointments, but in that hour he felt abundantly repaid. With firmer step and joyful heart he continued on his way. He would not complain of the past, nor fear for the future. Bonds and afflictions awaited him, he knew; but he knew also that it had been his to deliver souls from a bondage infinitely more terrible, and he rejoiced in his sufferings for Christ's sake.—"*The Acts of the Apostles*," *page 449.*

[5] Acts 28 : 15.

HOW GOD TRAINS HIS WORKERS

The Lord disciplines His workers, that they may be prepared to fill the places appointed them. He desires to fit them to do more acceptable service. There are those who wish to be a ruling power, and who need the sanctification of submission. God brings about a change in their lives. Perhaps He places before them duties that they would not choose. If they are willing to be guided by Him, He will give them grace and strength to perform these duties in a spirit of submission and helpfulness. Thus they are being qualified to fill places where their disciplined abilities will make them of great service.

Some God trains by bringing to them disappointment and apparent failure. It is His purpose that they shall learn to master difficulties. He inspires them with a determination to prove every apparent failure a success. Often men pray and weep because of the perplexities and obstacles that confront them. But if they will hold the beginning of their confidence steadfast unto the end, God will make their way clear. Success will come as they struggle against apparently insurmountable difficulties· and with success will come the greatest joy.

A life of monotony is not the most conducive to spiritual growth. Some can reach the highest standard of spirituality only through a change in the regular order of things. When in His providence God sees that changes are essential for the success of the character-building, He disturbs the smooth current of the life. He sees that a worker needs to be more closely associated with Him; and to bring this about, He separates him from friends and acquaintances. When He was preparing Elijah for translation, God moved him from place to place, that the prophet might not settle down at ease, and thus fail of gaining spiritual power. And it was God's design that Elijah's influence should be a power to help many souls to gain a wider, more helpful experience.

There are many who are not satisfied to serve God cheerfully in the place that He has marked out for them, or to do uncomplainingly the work that He has placed in their hands. It is right to be dissatisfied with the way in which we perform duty, but we are not to be dissatisfied with the duty itself because we would rather do something else. In His providence God places before human beings service that will be as medicine to their diseased minds. Thus He seeks to lead them to put aside the selfish preference, which, if gratified, would disqualify them for the work He has for them. If they accept and perform this service, their minds will be cured. If they refuse it, they will be left at strife with themselves and others.

Let those who are not permitted to rest in quietude, but who must be continually on the move, pitching their tent to-night in one place and to-morrow night in another place, remember that the Lord is leading them and that this is His way of helping them to form perfect characters. In all the changes that they are required to make, God is to be recognized as their companion, their guide, their dependence.

TAKE TIME TO TALK WITH GOD

Special instruction has been given me in regard to our ministers. It is not God's will that they should seek to be rich. They should not engage in worldly enterprises; for this disqualifies them for giving their best powers to spiritual things. But they are to receive wages enough to support themselves and their families. They are not to have so many burdens laid upon them that they cannot give proper attention to the church in their own family; for it is their special duty to train their children for the Lord.

It is a great mistake to keep a minister constantly at work in business lines, going from place to place, and sitting up late at night in attendance at board meetings and committee meetings. This brings upon him weariness and discouragement. Ministers should have time to rest, to obtain from God's word the rich nourishment of the bread of life. They should have time to drink refreshing draughts of consolation from the stream of living water.

Let ministers and teachers remember that God holds them accountable to fill their office to the best of their ability, to bring into their work their very best powers. They are not to take up duties that conflict with the work that God has given them.

When ministers and teachers, pressed under the burden of financial responsibilities, enter the pulpit or the schoolroom with wearied brain and overtaxed nerves, what else can be expected than that common fire will be used instead of the sacred fire of God's kindling? The strained, tattered efforts disappoint the listeners and hurt the speaker. He has had no time to seek the Lord, no time to ask in faith for the unction of the Holy Spirit. . . .

I am instructed to say to my fellow-workers, If you would have the rich treasures of heaven, you must hold secret communion with God. Unless you do this, your soul will be as destitute of the Holy Spirit as were the hills of Gilboa of dew and rain. When you hurry from one thing to another, when you have so much to do that you cannot take time to talk with God, how can you expect power in your work?

The reason so many of our ministers preach tame, lifeless discourses is that they allow a variety of things of a worldly nature to take their time and attention. Unless there is constant growth in grace, we shall be wanting in words suitable for the occasion. Commune with your own heart, and then commune with God. Unless you do this, your efforts will be fruitless, made thus by unsanctified hurry and confusion.

Ministers and teachers, let your work be fragrant with rich spiritual grace. Do not make it common by mixing it with common things. Move onward and upward. Cleanse yourselves "from all filthiness of the flesh and spirit, perfecting holiness in the fear of God." [1]

We need to be converted daily. Our prayers should be more fervent; then they will be more effectual. Stronger and stronger should be our confidence that God's Spirit will be with us, making us pure and holy, as upright and fragrant as the cedar of Lebanon. —*"Testimonies for the Church," Vol. VII, pages 250-252.*

[1] 2 Cor. 7 : 1.

OUR GREATEST NEED

"Ye shall be witnesses unto Me." [1]   These words of Jesus have lost none of their force. Our Saviour calls for faithful witnesses in these days of religious formalism; but how few, even among the professed ambassadors for Christ, are ready to give a faithful, personal testimony for their Master! Many can tell what the great and good men of generations past have done, and dared, and suffered, and enjoyed. They become eloquent in setting forth the power of the gospel, which has enabled others to rejoice in trying conflicts, and to stand firm against fierce temptations. But while so earnest in bringing forward other Christians as witnesses for Jesus, they seem to have no fresh, timely experience of their own to relate.

Ministers of Christ, what have *you* to say for yourselves? What soul conflicts have *you* experienced that have been for your good, for the good of others, and for the glory of God? You who profess to be proclaiming the last solemn message of mercy to the world, what is your experience in the knowledge of the truth, and what has been its effect upon your own hearts? Does your character testify for Christ? Can you speak of the refining, ennobling, sanctifying influence of the truth as it is in Jesus? What have *you* seen, what have *you* known, of the power of Christ? This is the kind of witness for which the Lord calls, and for which the churches are suffering.

[1] Acts 1 : 8.

Without a living faith in Christ as a personal Saviour, it is impossible to make your faith felt in a skeptical world. If you would draw sinners out of the swift-running current, your own feet must not stand on slippery places.

We need constantly a fresh revelation of Christ, a daily experience that harmonizes with His teachings. High and holy attainments are within our reach. Continual progress in knowledge and virtue is God's purpose for us. His law is the echo of His own voice, giving to all the invitation, "Come up higher; be holy, holier still." Every day we may advance in perfection of Christian character.

Those who are engaged in service for the Master need an experience much higher, deeper, broader, than many have yet thought of having. Many who are already members of God's great family know little of what it means to behold His glory, and to be changed from glory to glory. Many have a twilight perception of Christ's excellence, and their hearts thrill with joy. They long for a fuller, deeper sense of the Saviour's love. Let these cherish every desire of the soul after God.

The Holy Spirit works with those who will be worked, moulds those who will be moulded, fashions those who will be fashioned. Give yourselves the culture of spiritual thoughts and holy communings. You have seen but the first rays of the early dawn of His glory. As you follow on to know the Lord, you will know that the "path of the righteous is as the light of dawn, that shineth more and more unto the perfect day." [2]

2 Prov. 4 : 18, R. V.

SELF-EXAMINATION

There is much in the conduct of ministers that they can improve. Many see and feel their lack, yet they seem to be ignorant of the influence they exert. They are conscious of their actions as they perform them, but suffer them to pass from their memory, and therefore do not reform.

Let ministers make the actions of each day a subject of careful thought and deliberate review, with the object of becoming better acquainted with their own habits of life. By a close scrutiny of every circumstance of the daily life, they would know better their own motives and the principles which govern them. This daily review of our acts, to see whether conscience approves or condemns, is necessary for all who wish to reach perfection of Christian character. Many acts which pass for good works, even deeds of benevolence, will, when closely investigated, be found to be prompted by wrong motives.

Many receive applause for virtues which they do not possess. The Searcher of hearts weighs the motives, and often deeds highly applauded by men are recorded by Him as springing from selfishness and base hypocrisy. Every act of our lives, whether excellent and praiseworthy, or deserving of censure, is judged by the Searcher of hearts according to the motives which prompted it.

Many neglect to look at themselves in the mirror which reveals the defects in the character; therefore deformity and sin exist, and are apparent to others, if not understood by those who are in fault. The hateful sin of selfishness exists to a great degree, even in some who profess to be devoted to the work of God. If they would compare their character with His requirements, especially with the great standard, God's holy law, they would ascertain, if earnest, honest searchers, that they are fearfully wanting. But some are not willing to look far enough or deep enough to see the depravity of their own hearts. They are wanting in very many respects, yet they remain in willing ignorance of their guilt.

He who understands well his own character, who is acquainted with the sin that most easily besets him, and the temptations that are the most likely to overcome him, should not expose himself needlessly, and invite temptation by placing himself on the enemy's ground. If duty calls him where circumstances are not favorable, he will have special help from God, and can thus go fully girded for a conflict with the enemy.

Self-knowledge will save many from falling into grievous temptations, and prevent many an inglorious defeat. In order to become acquainted with ourselves, it is essential that we faithfully investigate the motives and principles of our conduct, comparing our actions with the standard of duty revealed in God's word.

SELF-IMPROVEMENT

Ministers of age and experience should feel it their duty, as God's hired servants, to go forward, progressing every day, continually becoming more efficient in their work, and constantly gathering fresh matter to set before the people. Each effort to expound the gospel should be an improvement upon that which preceded it. Each year they should develop a deeper piety, a more tender spirit, a greater spirituality, and a more thorough knowledge of Bible truth. The greater their age and experience, the nearer should they be able to approach the hearts of the people, having a more perfect knowledge of them.—*"Testimonies for the Church," Vol. IV, page 270.*

God has no use for lazy men in His cause; He wants thoughtful, kind, affectionate, earnest workers. Active exertion will do our preachers good. Indolence is proof of depravity. Every faculty of the mind, every bone in the body, every muscle of the limbs, shows that God designed our faculties to be used, not to remain inactive. . . . Men who will unnecessarily take the hours of daylight for sleep, have no sense of the value of precious, golden moments. . . .

Persons who have not acquired habits of close industry and economy of time, should have set rules to prompt them to regularity and dispatch. George Washington was enabled to perform a great amount of business because he was thorough in preserving order and regularity. Every paper had its date and its place, and no time was lost in looking up what had been mislaid.

Men of God must be diligent in study, earnest in the acquirement of knowledge, never wasting an hour. Through persevering exertion they may rise to almost any degree of eminence as Christians, as men of power and influence. But many will never attain superior rank in the pulpit or in business, because of their unfixedness of purpose, and the laxness of the habits contracted in their youth. Careless inattention is seen in everything they undertake.

A sudden impulse now and then is not sufficient to accomplish a reformation in these ease-loving, indolent ones; this is a work which requires patient continuance in well-doing. Men of business can be truly successful only by having regular hours for rising, for prayer, for meals, and for retiring. If order and regularity are essential in worldly business, how much more so in the work of God!

The bright morning hours are wasted by many in bed. These precious hours, once lost, are gone never to return; they are lost for time and for eternity. Only one hour lost each day, and what a waste of time in the course of a year! Let the slumberer think of this, and pause to consider how he will give an account to God for lost opportunities.

IMPROVING ODD MOMENTS

Ministers should devote time to reading, to study, to meditation and prayer. They should store the mind with useful knowledge, committing to memory portions of Scripture, tracing out the fulfilment of the prophecies, and learning the lessons which Christ gave

His disciples. Take a book with you to read when traveling on the cars or waiting in the railway station. Employ every spare moment in doing something. In this way an effectual door will be closed against a thousand temptations. . . .

Many have failed, signally failed, where they might have made a success. They have not felt the burden of the work; they have taken things as leisurely as if they had a temporal millennium in which to work for the salvation of souls. . . . The cause of God is not so much in need of preachers as of earnest, persevering workers for the Master. God alone can measure the powers of the human mind. It was not His design that man should be content to remain in the lowlands of ignorance, but that he should secure all the advantages of an enlightened, cultivated intellect.

Every one should feel that there rests upon him an obligation to reach the height of intellectual greatness. While none should be puffed up because of the knowledge they have acquired, it is the privilege of all to enjoy the satisfaction of knowing that with every advance step they are rendered more capable of honoring and glorifying God. They may draw from an inexhaustible fountain, the Source of all wisdom and knowledge.

Having entered the school of Christ, the student is prepared to engage in the pursuit of knowledge without becoming dizzy from the height to which he is climbing. As he goes on from truth to truth, obtaining clearer and brighter views of the wonderful laws of science and of nature, he becomes enraptured with the amazing exhibitions of God's love to man. He sees with intelligent eyes the perfection, knowledge, and wisdom of God stretching beyond into infinity. As his mind enlarges and expands, pure streams of light pour into his soul. The more he drinks from the fountain of knowledge, the purer and happier his contemplation of God's infinity, and the greater his longing for wisdom sufficient to comprehend the deep things of God.

NEED OF MENTAL CULTURE

Mental culture is what we as a people need, and what we must have in order to meet the demands of the time. Poverty, humble origin, and unfavorable surroundings need not prevent the cultivation of the mind. . . .

Difficulties will be met in all studies; but never cease through discouragement. Search, study, and pray; face every difficulty manfully and vigorously; call the power of will and the grace of patience to your aid, and then dig more earnestly till the gem of truth lies before you, plain and beautiful, all the more precious because of the difficulties involved in finding it. Do not, then, continually dwell upon this one point, concentrating upon it all the energies of the mind, and constantly urging it upon the attention of others: but take another subject, and carefully examine that. Thus mystery after mystery will be unfolded to your comprehension.

Two valuable victories will be gained by this course. You will not only secure useful knowledge, but the exercise of the mind will increase your mental power. The key found to unlock one mystery, may reveal also other precious gems of knowledge heretofore undiscovered.

Many of our ministers can present to the people only a few doctrinal discourses. The same exertion and application which made them familiar with these points would enable them to gain an understanding of others. The prophecies and other doctrinal subjects should be thoroughly understood by all ministers. But some who have been preaching for years are content to confine themselves to a few subjects, being too indolent to search the Scriptures diligently and prayerfully, that they may become giants in the understanding of Bible doctrines and the practical lessons of Christ.

The minds of all should be stored with a knowledge of the truths of God's word, that they may be prepared, at any moment when required, to present from the storehouse things new and old. Minds have been crippled and dwarfed for want of zeal and earnest, severe taxation. The time has come when God says, Go forward, and cultivate the abilities I have given you.

The world is teeming with errors and fables. Novelties in the form of sensational dramas are continually arising to engross the mind; and absurd theories abound, which are destructive to moral and spiritual advancement. The cause of God needs men of intellect, men of thought, men well versed in the Scriptures, to meet the inflowing tide of opposition. We should give no sanction to arrogance, narrow-mindedness, and inconsistencies, although the garment of professed piety may be thrown over them. Those who have the sanctifying power of the truth upon their hearts will exert a persuasive influence. Knowing that the advocates of error cannot create or destroy truth, they can afford to be calm and considerate. . .

There are many, even among our preachers, who want to rise in the world without effort. They are ambitious to do some great work of usefulness, while they disregard the little, every-day duties which would render them helpful and make them ministers after Christ's order. They wish to do the work that others are doing, but have no relish for the discipline necessary to fit them for it. This yearning desire by both men and women to do something far in advance of their present capabilities, is causing them to make decided failures at the outset. They indignantly refuse to climb the ladder, wishing to be elevated by a less laborious process.—*"Testimonies for the Church," Vol. IV, pages 411-417.*

I am astonished that with the examples before us of what man may be and what he may do, we are not stimulated to greater exertion to emulate the good works of the righteous. Not all may occupy positions of prominence; yet all may fill positions of usefulness and trust, and may, by their persevering fidelity, do far more good than they have any idea that they can do.— *Id., page 399.*

The value of men and women is not to be estimated by the class of labor they perform. It is fixed by Him who paid the price for every soul. In charity, in simplicity, in integrity, all who have Christ formed within, the hope of glory, are to be workers together with God. They are God's husbandry, God's building.

The heart in which the love of Christ abides will constantly manifest more and more refinement; for the spring of life is love to God and man. Christ is

Christianity. This is glory to God in the highest, and on earth peace, good will toward men. This is the carrying out of God's purpose.

True Christian growth tends upward to the full stature of men and women in Christ. True culture, real refinement of thought and manners, is better obtained by learning lessons in the school of Christ, than by the most labored, painstaking effort to observe forms and set rules, when the heart is not under the discipline of the Spirit of God.

The follower of Jesus should be constantly improving in manners, in habits, in spirit, in labor. This is done by keeping the eye, not on mere outward, superficial attainments, but on Jesus. A transformation takes place in mind, in spirit, in character. The Christian is educated in the school of Christ to cherish the graces of His Spirit in all meekness and lowliness. He is fitting for the society of heavenly angels.

———◆———

Above all other people on the earth, the man whose mind is enlightened by the word of God will feel that he must give himself to greater diligence in the perusal of the Bible, and to a diligent study of the sciences; for his hope and his calling are greater than any other. The more closely man is connected with the Source of all knowledge and wisdom, the more he can be helped intellectually as well as spiritually. The knowledge of God is the essential education, and this knowledge every true worker will make it his constant study to obtain.—*"Counsels to Teachers," page 510.*

THE HOLY SPIRIT

"When He, the Spirit of truth, is come," "He will reprove the world of sin, and of righteousness, and of judgment." [1]

The preaching of the word is of no avail without the presence and aid of the Holy Spirit; for this Spirit is the only effectual teacher of divine truth. Only when the truth is accompanied to the heart by the Spirit, will it quicken the conscience or transform the life. A minister may be able to present the letter of the word of God; he may be familiar with all its commands and promises; but his sowing of the gospel seed will not be successful unless this seed is quickened into life by the dew of heaven. Without the co-operation of the Spirit of God, no amount of education, no advantages, however great, can make one a channel of light. Before one book of the New Testament had been written, before one gospel sermon had been preached after Christ's ascension, the Holy Spirit came upon the praying disciples. Then the testimony of their enemies was, "Ye have filled Jerusalem with your doctrine." [2]

GOD'S PROMISES SUBJECT TO CONDITIONS

Christ promised the gift of the Holy Spirit to His church, and the promise belongs as much to us as to the first disciples. But like every other promise, it is given on conditions. There are many who profess to believe and claim the Lord's promises; they talk about Christ and the Holy Spirit; yet they receive

[1] John 16 : 13, 8. [2] Acts 5 : 28.

no benefit, because they do not surrender their souls to the guidance and control of divine agencies.

We cannot use the Holy Spirit; the Spirit is to use us. Through the Spirit, God works in His people "to will and to do of His good pleasure." [3] But many will not submit to be led. They want to manage themselves. This is why they do not receive the heavenly gift. Only to those who wait humbly upon God, who watch for His guidance and grace, is the Spirit given. This promised blessing, claimed by faith, brings all other blessings in its train. It is given according to the riches of the grace of Christ, and He is ready to supply every soul according to the capacity to receive.

The impartation of the Spirit is the impartation of the life of Christ. Those only who are thus taught of God, those only who possess the inward working of the Spirit, and in whose life the Christ-life is manifested, can stand as true representatives of the Saviour.

THE HOLY SPIRIT AS AN EDUCATOR

God takes men as they are, and educates them for His service, if they will yield themselves to Him. The Spirit of God, received into the soul, quickens all its faculties. Under the guidance of the Holy Spirit, the mind that is devoted unreservedly to God, develops harmoniously, and is strengthened to comprehend and fulfil the requirements of God. The weak, vacillating character becomes changed to one of strength and steadfastness. Continual devotion establishes so close a relation between Jesus and His disciples that the Christian becomes like his Master in character. He

[3] Phil. 2:13.

has clearer, broader views. His discernment is more penetrative, his judgment better balanced. So quickened is he by the life-giving power of the Sun of Righteousness, that he is enabled to bear much fruit to the glory of God.

Christ promised that the Holy Spirit should abide with those who wrestle for victory over sin, to demonstrate the power of divine might by endowing the human agent with supernatural strength and instructing the ignorant in the mysteries of the kingdom of God. Of what avail would it be to us that the only begotten Son of God humbled Himself, endured the temptations of the wily foe, and died, the just for the unjust, if the Spirit had not been given as a constant, working, regenerating agent, to make effectual in each individual case what has been wrought out by the world's Redeemer?

The Holy Spirit enabled the disciples to exalt the Lord alone, and guided the pens of the sacred historians, that the record of the words and works of Christ might be given to the world. To-day this Spirit is constantly at work, seeking to draw the attention of men to the great sacrifice made upon the cross of Calvary, to unfold to the world the love of God to man, and to open to the convicted soul the promises of the Scriptures.

It is the Spirit that causes to shine into darkened minds the bright beams of the Sun of Righteousness; that makes men's hearts burn within them with an awakened realization of the truths of eternity; that presents before the mind the great standard of righteousness, and convinces of sin; that inspires faith in Him who alone can save from sin; that works to transform character by withdrawing the affections of men from those things which are temporal and perishable, and fixing them upon the eternal inheritance. The Spirit recreates, refines, and sanctifies human beings, fitting them to become members of the royal family, children of the heavenly King.

EFFECT OF RECEIVING THE SPIRIT

When one is fully emptied of self, when every false god is cast out of the soul, the vacuum is filled by the inflowing of the Spirit of Christ. Such a one has the faith that purifies the soul from defilement. He is conformed to the Spirit, and he minds the things of the Spirit. He has no confidence in self. Christ is all and in all. He receives with meekness the truth that is constantly being unfolded, and gives the Lord all the glory, saying, "God hath revealed them unto us by His Spirit." "Now we have received, not the spirit of the world, but the spirit which is of God; that we might know the things that are freely given to us of God." [4]

The Spirit that reveals, also works in him the fruits of righteousness. Christ is in him, "a well of water springing up into everlasting life." [5] He is a branch of the True Vine, and bears rich clusters of fruit to the glory of God. What is the character of the fruit borne? — The fruit of the Spirit is "love," not hatred; "joy," not discontent and mourning; "peace," not irritation, anxiety, and manufactured trials. It is "long-suffering, gentleness, goodness, faith, meekness, temperance." [6]

[4] 1 Cor. 2 : 10, 12.   [5] John 4 : 14.   [6] Gal. 5 : 22, 23.

Those who have this Spirit are earnest workers together with God; the heavenly intelligences co-operate with them, and they go weighted with the spirit of the message that they bear. They speak words of solid sense, and from the treasury of the heart bring forth pure, sacred things, after the example of Christ.

The message that we have to bear is not one that we need cringe to declare. Its advocates are not to seek to cover it, to conceal its origin and purpose. As those who have made solemn vows to God, and who have been commissioned as the messengers of Christ, as stewards of the mysteries of grace, we are under obligation to declare faithfully the whole counsel of God.

We are not to make less prominent the special truths that have separated us from the world, and made us what we are; for they are fraught with eternal interests. God has given us light in regard to the things that are now taking place, and with pen and voice we are to proclaim the truth to the world. But it is the life of Christ in the soul, it is the active principle of love imparted by the Holy Spirit, that alone will make our words fruitful. The love of Christ is the force and power of every message for God that ever fell from human lips.

NEARING THE END

Day after day is passing into eternity, bringing us nearer to the close of probation. As never before we must pray for the Holy Spirit to be more abundantly bestowed upon us, and we must look for its sanctifying influence to come upon the workers, that those for whom they labor may know that they have been with Jesus and have learned of Him.

We need spiritual eyesight, that we may see the designs of the enemy, and as faithful watchmen proclaim the danger. We need power from above, that we may understand, as far as the human mind can, the great themes of Christianity and their far-reaching principles.

Those who are under the influence of the Spirit of God will not be fanatical, but calm and steadfast, free from extravagance in thought, word, or deed. Amid the confusion of delusive doctrines, the Spirit of God will be a guide and a shield to those who have not resisted the evidences of truth, silencing every other voice but that which comes from Him who is the truth.

We are living in the last days, when error of a most deceptive character is accepted and believed, while truth is discarded. The Lord will hold both ministers and people responsible for the light shining upon them. He calls upon us to work diligently in gathering up the jewels of truth, and placing them in the framework of the gospel. In all their divine beauty they are to shine forth in the moral darkness of the world. This cannot be accomplished without the aid of the Holy Spirit, but with this aid we can do all things. When we are endowed with the Spirit, we take hold by faith of infinite power. There is nothing lost of that which comes from God. The Saviour of the world sends His messages to the soul, that the darkness of error may be dispelled. The work of the Spirit is immeasurably great. It is from this source that power and efficiency come to the worker for God.

10

DEVELOPMENT AND SERVICE

Christian life is more than many take it to be. It does not consist wholly in gentleness, patience, meekness, and kindliness. These graces are essential; but there is need also of courage, force, energy, and perseverance. The path that Christ marks out is a narrow, self-denying path. To enter that path and press on through difficulties and discouragements, requires men who are more than weaklings.

Men of stamina are wanted, men who will not wait to have their way smoothed and every obstacle removed; men who will inspire with fresh zeal the flagging efforts of dispirited workers; men whose hearts are warm with Christian love, and whose hands are strong to do their Master's work.

Some who engage in missionary service are weak, nerveless, spiritless, easily discouraged. They lack push. They have not those positive traits of character that give power to do something,— the spirit and energy that kindle enthusiasm. Those who would win success must be courageous and hopeful. They should cultivate not only the passive but the active virtues. While they are to give the soft answer that turns away wrath, they must possess the courage of a hero to resist evil. With the charity that endures all things, they need the force of character that will make their influence a positive power.

Some have no firmness of character. Their plans and purposes have no definite form and consistency. They are of but little practical use in the world. This weakness, indecision, and inefficiency should be overcome. There is in true Christian character an indomitableness that cannot be moulded or subdued by adverse circumstances. We must have moral backbone, an integrity that cannot be flattered, bribed, or terrified.

God desires us to make use of every opportunity for securing a preparation for His work. He expects us to put all our energies into its performance, and to keep our hearts alive to its sacredness and its fearful responsibilities.

Many who are qualified to do excellent work accomplish little because they attempt little. Thousands pass through life as if they had no great object for which to live, no high standard to reach. One reason of this is the low estimate which they place upon themselves. Christ paid an infinite price for us, and according to the price paid He desires us to value ourselves.

Be not satisfied with reaching a low standard. We are not what we might be, or what it is God's will that we should be. God has given us reasoning powers, not to remain inactive, or to be perverted to earthly and sordid pursuits, but that they may be developed to the utmost, refined, sanctified, ennobled, and used in advancing the interests of His kingdom. . . .

Remember that in whatever position you may serve, you are revealing motive, developing character. Whatever your work, do it with exactness, with diligence; overcome the inclination to seek an easy task.

The same spirit and principles that one brings into the daily labor will be brought into the whole life. Those who desire a fixed amount to do and a fixed salary, and who wish to prove an exact fit without the trouble of adaptation or training, are not the ones whom God calls to work in His cause. Those who study how to give as little as possible of their physical, mental, and moral power, are not the workers upon whom He can pour out abundant blessings. Their example is contagious. Self-interest is the ruling motive. Those who need to be watched and who work only as every duty is specified to them, are not the ones who will be pronounced good and faithful. Workers are needed who manifest energy, integrity, diligence; those who are willing to do anything that needs to be done.

Many become inefficient by evading responsibilities for fear of failure. Thus they fail of gaining that education which results from experience, and which reading and study and all the advantages otherwise gained, cannot give them.

Man can shape circumstances, but circumstances should not be allowed to shape the man. We should seize upon circumstances as instruments with which to work. We are to master them, but should not permit them to master us.

Men of power are often those who have been opposed, baffled, and thwarted. By calling their energies into action, the obstacles they meet prove to them positive blessings. They gain self-reliance. Conflict and perplexity call for the exercise of trust in God, and for that firmness which develops power.

Christ gave no stinted service. He did not measure His work by hours. His time, His heart, His soul and strength, were given to labor for the benefit of humanity. Through weary days He toiled, and through long nights He bent in prayer for grace and endurance that He might do a larger work. With strong crying and tears He sent His petitions to heaven, that His human nature might be strengthened, that He might be braced to meet the wily foe in all his deceptive workings, and fortified to fulfil His mission of uplifting humanity. To His workers He says, "I have given you an example, that ye should do as I have done." [1]

"The love of Christ," said Paul, "constraineth us." [2] This was the actuating principle of his conduct; it was his motive-power. If ever his ardor in the path of duty flagged for a moment, one glance at the cross caused him to gird up anew the loins of his mind, and press forward in the way of self-denial. In his labors for his brethren he relied much upon the manifestation of infinite love in the sacrifice of Christ, with its subduing, constraining power.

How earnest, how touching his appeal: "Ye know the grace of our Lord Jesus Christ, that, though He was rich, yet for your sakes He became poor, that ye through His poverty might be rich." [3] You know the height from which He stooped, the depth of humiliation to which He descended. His feet entered upon the path of sacrifice, and turned not aside until He had given His life. There was no rest for Him between the throne in heaven and the cross. His love for man led Him to welcome every indignity, and suffer every abuse.

Paul admonishes us to "look not every man on his own things, but every man also on the things of others." He bids us possess the mind "which was

---

[1] John 13 : 15.   [2] 2 Cor. 5 : 14.   [3] 2 Cor. 8 : 9.

also in Christ Jesus: who, being in the form of God, thought it not robbery to be equal with God: but made Himself of no reputation, and took upon Him the form of a servant, and was made in the likeness of men: and being found in fashion as a man, He humbled Himself, and became obedient unto death, even the death of the cross." [4] . . .

Every one who accepts Christ as his personal Saviour will long for the privilege of serving God. Contemplating what Heaven has done for him, his heart is moved with boundless love and adoring gratitude. He is eager to signalize his gratitude by devoting his abilities to God's service. He longs to show his love for Christ and for his purchased possession. He covets toil, hardship, sacrifice.

The true worker for God will do his best, because in so doing he can glorify his Master. He will do right in order to regard the requirements of God. He will endeavor to improve all his faculties. He will perform every duty as unto God. His one desire will be that Christ may receive homage and perfect service.

There is a picture representing a bullock standing between a plow and an altar, with the inscription "Ready for either"—ready to toil in the furrow, or to be offered on the altar of sacrifice. This is the position of the true child of God — willing to go where duty calls, to deny self, to sacrifice for the Redeemer's cause.—*"Ministry of Healing," pages 497-502.*

[4] Phil. 2:4-8.

FOR FURTHER STUDY

BIBLE STUDY

Test. Vol. II, pp. 498-506, 556.
Test. Vol. IV, pp. 498, 499, 526.
Test. Vol. V, p. 575.
Ed., pp. 123-192.
C. O. L., pp. 111-114, 124-134.

SECRET PRAYER

Desire, pp. 139-141, 362, 363.
C. O. L., pp. 139-180.
Acts, p. 564.

FAITH

Test. Vol. I, pp. 120, 121.
Test. Vol. II, pp. 510-516.
Test. Vol. III, pp. 273-293.
Test. Vol. IV, pp. 443-445.
Ed., pp. 105, 106, 118, 119, 150, 151, 253-261.
Desire, pp. 124-131, 426-431.
M. of H., pp. 59-72, 196, 198-200, 481.
C. O. L., pp. 62-69, 145-149.

COURAGE

Test. Vol. II, pp. 150-152.
M. of H., p. 196.
Acts, pp. 169, 170, 233-242, 393-395, 428-433.

HOW GOD TRAINS HIS WORKERS

M. of H., pp. 469-482.
Acts, pp. 17-24.
Counsels, pp. 406-410.

TAKE TIME TO TALK WITH GOD

Test. Vol. I, p. 434.
Desire, pp. 359-363.
M. of H., pp. 508-511.

OUR GREATEST NEED

M. of H., pp. 503-516.
Acts, pp. 539-556.

SELF-EXAMINATION

Test. Vol. II, pp. 517, 518, 552.
Test. Vol. IV, p. 371.
Test. Vol. V, p. 574.
C. O. L., pp. 158-163.
Acts, pp. 118-120.
Counsels, p. 419.

SELF-IMPROVEMENT

Test. Vol. II, pp. 498-522.
Test. Vol. IV, pp. 270, 443.
Test. Vol. V, pp. 265, 266.
Ed., pp. 262-271.
C. O. L., pp. 278-283, 325-365.
Acts, pp. 346-358.
Counsels, pp. 37, 38, 66, 67, 510.

Dangers

> "If thou put the brethren in remembrance of these things, thou shalt be a good minister of Jesus Christ."

THE DANGER OF REJECTING LIGHT

God intends that, even in this life, truth shall be ever unfolding to His people. There is only one way in which this knowledge can be obtained. We can attain to an understanding of God's word only through the illumination of that Spirit by which the Word was given. "The things of God knoweth no man, but the Spirit of God;" "for the Spirit searcheth all things, yea, the deep things of God." [1] And the Saviour's promise to His followers was, "When He, the Spirit of truth, is come, He will guide you into all truth. . . . For He shall receive of Mine, and shall show it unto you." [2] . . .

Peter exhorts his brethren to "grow in grace, and in the knowledge of our Lord and Saviour Jesus Christ." [3] Whenever the people of God are growing in grace, they will be constantly obtaining a clearer understanding of His word. They will discern new light and beauty in its sacred truths. This has been true in the history of the church in all ages, and thus it will continue to the end. But as real spiritual life declines, it has ever been the tendency to cease to advance in the knowledge of the truth. Men rest

[1] 1 Cor. 2:11, 10.   [2] John 16:13, 14.   [3] 2 Peter 3:18.

satisfied with the light already received from God's word, and discourage any further investigation of the Scriptures. They become conservative, and seek to avoid discussion.

The fact that there is no controversy or agitation among God's people, should not be regarded as conclusive evidence that they are holding fast to sound doctrine. There is reason to fear that they may not be clearly discriminating between truth and error. When no new questions are started by investigation of the Scriptures, when no difference of opinion arises which will set men to searching the Bible for themselves, to make sure that they have the truth, there will be many now, as in ancient times, who will hold to tradition, and worship they know not what.

I have been shown that many who profess to have a knowledge of present truth, know not what they believe. They do not understand the evidences of their faith. They have no just appreciation of the work for the present time. When the time of trial shall come, there are men now preaching to others, who will find, upon examining the positions they hold, that there are many things for which they can give no satisfactory reason. Until thus tested, they knew not their great ignorance.

And there are many in the church who take it for granted that they understand what they believe, but, until controversy arises, they do not know their own weakness. When separated from those of like faith, and compelled to stand singly and alone to explain their belief, they will be surprised to see how confused are their ideas of what they had accepted as truth. Certain it is that there has been among us a departure from the living God, and a turning to men, putting human wisdom in place of divine.

God will arouse His people; if other means fail, heresies will come in among them, which will sift them, separating the chaff from the wheat. The Lord calls upon all who believe His word to awake out of sleep. Precious light has come, appropriate for this time. It is Bible truth, showing the perils that are right upon us. This light should lead us to a diligent study of the Scriptures, and a most critical examination of the positions which we hold.

God would have all the bearings and positions of truth thoroughly and perseveringly searched, with prayer and fasting. Believers are not to rest in suppositions and ill-defined ideas of what constitutes truth. Their faith must be firmly founded upon the word of God, so that when the testing time shall come, and they are brought before councils to answer for their faith, they may be able to give a reason for the hope that is in them, with meekness and fear.

Agitate, agitate, agitate! The subjects which we present to the world must be to us a living reality. It is important that in defending the doctrines which we consider fundamental articles of faith, we should never allow ourselves to employ arguments that are not wholly sound. These may avail to silence an opposer, but they do not honor the truth. We should present sound arguments, that will not only silence our opponents, but will bear the closest and most searching scrutiny.

With those who have educated themselves as debaters, there is great danger that they will not handle the word of God with fairness. In meeting an opponent, it should be our earnest effort to present subjects in such a manner as to awaken conviction in his mind, instead of seeking merely to give confidence to the believer.

Whatever may be man's intellectual advancement, let him not for a moment think that there is no need of thorough and continuous searching of the Scriptures for greater light. As a people, we are called individually to be students of prophecy. We must watch with earnestness that we may discern any ray of light which God shall present to us. We are to catch the first gleamings of truth; and through prayerful study, clearer light may be obtained, which can be brought before others.

When God's people are at ease, and satisfied with their present enlightenment, we may be sure that He will not favor them. It is His will that they should be ever moving forward, to receive the increased and ever-increasing light which is shining for them.

The present attitude of the church is not pleasing to God. There has come in a self-confidence that has led them to feel no necessity for more truth and greater light. We are living at a time when Satan is at work on the right hand and on the left, before and behind us; and yet as a people we are asleep. God wills that a voice shall be heard arousing His people to action. —*"Testimonies for the Church," Vol. V, pages 703-709.*

THE TEST OF NEW LIGHT

Our brethren should be willing to investigate in a candid way every point of controversy. If a brother is teaching error, those who are in responsible positions ought to know it; and if he is teaching truth, they ought to take their stand at his side. We should all know what is being taught among us; for if it is truth, we need it. We are all under obligation to God to know what He sends us. He has given directions by which we may test every doctrine,—"To the law and to the testimony: if they speak not according to this word, it is because there is no light in them." [4] If the light presented meets this test, we are not to refuse to accept it because it does not agree with our ideas.

No one has said that we shall find perfection in any man's investigations; but this I do know, that our churches are dying for the want of teaching on the subject of righteousness by faith in Christ, and on kindred truths.

No matter by whom light is sent, we should open our hearts to receive it with the meekness of Christ. But many do not do this. When a controverted point is presented, they pour in question after question, without admitting a point when it is well sustained. O, may we act as men who want light! May God give us His Holy Spirit day by day, and let the light of His countenance shine upon us, that we may be learners in the school of Christ.

When a doctrine is presented that does not meet our minds, we should go to the word of God, seek the Lord in prayer, and give no place for the enemy to come in with suspicion and prejudice. We should never permit the spirit to be manifested that arraigned the priests and rulers against the Redeemer of the world. They complained that He disturbed the peo-

[4] Isa. 8 : 20.

ple, and they wished He would let them alone; for He caused perplexity and dissension. The Lord sends light to us to prove what manner of spirit we are of. We are not to deceive ourselves.

In 1844, when anything came to our attention that we did not understand, we kneeled down and asked God to help us take the right position; and then we were able to come to a right understanding and see eye to eye. There was no dissension, no enmity, no evil-surmising, no misjudging of our brethren. If we but knew the evil of the spirit of intolerance, how carefully would we shun it!

We are to be established in the faith, in the light of the truth given us in our early experience. At that time one error after another pressed in upon us; ministers and doctors brought in new doctrines. We would search the Scriptures with much prayer, and the Holy Spirit would bring the truth to our minds. Sometimes whole nights would be devoted to searching the Scriptures, and earnestly asking God for guidance. Companies of devoted men and women assembled for this purpose. The power of God would come upon me, and I was enabled clearly to define what is truth and what is error.

As the points of our faith were thus established, our feet were placed upon a solid foundation. We accepted the truth point by point, under the demonstration of the Holy Spirit. I would be taken off in vision, and explanations would be given me. I was given illustrations of heavenly things, and of the sanctuary, so that we were placed where light was shining on us in clear, distinct rays.

I know that the sanctuary question stands in righteousness and truth, just as we have held it for so many years. It is the enemy that leads minds off on side-tracks. He is pleased when those who know the truth become engrossed in collecting scriptures to pile around erroneous theories, which have no foundation in truth. The scriptures thus used are misapplied; they were not given to substantiate error, but to strengthen truth.

We must learn that others have rights as well as we ourselves. When a brother receives new light upon the Scriptures, he should frankly explain his position, and every minister should search the Scriptures with the spirit of candor, to see if the points presented can be substantiated by the Inspired Word. "The servant of the Lord must not strive; but be gentle unto all men, apt to teach, patient, in meekness instructing those that oppose themselves; if God peradventure will give them repentance to the acknowledging of the truth." [5]

Every soul must look to God with contrition and humility, that He may guide and lead and bless. We must not trust to others to search the Scriptures for us. Some of our leading brethren have frequently taken their position on the wrong side; and if God would send a message and wait for these older brethren to open the way for its advancement, it would never reach the people. These brethren will be found in this position until they become partakers of the divine nature to a greater extent than ever they have been in the past.

[5] 2 Tim. 2 : 24, 25.

There is sadness in heaven over the spiritual blindness of many of our brethren. Our younger ministers, who fill less important positions, must make decided efforts to come to the light, to sink the shaft deeper and still deeper in the mine of truth.

The rebuke of the Lord will rest upon those who would bar the way, that clearer light shall not come to the people. A great work is to be done, and God sees that our leading men have need of more light, that they may unite with the messengers whom He sends to accomplish the work that He designs shall be done. The Lord has raised up messengers, and endued them with His Spirit, and has said, "Cry aloud, spare not, lift up thy voice like a trumpet, and show My people their transgression, and the house of Jacob their sins." [6] Let no one run the risk of interposing between the people and the message of Heaven. This message will go to the people; and if there were no voice among men to give it, the very stones would cry out.

I call upon every minister to seek the Lord, to put away pride and strife for supremacy, and to humble the heart before God. It is the coldness of heart, the unbelief of those who ought to have faith, that keeps the churches in feebleness.

[6] Isa. 58 : 1.

A WARNING AGAINST FALSE TEACHING

At this time we need in the cause of God spiritual-minded men, men who are firm in principle, and who have a clear understanding of the truth. I have been instructed that it is not new and fanciful doctrines nor human suppositions which the people need, but the testimony of men who know and practice the truth, men who understand and obey the charge given to Timothy: "Preach the word; be instant in season, out of season; reprove, rebuke, exhort with all long-suffering and doctrine." [1]

My brethren, walk firmly, decidedly, your feet shod with the preparation of the gospel of peace. You may be sure that pure and undefiled religion is not a sensational religion. God has not laid upon any one the burden of encouraging an appetite for speculative doctrines and theories. Keep these things out of your teaching. Do not allow them to enter into your experience. Let not your life-work be marred by them.

A warning against false teaching is found in Paul's letter to the Colossians. The apostle declares that the hearts of the believers are to be "knit together in love, and unto all riches of the full assurance of understanding, to the acknowledgment of the mystery of God, and of the Father, and of Christ; in whom are hid all the treasures of wisdom and knowledge.

"And this I say," he continues, "lest any man should beguile you with enticing words. . . . As ye have therefore received Christ Jesus the Lord, so walk

1 2 Tim. 4:2.

ye in Him: rooted and built up in Him, and stablished
in the faith, as ye have been taught, abounding therein
with thanksgiving. Beware lest any man spoil you
through philosophy and vain deceit, after the tradition of men, after the rudiments of the world, and not
after Christ. For in Him dwelleth all the fulness of
the Godhead bodily. And ye are complete in Him,
which is the head of all principality and power." [2]

I am instructed to say to our people, Let us follow
Christ. Do not forget that He is to be our pattern
in all things. We may safely discard those ideas that
are not found in His teaching. I appeal to our ministers to be sure that their feet are planted on the
platform of eternal truth. Beware how you follow
impulse, calling it the Holy Spirit. Some are in danger of doing this. The word of God urges us to be
sound in the faith, able to give to every one who asks,
a reason of the hope that is in us.

DIVERTING MINDS FROM PRESENT DUTY

The enemy is seeking to divert the minds of our
brethren and sisters from the work of preparing a
people to stand in these last days. His sophistries
are designed to lead minds away from the perils and
duties of the hour. They estimate as of little value
the light that Christ came from heaven to give to
John for His people. They teach that the scenes just
before us are not of sufficient importance to receive
special attention. They make of no effect the truth
of heavenly origin, and rob the people of God of their
past experience, giving them instead a false science.
"Thus saith the Lord: Stand ye in the ways, and

[2] Col. 2: 2-10.

see, and ask for the old paths, where is the good way, and walk therein." [3]

Let none seek to tear away the foundations of our faith,— the foundations that were laid at the beginning of our work, by prayerful study of the Word and by revelation. Upon these foundations we have been building for more than fifty years. Men may suppose that they have found a new way, that they can lay a stronger foundation than that which has been laid; but this is a great deception. "Other foundation can no man lay than that is laid." [4] In the past, many have undertaken to build a new faith, to establish new principles; but how long did their building stand? It soon fell; for it was not founded upon the Rock.

Did not the first disciples have to meet the sayings of men? did they not have to listen to false theories; and then, having done all, to stand firm, saying, "Other foundation can no man lay than that is laid"? So we are to hold the beginning of our confidence steadfast unto the end.

Words of power have been sent by God and by Christ to this people, bringing them out from the world, point by point, into the clear light of present truth. With lips touched by holy fire, God's servants have proclaimed the message. The divine utterance has set its seal to the genuineness of the truth proclaimed.

A RENEWAL OF THE STRAIGHT TESTIMONY

The Lord calls for a renewal of the straight testimony borne in years past. He calls for a renewal of spiritual life. The spiritual energies of His people

[3] Jer. 6 : 16.   [4] 1 Cor. 3 : 11.

have long been torpid, but there is to be a resurrection from apparent death. By prayer and confession of sin we must clear the King's highway. As we do this, the power of the Spirit will come to us. We need the pentecostal energy. This will come; for the Lord has promised to send His Spirit as the all-conquering power.

Perilous times are before us. Every one who has a knowledge of the truth should awake, and place himself, body, soul, and spirit, under the discipline of God. The enemy is on our track. We must be wide awake, on our guard against him. We must put on the whole armor of God. We must follow the directions given through the Spirit of prophecy. We must love and obey the truth for this time. This will save us from accepting strong delusions. God has spoken to us through His word. He has spoken to us through the testimonies to the church, and through the books that have helped to make plain our present duty and the position we should now occupy. The warnings that have been given, line upon line, precept upon precept, should be heeded. If we disregard them, what excuse can we offer?

I beseech those who are laboring for God not to accept the spurious for the genuine. Let not human reasoning be placed where sanctifying truth should be. Christ is waiting to kindle faith and love in the hearts of His people. Let not erroneous theories receive countenance from the people who ought to be standing firm on the platform of eternal truth. God calls upon us to hold firmly to the fundamental principles that are based upon unquestionable authority.

THE WORD OF GOD OUR SAFEGUARD

Our watchword is to be, "To the law and to the testimony: if they speak not according to this word, it is because there is no light in them." [5] We have a Bible full of the most precious truth. It contains the alpha and the omega of knowledge. The Scriptures, given by inspiration of God, are "profitable for doctrine, for reproof, for correction, for instruction in righteousness: that the man of God may be perfect, thoroughly furnished unto all good works." [6] Take the Bible as your study-book. All can understand its instruction.

Christ calls upon His people to believe and practice His word. Those who receive and assimilate this word, making it a part of every action, of every attribute of character, will grow strong in the strength of God. It will be seen that their faith is of heavenly origin. They will not wander into strange paths. Their minds will not turn to a religion of sentimentalism and excitement. Before angels and before men, they will stand as those who have strong, consistent Christian characters.

In the golden censer of truth, as presented in Christ's teachings, we have that which will convict and convert souls. Proclaim, in the simplicity of Christ, the truths that He came to this world to proclaim, and the power of your message will make itself felt. Do not advocate theories or tests that Christ has never mentioned, and that have no foundation in the Bible. We have grand, solemn truths for the people. "It is written" is the test that must be brought home to every soul.

[5] Isa. 8 : 20.   [6] 2 Tim. 3 : 16, 17.

Let us go to the word of God for guidance. Let us seek for a "Thus saith the Lord." We have had enough of human methods. A mind trained only in worldly science will fail to understand the things of God; but the same mind, converted and sanctified, will see the divine power in the Word. Only the mind and heart cleansed by the sanctification of the Spirit can discern heavenly things.

Brethren, in the name of the Lord I call upon you to awake to your duty. Let your hearts be yielded to the power of the Holy Spirit, and they will be made susceptible to the teachings of the Word. Then you will be able to discern the deep things of God.

May God bring His people under the deep movings of His Spirit! May He arouse them to see their peril, and to prepare for what is coming upon the earth!

————◆————

We must not for a moment think that there is no more light, no more truth, to be given us. We are in danger of becoming careless, by our indifference losing the sanctifying power of truth, and composing ourselves with the thought, "I am rich, and increased with goods, and have need of nothing." [7] While we must hold fast to the truths which we have already received, we must not look with suspicion upon any new light that God may send.

[7] Rev. 3 : 17.

SOUND DOCTRINE

"The time will come," Paul wrote to Timothy, "when they will not endure sound doctrine; but after their own lusts shall they heap to themselves teachers, having itching ears; and they shall turn away their ears from the truth, and shall be turned unto fables. But watch thou in all things, endure afflictions, do the work of an evangelist, make full proof of thy ministry." [1]

"Sound doctrine" is Bible truth — truth that will promote piety and devotion, confirming God's people in the faith. Sound doctrine means much to the receiver; and it means much, too, to the teacher, the minister of righteousness; for wherever the gospel is preached, every laborer, whatever his line of service, is either true or untrue to his responsibility as the Lord's messenger.

Paul wrote again, "It is a faithful saying: For if we be dead with Him, we shall also live with Him: if we suffer, we shall also reign with Him: if we deny Him, He also will deny us: if we believe not, yet He abideth faithful: He cannot deny Himself. Of these things put them in remembrance, charging them before the Lord that they strive not about words to no profit, but to the subverting of the hearers." [2]

Some who in Paul's day listened to the truth, raised questions of no vital importance, presenting the ideas and opinions of men, and seeking to divert the mind of the teacher from the great truths of the gospel, to the discussion of non-essential theories and

[1] 2 Tim. 4 : 3-5.   [2] 2 Tim. 2 : 11-14.

the settlement of unimportant disputes. Paul knew that the laborer for God must be wise enough to see the design of the enemy, and refuse to be misled or diverted. The conversion of souls must be the burden of his work; he must preach the word of God, but avoid controversy.

"Study to show thyself approved unto God," he wrote, "a workman that needeth not to be ashamed, rightly dividing the Word of truth. But shun profane and vain babblings: for they will increase unto more ungodliness." [3]

The ministers of Christ to-day are in the same danger. Satan is constantly at work to divert the mind into wrong channels, so that the truth may lose its force upon the heart. And unless ministers and people practice the truth and are sanctified by it, they will allow speculation regarding questions of no vital importance to occupy the mind. This will lead to caviling and strife; for countless points of difference will arise.

Men of ability have devoted a lifetime of study and prayer to the searching of the Scriptures, and yet there are many portions of the Bible that have not been fully explored. Some passages of Scripture will never be perfectly comprehended until in the future life Christ shall explain them. There are mysteries to be unraveled, statements that human minds cannot harmonize. And the enemy will seek to arouse argument upon these points, which might better remain undiscussed.

A devoted, spiritual worker will avoid bringing up minor theoretical differences, and will devote his energies to the proclamation of the great testing truths

[3] 2 Tim. 2: 15, 16.

to be given to the world. He will point the people to the work of redemption, the commandments of God, the near coming of Christ; and it will be found that in these subjects there is food enough for thought.

In time past there have been presented to me for my opinion many non-essential, fanciful theories. Some have advocated the theory that believers should pray with their eyes open. Others teach that, because those who ministered anciently in sacred office were required, upon entering the sanctuary, to remove their sandals and wash their feet, believers now should remove their shoes when entering the house of worship. Still others refer to the sixth commandment, and declare that even the insects that torment human beings should not be killed. And some have put forth the theory that the redeemed will not have gray hair — as if this were a matter of any importance.

I am instructed to say that these theories are the production of minds unlearned in the first principles of the gospel. By such theories the enemy strives to eclipse the great truths for this time.

Those who in their preaching pass by the great truths of God's word to speak of minor matters, are not preaching the gospel, but are dealing in idle sophistry. Let not our ministers spend time in the discussion of such matters. Let those who have any question as to what they should teach, any question as to the subjects upon which they should dwell, go to the discourses of the great Teacher, and follow His lines of thought. The subjects that Jesus regarded as essential are the subjects that we are to urge home to-day. We are to encourage our hearers to dwell upon those subjects which are of eternal moment.

When at one time a brother came to me with the message that the world is flat, I was instructed to present the commission that Christ gave His disciples, "Go ye therefore, and teach all nations: . . . and, lo, I am with you alway, even unto the end." [4] In regard to such subjects as the flat-world theory, God says to every soul, "What is that to thee? follow thou Me. I have given you your commission. Dwell upon the great testing truths for this time, not upon matters that have no bearing upon our work."

Workers for God should not spend time speculating as to what conditions will prevail in the new earth. It is presumption to indulge in suppositions and theories regarding matters that the Lord has not revealed. He has made every provision for our happiness in the future life, and we are not to speculate regarding His plans for us. Neither are we to measure the conditions of the future life by the conditions of this life.

To my ministering brethren I would say, Preach the word. Do not bring to the foundation wood, hay, and stubble,— your own surmisings and speculations, which can benefit no one. Subjects of vital importance are revealed in the word of God, and these are worthy of our deepest thought. But we are not to search into matters on which God has been silent.

When questions arise upon which we are uncertain, let us ask, What saith the Scripture? And if the Scripture is silent upon the question at issue, let it not be made the subject of discussion. Let those who wish for something new, seek for that newness of life resulting from the new birth. Let them purify their souls by obeying the truth, and act in harmony with the instruction that Christ has given.

The only question asked in the judgment will be, "Have they been obedient to My commandments?" Petty strife and contention over questions of no importance has no part in God's great plan. Those who teach the truth should be men of solid minds, who will not lead their hearers into a field of thistles, as it were, and leave them there.

The sacrifice of Christ as an atonement for sin is the great truth around which all other truths cluster. In order to be rightly understood and appreciated, every truth in the word of God, from Genesis to Revelation, must be studied in the light that streams from the cross of Calvary. I present before you the great, grand monument of mercy and regeneration, salvation and redemption,— the Son of God uplifted on the cross. This is to be the foundation of every discourse given by our ministers.

———◆———

Men are needed for this time who can understand the wants of the people, and minister to their necessities. The faithful minister of Christ watches at every outpost, to warn, to reprove, to counsel, to entreat, and to encourage his fellow-men, laboring with the Spirit of God, which worketh in him mightily, that he may present every man perfect in Christ. Such a man is acknowledged in heaven as a minister, treading in the footsteps of his great Exemplar.— *"Testimonies for the Church," Vol. IV, page 416.*

FANATICISM

As the end draws near, the enemy will work with all his power to bring in fanaticism among us. He would rejoice to see Seventh-day Adventists going to such extremes that they would be branded by the world as a body of fanatics. Against this danger I am bidden to warn ministers and lay members. Our work is to teach men and women to build on a true foundation, to plant their feet on a plain "Thus saith the Lord."

In 1844 we had to meet fanaticism on every hand, but always the word came to me: "A great wave of excitement is an injury to the work. Keep your feet in the footprints of Christ." Under great excitement, strange work is done. There are those who improve this opportunity to bring in strange and fanciful doctrines. Thus the door is closed to the proclamation of sound doctrine.

Those who do the work of the Lord in the cities must close and bolt the doors against excitement and fanaticism. Ministers are not to issue notices of meetings so worded as to create an alarm. When the Lord is ready for the advanced denunciation of wicked cities, He will let His people know. But this will be after these cities have had an opportunity to hear and receive the word that is unto life eternal.

Our work now is to enlighten minds in regard to the truths of the Scriptures. Doors are open for the entrance of truth, and we are to avail ourselves of every opportunity to reach souls. We are to explain the truth, as did Christ, in many ways, by figures and parables; but we are to discourage anything of a fanatical nature.

The people must be taught to search the word of God for themselves. Pastors and teachers must point them to the strong fortress, into which the righteous may run and be safe. Those who are handling the great, grand, ennobling truths of the Word, must ever reveal a spirit deep, earnest, fervent, but calm and full of sound sense that the mouths of gainsayers may be stopped.

Those who are close students of the Word, following Christ in humility of soul, will not go to extremes. The Saviour never went to extremes, never lost self-control, never violated the laws of good taste. He knew when to speak and when to keep silent. He was always self-possessed. He never erred in His judgment of men or of truth. He was never deceived by appearances. He never raised a question that was not clearly appropriate, never gave an answer that was not right to the point. He silenced the voice of the caviling priests by penetrating beneath the surface and reaching the heart, flashing light into the mind and awakening the conscience.

Those who follow the example of Christ will not be extremists. They will cultivate calmness and self-possession. The peace that was seen in the life of Christ will be seen in their lives.

SELF-CONFIDENCE

Young men who have had only a few years of imperfect experience in the cause of present truth . . . should manifest a delicacy in taking positions contrary to the judgment and opinions of those whose lives have been interwoven with the cause of God and who have had an active part in this work for many years. God does not select to lead out in His sacred, important work, men of immature judgment and great self-confidence. Those who have not passed through the sufferings, trials, opposition, and privations that have been endured to bring the work to its present condition of prosperity, should cultivate modesty and humility. They should be careful how they become exalted, lest they be overthrown. They will be accountable for the clear light of truth which shines upon them.

I saw that God is displeased with the disposition that some have to murmur against those who have fought the heaviest battles for them, and who endured so much in the beginning of the message, when the work went hard. The experienced laborers,— those who toiled under the weight and the oppressive burdens when there were but few to help bear them,— God regards; and He has a jealous care for those who have proved faithful. He is displeased with those who are ready to find fault with and reproach the servants of God who have grown gray in building up the cause of present truth. Your reproaches and murmurings, young men, will surely stand against you in the day of God.

HUMILITY IN YOUNG MINISTERS

As long as God has not laid heavy responsibilities upon you, do not get out of your place, and rely upon your own independent judgment, and assume responsibilities for which you are not fitted. You need to cultivate watchfulness and humility, and to be diligent in prayer. The nearer you live to God, the more clearly will you discern your weaknesses and dangers. A practical view of the law of God, and clear discernment of the atonement of Christ, will give you a knowledge of yourselves, and will show you wherein you fail to perfect Christian character. . . .

In a degree you overlook the necessity of having a divine influence constantly with you. This is positively necessary in doing the work of God. If you neglect this, and pass on in self-confidence and self-sufficiency, you will be left to make very great blunders. You need constantly to cherish lowliness of mind and a spirit of dependence. He who feels his own weakness will look higher than himself, and will feel the need of constant strength from above. The grace of God will lead him to cherish a spirit of constant gratitude. He who is best acquainted with his own weakness will know that it is the matchless grace of God alone that triumphs over the rebellion of the heart.

You need to become acquainted with the weak as well as the strong points in your characters, that you may be constantly guarded lest you engage in enterprises and assume responsibilities for which God has never designed you. You should not compare your actions and measure your lives by any human standard, but with the rule of duty revealed in the Bible. . . .

You are too dependent upon your surroundings. If you have a large congregation, you are elated, and you desire to address them. But sometimes your congregations diminish, your spirits sink, and you have but little courage to labor. Surely, something is wanting. Your hold upon God is not firm enough. . . .

Christ sought for men wherever He could find them,— in the public streets, in private houses, in the synagogues, by the seaside. He toiled all day, preaching to the multitude, and healing the sick that were brought to Him; and frequently, after He had dismissed the people that they might return to their homes to rest and sleep, He spent the entire night in prayer, to come forth and renew His labors in the morning. . . .

You need to bring your soul into close communion with God by earnest prayer mixed with living faith. Every prayer offered in faith lifts the suppliant above discouraging doubts and human passions. Prayer gives strength to renew the conflict with the powers of darkness, to bear trials patiently, and to endure hardness as good soldiers of Christ.

While you take counsel with your doubts and fears, or try to solve everything that you cannot see clearly before you have faith, your perplexities will only increase and deepen. If you come to God, feeling helpless and dependent, as you really are, and in humble, trusting prayer make your wants known to Him whose knowledge is infinite, who sees everything in creation, and who governs everything by His will and word, He can and will attend to your cry, and will let light shine into your heart and all around you; for through sincere prayer your soul is brought into connection with the mind of the Infinite. You may have no remarkable evidence at the time that the face of your Redeemer is bending over you in compassion and love, but this is even so. You may not feel His visible touch, but His hand is upon you in love and pitying tenderness. . . .

You have need of constant watchfulness, lest Satan beguile you through his subtlety, corrupt your minds, and lead you into inconsistencies and gross darkness. Your watchfulness should be characterized by a spirit of humble dependence upon God. It should not be carried on with a proud, self-reliant spirit, but with a deep sense of your personal weakness, and a childlike trust in the promises of God.

DAYS OF CONFLICT AND SOUL-ANGUISH

It is now an easy and pleasant task to preach the truth of the third angel's message, in comparison with what it was when the message first started, when the numbers were few, and we were looked upon as fanatics. Those who bore the responsibility of the work in the rise and early progress of the message, knew what conflict, distress, and soul-anguish are. Night and day the burden was heavy upon them. They thought not of rest or convenience, even when they were pressed with suffering and disease. The shortness of time called for activity, and the laborers were few.

Frequently, when brought into strait places, the entire night was spent in earnest, agonizing prayer, with tears, for help from God, and for light to shine upon His word. When the light did come, and the clouds were driven back, what joy and grateful happiness rested upon the anxious, earnest seekers! Our gratitude to God was as complete as had been our earnest, hungering cry for light. Some nights we could not sleep because our hearts were overflowing with love and gratitude to God.

Men who now go forth to preach the truth, have things made ready to their hand. They cannot experience such privations as the laborers in present truth endured before them. The truth has been brought out link after link, till it forms a clear, connected chain. To bring the truth out in such clearness and harmony has required careful research. Opposition, the most bitter and determined, drove the servants of God to the Lord and to their Bibles. Precious indeed to them was the light which came from God. . . .

In the final victory, God will have no use for those persons who are nowhere to be found in time of peril and danger, when the strength, courage, and influence of all are required to make a charge upon the enemy. Those who stand like faithful soldiers to battle against wrong and to vindicate the right, warring against principalities and powers, against the rulers of the darkness of this world, against spiritual wickedness in high places, will each receive the commendation from the Master, "Well done, good and faithful servant; . . . enter thou into the joy of thy Lord." [1] —"*Testimonies for the Church,*" *Vol. III, pages 320-327.*

He who loses sight of his entire dependence upon God is sure to fall. We are contending with those who are stronger than we. Satan and his hosts are constantly watching to assail us with temptations,

[1] Matt. 25 : 23.

and in our own strength and wisdom it is impossible for us to withstand them. Hence, whenever we permit our hearts to be drawn away from God, whenever we indulge self-exaltation or self-dependence, we are sure to be overthrown.

The world will never know the work secretly going on between the soul and God, nor the inward bitterness of spirit, the self-loathing, and the constant efforts to control self; but many of the world will be able to appreciate the result of these efforts.

Those who have the deepest experience in the things of God, are the farthest removed from pride or self-exaltation. It is when men have the most exalted conceptions of the glory and excellence of Christ, that self is abased, and they feel that the lowest place in His service is too honorable for them.

The Lord wants us to come up into the mount, more directly into His presence. We are coming to a crisis which, more than any previous time since the world began, will demand the entire consecration of every one who has named the name of Christ.

May God make His servants wise through the divine illumination, that the impress of man may not be seen on any of the great and important enterprises before us.

WORDS OF CAUTION

Christ said to His disciples, "Behold, I send you forth as sheep in the midst of wolves: be ye therefore wise as serpents, and harmless as doves." [1]

Satan's attacks against the advocates of the truth will wax more bitter and determined to the very close of time. As in Christ's day the chief priests and rulers stirred up the people against Him, so to-day the religious leaders will excite bitterness and preju- dice against the truth for this time. The people will be led to acts of violence and opposition which they would never have thought of had they not been im- bued with the animosity of professed Christians against the truth.

HOW TO MEET BITTER ATTACKS

What course shall the advocates of truth pursue? They have the unchangeable, eternal word of God, and they should reveal the fact that they have the truth as it is in Jesus. Their words must not be rug- ged or sharp. In their presentation of truth they must manifest the love and meekness and gentleness of Christ. Let the truth do the cutting; the word of God is as a sharp, two-edged sword, and will cut its way to the heart. Those who know that they have the truth should not, by the use of harsh and severe expressions, give Satan one chance to misinterpret their spirit.

As a people, we must stand as did the world's Redeemer. When in controversy with Satan in re- gard to the body of Moses, Christ "durst not bring

[1] Matt. 10 : 16.

against him a railing accusation." [2] He had every provocation to do this, and Satan was disappointed because he could not arouse in Christ a spirit of retaliation. Satan was ready to misinterpret everything that was done by Jesus; and the Saviour would give him no occasion, not the semblance of an excuse. He would not turn from His straightforward course of truth in order to follow the wanderings, and twistings, and turnings, and prevarications of Satan.

We read in the prophecy of Zechariah that when Satan with all his synagogue stood up to resist the prayers of Joshua, the high priest, and to resist Christ, who was about to show decided favor to Joshua, the Lord said to Satan, "The Lord rebuke thee, O Satan; even the Lord that hath chosen Jerusalem rebuke thee: is not this a brand plucked out of the fire?" [3]

The course of Christ in dealing with even the adversary of souls should be an example to us in all our intercourse with others,— never to bring a railing accusation against any; much less should we employ harshness or severity toward those who may be as anxious to know the right way as we are ourselves.

MAKING ALLOWANCE FOR OTHERS

Those who have been educated in the truth by precept and example, should make great allowance for others who have had no knowledge of the Scriptures except through the interpretations given by ministers and church-members, and who have received traditions and fables as Bible truth. They are surprised by the presentation of truth; it is as a new revelation to them, and they cannot bear to have

<hr>

[2] Jude 9.   [3] Zech. 3 : 2.

all the truth, in its most striking character, presented to them at the outset. All is new and strange, and wholly unlike that which they have heard from their ministers; and they are inclined to believe what the ministers have told them,— that Seventh-day Adventists are infidels, and do not believe the Bible. Let the truth be presented as it is in Jesus, line upon line, precept upon precept, here a little and there a little.

NOT TO HEDGE UP THE WAY

Let not those who write for our papers make unkind thrusts and allusions that will certainly do harm, and that will hedge up the way, and hinder us from doing the work that we should do in order to reach all classes, the Catholics included. It is our work to speak the truth in love, and not to mix in with the truth the unsanctified elements of the natural heart, and speak things that savor of the same spirit possessed by our enemies. All sharp thrusts will come back upon us in double measure when the power is in the hands of those who can exercise it for our injury.

Over and over the message has been given to me, that we are not to say one word, not to publish one sentence, especially by way of personalities,— unless positively essential in vindicating the truth,— that will stir up our enemies against us, and arouse their passions to a white heat. Our work will soon be closed up; and soon the time of trouble, such as never was, will come upon us, of which we have but little idea.

The Lord wants His workers to represent Him, the great missionary worker. The manifestation of rashness always does harm. The proprieties essential for Christian life must be learned daily in the school of Christ. He who is careless and heedless in uttering words or in writing words for publication to be sent broadcast into the world, sending forth expressions that can never be taken back, is disqualifying himself to be entrusted with the sacred work that devolves upon Christ's followers at this time. Those who practice giving harsh thrusts, are forming habits that will strengthen by repetition, and will have to be repented of. We should carefully examine our ways and our spirit, and see in what manner we are doing the work given us of God, a work which involves the destiny of souls. The very highest obligation is resting upon us.

Satan is standing ready, burning with zeal to inspire the whole confederacy of satanic agencies, that he may cause them to unite with evil men, and bring upon the believers of truth speedy and severe suffering. Every unwise word that is uttered by our brethren will be treasured up by the prince of darkness. How dare finite human intelligences speak careless and venturesome words that will stir up the powers of hell against the saints of God, when Michael the archangel durst not bring against Satan a railing accusation, but said, "The Lord rebuke thee"?

It will be impossible for us to avoid difficulties and suffering. Jesus said, "It must needs be that offenses come; but woe to that man by whom the offense cometh." [4] But because offenses will come, we should be careful not to stir up the natural temperament of those who love not the truth, by unwise words, and by the manifestation of an unkind spirit.

[4] Matt. 18:7.

Precious truth must be presented in its native force. The deceptive errors that are wide-spread, and that are leading the world captive, are to be unveiled. Every effort possible is being made to ensnare souls with subtle reasonings, to turn them from the truth to fables, and to prepare them to be deceived by strong delusions. But while these deceived souls turn from the truth to error, do not speak to them one word of censure. Seek to show them their danger, and to reveal to them how grievous is their course of action toward Jesus Christ; but let it be done in pitying tenderness. By a proper manner of labor some of the souls who are ensnared by Satan may be recovered from his power. But do not blame and condemn them. To ridicule the position held by those who are in error, will not open their blind eyes, nor attract them to the truth.

When men lose sight of Christ's example, and do not pattern after His manner of teaching, they become self-sufficient, and go forth to meet Satan with his own manner of weapons. The enemy knows well how to turn his weapons upon those who use them. Jesus spoke only words of pure truth and righteousness.

If ever a people needed to walk in humility before God, it is His church, His chosen ones in this generation. We all need to bewail the dulness of our intellectual faculties, the lack of appreciation of our privileges and opportunities. We have nothing whereof to boast. We grieve the Lord Jesus Christ by our harshness, by our unchristlike thrusts. We need to become complete in Him.

It is true that we are commanded to "cry aloud, spare not, lift up thy voice like a trumpet, and show

My people their transgression, and the house of Jacob their sins." [5] This message must be given; but we should be careful not to thrust and crowd and condemn those who have not the light that we have. We should not go out of our way to make hard thrusts at Catholics. Among the Catholics there are many who are most conscientious Christians, and who walk in all the light that shines upon them; and God will work in their behalf. Those who have had great privileges and opportunities, but who have failed to improve their physical, mental, and moral powers, and have lived to please themselves, refusing to bear their responsibility, are in greater danger and in greater condemnation before God, than those who are in error upon doctrinal points, yet who seek to live to do good to others.

Do not censure others; do not condemn them If we allow selfish considerations, false reasoning, and false excuses to bring us into a perverse state of mind and heart, so that we do not know the ways and will of God, we shall be far more guilty than the open sinner. We need to be very cautious in order that we may not condemn those who, before God, are less guilty than ourselves.—*"Testimonies for the Church," Vol. IX, pages 239-244.*

[5] Isa. 58 : 1.

NO RESPECT OF PERSONS WITH GOD

The religion of Christ uplifts the receiver to a higher plane of thought and action, while at the same time it presents the whole human race as alike the objects of the love of God, being purchased by the sacrifice of His Son. At the feet of Jesus, the rich and the poor, the learned and the ignorant, meet together, with no thought of caste or worldly pre-eminence. All earthly distinctions are forgotten as we look upon Him whom our sins have pierced. The self-denial, the condescension, the infinite compassion of Him who was highly exalted in heaven, puts to shame human pride, self-esteem, and social caste. Pure, undefiled religion manifests its heaven-born principles in bringing into oneness all who are sanctified through the truth. All meet as blood-bought souls, alike dependent upon Him who has redeemed them to God.

TALENTS

The Lord has lent men talents to improve. Those whom He has entrusted with money are to bring their talent of means to the Master. Men and women of influence are to use that which God has given them. The ones whom He has endowed with wisdom are to bring to the cross of Christ this gift to be used to His glory.

And the poor have their talent, which perhaps may be larger than any other mentioned. It may be simplicity of character, humility, tried virtue, confidence in God. Through patient toil, through their entire dependence upon God, they are pointing those with whom they associate to Jesus, their Redeemer. They have a heart full of sympathy for the poor, a home for the needy and oppressed, and their testimony is clear and decided as to what Jesus is to them. They seek for glory, honor, and immortality, and their reward will be eternal life.

HUMAN BROTHERHOOD

In the human brotherhood it takes all kinds of talents to make a perfect whole; and the church of Christ is composed of men and women of varied talents, and of all ranks and all classes. God never designed that the pride of men should dissolve that which His own wisdom had ordained,— the combination of all classes of minds, of all the varied talents that make a complete whole. There should be no depreciating of any part of God's great work, whether the agencies are high or lowly. All have their part to act in diffusing light in different degrees.

There should be no monopolizing of what belongs, in a measure, to all, high and low, rich and poor, learned and unlearned. Not a ray of light must be undervalued, not a ray shut out, not a gleam unrecognized, or even acknowledged reluctantly. Let all act their part for truth and righteousness. The interests of the different classes of society are indissolubly united. We are all woven together in the great web of humanity, and we cannot, without loss, withdraw our sympathies from one another. It is impossible for a healthy influence to be maintained in the church when this common interest and sympathy does not exist.

EXCLUSIVENESS

There is no caste with God. He ignores everything of the kind. All souls are of value with Him. Laboring for the salvation of the soul is employment worthy of the highest honor. It matters not what may be the form of our labor, or among what class, whether high or low. In God's sight these distinctions will not affect its true worth. The sincere, earnest, contrite soul, however ignorant, is precious in the sight of the Lord. He places His own signet upon men, judging, not by their rank, not by their wealth, not by their intellectual greatness, but by their oneness with Christ. The unlearned, the outcast, the slave, if he has made the most of his opportunities and privileges, if he has cherished the light given him of God, has done all that is required. The world may call him ignorant, but God calls him wise and good, and thus his name stands registered in the books of heaven. God will fit him up to do Him honor, not only in heaven, but on the earth.

The divine rebuke is upon him who refuses the companionship of those whose names are written in the Lamb's book of life, simply because they are not rich, learned, or honored in this world. Christ, the Lord of glory, is satisfied with those who are meek and lowly in heart, however humble may be their calling, whatever their rank or degree of intelligence.

TRAINING FOR SERVICE

How many useful and honored workers in God's cause have received a training amid the humble duties of the most lowly positions in life! Moses was the prospective ruler of Egypt, but God could not take him from the king's court to do the work appointed him. Only when he had been for forty years a faithful shepherd was he sent to be the deliverer of his people. Gideon was taken from the threshing-floor to be the instrument in the hands of God for delivering the armies of Israel. Elisha was called to leave the plow and do the bidding of God. Amos was a husbandman, a tiller of the soil, when God gave him a message to proclaim.

All who become co-workers with Christ will have a great deal of hard, uncongenial labor to perform, and their lessons of instruction should be wisely chosen, and adapted to their peculiarities of character, and the work which they are to pursue.

CARE IN TRAINING THE YOUTH

The Lord has presented to me, in many ways and at various times, how carefully we should deal with the young,— that it requires the finest discrimination to deal with minds. Every one who has to do with the education and training of youth, needs to live very close to the great Teacher, to catch His spirit and manner of work. Lessons are to be given which will affect their character and life-work.

They should be taught that the gospel of Christ tolerates no spirit of caste, that it gives no place to unkind judgment of others, which tends directly to self-exaltation. The religion of Jesus never degrades the receiver, nor makes him coarse and rough; nor does it make him unkind in thought and feeling toward those for whom Christ died.

There is danger of attaching too much importance to the matter of etiquette, and diverting much time to education upon the subject of manner and form, that can never be of great use to many youth. Some are in danger of making the externals all-important, of overestimating the value of mere conventionalities. The results will not warrant the expenditure of the time and thought given to these matters. Some who are trained to give much attention to these things, manifest little true respect or sympathy for anything, however excellent, that fails to meet their standard of conventionality.

Anything that would encourage ungenerous criticism, a disposition to notice and expose every defect or error, is wrong. It fosters distrust and suspicion, which are contrary to the character of Christ, and detrimental to the mind thus exercised. Those who are engaged in this work, gradually depart from the true spirit of Christianity.

The most essential, enduring education is that which will develop the nobler qualities, which will encourage a spirit of universal kindliness, leading the youth to think no evil of any one, lest they misjudge motives and misinterpret words and actions. The time devoted to this kind of instruction will yield fruit to everlasting life.

CHRIST'S EXAMPLE A REBUKE TO EXCLUSIVENESS

In every age since Christ was among men, there have been some who chose to seclude themselves from others, manifesting a Pharisaical desire for pre-eminence. Shutting themselves away from the world, they have not lived to bless their fellow-men.

There is no example in the life of Christ for this self-righteous bigotry; His character was genial and beneficent. There is not a monastic order upon earth from which He would not have been excluded for overstepping the prescribed rules. In every religious denomination, and in almost every church, are to be found erratics who would have blamed Him for His liberal mercies. They would have found fault with Him because He ate with publicans and sinners; they would have accused Him of worldly conformity in attending a wedding feast, and would have censured Him unmercifully for permitting His friends to make a supper in honor of Him and His disciples.

But on these very occasions, by His teachings, as well as by His generous conduct, He was enshrining Himself in the hearts of those whom He honored with His presence. He was giving them an opportunity to become acquainted with Him, and to see the marked contrast between His life and teachings and those of the Pharisees.

Those with whom God has entrusted His truth, must possess the same beneficent spirit that Christ manifested. They must adopt the same broad plans of action. They should have a kind, generous spirit toward the poor, and in a special sense feel that they are God's stewards. They must hold all they have — property, mental powers, spiritual strength — as not their own, but only lent them to advance the cause of Christ in the earth. Like Christ, they should not shun the society of their fellow-men, but should seek it with the purpose of bestowing upon others the heavenly benefits they have received from God.

Do not be exclusive. Do not seek out a few with whom you delight to associate, and leave others to take care of themselves. Suppose you do see weakness in one and folly in another; do not stand aloof from them, and associate with those only who you think are about perfect.

The very souls you despise need your love and sympathy. Do not leave a weak soul to struggle alone, to wrestle with the passions of his own heart without your help and prayers, but consider yourself, lest you also be tempted. If you do this, God will not leave you to your own weakness. You may have sins greater in His sight than the sins of those you condemn. Do not stand off and say, "I am holier than thou."

Christ has thrown His divine arm around the human race. He has brought His divine power to man, that He might encourage the poor, sin-sick, discouraged soul to reach up for a higher life. O, we need more of Christ's spirit, and much less of self! We need the converting power of God upon our hearts daily. We need the mellowing spirit of Christ, to subdue and soften our souls. The only way for those to do who feel that they are whole, is to fall upon the Rock and be broken. Christ can change you into His likeness, if you will submit yourself to Him.

———◆———

If we follow in Christ's footsteps, we must come close to those who need our ministry. We must open the Bible to the understanding, present the claims of God's law, read the promises to the hesitating, arouse the careless, strengthen the weak.

SECLUSION

The incessant reading and writing of many ministers unfits them for pastoral work. They consume valuable time in abstract study, which should be expended in helping the needy at the right moment. Some ministers have given themselves to the work of writing during a period of decided religious interest, and sometimes these writings have had no special connection with the work in hand. At such times it is the duty of the minister to use his entire strength in pushing forward the present interest. His mind should be clear, and centered upon the one object of saving souls. Should his thoughts be preoccupied with other subjects, many might be lost to the cause who could have been saved by timely instruction.

When the temptation comes to seclude themselves, and to indulge in reading and writing at a time when other duties claim their immediate attention, ministers should be strong enough to deny self, and devote themselves to the work that lies directly before them. This is undoubtedly one of the most trying tests that a studious mind is called to undergo.

The duties of a pastor are often shamelessly neglected because the minister lacks strength to sacrifice his personal inclinations for seclusion and study. The pastor should visit from house to house among his flock, teaching, conversing, and praying with each family, and looking out for the welfare of their souls. Those who have manifested a desire to become acquainted with the principles of our faith should not be neglected, but thoroughly instructed in the truth.

Certain ministers who have been invited to houses by the heads of families, have spent the few hours of their visit in secluding themselves in an unoccupied room to indulge their inclination for reading and writing. The family that entertained them derived no benefit from the visit. The ministers accepted the hospitality extended them without giving an equivalent in the labor that was so much needed.

People are easily reached through the avenues of the social circle. But many ministers dread the task of visiting; they have not cultivated social qualities, have not acquired that genial spirit that wins its way to the hearts of the people.

Those who seclude themselves from the people are in no condition to help them. A skilful physician must understand the nature of various diseases, and must have a thorough knowledge of the human structure. He must be prompt in attending to the patients. He knows that delays are dangerous. When his experienced hand is laid upon the pulse of the sufferer, and he carefully notes the peculiar indication of the malady, his previous knowledge enables him to determine the nature of the disease, and the treatment necessary to arrest its progress.

As the physician deals with physical disease, so does the pastor minister to the sin-sick soul. And his work is as much more important than that of the physician as eternal life is more valuable than temporal existence. The pastor meets with an endless variety of temperaments; and it is his duty to become acquainted with the members of the families that listen to his teachings, in order to determine what means will best influence them in the right direction.

MINISTERS AND COMMERCIAL BUSINESS

Ministers cannot do acceptable work for God, and at the same time carry the burden of large personal business enterprises. Such a division of interest dims their spiritual perception. The mind and heart are occupied with earthly things, and the service of Christ takes a second place. They seek to shape their work for God by their circumstances, instead of shaping circumstances to meet the demands of God.

The energies of the minister are all needed for his high calling. His best powers belong to God. He should not engage in speculation, or in any other business that would turn him aside from his great work. "No man that warreth," Paul declared, "entangleth himself with the affairs of this life; that he may please Him who hath chosen him to be a soldier."[1] Thus the apostle emphasized the minister's need of unreserved consecration to the Master's service.

The minister who is wholly consecrated to God refuses to engage in business that would hinder him from giving himself fully to his sacred calling. He is not striving for earthly honor or riches; his one purpose is to tell others of the Saviour, who gave Himself to bring to human beings the riches of eternal life. His highest desire is not to lay up treasure in this world, but to bring to the attention of the indifferent and disloyal the realities of eternity. He may be asked to engage in enterprises which promise large worldly gain, but to such temptations he returns the

[1] 2 Tim. 2 : 4.

answer, "What shall it profit a man, if he shall gain the whole world, and lose his own soul?" [2]

Satan presented this inducement to Christ, knowing that if He accepted it, the world would never be ransomed. And under different guises he presents the same temptation to God's ministers to-day, knowing that those who are beguiled by it will be false to their trust.

It is not God's will that His ministers should seek to be rich. Regarding this Paul wrote to Timothy: "The love of money is the root of all evil: which while some coveted after, they have erred from the faith, and pierced themselves through with many sorrows. But thou, O man of God, flee these things; and follow after righteousness, godliness, faith, love, patience, meekness." [3] By example as well as by precept, the ambassador for Christ is to "charge them that are rich in this world, that they be not high-minded, nor trust in uncertain riches, but in the living God, who giveth us richly all things to enjoy; that they do good, that they be rich in good works, ready to distribute, willing to communicate; laying up in store for themselves a good foundation against the time to come, that they may lay hold on eternal life." [4] —*"The Acts of the Apostles," pages 365-367.*

———

Ministers cannot carry the burden of the work while at the same time they are carrying the burden of farms or other business enterprises, having their hearts on their earthly treasure. Their spiritual discernment is dimmed. They cannot appreciate the wants of the cause of God, and therefore cannot put

[2] Mark 8:36. [3] 1 Tim. 6:10, 11. [4] 1 Tim. 6:17-19.

forth well-directed efforts to meet its emergencies and to advance its interests. The want of a full consecration to the work on the part of the minister is soon felt all through the field where he labors. If his own standard is low, he will not bring others to accept a higher one.

LAND AND MINING SPECULATION

The Lord cannot glorify His name through ministers who attempt to serve God and mammon. We are not to urge men to invest in mining stock, or in city lots, holding out the inducement that the money invested will be doubled in a short time. Our message for this time is, "Sell that ye have, and give alms; provide yourselves bags which wax not old, a treasure in the heavens that faileth not, where no thief approacheth, neither moth corrupteth. For where your treasure is, there will your heart be also." [5]

Just before the Israelites entered the land of Canaan, Satan sought to seduce them, and lead them into idolatry, thinking to compass their ruin. He works in the same way in our day. There are young men whom God would accept as workers together with Him, but they have become absorbed in the real-estate craze, and have sold their interest in the truth for the prospect of worldly advantage.

There are many who hold themselves away from the service of God, because they desire worldly gain; and Satan uses them to lead others astray. The tempter comes to men as he came to Jesus, presenting the glory of the world; and when a measure of success attends their ventures, they become greedy for

[5] Luke 12 : 33, 34.

more gain, lose their love for the truth, and their spirituality dies. The immortal inheritance, the love of Jesus, is eclipsed to their vision by the fleeting prospects of this world.

The people will seldom rise higher than their minister. A world-loving spirit in him has a tremendous influence upon others. The people make his deficiencies an excuse to cover their own world-loving spirit. They quiet their consciences, thinking that they may be free to love the things of this life and be indifferent to spiritual things, because their ministers are so. They deceive their own souls, and remain in friendship with the world, which the apostle declares to be "enmity against God." [6] Ministers should be examples to the flock. They should manifest an undying love for souls, and the same devotion to the cause which they desire to see in the people.—*"Testimonies for the Church," Vol. II, pages 645, 646.*

We are nearing the close of time. We want not only to teach present truth in the pulpit, but to live it out of the pulpit. Examine closely the foundation of your hope of salvation. While you stand in the position of a herald of truth, a watchman upon the walls of Zion, you cannot have your interest interwoven with mining or real-estate business, and at the same time do effectually the sacred work committed to your hands. Where the souls of men are at stake, where eternal things are involved, the interest cannot safely be divided. — *"Testimonies for the Church," Vol. V, page 530.*

[6] Rom. 8:7

FOR FURTHER STUDY

THE DANGER OF REJECTING LIGHT	Test. Vol. II, pp. 694, 695. Test. Vol. V, p. 144. Test. Vol. VIII, pp. 192-194. Desire, pp. 322, 489, 490, 580-588. E. W., pp. 61-64.
A WARNING AGAINST FALSE TEACHING	Test. Vol. IX, pp. 67, 68. E. W., pp. 100-102, 123-125, 258-261. Ed., pp. 230, 231. C. O. L., pp. 39, 40. M. of H., pp. 427-438. Desire, pp. 212, 213, 456, 478. Acts, pp. 319-321, 383-388, 473-475, 502, 503, 535, 536, 553-556, 580, 581.
SOUND DOCTRINE	Test. Vol. VIII, pp. 279, 290-304, 309-311. Test. Vol. IX, pp. 67-69. Desire, p. 827. Acts, pp. 473-475, 502-508, 553-556.
FANATICISM	Test. Vol. I, pp. 228-232. Test. Vol. II, pp. 553-557. Test. Vol. III, pp. 315, 316. Test. Vol. V, pp. 305, 306, 647-649. Test. Vol. VIII, pp. 292, 293. Acts, pp. 347, 348.
SELF-CONFIDENCE	Test. Vol. I, pp. 621-628. Test. Vol. III, pp. 307, 308, 320-327, 449-459, 464. Test. Vol. IV, p. 608. Test. Vol. V, pp. 214, 219. M. of H., pp. 150, 151. C. O. L., pp. 150-163.
WORDS OF CAUTION	Test. Vol. II, pp. 134-136, 220. Test. Vol. III, pp. 424-428, 461-463, 570, 575. Test. Vol. IV, pp. 262, 263. Test. Vol. VI, pp. 120-123. Test. Vol. VII, pp. 150-158. Test. Vol. IX, pp. 147-149.

Methods

"There is a man whose labor is
in wisdom, and in knowledge,
and in equity."

LABOR IN THE CITIES

In connection with the proclamation of the message in large cities, there are many kinds of work to be done by laborers with varied gifts. Some are to labor in one way, some in another. The Lord desires that the cities shall be worked by the united efforts of laborers of different capabilities. All are to look to Jesus for direction, not depending on man for wisdom, lest they be led astray. As laborers together with God, they should seek to be in harmony with one another. There should be frequent councils, and earnest, whole-hearted co-operation. Yet all are to look to Jesus for wisdom, not depending upon men alone for direction.

The Lord has given to some ministers the ability to gather and to hold large congregations. This calls for the exercise of tact and skill. In the cities of to-day, where there is so much to attract and please, the people can be interested by no ordinary efforts. Ministers of God's appointment will find it necessary to put forth extraordinary efforts in order to arrest the attention of the multitudes. And when they succeed in bringing together a large number of people, they must bear messages of a character so out of the usual order that the people will be aroused and warned.

They must make use of every means that can possibly be devised for causing the truth to stand out clearly and distinctly. The testing message for this time is to be borne so plainly and decidedly as to startle the hearers, and lead them to desire to study the Scriptures.

Those who do the work of the Lord in the cities must put forth calm, steady, devoted effort for the education of the people. While they are to labor earnestly to interest the hearers, and to hold this interest, yet at the same time they must carefully guard against anything that borders on sensationalism. In this age of extravagance and outward show, when men think it necessary to make a display in order to gain success, God's chosen messengers are to show the fallacy of spending means needlessly for effect. As they labor with simplicity, humility, and graceful dignity, avoiding everything of a theatrical nature, their work will make a lasting impression for good.

There is a necessity, it is true, for expending money judiciously in advertising the meetings, and in carrying forward the work solidly. Yet the strength of every worker will be found to lie, not in these outward agencies, but in trustful dependence upon God, in earnest prayer to Him for help, in obedience to His word. Much more prayer, much more Christlikeness, much more conformity to God's will, is to be brought into the Lord's work. Outward show and extravagant outlay of means will not accomplish the work to be done.

God's work is to be carried forward with power. We need the baptism of the Holy Spirit. We need to understand that God will add to the ranks of His people men of ability and influence who are to act their part in warning the world. Not all in the world are lawless and sinful. God has many thousands who have not bowed the knee to Baal. There are God-fearing men and women in the fallen churches. If this were not so, we would not be given the message to bear: "Babylon the great is fallen, is fallen." "Come out of her, My people." [1] Many of the honest in heart are gasping for a breath of life from heaven. They will recognize the gospel when it is brought to them in the beauty and simplicity with which it is presented in God's word. . . .

TEACHING THE PRINCIPLES OF HEALTH REFORM

As a people we have been given the work of making known the principles of health reform. There are some who think that the question of diet is not of sufficient importance to be included in their evangelistic work. But such make a great mistake. God's word declares, "Whether therefore ye eat, or drink, or whatsoever ye do, do all to the glory of God." [2] The subject of temperance, in all its bearings, has an important place in the work of salvation.

In connection with our city missions there should be suitable rooms where those in whom an interest has been awakened can be gathered for instruction. This necessary work is not to be carried on in such a meager way that an unfavorable impression will be made on the minds of the people. All that is done should bear favorable witness to the Author of truth, and should properly represent the sacredness and

[1] Rev. 18 : 2, 4.   [2] 1 Cor. 10 : 31.

importance of the truths of the third angel's message. . . .

The work of health reform is the Lord's means for lessening suffering in our world and for purifying His church. Teach the people that they can act as God's helping hand, by co-operating with the Master-worker in restoring physical and spiritual health. This work bears the signature of Heaven, and will open doors for the entrance of other precious truths. There is room for all to labor who will take hold of this work intelligently.

Keep the work of health reform to the front, is the message I am instructed to bear. Show so plainly its value that a wide-spread need for it will be felt. Abstinence from all hurtful food and drink is the fruit of true religion. He who is thoroughly converted will abandon every injurious habit and appetite. By total abstinence he will overcome his desire for health-destroying indulgences. . . .

WORK FOR THE WEALTHY CLASSES

The servants of Christ should labor faithfully for the rich men in our cities, as well as for the poor and lowly. There are many wealthy men who are susceptible to the influences and impressions of the gospel message, and who, when the Bible and the Bible alone is presented to them as the expositor of Christian faith and practice, will be moved by the Spirit of God to open doors for the advancement of the gospel. They will reveal a living faith in the word of God, and will use their entrusted means to prepare the way of the Lord, to make straight in the desert a highway for our God.

For years the perplexing question has been before us, How can we raise funds adequate for the support of the missions which the Lord has gone before us to open? We read the plain commands of the gospel, and the missions, in both home and foreign fields, present their necessities. The indications, yea, the positive revelations, of Providence unite in urging us to do quickly the work that is waiting to be done.

The Lord desires that moneyed men shall be converted, and act as His helping hand in reaching others. He desires that those who can help in the work of reform and restoration shall see the precious light of truth, be transformed in character, and be led to use their entrusted capital in His service. He would have them invest the means He has lent them, in doing good, in opening the way for the gospel to be preached to all classes, nigh and afar off.

Will not heaven be appreciated by the worldly wise men? — O, yes; there they will find rest and peace and repose from all trifling, all ambition, all self-serving. Urge them to seek for the peace and happiness and joy that Christ is longing to bestow upon them. Urge them to give their attention to securing the richest gift that can be given to mortal man,— the robe of Christ's righteousness. Christ offers them a life that measures with the life of God, and a far more exceeding and eternal weight of glory. If they accept Christ, they will have the highest honor—honor which the world can neither give nor take away. They will find that in the keeping of the commandments of God there is great reward.

The compassionate Redeemer bids His servants give to rich and poor the call to the supper. Go out into the highways and the hedges, and by your persevering, determined efforts, compel them to come in. Let ministers of the gospel take hold of these worldly moneyed men, and bring them to the banquet of truth that Christ has prepared for them. He who gave His precious life for them says, "Bring them in, and seat them at My table, and I will serve them."

Ministers of Christ, link yourselves up with this class. Pass them not by as hopeless. Work with all the persuasion possible, and as the fruit of your faithful efforts you will see in the kingdom of heaven men and women who will be crowned as overcomers, to sing the triumphant song of the conqueror. "They shall walk with Me in white," says the First and the Last; "for they are worthy." [3]

Altogether too little effort has been put forth for men in responsible places in the world. Many of them possess superior qualifications; they have means and influence. These are precious gifts, entrusted to them by the Lord to be increased and used for the good of others.

Seek to save men of wealth. Entreat them to return to the Lord the treasures He has lent them in trust, that in New York and other great cities there may be established centers of influence from which Bible truth in its simplicity shall go forth to the people. Persuade men to lay up their treasures beside the throne of God by returning to the Lord their substance, enabling His workers to do good and to advance His glory.

[3] Rev. 3:4.

ENLARGING OUR FORCES

The strength of an army is measured largely by the efficiency of the men in the ranks. A wise general instructs his officers to train every soldier for active service. He seeks to develop the highest efficiency on the part of all. If he were to depend on his officers alone, he could never expect to conduct a successful campaign. He counts on loyal and untiring service from every man in his army. The responsibility rests largely upon the men in the ranks.

And so it is in the army of Prince Emmanuel. Our General, who has never lost a battle, expects willing, faithful service from every one who has enlisted under His banner. In the closing controversy now waging between the forces for good and the hosts of evil, He expects all, laymen as well as ministers, to take part. All who have enlisted as His soldiers are to render faithful service as minutemen, with a keen sense of the responsibility resting upon them individually.

Those who have the spiritual oversight of the church should devise ways and means by which an opportunity may be given to every member of the church to act some part in God's work. Too often in the past this has not been done. Plans have not been clearly laid and fully carried out, whereby the talents of all might be employed in active service. There are but few who realize how much has been lost because of this.

The leaders in God's cause, as wise generals, are to lay plans for advance moves all along the line. In their planning they are to give special study to the work that can be done by the laity for their friends and neighbors. The work of God in this earth can never be finished until the men and women comprising our church membership rally to the work, and unite their efforts with those of ministers and church officers. . . .

CENTERS OF COMMERCE AND TRAVEL

In these days of travel, the opportunities for coming in contact with men and women of all classes, and of many nationalities, are much greater than in the days of Israel. The thoroughfares of travel have multiplied a thousand-fold. God has wonderfully prepared the way. The agency of the printing-press, with its manifold facilities, is at our command. Bibles, and publications in many languages, setting forth the truth for this time, are at our hand, and can be swiftly carried to every part of the world.

Christians who are living in the great centers of commerce and travel have special opportunities. Believers in these cities can work for God in the neighborhood of their homes.

In the world-renowned health resorts and centers of tourist traffic, crowded with many thousands of seekers after health and pleasure, there should be stationed ministers and canvassers capable of arresting the attention of the multitudes. Let these workers watch their chance for presenting the message for this time, and hold meetings as they have opportunity. Let them be quick to seize opportunities to speak to the people. Accompanied by the power of the Holy Spirit, let them meet the people with the message borne by John the Baptist, "Repent ye: for the kingdom of heaven is at hand." [4]

[4] Matt. 3 : 2.

The word of God is to be presented with clearness and power, that those who have ears to hear may hear the truth. Thus the gospel of present truth will be placed in the way of those who know it not, and it will be accepted by not a few, and carried by them to their own homes in all parts of the world.

We are to give the last warning of God to men, and what should be our earnestness in studying the Bible, and our zeal in spreading the light! Let every soul who has received the divine illumination seek to impart it. Let the workers go from house to house, opening the Bible to the people, circulating the publications, telling others of the light that has blessed their own souls. Let literature be distributed judiciously, on the trains, in the street, on the great ships that ply the sea, and through the mails. . . .

I am instructed to point our ministers to the unworked cities, and to urge them by every possible means to open the way for the presentation of the truth. In some of the cities where the message of the second coming of the Lord was first given, we are compelled to take up the work as if it were a new field. How much longer will these barren fields, these unworked cities, be passed by? Without delay, the sowing of the seed should begin in many, many places.—*"Testimonies for the Church," Vol. IX. pages 109–123.*

COUNSEL REGARDING THE WORK
IN CITIES

There is a vast amount of work to be done in proclaiming the truth for this time to those who are dead in trespasses and sins. Most startling messages will be borne by men of God's appointment, messages of a character to warn the people, to arouse them. And while some will be provoked by the warning, and led to resist the light and evidence, we are to see from this that we are giving the testing message for this time.

Messages will be given out of the usual order. The judgments of God are in the land. While city missions must be established where colporteurs, Bible-workers, and practical medical missionaries may be trained to reach certain classes, we must also have, in our cities, consecrated evangelists through whom a message is to be borne so decidedly as to startle the hearers. . . .

The time has come to make decided efforts in places where the truth has not yet been proclaimed. How shall the Lord's work be done? In every place that is entered, a solid foundation is to be laid for permanent work. The Lord's methods are to be followed. It is not for you to be intimidated by outward appearances, however forbidding they may be. It is for you to carry forward the work as the Lord has said it should be carried. Preach the word, and the Lord by His Holy Spirit will send conviction to the minds of the hearers. The word is, "They went forth, and preached everywhere, the Lord working with them, and confirming the word with signs following." [1]

Many workers are to act their part, doing house-to-house work, and giving Bible-readings in families. They are to show their growth in grace by submission to the will of Christ. Thus they will gain a rich experience. As in faith they receive, believe, and obey Christ's word, the efficiency of the Holy Spirit will be seen in their life-work. There will be an intensity of earnest effort. There will be cherished a faith that works by love, and purifies the soul. The fruits of the Spirit will be seen in the life. . . .

There is need of all the instruction that our missions can give. Continue your work in the power of the same Spirit that led in its establishment. By opening the Scriptures, by praying, by exercising faith, educate the people in the way of the Lord; and there will be built up a church founded on the rock Christ Jesus. . .

Carry forward your work in humility. Never rise above the simplicity of the gospel of Christ. Not in the art of display, but in lifting up Christ, the sin-pardoning Redeemer, will you find success in winning souls. As you work for God in humility and lowliness of heart, He will manifest Himself to you.

THEATRICAL DEVICES

By the use of charts, symbols, and representations of various kinds, the minister can make the truth stand out clearly and distinctly. This is a help, and in harmony with the word of God. But when the

[1] Mark 16 : 20.

worker makes his labors so expensive that others are unable to secure from the treasury sufficient means to support them in the field, he is not working in harmony with God's plan.

The work in the large cities is to be done after Christ's order, not after the order of a theatrical performance. It is not a theatrical performance that glorifies God, but the presentation of the truth in the love of Christ.

PRELIMINARIES

Do not divest the truth of its dignity and impressiveness by preliminaries that are more after the order of the world than after the order of heaven. Let your hearers understand that you hold meetings, not to charm their senses with music and other things, but to preach the truth in all its solemnity, that it may come to them as a warning, arousing them from their death-like sleep of self-indulgence. It is the naked truth that like a sharp, two-edged sword cuts both ways. It is this that will arouse those who are dead in trespasses and sins.

He who gave His life to save men and women from idolatry and self-indulgence, left an example to be followed by all who take up the work of presenting the gospel to others. God's servants in this age have been given most solemn truths to proclaim, and their actions and methods and plans must correspond to the importance of their message. If you are presenting the word in Christ's way, your audience will be deeply impressed with the truths you teach. The conviction will come to them that this is the word of the living God.

FORMALITY IN WORSHIP

In their efforts to reach the people, the Lord's messengers are not to follow the ways of the world. In the meetings that are held, they are not to depend on worldly singers and theatrical display to awaken an interest. How can those who have no interest in the word of God, who have never read His word with a sincere desire to understand its truths, be expected to sing with the spirit and the understanding? How can their hearts be in harmony with the words of sacred song? How can the heavenly choir join in music that is only a form?

The evil of formal worship cannot be too strongly depicted, but no words can properly set forth the deep blessedness of genuine worship. When human beings sing with the spirit and the understanding, heavenly musicians take up the strain, and join in the song of thanksgiving. He who has bestowed upon us all the gifts that enable us to be workers together with God, expects His servants to cultivate their voices, so that they can speak and sing in a way that all can understand. It is not loud singing that is needed, but clear intonation, correct pronunciation, and distinct utterance. Let all take time to cultivate the voice, so that God's praise can be sung in clear, soft tones, not with harshness and shrillness that offend the ear. The ability to sing is the gift of God; let it be used to His glory.

In the meetings held, let a number be chosen to take part in the song service. And let the singing be accompanied with musical instruments skilfully handled. We are not to oppose the use of instruments of music in our work. This part of the service is to be carefully conducted; for it is the praise of God in song. The singing is not always to be done by a few. As often as possible, let the entire congregation join. . . .

HOLDING TO THE AFFIRMATIVE

Often, as you seek to present the truth, opposition will be aroused; but if you seek to meet the opposition with argument, you will only multiply it, and this you cannot afford to do. Hold to the affirmative. Angels of God are watching you, and they understand how to impress those whose opposition you refuse to meet with arguments. Dwell not on the negative points of questions that arise, but gather to your minds affirmative truths, and fasten them there by much study, earnest prayer, and heart consecration. Keep your lamps trimmed and burning, and let bright rays shine forth, that men, beholding your good works, may be led to glorify your Father who is in heaven.

If Christ had not held to the affirmative in the wilderness of temptation, He would have lost all that He desired to gain. Christ's way is the best way to meet our opponents. We strengthen their arguments when we repeat what they say. Keep always to the affirmative. It may be that the very man who is opposing you will carry your words home, and be converted to the sensible truth that has reached his understanding.

I have often said to our brethren: Your opponents will make statements about your work that are false. Do not repeat their statements, but hold to your assertions of the living truth; and angels of God will open the way before you. We have a great work to carry forward, and we must carry it in a sensible way. Let us never get excited, or allow evil feelings to arise. Christ did not do this, and He is our example in all things. For the work given us to do we need much more of heavenly, sanctified, humble wisdom, and much less of self. We need to lay hold firmly on divine power.

Those who have departed from the faith will come to our congregations to divert our attention from the work that God would have done. You cannot afford to turn your ears from the truth to fables. Do not stop to try to convert the one who is speaking words of reproach against your work, but let it be seen that you are inspired by the Spirit of Jesus Christ; and angels of God will put into your lips words that will reach the hearts of the opposers. If these men persist in pressing their way in, those who are of a sensible mind in the congregation will understand that yours is the higher standard. So speak that it will be known that Jesus Christ is speaking through you.—*"Testimonies for the Church," Vol. IX, pages 137-149.*

———◆———

There are those who have a special gift of song, and there are times when a special message is borne by one singing alone, or by several uniting in song. But the singing is seldom to be done by a few. The ability to sing is a talent of influence, which God desires all to cultivate and use to His name's glory.— *"Testimonies for the Church," Vol. VII, pages 115, 116.*

MEDICAL MISSIONARY WORK IN CITIES

Medical missionary evangelistic work should be carried forward in a most prudent and thorough manner. The solemn, sacred work of saving souls is to advance in a way that is modest, and yet elevated. Where are the working forces? Men and women who are thoroughly converted, men and women of discernment and keen foresight, should act as directors. Good judgment must be exercised in employing persons to do this special work,— persons who love God and who walk before Him in all humility, persons who will be effective agencies in God's hand for the accomplishment of the object He has in view,— the uplifting and saving of human beings.

Medical missionary evangelists will be able to do excellent pioneer work. The work of the minister should blend fully with that of the medical missionary evangelist. The Christian physician should regard his work as exalted as that of the ministry. He bears a double responsibility; for in him are combined the qualifications of both physician and gospel minister. His is a grand, a sacred, and a very necessary work.

The physician and the minister should realize that they are engaged in the same work. They should labor in perfect harmony. They should counsel together. By their unity they will bear witness that God has sent His only begotten Son into the world to save all who will believe in Him as their personal Saviour.

Physicians whose professional abilities are above those of the ordinary doctor, should engage in the service of God in the large cities. They should seek to reach the higher classes. . . . Medical missionaries who labor in evangelistic lines are doing a work of as high an order as are their ministerial fellow-laborers. The efforts put forth by these workers are not to be limited to the poorer classes. The higher classes have been strangely neglected. In the higher walks of life will be found many who will respond to the truth, because it is consistent, because it bears the stamp of the high character of the gospel. Not a few of the men of ability thus won to the cause will enter energetically into the Lord's work.

The Lord calls upon those who are in positions of trust, those to whom He has entrusted His precious gifts, to use their talents of intellect and means in His service. Our workers should present before these men a plain statement of our plan of labor, telling them what we need in order to help the poor and needy and to establish this work on a firm basis. Some of these will be impressed by the Holy Spirit to invest the Lord's means in a way that will advance His cause. They will fulfil His purpose by helping to create centers of influence in the large cities. Interested workers will be led to offer themselves for various lines of missionary effort.

THE HEALTH WORK

Hygienic restaurants will be established. But with what carefulness should this work be done! Every hygienic restaurant should be a school. The workers connected with it should be constantly studying and experimenting, that they may make improvements in the preparation of healthful foods.

In the cities this work of instruction may be carried forward on a much larger scale than in smaller places. But in every place where there is a church, instruction should be given in regard to the preparation of simple, wholesome foods for the use of those who wish to live in accordance with the principles of health. And the church-members should impart to the people of their neighborhoods the light they receive on this subject. . . .

Cooking-schools are to be established in many places. This work may begin in a humble way, but as intelligent cooks do their best to enlighten others, the Lord will give them skill and understanding. The word of the Lord is, "Forbid them not; for I will reveal Myself to them as their Instructor." God will work with those who carry out His plans, teaching the people how to bring about a reformation in their diet by the preparation of healthful, inexpensive foods. Thus the poor will be encouraged to adopt the principles of health reform. And they will be helped to become industrious and self-reliant.

It has been presented to me that men and women of capability were being taught of God how to prepare wholesome, palatable foods in an acceptable manner. Many of these were young, and there were also those of mature age. I have been instructed to encourage the conducting of cooking-schools in all places where medical missionary work is being done. Every inducement to lead the people to reform must be held out before them. Let as much light as possible shine upon them. Teach them to make every improvement that they can in the preparation of food, and encourage them to impart to others that which they learn. . . .

From the record of the Lord's miracles in providing wine at the wedding feast and in feeding the multitude, we may learn a lesson of the highest importance. The health-food business is one of the Lord's own instrumentalities to supply a necessity. The heavenly Provider of all foods will not leave His people in ignorance in regard to the preparation of the best foods for all times and occasions.—*"Testimonies for the Church," Vol. VII, pages 110-114.*

————◆————

Christ's method alone will give true success in reaching the people. The Saviour mingled with men as one who desired their good. He showed His sympathy for them, ministered to their needs, and won their confidence. Then He bade them, "Follow Me."

There is need of coming close to the people by personal effort. If less time were given to sermonizing, and more time were spent in personal ministry, greater results would be seen. The poor are to be relieved, the sick cared for, the sorrowing and the bereaved comforted, the ignorant instructed, the inexperienced counseled. We are to weep with those that weep, and rejoice with those that rejoice. Accompanied by the power of persuasion, the power of prayer, the power of the love of God, this work will not, cannot, be without fruit.—*"Ministry of Healing," pages 143, 144.*

THE CITY MISSION TRAINING-SCHOOL

Of equal importance with public effort is house-to-house work in the homes of the people. In large cities there are certain classes who cannot be reached by public meetings. These must be searched out as the shepherd searches for his lost sheep. Diligent personal effort must be put forth in their behalf. When personal work is neglected, many precious opportunities are lost, which, were they improved, would advance the work decidedly.

Again, as the result of the presentation of truth in large congregations, a spirit of inquiry is awakened, and it is especially important that this interest be followed by personal labor. Those who desire to investigate the truth need to be taught to study diligently the word of God. Some one must help them to build on a sure foundation. At this critical time in their religious experience, how important it is that wisely directed Bible-workers come to their help, and open to their understanding the treasure-house of God's word!

A well-balanced work can be carried on best in the cities when a Bible school for the training of workers is in progress while public meetings are being held. Connected with this training-school or city mission should be experienced laborers of deep spiritual understanding, who can give the Bible-workers daily instruction, and who can also unite whole-heartedly in the general public effort. And as men and women are converted to the truth, those standing at the head of the mission should, with much prayer, show these new converts how to experience the power of the truth in their hearts. Such a mission, if conducted by those who know how to manage wisely, will be a light shining in a dark place.

Missions are essential as the foundation of missionary effort in our cities; but let it never be forgotten that those standing at the head of them are to guard every point, that all may be done to the honor of God. In these missions young men and women are to receive a training that will qualify them to work for the Master. But if they do not possess solidity of character and a spirit of consecration, all effort to fit them for the work will prove a failure. Without a high sense of propriety, of sobriety, of the sacredness of the truth and the exalted character of the work, they cannot succeed. The same is true of the older workers. Unless they are sanctified by the truth, they cannot give those under their charge an education that will elevate, ennoble, and refine them.

Our missions must be kept free from all wrong practices, all coarseness, all carelessness. Everything connected with them should be above reproach. Every one who has any part to act in them should be an example to believers. There is need that many moments be spent in secret prayer, in close communion with God. Thus only can victories be won. Every arrangement of the mission should be such as to garrison the soul against yielding to temptation. Every unholy passion must be kept under the control of sanctified reason, through the grace abundantly bestowed by God.

When a man who is counted worthy to fill a position of trust in one of our institutions or in a mission, betrays his trust and gives himself into the hands of Satan as an instrument of unrighteousness, to sow the seeds of evil, he is a traitor of the worst type. From one such tainted, polluted mind the youth often receive the impure thoughts that lead to a life of shame and defilement.

The men and women at the head of a mission need close connection with God, in order to keep themselves pure and to know how to manage the youth discreetly, so that the thoughts of all shall be untainted, uncorrupted. Let the lessons given be of an elevated, ennobling character, that the mind may be filled with pure, Christlike thoughts. "Every man that hath this hope in him purifieth himself, even as He is pure." [1] As God is pure in His sphere, so man is to be pure in his. And he will be pure if Christ is formed within, the hope of glory; for he will imitate Christ's life and reflect His character.

When a mission is established in a city, our people should take an interest in it, showing this interest in a practical, substantial way. The mission workers labor hard and self-sacrificingly, and they do not receive large wages. Let not our people think that the conducting of city missions is an easy work, or one that brings financial profit. Often the missions are carried on with no means in sight, by men and women who from day to day beseech God to send them means with which to advance the work.

[1] 1 John 3 : 3.

THOROUGHNESS

A solemn responsibility rests upon the ministers of Christ to do their work with thoroughness. They should lead young disciples along wisely and judiciously, step by step, onward and upward, until every essential point has been brought before them. Nothing should be kept back. But not all points of truth should be given in the first few meetings. Gradually, cautiously, his own heart imbued with the Spirit of God, the teacher should give his hearers meat in due season.

Ministers should not feel that their work is finished until those who have accepted the theory of the truth realize indeed the influence of its sanctifying power, and are truly converted. When the word of God, as a sharp, two-edged sword, cuts its way to the heart and arouses the conscience, many suppose that this is enough; but the work is only begun. Good impressions have been made, but unless these impressions are deepened by careful, prayerful effort, Satan will counteract them. Let not the laborers rest content with what has been done. The plowshare of truth must go deeper, and this it will surely do if thorough efforts are made to direct the thoughts and establish the convictions of those who are studying the truth.

Too often the work is left in an unfinished state, and in many such cases it amounts to nothing. Sometimes, after a company of people has accepted the truth, the minister thinks that he must immediately go to a new field; and sometimes, without proper investigation, he is authorized to go. This is wrong; he should finish the work begun; for in leaving it incomplete, more harm than good is done. No field is so unpromising as one that has been cultivated just enough to give the weeds a more luxuriant growth. By this method of labor many souls have been left to the buffeting of Satan and the opposition of members of other churches who have rejected the truth; and many are driven where they can never again be reached. A minister might better not engage in the work unless he can bind it off thoroughly.

Upon all new converts should be impressed the truth that abiding knowledge can be gained only by earnest labor and persevering study. As a rule, those who are converted to the truth we preach have not previously been diligent students of the Scriptures; for in the popular churches there is little real study of the word of God. The people look to the ministers to search the Scriptures for them and to explain what they teach.

Many accept the truth without digging down deep to understand its foundation principles; and when it is opposed, they forget the arguments and evidences that sustain it. They have been led to believe the truth, but have not been fully instructed as to what truth is, or carried forward from point to point in the knowledge of Christ. Too often their piety degenerates into a form, and when the appeals that first aroused them are no longer heard, they become spiritually dead. Unless those who receive the truth are thoroughly converted, unless there is a radical change in the life and character, unless the soul is riveted to the eternal Rock, they will not endure the test of trial. After the minister leaves and the novelty has worn off, the truth loses its power to charm, and they exert no holier influence than before.

God's work is not to be done in a bungling, slipshod manner. When a minister enters a field, he should work that field thoroughly. He should not be satisfied with his success until he can, through earnest labor and the blessing of Heaven, present to the Lord converts who have a true sense of their responsibility, and who will do their appointed work. If he has properly instructed those under his care, when he leaves for other fields of labor the work will not ravel out; it will be bound off so firmly as to be secure.

The minister has no sanction for confining his labors to the pulpit, leaving his hearers unhelped by personal effort. He should seek to understand the nature of the difficulties in the minds of the people. He should talk and pray with those who are interested, giving them wise instruction, to the end that he "may present every man perfect in Christ." [1] His Bible teaching should have a directness and force that will send conviction home to the conscience. The people know so little of the Bible that practical, definite lessons should be given concerning the nature of sin and its remedy.

A laborer should never leave some portion of the work undone because it is not agreeable to perform, thinking that the minister coming next will do it for him. When this is the case, if a second minister follows the first, and presents the claims that God has upon His people, some draw back, saying, "The minister who brought us the truth did not mention

[1] Col. 1 : 28.

these things." And they become offended because of the word. Some refuse to accept the tithing system; they turn away, and no longer walk with those who believe and love the truth. When other lines are opened before them, they answer, "It was not so taught us," and they hesitate to move forward. How much better it would have been if the first messenger of truth had faithfully and thoroughly educated these converts in regard to all essential matters, even if fewer had been added to the church under his labors. God would be better pleased to have six thoroughly converted to the truth than to have sixty make a profession and yet not be truly converted.

It is part of the minister's work to teach those who accept the truth through his efforts, to bring the tithe to the storehouse, as an acknowledgment of their dependence upon God. The new converts should be fully enlightened as to their duty to return to the Lord His own. The command to pay tithe is so plain that there is no semblance of excuse for disregarding it. He who neglects to give instruction on this point, leaves undone a most important part of his work.

Ministers must also impress upon the people the importance of bearing other burdens in connection with the work of God. No one is exempt from the work of benevolence. The people must be taught that every department of the cause of God should enlist their support and engage their interest. The great missionary field is open before us, and this subject must be agitated, agitated, again and again. The people must be made to understand that it is not the hearers, but the doers of the Word, who will gain eternal life. And they are to be taught also that those who become partakers of the grace of Christ are not only to communicate of their substance for the advancement of the truth, but are to give themselves to God without reserve.

Some ministers are easily diverted from their work. They become discouraged, or are drawn away by their home ties, and leave a growing interest to die for want of attention. The loss sustained by the cause in this way can scarcely be estimated. When an effort to proclaim the truth is made, the minister in charge should feel responsible to act his part in faithfully carrying it forward. If his labors appear to be without result, he should seek by earnest prayer to discover if they are what they should be. He should humble his soul before God in self-examination, and by faith cling to the divine promises, humbly continuing his efforts till he is satisfied that he has faithfully discharged his duty, and done everything in his power to gain the desired result.

———◆———

God does not accept the most splendid service unless self is laid upon the altar, a living, consuming sacrifice. The root must be holy, else there can be no sound, healthy fruit, which alone is acceptable to God. . . . While worldly ambitions, worldly projects, and the greatest plans and purposes of men, will perish like the grass, "they that be wise shall shine as the brightness of the firmament; and they that turn many to righteousness as the stars forever and ever." [2] —*"Testimonies for the Church," Vol. VII, pages 248, 249.*

[2] Dan. 12 : 3.

MEETING OPPOSITION

Our ministers and teachers are to represent the love of God to a fallen world. With hearts melted in tenderness let the word of truth be spoken. Let all who are in error be treated with the gentleness of Christ. If those for whom you labor do not immediately grasp the truth, do not censure, do not criticize or condemn. Remember that you are to represent Christ in His meekness and gentleness and love.

We must expect to meet unbelief and opposition. The truth has always had to contend with these elements. But though you should meet the bitterest opposition, do not denounce your opponents. They may think, as did Paul, that they are doing God service; and to such we must manifest patience, meekness, and long-suffering.

Let us not feel that we have heavy trials to bear, severe conflicts to endure, in representing unpopular truth. Think of Jesus and what He has suffered for you, and be silent. Even when abused and falsely accused, make no complaint; speak no word of murmuring; let no thought of reproach or discontent enter your mind. Take a straightforward course, "having your conversation honest among the Gentiles: that, whereas they speak against you as evildoers, they may by your good works, which they shall behold, glorify God in the day of visitation." [1] . . .

You should conduct yourself with meekness toward those who are in error, for were not you yourself recently in blindness in your sins? And because of

[1] 1 Peter 2 : 12.

the patience of Christ toward you, should you not be tender and patient toward others? God has given us many admonitions to manifest great kindness toward those who oppose us, lest we influence a soul in the wrong direction.

Our life must be hid with Christ in God. We must know Christ personally. Then only can we rightly represent Him to the world. Let the prayer constantly ascend, "Lord, teach me how to do as Jesus would do, were He in my place." Wherever we are, we must let our light shine forth to the glory of God in good works. This is the great, important interest of our life.

WISDOM IN CONDEMNING WRONG

The Lord wants His people to follow other methods than that of condemning wrong, even though the condemnation is just. He wants us to do something more than to hurl at our adversaries charges that only drive them farther from the truth. The work which Christ came to do in our world was not to erect barriers, and constantly thrust upon the people the fact that they were wrong. He who expects to enlighten a deceived people must come near to them and labor for them in love. He must become a center of holy influence.

In the advocacy of truth the bitterest opponents should be treated with respect and deference. Some will not respond to our efforts, but will make light of the gospel invitation. Others, even those whom we suppose to have passed the boundary of God's mercy, will be won to Christ. The very last work in the controversy may be the enlightenment of those who have not rejected light and evidence, but who have been in midnight darkness, and have in ignorance worked against the truth. Therefore treat every man as honest. Speak no word, do no deed, that will confirm any in unbelief.

If any one shall seek to draw the workers into debate or controversy on political or other questions, take no heed to either persuasion or challenge. Carry forward the work of God firmly and strongly, but in the meekness of Christ, and as quietly as possible. Let no human boasting be heard. Let no sign of self-sufficiency be made. Let it be seen that God has called us to handle sacred trusts; preach the word, be diligent, earnest, and fervent.

The influence of your teaching would be tenfold greater if you were careful of your words. Words that should be a savor of life unto life may by the spirit which accompanies them be made a savor of death unto death. And remember that if by your spirit or your words you close the door to even one soul, that soul will confront you in the judgment.

Do not, when referring to the Testimonies, feel it your duty to drive them home. In reading them, be sure not to mix in your filling of words; for this makes it impossible for the hearers to distinguish between the word of the Lord to them and your words. Be sure that you do not make the word of the Lord offensive.

We long to see reforms; and because we do not see that which we desire, an evil spirit is too often allowed to cast drops of gall into our cup, and thus others are embittered. By our ill-advised words their spirit is chafed, and they are stirred to rebellion.

Every sermon you preach, every article you write, may be all true; but one drop of gall in it will be poison to the hearer or the reader. Because of that drop of poison, one will discard all your good and acceptable words. Another will feed on the poison; for he loves such harsh words. He follows your example, and talks just as you talk. Thus the evil is multiplied.

Those who present the eternal principles of truth need the holy oil emptied from the two olive branches into the heart. This will flow forth in words that will reform but not exasperate. The truth is to be spoken in love. Then the Lord Jesus by His Spirit will supply the force and the power. That is His work.— *"Testimonies for the Church," Vol. VI, pages 120-123.*

HOW TO DEAL WITH OBJECTIONS

Time and strength can be better employed than in dwelling at length upon the quibbles of our opponents who deal in slander and misrepresentation. While precious time is employed in following the crooks and turns of dishonest opponents, the people who are open to conviction are dying for want of knowledge. A train of senseless quibbles of Satan's own invention is brought before minds, while the people are crying for food — for meat in due season.

It takes those who have trained their minds to war against the truth, to manufacture quibbles. And we are not wise to take them from their hands, and pass them out to thousands who would never have thought of them had we not published them to the world.

The plan of Christ's teaching should be ours. He was plain and simple, striking directly at the root of the matter, and the minds of all were met. It is not the best policy to be so very explicit, and say all upon a point that can be said, when a few arguments will cover the ground, and be sufficient for all practical purposes, to convince or silence opponents.

You may remove every prop to-day, and close the mouths of objectors so that they can say nothing, and to-morrow they will go over the same ground again. Thus it will be, over and over, because they do not love the truth, and will not come to the light, lest their darkness and error should be removed from them.

Christ's ministry lasted only three years, but a great work was done in that short period. In these last days there is a great work to be done in a short time. While many are getting ready to do something, souls will perish for lack of light and knowledge.

If men who are engaged in presenting and defending the truth of the Bible, undertake to investigate and show the fallacy and inconsistency of men who dishonestly turn the truth of God into a lie, Satan will stir up opponents enough to keep their pens constantly employed, while other branches of the work will be left to suffer. We must have more of the spirit of those men who were engaged in building the walls of Jerusalem. We are doing a great work, and cannot come down. If Satan can keep men answering the objections of opponents, thus hindering them from doing the most important work for the present time, his object is accomplished.

DISCUSSIONS NOT TO BE SOUGHT *

Young preachers should avoid discussions, for these do not increase spirituality or humbleness of mind. In some cases, it may be necessary to meet a proud boaster against the truth of God in open debate; but generally these discussions, either oral or written, result in more harm than good. After a discussion, the greater responsibility rests upon the minister to keep up the interest. He should beware of the reaction which is liable to take place after a religious excitement, and not yield to discouragement. . . .

Generally, the influence of discussions upon our ministers is to make them self-sufficient, exalted in their own estimation. This is not all. Those who love to debate are unfitted for being pastors to the flock. They have trained their minds to meet opponents, and to say sarcastic things; and they cannot come down to meet hearts that are sorrowing, and that need to be comforted. . . .

In the presentation of unpopular truth, which involves a heavy cross, preachers should be careful that every word is as God would have it. Their words should never cut. They should present the truth in humility, with the deepest love for souls, and an earnest desire for their salvation, and let the truth cut. —*"Testimonies for the Church," Vol. III, pages 213-218.*

Discussions cannot always be avoided. . . . People who love to see opponents combat, may clamor

* From a personal testimony.

for discussion. Others, who have a desire to hear the evidences on both sides, may urge discussion in all honesty of motive; but whenever discussions can be avoided, they should be. They generally strengthen combativeness, and weaken that pure love and sacred sympathy which should ever exist in the hearts of Christians, although they may differ in opinion.

In this age of the world a demand for a discussion is not real evidence of earnest desire on the part of the people to investigate the truth, but comes through the love of novelty and the excitement which generally attends discussions. God is seldom glorified or the truth advanced in these combats. Truth is too solemn, too momentous in its results, to make it a small matter whether it is received or rejected. To discuss truth for the sake of showing opponents the skill of the combatants, is ever poor policy; for it does very little to advance the truth.

Opponents of the truth will show skill in misstating the positions of its defenders. . . . They will generally deride sacred truth, and place it in so false a light before the people that minds that are darkened by error and polluted by sin, do not discern the motives and objects of these designing men in thus covering up and falsifying important truth. Because of the men who engage in them, there are few discussions that it is possible to conduct upon right principles. Sharp thrusts are too frequently given, personalities are indulged in, and often both parties descend to sarcasm and witticism. The love of souls is lost in the greater desire for the mastery. Prejudice, deep and bitter, is often the result. . . .

Many choose darkness rather than light, because their deeds are evil. But there are those who, if the truth had been presented in a different manner, under different circumstances, giving them a fair chance to weigh the arguments for themselves, and to compare scripture with scripture, would have been charmed by its clearness, and would have taken hold of it.

It has been very indiscreet for our ministers to publish to the world the wily sophistry of error, furnished by designing men to cover up and make of no effect the solemn, sacred truth of Jehovah. These crafty men who lie in wait to deceive the unwary, give their strength of intellect to perverting the word of God. The inexperienced and unsuspecting are deceived to their ruin. It has been a great error to publish to all the arguments wherewith opponents battle against the truth of God; for in so doing minds of every class are furnished with arguments which many of them had never thought of. Some one must render an account for this unwise generalship.

Arguments against the sacred truth, subtle in their influence, affect minds that are not well informed in regard to the strength of the truth. The moral sensibilities of the community at large are blunted by familiarity with sin. Selfishness, dishonesty, and the varied sins which prevail in this degenerate age, have blunted the senses to eternal things, so that God's truth is not discerned. In giving publicity to the erroneous arguments of our opponents, truth and error are placed upon a level in the minds of the people, when, if they could have the truth before them in its clearness long enough to see and realize its sacredness and importance, they would be convinced of the strong arguments in its favor, and would then be prepared to meet the arguments urged by opposers.

Those who are seeking to know the truth and to understand the will of God, who are faithful to the light, and zealous in the performance of their daily duties, will surely know of the doctrine; for they will be guided into all truth.—*"Testimonies for the Church," Vol. III, pages 424-427.*

Whenever it is necessary for the advancement of the cause of truth and the glory of God, that an opponent be met, now carefully, and with what humility should they [the advocates of truth] go into the conflict. With heart-searching, confession of sin, and earnest prayer, and often fasting for a time, they should entreat that God would especially help them, and give His saving, precious truth a glorious victory, that error might appear in its true deformity, and its advocates be completely discomfited. . . .

Never should you enter upon a discussion, where so much is at stake, relying upon your aptness to handle strong arguments. If it cannot be well avoided, enter the conflict, but enter upon it with firm trust in God, and in the spirit of humility, in the spirit of Jesus, who has bidden you learn of Him who is meek and lowly in heart.— *Id., Vol. I, pages 624-626.*

DEFECTIVE METHODS

There are many men of good minds, intelligent in regard to the Scriptures, whose usefulness is greatly hindered by their defective method of labor. Some who engage in the work of saving souls, fail to secure the best results because they do not carry out with thoroughness the work that they began with much enthusiasm. Others cling tenaciously to preconceived notions, making these prominent, and thereby fail to conform their teaching to the actual needs of the people. Many do not realize the necessity of adapting themselves to circumstances, and meeting the people where they are. They do not identify themselves with those whom they wish to help to reach the Bible standard of Christianity. Some fail of success because they trust to the strength of argument alone, and do not cry earnestly to God for His wisdom to direct them and His grace to sanctify their efforts.

Ministers should be careful not to expect too much from those who are still groping in the darkness of error. They should do their work well, relying upon God to impart to inquiring minds the mysterious, quickening influence of His Holy Spirit, knowing that without this their labors will be unsuccessful. They should be patient and wise in dealing with minds, remembering how manifold are the circumstances that have developed such different traits in individuals. They should strictly guard themselves also, lest self get the supremacy, and Jesus be left out of the question.

Some ministers fail of success because they do not give their undivided interest to the work, when very much depends upon persistent, well-directed labor. They are not true laborers; they do not pursue their work outside of the pulpit. They shirk the duty of going from house to house and laboring wisely in the home circle. They need to cultivate that rare Christian courtesy which would render them kind and considerate toward the souls under their care, working for them with true earnestness and faith, teaching them the way of life.

There are in the ministry men who gain apparent success by swaying minds through human influence. They play upon the feelings at will, making their hearers weep, and in a few minutes laugh. Under labor of this kind, many are moved by impulse to profess Christ, and there is thought to be a wonderful revival; but when the test comes, the work does not endure. Feelings are stirred, and many are borne along by the tide that seems to be setting heavenward; but in the strong current of temptation they quickly float back as driftwood. The laborer is self-deceived, and he misleads his hearers.

Ministers should be guarded, lest they thwart the purposes of God by plans of their own. Many are in danger of narrowing down the work of God, and confining their labor to certain localities, and not cultivating a special interest for the cause in all its various departments.

There are some who concentrate their minds upon one subject, to the exclusion of others which may be of equal importance. They are one-idea men. All the strength of their being is concentrated upon the subject on which the mind is exercised for the time. This one favorite theme is the burden of their thoughts and conversation. Every other consideration is lost sight of. All the evidence that has a bearing upon that subject is eagerly appropriated, and dwelt upon at so great length that minds are wearied in following them.

———

Some ministers make the mistake of supposing that success depends on drawing a large congregation by outward display, and then delivering the message of truth in a theatrical style. But this is using common fire instead of the sacred fire of God's kindling. The Lord is not glorified by this manner of working. Not by startling notices and expensive display is His work to be carried to completion, but by following Christlike methods. "Not by might, nor by power, but by My Spirit, saith the Lord of hosts." [1] It is the naked truth which, like a sharp, two-edged sword, cuts both ways, arousing to spiritual life those who are dead in trespasses and sins. Men will recognize the gospel when it is brought to them in a way that is in harmony with God's purposes.

[1] Zech. 4 : 6.

THE TEMPERANCE WORK

Of all who claim to be numbered among the friends of temperance, Seventh-day Adventists should stand in the front ranks. For many years a flood of light concerning the principles of true reform has been shining on our pathway, and we are accountable before God to let this light shine to others. Years ago we regarded the spread of temperance principles as one of our most important duties. It should be so to-day. Our schools and sanitariums are to reveal the power of the grace of Christ to transform the whole being,— body, soul, and spirit. Our sanitariums and other educational institutions should be centers of light and blessing in the cause of every true reform.

We need at this time to show a decided interest in the workers of the Woman's Christian Temperance Union. None who claim to have a part in the work of God, should lose interest in the grand object of this organization in temperance lines. It would be a good thing if at our camp-meetings we should invite the members of the W. C. T. U. to take part in our exercises. This would help them to become acquainted with the reasons of our faith, and open the way for us to unite with them in the temperance work. If we will do this, we shall come to see that the temperance question means more than many of us have supposed.

In some matters, the workers of the W. C. T. U. are far in advance of our leaders. The Lord has in that organization precious souls, who can be a great help to us in our efforts to advance the temperance movement. And the education our people have had in Bible truth and in a knowledge of the requirements of the law of Jehovah, will enable our sisters to impart to these noble temperance advocates that which will be for their spiritual welfare. Thus a union and sympathy will be created where in the past there has sometimes existed prejudice and misunderstanding. I have been surprised as I have seen the indifference of some of our leaders to this organization. We cannot do a better work than to unite, so far as we can do so without compromise, with the W. C. T. U. workers.

We have a work to do along temperance lines besides that of speaking in public. We must present our principles in pamphlets and in our papers. We must use every possible means of arousing our people to their duty to get into connection with those who know not the truth. The success we have had in missionary work has been fully proportionate to the self-denying, self-sacrificing efforts we have made. The Lord alone knows how much we might have accomplished if as a people we had humbled ourselves before Him and proclaimed the temperance truth in clear, straight lines. . . .

A RIGHT USE OF THE GIFTS OF PROVIDENCE

Our Creator has bestowed His bounties upon man with a liberal hand. Were all these gifts of Providence wisely and temperately employed, poverty, sickness, and distress would be well-nigh banished

13

from the earth. But alas, we see on every hand the blessings of God changed to a curse by the wickedness of men.

There is no class guilty of greater perversion and abuse of His precious gifts than are those who employ the products of the soil in the manufacture of intoxicating liquors. The nutritive grains, the healthful, delicious fruits, are converted into beverages that pervert the senses and madden the brain. As a result of the use of these poisons, thousands of families are deprived of the comforts and even the necessaries of life, acts of violence and crime are multiplied, and disease and death hurry myriads of victims to a drunkard's grave.

This work of destruction is carried on under the protection of the laws of the land! For a paltry sum, men are licensed to deal out to their fellow-men the potion that shall rob them of all that makes this life desirable and of all hope of the life to come. Neither the law-maker nor the liquor-seller is ignorant of the result of his work. At the hotel bar, in the beer-garden, at the saloon, the slave of appetite expends his means for that which is destructive to reason, health, and happiness. The liquor-seller fills his till with the money that should provide food and clothing for the family of the poor drunkard.

This is the worst kind of robbery. Yet men in high positions in society and in the church lend their influence in favor of license laws! . . . Thus society is corrupted, work-houses and prisons are crowded with paupers and criminals, and the gallows is supplied with victims. The evil ends not with the drunkard and his unhappy family. The burdens of taxation are increased, the morals of the young are imperiled, the property and even the life of every member of society is endangered. But the picture may be presented never so vividly, and yet it falls short of the reality. No human pen can fully delineate the horrors of intemperance. . . .

THE CAUSE OF MORAL PARALYSIS

How can Christian men and women tolerate this evil? . . . There is a cause for the moral paralysis upon society. Our laws sustain an evil which is sapping their very foundations. Many deplore the wrongs which they know exist, but consider themselves free from all responsibility in the matter. This cannot be. Every individual exerts an influence in society. In our favored land, every voter has some voice in determining what laws shall control the nation. Should not that influence and that vote be cast on the side of temperance and virtue? . . .

We may call upon the friends of the temperance cause to rally to the conflict, and seek to press back the tide of evil that is demoralizing the world; but of what avail are all our efforts while liquor-selling is sustained by law? Must the curse of intemperance forever rest like a blight upon our land? Must it every year sweep like a devouring fire over thousands of happy homes?

We talk of the results, tremble at the results, and wonder what we can do with the terrible results, while too often we tolerate and even sanction the cause. The advocates of temperance fail to do their whole duty unless they exert their influence by precept and example — by voice and pen and vote —

in favor of prohibition and total abstinence. We need not expect that God will work a miracle to bring about this reform, and thus remove the necessity for our exertion. We ourselves must grapple with this giant foe, our motto, No compromise and no cessation of our efforts till the victory is gained. . . .

What can be done to press back the inflowing tide of evil? Let laws be enacted and rigidly enforced prohibiting the sale and the use of ardent spirits as a beverage. Let every effort be made to encourage the inebriate's return to temperance and virtue. But even more than this is needed to banish the curse of inebriety from our land. Let the appetite for intoxicating liquors be removed, and their use and sale is at an end. This work must to a great degree devolve upon parents. Let them, by observing strict temperance themselves, give the right stamp of character to their children, and then educate and train these children, in the fear of God, to habits of self-denial and self-control. Youth who have been thus trained will have moral stamina to resist temptation, and to control appetite and passion. They will stand unmoved by the folly and dissipation that are corrupting society.

The prosperity of a nation is dependent upon the virtue and intelligence of its citizens. To secure these blessings, habits of strict temperance are indispensable. The history of ancient kingdoms is replete with lessons of warning for us. Luxury, self-indulgence, and dissipation prepared the way for their downfall. It remains to be seen whether our own republic will be admonished by their example, and avoid their fate.— *Review and Herald, Nov. 8, 1881.*

RELIGIOUS LIBERTY

The principle for which the disciples stood so fearlessly when, in answer to the command not to speak any more in the name of Jesus, they declared, "Whether it be right in the sight of God to hearken unto you more than unto God, judge ye,"[1] is the same that the adherents of the gospel struggled to maintain in the days of the Reformation. When in 1529 the German princes assembled at the Diet of Spires, there was presented the emperor's decree restricting religious liberty, and prohibiting all further dissemination of the reformed doctrines. It seemed that the hope of the world was about to be crushed out. Would the princes accept the decree? Should the light of the gospel be shut out from the multitudes still in darkness? Mighty issues for the world were at stake. Those who had accepted the reformed faith met together, and their unanimous decision was, "Let us reject this decree. In matters of conscience the majority has no power."[2]

This principle we in our day are firmly to maintain. The banner of truth and religious liberty held aloft by the founders of the gospel church and by God's witnesses during the centuries that have passed since then, has, in this last conflict, been committed to our hands. The responsibility for this great gift rests with those whom God has blessed with a knowledge of His word. We are to receive this word as supreme authority. We are to recognize human government

---

[1] Acts 4 : 19.

[2] D'Aubigné : " History of the Reformation," book 13, chap. 5.

as an ordinance of divine appointment, and teach obedience to it as a sacred duty, within its legitimate sphere. But when its claims conflict with the claims of God, we must obey God rather than men. God's word must be recognized as above all human legislation. A "Thus saith the Lord" is not to be set aside for a "Thus saith the church" or a "Thus saith the state." The crown of Christ is to be lifted above the diadems of earthly potentates.

We are not required to defy authorities. Our words, whether spoken or written, should be carefully considered, lest we place ourselves on record as uttering that which would make us appear antagonistic to law and order. We are not to say or do anything that would necessarily close up our way. We are to go forward in Christ's name, advocating the truths committed to us. If we are forbidden by men to do this work, then we may say, as did the apostles, "Whether it be right in the sight of God to hearken unto you more than unto God, judge ye. For we cannot but speak the things which we have seen and heard." [3] —*"The Acts of the Apostles," pages 68, 69.*

———◆———

Luther's pen was a power, and his writings, scattered broadcast, stirred the world. The same agencies are at our command, with facilities multiplied a hundred-fold. Bibles, publications in many languages, setting forth the truth for this time, are at our hand, and can be swiftly carried to all the world. We are to give the last warning of God to men, and what should be our earnestness in studying the Bible, and our zeal in spreading the light! —*"Testimonies for the Church," Vol. VI, page 403.*

[3] Acts 4 : 19, 20.

OUR ATTITUDE IN REGARD TO POLITICS

To the Teachers and Managers of our Schools: —

Those who have charge of our institutions and our schools should guard themselves diligently, lest by their words and sentiments they lead the students into false paths. Those who teach the Bible in our churches and our schools are not at liberty to unite in making apparent their prejudices for or against political men or measures, because by so doing they stir up the minds of others, leading each to advocate his favorite theory. There are among those professing to believe present truth, some who will thus be stirred up to express their sentiments and political preferences, so that division will be brought into the church.

The Lord would have His people bury political questions. On these themes silence is eloquence. Christ calls upon His followers to come into unity on the pure gospel principles which are plainly revealed in the word of God. We cannot with safety vote for political parties; for we do not know whom we are voting for. We cannot with safety take part in any political scheme. We cannot labor to please men who will use their influence to repress religious liberty, and to set in operation oppressive measures to lead or compel their fellow-men to keep Sunday as the Sabbath. The first day of the week is not a day to be reverenced. It is a spurious sabbath, and the members of the Lord's family cannot participate with the men who exalt this day, and violate the law of

God by trampling upon His Sabbath. The people of God are not to vote to place such men in office; for when they do this, they are partakers with them of the sins which they commit while in office.

We are not to compromise principle by yielding to the opinions and prejudices which we may have encouraged before we united with God's commandment-keeping people. We have enlisted in the army of the Lord, and we are not to fight on the enemy's side, but on the side of Christ, where we can be a united whole, in sentiment, in action, in spirit, in fellowship. Those who are Christians indeed will be branches of the true vine, and will bear the same fruit as the vine. They will act in harmony, in Christian fellowship. They will not wear political badges, but the badge of Christ.

What are we to do, then?—Let political questions alone. "Be ye not unequally yoked together with unbelievers: for what fellowship hath righteousness with unrighteousness? and what communion hath light with darkness? and what concord hath Christ with Belial? or what part hath he that believeth with an infidel?"[1] What can there be in common between these parties? There can be no fellowship, no communion.

The word "fellowship" means participation, partnership. God employs the strongest figures to show that there should be no union between worldly parties and those who are seeking the righteousness of Christ. What communion can there be between light and darkness, truth and unrighteousness? None whatever. Light represents righteousness; darkness, unrighteousness. Christians have come out of darkness into the

[1] 2 Cor. 6:14, 15.

light. They have put on Christ, and they wear the badge of truth and obedience. They are governed by the elevated and holy principles which Christ expressed in His life. . . .

Those teachers in the church or in the school who distinguish themselves by their zeal in politics, should be relieved of their work and responsibilities without delay; for the Lord will not co-operate with them. The tithe should not be used to pay any one for speechifying on political questions. Every teacher, minister, or leader in our ranks who is stirred with a desire to ventilate his opinions on political questions, should be converted by a belief in the truth, or give up his work. His influence must tell as a laborer together with God in winning souls to Christ, or his credentials must be taken from him. If he does not change, he will do harm, and only harm. . . .

"BE YE SEPARATE"

I call upon my brethren who are appointed to educate, to change their course of action. It is a mistake for you to link your interests with any political party, to cast your vote with them or for them. Those who stand as educators, as ministers, as laborers together with God in any line, have no battles to fight in the political world. Their citizenship is in heaven. The Lord calls upon them to stand as a separate and peculiar people. He would have no schisms in the body of believers. His people are to possess the elements of reconciliation.

Is it their work to make enemies in the political world? — No, no. They are to stand as subjects of Christ's kingdom, bearing the banner on which is inscribed, "The commandments of God, and the faith of Jesus." They are to carry the burden of a special work, a special message. We have a personal responsibility, and this is to be revealed before the heavenly universe, before angels, and before men. God does not call upon us to enlarge our influence by mingling with society, by linking up with men on political questions, but by standing as individual parts of His great whole, with Christ as our head. Christ is our Prince, and as His subjects we are to do the work appointed us by God. . . .

The question may be asked, Are we to have no union whatever with the world? The word of the Lord is to be our guide. Any connection with infidels and unbelievers that would identify us with them, is forbidden by the Word. We are to come out from among them, and be separate. In no case are we to link ourselves with them in their plans of work. But we are not to live reclusive lives. We are to do worldlings all the good we possibly can.

Christ has given us an example of this. When invited to eat with publicans and sinners, He did not refuse; for in no other way than by mingling with them could He reach this class. But on every occasion . . . He opened up themes of conversation which brought things of eternal interest to their minds. And He enjoins us, "Let your light so shine before men, that they may see your good works, and glorify your Father which is in heaven." [2]

On the temperance question, take your position without wavering. Be as firm as a rock. Be not partakers of other men's sins. . . .

[2] Matt. 5 : 16.

There is a large vineyard to be cultivated; but while Christians are to work among unbelievers, they are not to appear like worldlings. They are not to spend their time talking politics or acting politics; for by so doing they give the enemy opportunity to come in and cause variance and discord. Those in the ministry who desire to stand as politicians, should have their credentials taken from them; for this work God has not given to high or low among His people.

God calls upon all who minister in word and doctrine to give the trumpet a certain sound. All who have received Christ, ministers and lay members, are to arise and shine; for great peril is right upon us. Satan is stirring up the powers of earth. Everything in this world is in confusion. God calls upon His people to hold aloft the banner bearing the message of the third angel. . . .

God's children are to separate themselves from politics, from any alliance with unbelievers. They are not to link their interests with the interests of the world. "Give proof of your allegiance to Me," He says, "by standing as My chosen heritage, as a people zealous of good works." Do not take part in political strife. Separate from the world, and refrain from bringing into the church or school ideas that will lead to contention and disorder. Dissension is the moral poison taken into the system by human beings who are selfish. God wants His servants to have clear perceptions, true and noble dignity, that their influence may demonstrate the power of truth.

The Christian life is not to be a haphazard, emotional life. True Christian influence, exerted for the accomplishment of the work God has appointed, is a precious agency, and it must not be united with politics, or bound up in a confederacy with unbelievers. God is to be the center of attraction. Every mind that is worked by the Holy Spirit will be satisfied with Him.— *MS., June 16, 1899.*

"None of us liveth to himself." [3] Let those who are tempted to take part in politics, remember that every move they make has its influence upon others. When ministers or others in responsible positions make remarks in regard to these matters, they cannot gather up the thoughts they have planted in human minds. Under Satan's temptations they have set in operation a train of circumstances leading to results of which they little dream. An act, a word, a thought, cast into the minds of the great concourse of humanity, if it bears the heavenly endorsement, will yield a harvest of precious fruit; but if it is inspired by Satan, it will cause the root of bitterness to spring up, whereby many will be defiled. Then let the stewards of God's grace in any line of service, beware how they mingle the common with the sacred.

Again and again Christ had been asked to decide legal and political questions; but He refused to interfere in temporal matters. . . . He stood in our world as the Head of the great spiritual kingdom that He came to our world to establish,— the kingdom of righteousness. His teaching made plain the ennobling, sanctifying principles that govern this kingdom. He showed that justice and mercy and love are the controlling powers in Jehovah's kingdom.— *"Testimonies for the Church," Vol. IX, page 218.*

[3] Rom. 14: 7.

WORK FOR THE JEWS

At the time when Jerusalem was destroyed and the temple laid in ruins, many thousands of the Jews were sold to serve as bondmen in heathen lands. Like wrecks on a desert shore, they were scattered among the nations. For eighteen hundred years the Jews have wandered from land to land throughout the world, and in no place have they been given the privilege of regaining their ancient prestige as a nation. Maligned, hated, persecuted, from century to century theirs has been a heritage of suffering.

Notwithstanding the awful doom pronounced upon the Jews as a nation at the time of their rejection of Jesus of Nazareth, there have lived from age to age many noble, God-fearing Jewish men and women who have suffered in silence. God has comforted their hearts in affliction, and has beheld with pity their terrible situation. He has heard the agonizing prayers of those who have sought Him with all the heart for a right understanding of His word. Some have learned to see in the lowly Nazarene whom their forefathers rejected and crucified, the true Messiah of Israel. As their minds have grasped the significance of the familiar prophecies so long obscured by tradition and misinterpretation, their hearts have been filled with gratitude to God for the unspeakable gift He bestows upon every human being who chooses to accept Christ as a personal Saviour.

It is to this class that Isaiah referred in his prophecy, "A remnant shall be saved." [1] From Paul's day

[1] See Isa. 10 : 20-22.

to the present time, God by His Holy Spirit has been calling after the Jew as well as the Gentile. "There is no respect of persons with God," [2] declared Paul. The apostle regarded himself as "debtor both to the Greeks, and to the barbarians," [3] as well as to the Jews; but he never lost sight of the decided advantages possessed by the Jews over others, "chiefly, because that unto them were committed the oracles of God." [4] "The gospel," he declared, "is the power of God unto salvation to every one that believeth; to the Jew first, and also to the Greek. For therein is the righteousness of God revealed from faith to faith: as it is written, The just shall live by faith." [5] It is of this gospel of Christ, equally efficacious for Jew and Gentile, that Paul in his epistle to the Romans declared he was not ashamed.

When this gospel shall be presented in its fulness to the Jews, many will accept Christ as the Messiah. Among Christian ministers there are only a few who feel called upon to labor for the Jewish people; but to those who have been often passed by, as well as to all others, the message of mercy and hope in Christ is to come.

In the closing proclamation of the gospel, when special work is to be done for classes of people hitherto neglected, God expects His messengers to take particular interest in the Jewish people whom they find in all parts of the earth. As the Old Testament Scriptures are blended with the New in an explanation of Jehovah's eternal purpose, this will be to many of the Jews as the dawn of a new creation, the resurrection of the soul. As they see the Christ

[2] Rom. 2:11.   [3] Rom. 1:14.   [4] Rom. 3:2.   [5] Rom. 1:16, 17.

of the gospel dispensation portrayed in the pages of the Old Testament Scriptures, and perceive how clearly the New Testament explains the Old, their slumbering faculties will be aroused, and they will recognize Christ as the Saviour of the world. Many will by faith receive Him as their Redeemer. To them will be fulfilled the words, "As many as received Him, to them gave He power to become the sons of God, even to them that believe on His name." [6]

Among the Jews are some who, like Saul of Tarsus, are mighty in the Scriptures, and these will proclaim with wonderful power the immutability of the law of God. The God of Israel will bring this to pass in our day. His arm is not shortened that it cannot save. As His servants labor in faith for those who have long been neglected and despised, His salvation will be revealed.

"Thus saith the Lord, who redeemed Abraham, concerning the house of Jacob, Jacob shall not now be ashamed, neither shall his face now wax pale. But when he seeth his children, the work of Mine hands, in the midst of him, they shall sanctify My name, and sanctify the Holy One of Jacob, and shall fear the God of Israel. They also that erred in spirit shall come to understanding, and they that murmured shall learn doctrine." [7]—"*The Acts of the Apostles*," *pages 379-382.*

[6] John 1 : 12.   [7] Isa. 29 : 22-24.

IMPORTANCE OF THE CAMP-MEETING

The camp-meeting is one of the most important agencies in our work. It is one of the most effective methods of arresting the attention of the people, and reaching all classes with the gospel invitation. . . .

If our camp-meetings are conducted as they should be, they will indeed be a light in the world. They should be held in the large cities and towns where the message of truth has not been proclaimed. And they should continue for two or three weeks. It may sometimes be advisable to hold a camp-meeting for several successive seasons in the same place; but as a rule the place of meeting should be changed from year to year. Instead of having mammoth camp-meetings in a few localities, more good would be done by having smaller meetings in many places. Thus the work will be constantly extending into new fields. . . .

A mistake has been made in holding camp-meetings in out-of-the-way places, and in continuing in the same place year after year. This has been done to save expense and labor; but the saving should be made in other lines. In new fields especially, a dearth of means often makes it difficult to meet the expense of a camp-meeting. Careful economy should be exercised, and inexpensive plans devised; for much can be saved in this way. But let not the work be crippled. This method of presenting the truth to the people is by the devising of our God. When souls are to be labored for, and the truth is to be brought before those who know it not, the work must not be hindered in order to save expense. . . .

[400]

SECURING ATTENDANCE

At one time as we were preparing to hold a camp-meeting near a large city where our people were but little known, I seemed one night to be in an assembly met for consultation as to the work to be done before the meeting. It was proposed to make large efforts, and incur heavy expense for distributing notices and papers. Arrangements were being made to do this, when One who is wise in counsel said:

"Set your tents, begin your meetings, then advertise; and more will be accomplished. The truth spoken by the living preacher will have greater influence than the same matter will have when published in the papers. But both methods combined will have still greater force.

"It is not the best plan to follow one line of effort year after year. Change the order of things. When you give time and opportunity, Satan is prepared to rally his forces, and he will work to destroy every soul possible.

"Do not arouse opposition before the people have had opportunity to hear the truth and know what they are opposing. Reserve your means to do a strong work after the meeting rather than before. If a press can be secured to be worked during the meeting, printing leaflets, notices, and papers for distribution, it will have a telling influence."

At some of our camp-meetings, strong companies of workers have been organized to go out into the city and its suburbs to distribute literature and invite people to the meetings. By this means hundreds of persons were secured as regular attendants during the last half of the meeting, who otherwise might have thought little about it. We must take every justifiable means of bringing the light before the people. . . .

Those who have become interested have to meet sophistry and misrepresentation from popular ministers, and they know not how to answer these things. The truth presented by the living preacher should be published in as compact a form as possible, and circulated widely. So far as practicable, let the important discourses given at our camp-meetings be published in the newspapers. Thus the truth which was placed before a limited number may find access to many minds. And where the truth has been misrepresented, the people will have an opportunity of knowing just what the minister said. . . .

BUSINESS MATTERS

As far as possible, our camp-meetings should be wholly devoted to spiritual interests. They should not be made occasions for the transaction of business. Workers are gathered from all parts of the field, and it seems a favorable opportunity for considering business matters connected with the various branches of the work, and for the training of workers in different lines.

All these interests are important, but when they are attended to at a camp-meeting, but little opportunity remains for dealing with the practical relation of truth to the soul. Ministers are diverted from their work of building up the children of God in the most holy faith, and the camp-meeting does not meet the end for which it was appointed.

Many meetings are conducted in which the larger number of the people have no interest; and if they could attend them all, they would go away wearied instead of being refreshed and benefited. Many are disappointed at the failure of their expectation to receive help from the camp-meeting. Those who came for enlightenment and strength return to their homes little better fitted to work in their families and churches than before attending the meeting.

Business matters should be attended to by those specially appointed for this work. And as far as possible they should be brought before the people at some other time than the camp-meeting. Instruction in canvassing, in Sabbath-school work, and in the details of tract and missionary work, should be given in the home churches, or in meetings specially appointed. The same principle applies to cooking-schools. While these are all right in their place, they should not occupy the time of our camp-meetings.

The presidents of conferences and the ministers should give themselves to the spiritual interests of the people, and should therefore be excused from the mechanical labor attendant upon the meeting. The ministers should be ready to act as teachers and leaders in the work of the camp when occasion requires; but they should not be wearied out. They should feel refreshed, and be in a cheerful frame of mind; for this is essential for the best good of the meeting. They should be able to speak words of cheer and courage, and to drop seeds of spiritual truth into the soil of honest hearts. . . .

THE TRAINING OF YOUNG WORKERS

Those who are in training for work in the cause in any line, should improve every opportunity to work at the camp-meeting. Wherever camp-meetings are held, young men who have received an education in medical lines should feel it their duty to act a part. They should be encouraged not only to work in medical lines, but also to speak upon the points of present truth, giving the reason why we are Seventh-day Adventists. These young men, if given an opportunity to work with older ministers, will receive much help and blessing. . . .

Properly conducted, the camp-meeting is a school where pastors, elders, and deacons can learn to do more perfect work for the Master. It should be a school where the members of the church, old and young, are given an opportunity to learn the way of the Lord more perfectly, a place where believers can receive an education that will help them to help others. . . .

———————

One night, previous to an important meeting, I seemed in my sleeping hours to be in meeting with my brethren, listening to One who spoke as having authority. He said:

"Many souls will attend this meeting who are honestly ignorant of the truths that will be presented. They will listen and become interested, because Christ is drawing them; conscience tells them that what they hear is true, for it has the Bible for its foundation. The greatest care is needed in dealing with these souls.

"Let such portions of the message be dealt out to them as they may be able to grasp and appropriate. Though it should appear strange and startling, many will recognize with joy that new light is shed on the word of God; whereas, if new truths were presented in so large a measure that they could not comprehend them, some would go away and never come again. Some, in their efforts to tell it to others, would misrepresent what they had heard. Some would so wrest the Scriptures as to confuse other minds.

"Those who will study the manner of Christ's teaching, and educate themselves to follow His way, will attract and hold large numbers now, as Christ held the people in His day. At every meeting, Satan will be on the ground, that he may obtrude his hellish shadow between man and God, to intercept every ray of light that might shine on the soul. But when the truth in its practical character is urged upon the people because you love them, souls will be convicted, because the Holy Spirit of God will impress their hearts.

"Arm yourselves with humility; pray that angels of God may come close to your side to impress the mind; for it is not you that work the Holy Spirit, but the Holy Spirit must work you. It is the Holy Spirit that makes the truth impressive. Keep practical truth ever before the people."

Do not make prominent those features of the message which are a condemnation of the customs and practices of the people, until they have an opportunity to know that we are believers in Christ, that we believe in His divinity and in His pre-existence. Let the testimony of the world's Redeemer be dwelt upon. He says, "I Jesus have sent Mine angel to testify unto you these things in the churches." [1] . . .

Whenever practicable, every important discourse should be followed by a Bible study. Here the points

[1] Rev. 22 : 16.

that have been presented can be applied, questions can be asked, and right ideas inculcated. More time should be devoted to patiently educating the people, giving them opportunity to express themselves. It is instruction that men need, line upon line and precept upon precept.

Special meetings also should be held for those who are becoming interested in the truths presented, and who need instruction. To these meetings the people should be invited, and all, both believers and unbelievers, should have an opportunity to ask questions on points not fully understood. Give all an opportunity to speak of their perplexities, for they will have them. In all the sermons and in all the Bible studies, let the people see that on every point a plain "Thus saith the Lord" is given for the faith and doctrines which we advocate.

This was the method of Christ's teaching. As He spoke to the people, they would question as to His meaning. To those who were humbly seeking for light, He was always ready to explain His words. But Christ did not encourage criticism or caviling, nor should we. When men try to provoke a discussion of controverted points of doctrine, tell them that the meeting was not appointed for that purpose. When you do answer a question, be sure to have the hearers see and acknowledge that it is answered. Do not let a question drop, telling them to ask it again. Feel your way step by step, and know how much you have gained.—*"Testimonies for the Church," Vol. VI, pages 31-69.*

LESS PREACHING, MORE TEACHING

At our camp-meetings, one or two laborers should not be required to do all the preaching and all the teaching in Bible lines. At times, greater good can be accomplished by breaking up the large congregation into sections. Thus the educator in Bible truth can come closer to the people than in a large assembly.

There is much more preaching than there should be at our camp-meetings. This brings a heavy burden upon the ministers, and as a consequence much that requires attention is neglected. Many little things that open the door to serious evils are passed by unnoticed. The minister is robbed of physical strength, and deprived of the time he needs for meditation and prayer, in order to keep his own soul in the love of God. And when so many discourses are crowded in, one after another, the people have no time to appropriate what they hear. Their minds become confused, and the services seem to them tedious and wearisome.

There should be less preaching, and more teaching. There are those who want more definite light than they receive from hearing the sermons. Some need a longer time than do others to understand the points presented. If the truth presented could be made a little plainer, they would see it and take hold of it, and it would be like a nail fastened in a sure place.

It has been shown me that our camp-meetings are to increase in interest and success. As we approach the end, I have seen that in these meetings there will be less preaching, and more Bible study. There will be little groups all over the grounds, with their Bibles in their hands, and different ones leading out in a free, conversational study of the Scriptures.

This was the method that Christ taught His disciples. When the great throngs gathered about the Saviour, He would give instruction to the disciples and to the multitude. Then after the discourse, the disciples would mingle with the people, and repeat to them what Christ had said. Often the hearers had misapplied Christ's words, and the disciples would tell them what the Scriptures said, and what Christ had taught that they said.— *"Testimonies for the Church,"* *Vol. VI, pages 87, 88.*

———◆———

The great Teacher brought His hearers in contact with nature, that they might listen to the voice which speaks in all created things; and as their hearts became tender and their minds receptive, He helped them to interpret the spiritual teaching of the scenes upon which their eyes rested. The parables, by means of which He loved to teach lessons of truth, show how open His spirit was to the influences of nature, and how He delighted to gather the spiritual teaching from the surroundings of daily life. The birds of the air, the lilies of the field, the sower and the seed, the shepherd and the sheep,— with these Christ illustrated immortal truth. He drew illustrations also from the events of life, facts of experience familiar to the hearers,— the leaven, the hid treasure, the pearl, the fishing net, the lost coin, the prodigal son, the houses on the rock and the sand. In His lessons there was something to interest every mind, to appeal to every heart.—*"Christ's Object Lessons," page 102.*

SOWING AND REAPING

"One soweth, and another reapeth." [1] The Saviour spoke these words in anticipation of the ordination and sending forth of His disciples. Throughout Judea, Christ had been sowing the seeds of truth. Clearly and distinctly He had outlined the plan of salvation; for the truth never languished on His lips. The earthly work of the great Teacher was soon to close. The disciples were to follow after, reaping where He had sown, that both the Sower and the reapers might rejoice together.

To-day in His great harvest-field God has need of sowers and of reapers. Let those who go forth into the work, some to sow and some to reap, remember that they are never to take to themselves the glory for the success of their work. God's appointed agencies have been before them, preparing the way for the sowing of the seed and the reaping of the harvest. "I sent you to reap that whereon ye bestowed no labor," Christ said; "other men labored, and ye are entered into their labors." [1]

"He that reapeth receiveth wages, and gathereth fruit unto life eternal: that both he that soweth and he that reapeth may rejoice together." [1] Read these words carefully. Study their meaning; for they outline God's plan. Those who sow the seed, presenting before large and small gatherings the testing truth for this time, at the cost of much labor, may not always gather the harvest. Often the Lord's workers are bitterly opposed, and their work is hindered.

[1] John 4 : 37, 38, 36.

They do their best; with earnest, painstaking effort they sow the good seed. But the element of opposition becomes fiercer and fiercer. Some of the hearers may be convinced of the truth, but they are intimidated by the opposition shown, and they have not the courage to acknowledge their convictions.

The lives of the workers may be endangered by those who are controlled by Satan. It is then their privilege to follow the example of their Master, and go to another place. "Ye shall not have gone over the cities of Israel," Christ said, "till the Son of man be come."[2] Let the messengers of truth pass on to another field. Here may be a more favorable opportunity for work, and they may successfully sow the seed of truth and reap the harvest. The report of their success will find its way to the place where the work was apparently unsuccessful, and the next messenger of truth who goes there will be more favorably received.

The seed sown in trial and discouragement will be seen to have life and vitality. Adversity, sorrow, loss of property, the changes of God's providence, recall with vivid distinctness the words spoken years before by the faithful servant of God. The seed sown springs up and bears fruit.

God has need of wise men and women who will labor earnestly to accomplish the work committed to them. He will use them as His instruments in the conversion of souls. Some will sow, and some will reap the harvest of the seed sown. Let every one do his best to improve his talents, that God may use him either as a sower or as a reaper.

[2] Matt. 10 : 23.

FOR FURTHER STUDY

LABOR IN THE CITIES

Test. Vol. VII, pp. 34-41.
Test. Vol. IX, pp. 137-152.
C. O. L., pp. 219-237.

MEDICAL MISSIONARY WORK
IN CITIES

Test. Vol. VI, pp. 234-242, 254-
260, 288-293.
Test. Vol. VIII, pp. 158-171.
Test. Vol. IX, pp. 167-172.
M. of H., pp. 139-216.

THE CITY MISSION TRAINING
SCHOOL

Test. Vol. V, pp. 368-385.

THOROUGHNESS

Test. Vol. II, pp. 621, 622.
Test. Vol. III, p. 228.
Test. Vol. IV, pp. 261-265.
Test. Vol. V, pp. 254-256.

MEETING OPPOSITION

Test. Vol. III, pp. 570-575.
Test. Vol. IX, pp. 141-152, 204-
216.
Acts, pp. 546-556.

DISCUSSIONS NOT TO BE
SOUGHT

Test. Vol. I, pp. 428, 623-627.
Test. Vol. III, p. 203.
Test. Vol. V, p. 708.
Acts, pp. 243-254.

DEFECTIVE METHODS

Test. Vol. III, pp. 34-39.
Ed., pp. 76-96, 119, 120, 185-
192, 230-239.

THE TEMPERANCE WORK

Test. Vol. VI, pp. 110, 111.
M. of H., pp. 171-182, 325-346.

RELIGIOUS LIBERTY

Test. Vol. VI, pp. 394-403.
Test. Vol. IX, pp. 227-244.

OUR ATTITUDE IN REGARD
TO POLITICS

Test. Vol. VII, p. 252.
Test. Vol. IX, pp. 216-218.

Conference Responsibilities

"It is required . . . that a
man be found faithful."

CONFERENCE PRESIDENTS *

The Lord has been pleased to present before me many things in regard to the calling and labor of our ministers, especially those who have been appointed as presidents of conferences. Great care should be exercised in the selection of men for these positions of trust. There should be earnest prayer for divine enlightenment.

Those who are thus appointed as overseers of the flock should be men of good repute; men who give evidence that they have not only a knowledge of the Scriptures, but an experience in faith, in patience, that in meekness they may instruct those who oppose the truth. They should be men of thorough integrity, not novices, but intelligent students of the Word, able to teach others also, bringing from the treasure-house things new and old; men who in character, in words, in deportment, will be an honor to the cause of Christ, teaching the truth, living the truth, growing up to the full stature in Christ Jesus. This means the development and strengthening of every faculty by exercise, that the workers may become qualified to bear larger responsibilities as the work increases.

---

* From a sermon delivered at the General Conference of 1883.

The Lord Jesus connected Judas and Peter with Himself, not because they were defective in character, but notwithstanding their defects. He would give them an opportunity to learn in His school, meekness and lowliness of heart, that they might become co-laborers with Him. And if they would improve these opportunities, if they would be willing to learn, willing to see their deficiencies, and in the light of a pure example to become all that Christ would have them, then they would be a great blessing to the church.

Thus the Lord Jesus is still dealing with men. Some who are imperfect in character are connected with solemn, sacred interests; and when chosen for a special work, they should not feel that their own wisdom is sufficient, that they need not be counseled, reproved, and instructed. Brethren, if you feel thus, you will separate from the Source of your strength, and will be in peril. You may be left to your own supposed sufficiency, to do as Judas did,— betray your Lord. . . .

LOOKING TO MEN FOR COUNSEL

Some of our conferences are weak in Christian experience because their leading men — and the people have followed their example — have sought for the approval of man with far greater anxiety than for the approval of God. They have looked to man for help and counsel more than to God. They have made men their burden-bearers, and have accepted human wisdom just when and where they should have depended upon God. And too often those of whom they sought counsel needed help themselves; for their souls were not right with God. The presidents of our conferences have become weak and inefficient by making flesh their arm. Trust in the wisdom of man does not facilitate growth in grace and in the knowledge of Christ.

Brethren, when perplexities arise in your conference, when emergencies are to be met, do not let these dark clouds drift into the General Conference if you can possibly avoid it. The president of the General Conference should not be burdened with the affairs of the State conferences, as has been the case in the past. If you, with your associates in the work, cannot adjust the troubles and difficulties that arise in your conference, how do you think that one man can do this work for all the conferences? Why should you pour all your perplexities and discouragements into the burdened mind and heart of the president of the General Conference? He cannot understand the situation as well as do you who are on the ground. If you shirk responsibility and crosses and burden-bearing, hard thinking and earnest praying, and look to the president of the General Conference to do your work and help you out of your difficulties, cannot you see that you lay upon him burdens that will imperil his life? Have you not mind and ability as well as he? You should not neglect any part of the work because it calls for earnest, cross-bearing effort.

I repeat, Do not throw your burdens upon the president of the General Conference. Do not expect him to take up your dropped stitches and bind off your work. Resolve that you will bear your own burdens through Christ who strengthens you.

The president of the General Conference, if he is walking in the counsel of God, will not encourage his brethren to look to him to define their duty, but will direct them to the only Source that is untainted with the errors of humanity. He will refuse to be mind and conscience for others. . . .

The one who is the object of this undue confidence is exposed to strong temptations. Satan will, if possible, lead him to be self-confident, in order that human defects may mar the work. He will be in danger of encouraging his brethren in their dependence upon him, and of feeling that all things that pertain to the movements of the cause must be brought to his notice. Thus the work will bear the impress of man instead of the impress of God.

But if all will learn to depend upon God for themselves, many dangers that assail the one who stands at the head of the work will be averted. If he errs, if he permits human influence to sway his judgment, or yields to temptation, he can be corrected and helped by his brethren. And those who learn to go to God for themselves for help and counsel, are learning lessons that will be of the highest value to them.

If the officers of a conference would bear successfully the burdens laid upon them, they must pray, they must believe, they must trust God to use them as His agents in keeping the churches of the conference in good working order. This is their part of the vineyard to cultivate. There must be far more personal responsibility, far more thinking and planning, far more mental power brought into the labor put forth for the Master. This would enlarge the capacity of the mind, and give keener perceptions as to what to do and how.

Brethren, you will have to wrestle with difficulties, carry burdens, give advice, plan and execute, constantly looking to God for help. Pray and labor, labor and pray; as pupils in the school of Christ, learn of Jesus.

The Lord has given us the promise, "If any of you lack wisdom, let him ask of God, that giveth to all men liberally, and upbraideth not; and it shall be given him." [1] It is in the order of God that those who bear responsibilities should often meet together to counsel with one another, and to pray earnestly for that wisdom which He alone can impart. Talk less; much precious time is lost in talk that brings no light. Let brethren unite in fasting and prayer for the wisdom that God has promised to supply liberally. Make known your troubles to God. Tell Him, as did Moses, "I cannot lead this people unless Thy presence shall go with me." And then ask still more; pray with Moses, "Show me Thy glory." [2] What is this glory? — The character of God. This is what He proclaimed to Moses.

Let the soul in living faith fasten upon God. Let the tongue speak His praise. When you associate together, let the mind be reverently turned to the contemplation of eternal realities. Thus you will be helping one another to be spiritually minded. When your will is in harmony with the divine will, you will be in harmony with one another; you will have Christ by your side as a counselor.

Enoch walked with God. So may every laborer for Christ. You may say with the psalmist, "I have set the Lord always before me: because He is at my

[1] James 1 : 5. [2] Ex. 33 : 18.

14

right hand, I shall not be moved." [3] While you feel that you have no sufficiency of yourself, your sufficiency will be in Jesus. If you expect all your counsel and wisdom to come from men, mortal and finite like yourselves, you will receive only human help. If you go to God for help and wisdom, He will never disappoint your faith.

The presidents of the State conferences have the same God that the president of the General Conference has, and they may go to the Source of wisdom for themselves, instead of depending upon one man, who has to obtain his light from the same source.

It may be argued that the Lord gives special wisdom to those entrusted with important responsibilities. True, if they walk humbly with Him, He will give them help for their work; and He will give you help for yours, if you seek it in the same spirit. If the Lord in His providence has placed important responsibilities upon you, He will fit you to bear these burdens, if you go to Him in faith for strength to do this. When you put your trust in Him, and depend upon His counsel, He will not leave you to your own finite judgment, to make imperfect plans and decided failures.

MAKE NO MAN YOUR CONFESSOR

Every one needs a practical experience in trusting God for himself. Let no man become your confessor; open the heart to God; tell Him every secret of the soul. Bring to Him your difficulties, small and great, and He will show you a way out of them all. He alone can know how to give the very help you need.

[3] Ps. 16 : 8.

And when, after a trying season, help comes to you, when the Spirit of God is manifestly at work for you, what a precious experience you gain! You are obtaining faith and love, the gold that the True Witness counsels you to buy of Him. You are learning to go to God in all your troubles; and as you learn these precious lessons of faith, you will teach the same to others. Thus you may be continually leading the people to a higher plane of experience.

The president of a State conference is, by his manner of dealing, educating the ministers under him, and together they can so educate the churches that it will not be necessary to call the ministers of the conference from the field to settle difficulties and dissensions in the church. If the officers in the conference will, as faithful servants, perform their Heaven-appointed duties, the work in our conferences will not be left to become entangled in such perplexities as heretofore. And in laboring thus, the workers will become solid, responsible men, who will not fail nor be discouraged in a hard place.

There is One who is mighty to save to the uttermost all who come unto Him. Is not the promise broad and full, "Come unto Me, all ye that labor and are heavy laden, and I will give you rest"? [4] Why are we so unwilling to come directly to the Source of our strength? Have we not departed from the Lord in this? Should not our ministers and the presidents of our conferences learn whence cometh their help? . . .

A CHANGE OF LABORERS

The question is asked me if it is not a mistake to remove the president of a State conference to a

[4] Matt. 11 : 28.

new field when many of the people under his present charge are unwilling to give him up.

The Lord has been pleased to give me light on this question. I have been shown that ministers should not be retained in the same district year after year, nor should the same man long preside over a conference. A change of gifts is for the good of our conferences and churches.

Ministers have sometimes felt unwilling to change their field of labor; but if they understood all the reasons for making changes, they would not draw back. Some have pleaded to remain one year longer in the same field, and frequently the request has been respected. They have claimed to have plans for accomplishing a greater work than heretofore. But at the close of the year there was a worse state of things than before. If a minister has been unfaithful in his work, it is not likely that he will mend the matter by remaining. The churches become accustomed to the management of that one man, and think they must look to him instead of to God. His ideas and plans have a controlling power in the conference.

The people may see that he errs in judgment, and because of this they learn to place a low estimate upon the ministry. If they would look to God, and depend upon heavenly wisdom, they would be gaining an experience of the highest value, and would themselves be able, in many respects at least, to supply what is lacking in him who is the overseer of the flock. But too often things are left to drift as they will, the president being held responsible for the condition of the churches in the conference, while the church-members settle down, indifferent, lukewarm, doing nothing to bring things into order.

The president may not feel the importance of sanctifying himself, that others may be sanctified. He may be an unfaithful watchman, preaching to please the people. Many are strong in some points of character, while they are weak and deficient in others. As the result, a want of efficiency is manifest in some parts of the work. Should the same man continue as president of a conference year after year, his defects would be reproduced in the churches under his labors. But one laborer may be strong where his brother is weak, and so by exchanging fields of labor, one may, to some extent, supply the deficiencies of another.

If all were fully consecrated to God, these marked imperfections of character would not exist; but since the laborers do not meet the divine standard, since they weave self into all their work, the best thing, both for themselves and for the churches, is to make frequent changes. And, on the other hand, if a laborer is spiritually strong, he is, through the grace of Christ, a blessing to the churches, and his labors are needed in different conferences.

———◆———

We are in times of peculiar danger from foes without and within, and God would have you alive to everything concerning your special work. You need not try to do anything without the special help of your heavenly Father. He is waiting for you to call, that He may say, "Here I am." If you will seek, He says He will be found of you; His strength, His grace, and His righteousness will be given to the humble, contrite one who seeks Him with all the heart.

MINISTERS AND BUSINESS MATTERS

I have been instructed in regard to the importance of our ministers' keeping free from responsibilities that should be largely borne by business men. In the night season I was in an assembly consisting of a number of our brethren who bear the burden of the work. They were deeply perplexed over financial affairs, and were consulting as to how the work could be managed most successfully. Some thought that the number of workers might be limited, and yet all the results essential be realized. One of the brethren occupying a position of responsibility was explaining his plans, and stating what he desired to see accomplished. Several others presented matters for consideration. Then One of dignity and authority arose, and proceeded to state principles for our guidance. To several ministers the Speaker said:

"Your work is not the management of financial matters. It is not wise for you to undertake this. God has burdens for you to bear, but if you carry lines of work for which you are not adapted, your efforts in presenting the Word will prove unsuccessful. This will bring upon you discouragement that will disqualify you for the very work you should do,— a work requiring careful discrimination and sound, unselfish judgment."

Those who are employed to write and to speak the Word should attend fewer committee meetings. They should entrust many minor matters to men of business ability, and thus avoid being kept on a constant strain that robs the mind of its natural vigor.

They should give far more attention to the preservation of physical health; for vigor of mind depends largely upon vigor of body. Proper periods of sleep and rest and an abundance of physical exercise are essential to health of body and mind. To rob nature of her hours for rest and recuperation, by allowing one man to do the work of four, or of three, or even of two, will result in irreparable loss.

EDUCATION IN BUSINESS LINES

Those who think that a man's fitness for a certain position qualifies him to fill several other positions, are liable to make mistakes when planning for the advancement of the work. They are liable to place upon one the cares and burdens that should be divided among several.

Experience is of great value. The Lord desires to have men of intelligence connected with His work, men qualified for various positions of trust in our conferences and institutions. Especially are consecrated business men needed, men who will carry the principles of truth into every business transaction. Those placed in charge of financial affairs should not assume other burdens, burdens that they are incapable of bearing; nor is the business management to be entrusted to incompetent men. Those in charge of the work have erred sometimes in permitting the appointment of men devoid of tact and ability to manage important financial interests.

Men of promise in business lines should develop and perfect their talents by most thorough study and training. They should be encouraged to place themselves where, as students, they can rapidly gain a knowledge of right business principles and methods. Not one business man now connected with the cause needs to be a novice. If men in any line of work ought to improve their opportunities to become wise and efficient, it is those who are using their ability in the work of building up the kingdom of God in our world. In view of the fact that we are living so near the close of this earth's history, there should be greater thoroughness in labor, more vigilant waiting, watching, praying, and working. The human agent should strive to attain perfection, that he may be an ideal Christian, complete in Christ Jesus.

RIGHT PRINCIPLES ESSENTIAL

Those who labor in business lines should take every precaution against falling into error through wrong principles or methods. Their record may be like that of Daniel in the courts of Babylon. When all his business transactions were subjected to the closest scrutiny, not one faulty item could be found. The record of his business life, incomplete though it is, contains lessons worthy of study. It reveals the fact that a business man is not necessarily a scheming, policy man. He may be a man instructed of God at every step. Daniel, while prime minister of the kingdom of Babylon, was a prophet of God, receiving the light of heavenly inspiration. His life is an illustration of what every Christian business man may be. . . .

At this time God's cause is in need of men and women who possess rare qualifications and good administrative powers; men and women who will make patient, thorough investigation of the needs of the work in various fields; those who have a large capacity for work; those who possess warm, kind hearts, cool heads, sound sense, and unbiased judgment; those who are sanctified by the Spirit of God, and can fearlessly say No, or Yea and amen, to propositions; those who have strong convictions, clear understanding, and pure, sympathetic hearts; those who practice the words, "All ye are brethren;" [1] those who strive to uplift and restore fallen humanity.—"*Testimonies for the Church,*" *Vol. VII, pages 246-249.*

———◆———

Not a few ministers are neglecting the very work that they have been appointed to do. Why are those who are set apart for the work of the ministry placed on committees and boards? Why are they called upon to attend so many business meetings, many times at great distance from their fields of labor? Why are not business matters placed in the hands of business men? The ministers have not been set apart to do this work. The finances of the cause are to be managed by men of ability; but ministers are set apart for another line of work. . . .

Ministers are not to be called hither and thither to attend board meetings for the purpose of deciding common business questions. Many of our ministers have done this work in the past, but it is not the work in which the Lord wishes them to engage. Too many financial burdens have been placed on them. When they try to carry these burdens, they neglect to fulfil the gospel commission. God looks upon this as a dishonor to His name.—"*Testimonies for the Church,*" *Vol. VII, pages 254, 255.*

[1] Matt. 23 : 8.

CARE FOR WORKERS

Some provision should be made for the care of ministers and others of God's faithful servants who through exposure or overwork in His cause have become ill and need rest and restoration, or who through age or loss of health are no longer able to bear the burden and heat of the day. Ministers are often appointed to a field of labor that they know will be detrimental to their health; but, unwilling to shun trying places, they venture, hoping to be a help and blessing to the people. After a time they find their health failing. A change of climate and of work is tried, without bringing relief; and then what are they to do?

These faithful laborers, who for Christ's sake have given up worldly prospects, choosing poverty rather than pleasure or riches; who, forgetful of self, have labored earnestly to win souls to Christ; who have given liberally to advance various enterprises in the cause of God, and have then sunk down in the battle, wearied and ill, and with no means of support, must not be left to struggle on in poverty and suffering, or to feel that they are paupers. When sickness or infirmity comes upon them, let not our workers be burdened with the anxious query, "What will become of my wife and little ones, now that I can no longer labor and supply their necessities?" It is but just that provision be made to meet the needs of these faithful laborers, and the needs of those who are dependent on them.

Generous provision is made for veterans who have fought for their country. These men bear the scars and life-long infirmities that tell of their perilous conflicts, their forced marches, their exposure to storms, their suffering in prison. All these evidences of their loyalty and self-sacrifice give them a just claim upon the nation they have helped to save,— a claim that is recognized and honored. But what provision have Seventh-day Adventists made for the soldiers of Christ?

Our people have not felt as they should the necessity of this matter, and it has therefore been neglected. The churches have been thoughtless, and though the light of the word of God has been shining upon their pathway, they have neglected this most sacred duty. The Lord is greatly displeased with this neglect of His faithful servants. Our people should be as willing to assist these persons when in adverse circumstances as they have been to accept their means and services when in health.

God has laid upon us the obligation of giving special attention to the poor among us. But these ministers and workers are not to be ranked with the poor. They have laid up for themselves a treasure in the heavens that faileth not. They have served the conference in its necessity, and now the conference is to serve them.

When cases of this kind come before us, we are not to pass by on the other side. We are not to say, "Be ye warmed and filled," [1] and then take no active measures to supply their necessities. This has been done in the past, and thus in some cases Seventh-day Adventists have dishonored their profession of faith, and

[1] James 2 : 16.

have given the world opportunity to reproach the cause of God.

It is now the duty of God's people to roll back this reproach by providing these servants of God with comfortable homes, with a few acres of land, on which they can raise their own produce, and feel that they are not dependent on the charities of their brethren. With what pleasure and peace would these worn laborers look to a quiet little home where their just claims to its rest would be recognized! . . .

OUR SANITARIUMS A REFUGE FOR WORKERS

Often these ministers need special care and treatment. Our sanitariums should be a refuge for such, and for all our worn workers who need rest. Rooms should be provided where they can have a change and rest, without continual anxiety as to how they are to meet the expense. When the disciples were worn with labor, Christ said to them, "Come ye yourselves apart, . . . and rest awhile." [2] He would have arrangements made whereby His servants now may have opportunity to rest and recover strength. Our sanitariums are to be open to our hard-working ministers, who have done all in their power to secure funds for the erection and support of these institutions; and at any time when they are in need of the advantages here offered, they should be made to feel at home.

These workers should not at any time be charged a high price for board and treatment, neither should they be regarded as beggars, or in any way made to feel as such by those whose hospitality they receive. To manifest liberality in the use of the facilities God has provided for His worn and overworked servants,

[2] Mark 6 : 31.

is genuine medical missionary work in His sight. God's workers are bound to Him, and when they are received, it should be remembered that Christ is received in the person of His messengers. He requires this, and is dishonored and displeased when they are treated indifferently or dealt with in a small or selfish manner. God's blessing will not attend close dealing with any of His chosen ones.

Among the medical fraternity there has not always been a keenness of perception to discern these matters. Some have not regarded them as they should. May the Lord sanctify the perception of those who have charge of our institutions, that they may know who should have true sympathy and care. That branch of the cause for which these worn-out laborers have worked should show an appreciation of their labor by helping them in their time of need, thus sharing largely with the sanitarium the burden of expense. Some workers are so situated as to be able to lay by a little from their salary; and this they should do, if possible, to meet an emergency; yet even these should be welcome as a blessing to the sanitarium.

But most of our workers have many and great obligations to meet. At every turn, when means are needed, they are called upon to do something, to lead out, that the influence of their example may stimulate others to liberality, and the cause of God be advanced. They feel such an intense desire to plant the standard in new fields that many even hire money to help in various enterprises. They have not given grudgingly, but have felt that it was a privilege to work for the advancement of the truth. By thus responding to calls for means, they are often left with very little surplus.

The Lord has kept an accurate account of their liberality to the cause. He knows what a good work they have done, a work of which the younger laborers have no conception. He has been cognizant of all the privation and self-denial they have endured. He has marked every circumstance of these cases. It is all written in the books. These workers are a spectacle before the world, before angels, and before men; and they are an object-lesson to test the sincerity of our religious principles. The Lord would have our people understand that the pioneers in this work deserve all that our institutions can do for them. God calls upon us to understand that those who have grown old in His service deserve our love, our honor, our deepest respect.

A WORKERS' FUND

A fund should be raised for such workers as are no longer able to labor. We cannot be clear before God unless we make every reasonable effort in this matter, and that without delay. There are some among us who will not see the necessity of this move; but their opposition should have no influence with us. Those who purpose in their hearts to be right and to do right, should move steadily forward for the accomplishment of a good work, a work that God requires to be done.—"*Testimonies for the Church*," *Vol. VII, pages 290-294.*

HOUSES OF WORSHIP

When an interest is aroused in any town or city, that interest should be followed up. The place should be thoroughly worked, until a humble house of worship stands as a sign, a memorial of God's Sabbath, a light amid the moral darkness. These memorials are to stand in many places as witnesses to the truth. God in His mercy has provided that the messengers of the gospel shall go to all countries, tongues, and peoples, until the standard of truth shall be established in all parts of the inhabited world.

Wherever a company of believers is raised up, a house of worship should be built. Let not the workers leave the place without accomplishing this.

In many places where the message has been preached, those who have accepted it are in limited circumstances, and can do but little toward securing advantages that would give character to the work. Often this renders it difficult to extend the work. As persons become interested in the truth, they are told by the ministers of other churches,— and these words are echoed by the church-members,—"These people have no church, and you have no place of worship. You are a small company, poor and unlearned. In a short time the ministers will go away, and then the interest will die down. Then you will give up all these new ideas which you have received." Can we suppose that this will not bring strong temptation to those who see the reasons of our faith and are convicted by the Spirit of God in regard to present truth?

It has to be often repeated, that from a small beginning large interests may grow. If wisdom and sanctified judgment and skilful generalship are manifested by us in building up the interests of our Redeemer's kingdom, we shall do all in our power to assure the people of the stability of our work. Humble sanctuaries will be erected, where those who accept the truth may find a place to worship God according to the dictates of their own conscience.

Whenever it is possible, let our church buildings be dedicated to God free of debt. When a church is raised up, let the members arise and build. Under the direction of a minister who is guided by the advice of his fellow-ministers, let the newly converted ones work with their own hands, saying, "We need a meeting-house, and we must have it." God calls upon His people to make cheerful, united efforts in His cause. Let this be done, and soon will be heard the voice of thanksgiving, "See what the Lord hath wrought!"

There are some cases, however, in which a young church may not be able at once to bear the whole burden of erecting a house of worship. In these cases let the brethren in other churches help them. In some cases it may be better to hire some money than not to build. If a man has money, and, after giving what he can, will make a loan, either without interest or at a low rate, it would be right to use the money until the indebtedness can be lifted. But I repeat, If possible, church buildings should be dedicated free of debt.

In our churches the pews should not be rented. The wealthy are not to be honored above the poor. Let no distinction be made. "All ye are brethren." [1]

[1] Matt. 23 : 8.

In none of our buildings should we seek to make a display, for this would not advance the work. Our economy should testify to our principles. We should employ methods of work that are not transient. Everything should be done solidly. . . .

The lax way which some churches have of incurring debts and keeping in debt, was presented before me. In some cases a continual debt is upon the house of God. There is a continual interest to be paid. These things should not and need not be. If there is that wisdom and tact and zeal manifested for the Master which God requires, there will be a change in these things. The debts will be lifted. God calls for offerings from those who can give, and even the poorer members can do their little. Self-denial will enable all to do something. Both old and young, parents and children, are to show their faith by their works. Let the necessity that each act a part be most strenuously impressed upon the members of the church. Let every one do his best. When there is a will to do, God will open the way. He does not design that His cause shall be trammeled with debt.

God calls for self-sacrifice. This will bring not only financial but spiritual prosperity. Self-denial and self-sacrifice will work wonders in advancing the spirituality of the church. . . .

The test question for every Christian to ask himself is, "Have I, in my inmost soul, supreme love for Christ? Do I love His tabernacle? Will not the Lord be honored by my making His sacred institution my first consideration? Is my love for God and my Redeemer strong enough to lead me to deny self? When tempted to indulge in pleasure and selfish enjoyment, shall I not say, No, I will spend nothing for my own gratification while the house of God is burdened with debt?"

Our Redeemer claims far more than we give Him. Self interposes its desire to be first; but the Lord claims the whole heart, the entire affections. He will not come in as second. And should not Christ have our first and highest consideration? Should He not demand this token of our respect and loyalty? These things underlie our very heart-life, in the home circle and in the church. If the heart, the soul, the strength, the life, is surrendered wholly to God, if the affections are given wholly to Him, we shall make Him supreme in all our service. When we are in harmony with God, the thought of His honor and glory comes before everything else. No person is preferred before Him in our gifts and offerings. We have a sense of what it means to be partners with Christ in the sacred firm.

The house where God meets with His people will be dear and sacred to every one of His loyal children. It will not be left crippled with debt. To allow such a thing would appear almost like a denial of your faith. You will be ready to make a great personal sacrifice if only you may have a house free from debt, where God can meet with and bless His people.

Every debt upon every house of worship among us may be paid if the members of the church will plan wisely and put forth earnest, zealous effort to cancel the debt. And in every case where a debt is lifted, let there be a service of thanksgiving, which shall be as a re-dedication to God of His house.—*"Testimonies for the Church," Vol. VI, pages 100-104.*

The need for a meeting-house where there is a newly formed company of believers, has been presented before me in a panoramic view. I saw workmen building humble houses of worship. Those newly come to the faith were helping with willing hands, and those who had means were assisting with their means. In the basement of the church, above ground, a schoolroom was prepared for the children, and a teacher was sent there to take charge. The numbers in the school were not large, but it was a happy beginning. I heard the songs of children and of parents: "Except the Lord build the house, they labor in vain that build it: except the Lord keep the city, the watchman waketh but in vain." "Praise ye the Lord. Praise the Lord, O my soul. While I live will I praise the Lord: I will sing praises unto my God while I have any being." [2]

The establishment of churches, the erection of meeting-houses and school-buildings, was extended from city to city, and the tithe was increasing to carry forward the work. Plants were made not only in one place, but in many places, and the Lord was working to increase His forces.

In this work all classes will be reached. When the Holy Spirit works among us, souls who are unready for Christ's appearing are convicted. Many come to our meetings and are converted who for years have

[2] Ps. 127 : 1 ; 146 : 1, 2.

not attended meetings in any church. The simplicity of the truth reaches their hearts. The tobacco devotees sacrifice their idol, and the liquor drinker his liquor. They could not do this if they did not by faith grasp the promises of God for the forgiveness of their sins.

The truth as it is in the Word comes before high and low, rich and poor, and those who receive the message become workers with us and with God, and a strong force is raised up to labor harmoniously. This is our work. It is not to be neglected in any of our camp-meeting labor. It is a part of every gospel mission. Instead of setting every talent to work for the lowest outcasts, we should seek in every place to raise up a company of believers who will unite with us in uplifting the standard of truth, and working for rich and poor. Then as churches are established, there will be an increase of helpers to labor for the destitute and the outcast.— *General Conference Bulletin, March, 1899.*

———◆———

Many not of our faith are longing for the very help that Christians are in duty bound to give. If God's people would show a genuine interest in their neighbors, many would be reached by the special truths for this time. Nothing will or ever can give character to the work like helping people just where they are.—"*Testimonies for the Church*," *Vol. VI page 280.*

EXAMINATION FOR THE MINISTRY

Men should not be encouraged to go into the field as ministers without unmistakable evidence that God has called them. The Lord will not entrust the burden for His flock to unqualified individuals. Those whom God calls must be men of deep experience, tried and proved, men of sound judgment, men who will dare to reprove sin in the spirit of meekness, men who understand how to feed the flock. God knows the heart, and He knows whom to select.—*"Testimonies for the Church," Vol. I, page 209.*

There has been too little done in examining ministers; and for this very reason churches have had the labors of unconverted, inefficient men, who have lulled the members to sleep, instead of awakening them to greater zeal and earnestness in the cause of God. There are ministers who come to the prayer-meeting, and pray the same old, lifeless prayers over and over; they preach the same dry discourses from week to week and from month to month. They have nothing new and inspiring to present to their congregations, and this is evidence that they are not partakers of the divine nature. Christ is not abiding in the heart by faith.

Those who claim to keep and teach the holy law of God, and yet are continually transgressing that law, are stumbling-blocks both to sinners and to believers in the truth. The loose, lax way in which many regard the law of Jehovah and the gift of His Son, is an insult to God. The only way in which we can correct this wide-spread evil, is to examine closely every one who would become a teacher of the Word. Those upon whom this responsibility rests, should acquaint themselves with his history since he professed to believe the truth. His Christian experience and his knowledge of the Scriptures, the way in which he holds present truth, should all be understood. No one should be accepted as a laborer in the cause of God, until he makes it manifest that he has a real, living experience in the things of God.

Those who are about to enter upon the sacred work of teaching Bible truth to the world, should be carefully examined by faithful, experienced persons. After they have had some experience, there is still another work to be done for them: they should be presented before the Lord in earnest prayer, that He may indicate by His Holy Spirit whether they are acceptable to Him. The apostle says, "Lay hands suddenly on no man." [1] In the days of the apostles, the ministers of God did not dare to rely upon their own judgment in selecting or accepting men to take the solemn and sacred position of mouthpiece for God. They chose the men whom their judgment accepted, and then placed them before the Lord to see if He would accept them to go forth as His representatives. No less than this should be done now.

In many places we meet men who have been hurried into responsible positions as elders of the church, when they are not qualified for such a position. They

[1] 1 Tim. 5 : 22.

have not proper government over themselves. Their influence is not good. The church is in trouble continually in consequence of the defective character of the leaders. Hands have been laid too suddenly upon these men.

Ministers of God should be men of good repute, capable of discreetly managing an interest after they have aroused it. We stand in great need of competent men, who will bring honor instead of disgrace upon the cause which they represent.

Ministers should be examined especially to see if they have an intelligent understanding of the truth for this time, so that they can give a connected discourse upon the prophecies or upon practical subjects. If they cannot clearly present Bible subjects, they need to be hearers and learners still. In order to be teachers of Bible truth, they should earnestly and prayerfully search the Scriptures, and become conversant with them. All these things should be carefully and prayerfully considered before men are sent into the field of labor.—*"Testimonies for the Church," Vol. IV, pages 406, 407.*

In Timothy, Paul saw one who appreciated the sacredness of the work of a minister, who was not appalled at the prospect of suffering and persecution, and who was willing to be taught. Yet the apostle did not venture to take the responsibility of giving Timothy, an untried youth, a training in the gospel ministry, without first fully satisfying himself in regard to his character and his past life.

Timothy's father was a Greek and his mother a Jewess. From a child he had known the Scriptures. The piety that he saw in his home life was sound and sensible. The faith of his mother and his grandmother in the sacred oracles was to him a constant reminder of the blessing in doing God's will. The word of God was the rule by which these two godly women had guided Timothy. The spiritual power of the lessons that he had received from them kept him pure in speech and unsullied by the evil influences with which he was surrounded. Thus his home instructors had co-operated with God in preparing him to bear burdens.

Paul saw that Timothy was faithful, steadfast, and true, and he chose him as a companion in labor and travel. Those who had taught Timothy in his childhood were rewarded by seeing the son of their care linked in close fellowship with the great apostle. . . .

Paul loved Timothy, his "own son in the faith." [2] The great apostle often drew the younger disciple out, questioning him in regard to Scripture history; and as they traveled from place to place, he carefully taught him how to do successful work. Both Paul and Silas, in all their association with Timothy, sought to deepen the impression that had already been made upon his mind, of the sacred, serious nature of the work of the gospel minister.—*"Acts of the Apostles,"* pages 203, 204.

In his work, Timothy constantly sought Paul's advice and instruction. He did not move from impulse, but exercised consideration and calm thought, inquiring at every step, Is this the way of the Lord? —*Idem, page 205.*

[2] 1 Tim. 1 : 2.

ORDINATION

"There were in the church that was at Antioch certain prophets and teachers; as Barnabas, and Simeon that was called Niger, and Lucius of Cyrene, and Manaen, . . . and Saul. As they ministered to the Lord, and fasted, the Holy Ghost said, Separate Me Barnabas and Saul for the work whereunto I have called them." [1] Before being sent forth as missionaries to the heathen world, these apostles were solemnly dedicated to God by fasting and prayer and the laying on of hands. Thus they were authorized by the church, not only to teach the truth, but to perform the rite of baptism, and to organize churches, being invested with full ecclesiastical authority.

The Christian church was at this time entering upon an important era. The work of proclaiming the gospel message among the Gentiles was now to be prosecuted with vigor; and as a result, the church was to be strengthened by a great ingathering of souls. The apostles who had been appointed to lead out in this work, would be exposed to suspicion, prejudice, and jealousy. Their teachings concerning the breaking down of "the middle wall of partition" [2] that had so long separated the Jewish and the Gentile world, would naturally subject them to the charge of heresy; and their authority as ministers of the gospel would be questioned by many zealous, believing Jews.

God foresaw the difficulties that His servants would be called to meet; and in order that their work

[1] Acts 13 : 1, 2. [2] Eph. 2 : 14.

should be above challenge, He instructed the church by revelation to set them apart publicly to the work of the ministry. Their ordination was a public recognition of their divine appointment to bear to the Gentiles the glad tidings of the gospel.

Both Paul and Barnabas had already received their commission from God Himself, and the ceremony of the laying on of hands added no new grace or virtual qualification. It was an acknowledged form of designation to an appointed office, and a recognition of one's authority in that office. By it the seal of the church was set upon the work of God.

To the Jew, this form was a significant one. When a Jewish father blessed his children, he laid his hands reverently upon their heads. When an animal was devoted to sacrifice, the hand of the one invested with priestly authority was laid upon the head of the victim. And when the ministers of the church of believers in Antioch laid their hands upon Paul and Barnabas, they by that action asked God to bestow His blessing upon the chosen apostles, in their devotion to the specific work to which they had been appointed.

At a later date, the rite of ordination by the laying on of hands was greatly abused; unwarrantable importance was attached to the act, as if a power came at once upon those who received such ordination, which immediately qualified them for any and all ministerial work. But in the setting apart of these two apostles, there is no record indicating that any virtue was imparted by the mere act of laying on of hands. There is only the simple record of their ordination, and of the bearing that it had on their future work.

The circumstances connected with the separation of Paul and Barnabas by the Holy Spirit to a definite line of service, show clearly that the Lord works through appointed agencies in His organized church. Years before, when the divine purpose concerning Paul was first revealed to him by the Saviour Himself, Paul was immediately afterward brought into contact with members of the newly organized church at Damascus. Furthermore, the church at that place was not long left in darkness as to the personal experience of the converted Pharisee. And now, when the divine commission given at that time was to be more fully carried out, the Holy Spirit, again bearing witness concerning Paul as a chosen vessel to bear the gospel to the Gentiles, laid upon the church the work of ordaining him and his fellow-laborer. As the leaders of the church in Antioch "ministered to the Lord, and fasted, the Holy Ghost said, Separate Me Barnabas and Saul for the work whereunto I have called them."

God has made His church on the earth a channel of light, and through it He communicates His purposes and His will. He does not give to one of His servants an experience independent of and contrary to the experience of the church itself. Neither does He give one man a knowledge of His will for the entire church, while the church — Christ's body — is left in darkness. In His providence, He places His servants in close connection with His church, in order that they may have less confidence in themselves, and greater confidence in others whom He is leading out to advance His work.

There have ever been in the church those who are constantly inclined toward individual independence.

They seem unable to realize that independence of spirit is liable to lead the human agent to have too much confidence in himself, and to trust in his own judgment rather than to respect the counsel and highly esteem the judgment of his brethren, especially of those in the offices that God has appointed for the leadership of His people. God has invested His church with special authority and power, which no one can be justified in disregarding and despising; for he who does this despises the voice of God.

Those who are inclined to regard their individual judgment as supreme, are in grave peril. It is Satan's studied effort to separate such ones from those who are channels of light, through whom God has wrought to build up and extend His work in the earth. To neglect or despise those whom God has appointed to bear the responsibilities of leadership in connection with the advancement of the truth, is to reject the means that He has ordained for the help, encouragement, and strength of His people. For any worker in the Lord's cause to pass these by, and to think that his light must come through no other channel than directly from God, is to place himself in a position where he is liable to be deceived by the enemy, and overthrown. The Lord in His wisdom has arranged that by means of the close relationship that should be maintained by all believers, Christian shall be united to Christian, and church to church. Thus the human instrumentality will be enabled to co-operate with the divine. Every agency will be subordinate to the Holy Spirit, and all the believers will be united in an organized and well-directed effort to give to the world the glad tidings of the grace of God.

Paul regarded the occasion of his formal ordination as marking the beginning of a new and important epoch in his life-work. It was from this time that he afterward dated the beginning of his apostleship in the Christian church.—*"The Acts of the Apostles," pages 160-165.*

———♦———

It was at the ordination of the twelve that the first step was taken in the organization of the church that after Christ's departure was to carry on His work on the earth. Of this ordination the record says, "He goeth up into a mountain, and calleth unto Him whom He would: and they came unto Him. And He ordained twelve, that they should be with Him, and that He might send them forth to preach."[3] . . .

With gladness and rejoicing, God and the angels beheld this scene. The Father knew that from these men the light of heaven would shine forth; that the words spoken by them as they witnessed for His Son, would echo from generation to generation till the close of time.

The disciples were to go forth as Christ's witnesses, to declare to the world what they had seen and heard of Him. Their office was the most important to which human beings had ever been called, second only to that of Christ Himself. They were to be workers together with God for the saving of men. As in the Old Testament the twelve patriarchs stood as representatives of Israel, so the twelve apostles stand as representatives of the gospel church.— *Idem, pages 18, 19.*

[3] Mark 3 : 13, 14.

BUSINESS MEETINGS

In all our business meetings, as well as our social and religious meetings, we want Jesus by our side as a guide and counselor. There will be no tendency to lightness where the presence of the Saviour is recognized. Self will not be made prominent. There will be a realization of the importance of the work that is to be done. There will be a desire that the plans to be laid may be directed by Him who is mighty in counsel.

Could our eyes but be opened, we should behold angels of heaven in our assemblies. Could we but realize this, there would be no desire to hold to our own opinions upon unimportant points, which so often retard the progress of the meeting and the work. If there were more real praying done, if there were more solemn consideration given to weighty matters, the tone of our business meetings would be changed, elevated. All would feel that the assembly had met to lay plans for the advancement of the work, and that the object of the work is only to save souls.

All that we do and all that we say is transferred to the books of heaven. Let us not be guilty of bringing down God's work to the level of common business transactions. Our standard must be high; our minds must be elevated.

There are always a few who think, when their brethren are pulling forward, that it is their duty to pull back. They object to everything that is proposed, and make war on every plan that they have not themselves originated. Here is an opportunity for persons to develop inordinate self-confidence. They have never learned in the school of Christ the precious and all-important lesson of becoming meek and lowly. There is nothing harder for those who possess a strong will than to give up their own way, and submit to the judgment of others. It is difficult for such to become teachable, gentle, and easy to be entreated.

In our business meetings, it is important that precious time should not be consumed in debating points that are of small consequence. The habit of petty criticism should not be indulged; for it perplexes and confuses minds, and shrouds in mystery the things that are most plain and simple. If there is that love among brethren which will lead them to esteem others better than themselves, there will be a giving up of their own ways and wishes to others. It is our duty to study, daily and hourly, how we may answer the prayer of Christ, that His disciples may be one, as He and the Father are one. Precious lessons may be learned by keeping our Saviour's prayer before the mind, and by acting our part to fulfill His desire.

In our business connection with the work of God, and in handling sacred things, we cannot be too careful to guard against a spirit of irreverence; never, for an instant, should the word of God be used deceitfully, to carry a point which we are anxious to see succeed. Honor, integrity, and truth must be preserved at any cost to self. Our every thought, word, and action should be subject to the will of Christ.

Levity is not appropriate in meetings where the solemn work and word of God are under consideration. The prayer has been offered that Christ shall preside in the assembly, and impart His wisdom, His grace and righteousness. Is it consistent to take a course that will be grievous to His Spirit and contrary to His work?

Let us bear in mind that Jesus is in our midst. Then an elevating, controlling influence from the Spirit of God will pervade the assembly. There will be manifested that wisdom which is "from above," which is "first pure, then peaceable, . . . full of mercy and good fruits," [1] which cannot err. In all the plans and decisions there will be that charity that "seeketh not her own;" that is "not easily provoked;" that "thinketh no evil;" that "rejoiceth not in iniquity, but rejoiceth in the truth;" that "beareth all things, believeth all things, hopeth all things, endureth all things." [2]

———◆———

Let every one who sits in council and committee meetings write in his heart the words, "I am working for time and for eternity; and I am accountable to God for the motives that prompt me to action." Let this be his motto. Let the prayer of the psalmist be his prayer: "Set a watch, O Lord, before my mouth; keep the door of my lips. Incline not my heart to any evil thing." [3] —*"Testimonies for the Church," Vol. VII, pages 258, 259.*

[1] James 3 : 17.   [2] 1 Cor. 13 : 5-7.   [3] Ps. 141 : 3, 4.

PROPER REMUNERATION FOR MINISTERS

In this life those engaged in the ministry should receive fitting remuneration for their labor. They give their entire time, thought, and effort to the service of the Master; and it is not in the order of God that the wages paid them should be insufficient to supply the needs of their families. The minister who does his share according to his ability should receive his just due.

The men who decide what each worker shall receive are to strive earnestly to meet the mind of God in their decisions. Some who have served on auditing committees have lacked in discrimination and judgment. At times the committee has been composed of men who had no real understanding of the situation of the workers, and who have again and again brought real oppression and want into families by their wrong decisions. Their management has given occasion for the enemy to tempt and discourage the workers, and in some cases has driven them from the field.

Scrupulous care should be shown in settling the accounts of the laborers. Those who are chosen to act on the auditing committee should be men of clear perception, acquainted with the work they are handling. They should be "able men, such as fear God, men of truth, hating covetousness." [1]

The minister should have a margin to work upon, for there are many calls made upon his financial resources. In his work he frequently finds people so

[1] Ex. 18 : 21.

poor that they have little to eat and wear, and no proper sleeping accommodations. He must give succor to the very needy, to supply their hunger and cover their nakedness. He is also expected to lead out in good enterprises, to help in building churches, and in advancing the cause of God in other lands.

God's chosen missionary can have no settled abode, but must take his family from place to place, often from country to country. The character of his work makes this necessary. But this frequent moving places him under heavy expense. Then, too, in order to exert a good influence, his wife and children, and he himself, must set a fitting example of neat and becoming dress. Their personal appearance, their living quarters, their surroundings,— all must tell in favor of the truth they advocate. They must always appear cheerful and fresh, that they may bring sunshine to those who need help. They are often obliged to entertain their brethren, and while they find this a pleasure, it is also an additional expense.

It is a terrible injustice for an auditing committee to disappoint a worthy minister who is in need of every cent that he has been led to expect. The Lord declares, "I the Lord love judgment, I hate robbery for burnt-offering." [2] He would have His people reveal a liberal spirit in all their dealings with their fellows. The principle underlying His command to ancient Israel, "Thou shalt not muzzle the mouth of the ox that treadeth out the corn," [3] is a principle that should never be set aside by any who have to do with the remuneration of those who have given themselves to advance God's cause in the world, and who spend

[2] Isa. 61 : 8.   [3] 1 Cor. 9 : 9 ; see Deut. 25 : 4.

their strength in lifting the minds of men from the contemplation of earthly things to the heavenly. God loves these workers, and He would have men respect their rights.

The eight-hour system finds no place in the program of the minister of God. He must hold himself in readiness for service at any hour. He must keep up his life and energy; for if he is dull and languid, he cannot exert a saving influence. If he occupies a position of responsibility, he must be prepared to attend board and council meetings, spending hours in brain- and nerve-taxing labor, planning for the advancement of the cause. Work of this kind is a heavy tax on mind and body.

The minister who has a due appreciation of service, regards himself as God's minuteman. When, with Isaiah, he hears the voice of the Lord saying, "Whom shall I send, and who will go for us?" he responds, "Here am I; send me." [4] He cannot say, I am my own; I will do what I please with my time. No one who has given his life to God's work as His minister, lives for self. His work is to follow Christ, to be a willing agent and co-worker with the Master, receiving His Spirit day by day, and working as the Saviour worked, neither failing nor being discouraged. He is chosen of God as a faithful instrument to promote missionary work in all lands, and he must ponder well the path he follows.

Those who have never carried the burden of such work, and who suppose that the Lord's chosen and faithful ministers have an easy time, should bear in mind that sentinels for God are on duty constantly.

[4] Isa. 6 : 8.

Their labor is not measured by hours. When their accounts are audited, if selfish men, with voice or stroke of pen, limit them unduly in their wages, a great wrong is done.

Those who are bearing administrative burdens in connection with God's cause, can afford to be fair and true; they can afford to deal on right principles. When in a time of financial stress it is thought that wages must be reduced, let a circular be published setting forth the true situation, and then let those employed by the conference be asked whether, under the circumstances, they could do with less for their support. All the arrangements made with those in God's service should be regarded as a sacred transaction between man and his fellow-man. Men have no right to treat the workers as if they were inanimate objects, with no voice or expression of their own.

THE MINISTER'S WIFE

The minister is paid for his work, and this is well. And if the Lord gives the wife as well as the husband the burden of labor, and she devotes her time and strength to visiting from family to family and opening the Scriptures to them, although the hands of ordination have not been laid upon her, she is accomplishing a work that is in the line of ministry. Then should her labors be counted as naught?

Injustice has sometimes been done to women who labor just as devotedly as their husbands, and who are recognized by God as being necessary to the work of the ministry. The method of paying men-laborers, and not paying their wives who share their labors with them, is a plan not according to the Lord's order, and if carried out in our conferences, is liable to discourage our sisters from qualifying themselves for the work they should engage in. God is a God of justice, and if the ministers receive a salary for their work, their wives, who devote themselves just as disinterestedly to the work, should be paid in addition to the wages their husbands receive, even though they may not ask for this.

Seventh-day Adventists are not in any way to belittle woman's work. If a woman puts her housework in the hands of a faithful, prudent helper, and leaves her children in good care, while she engages in the work, the conference should have wisdom to understand the justice of her receiving wages.

———◆———

The Lord has a work for women as well as men to do. They may accomplish a good work for God if they will first learn in the school of Christ the precious, all-important lesson of meekness. They must not only bear the name of Christ, but possess His Spirit. They must walk even as He walked, purifying their souls from everything that defiles. Then they will be able to benefit others by presenting the all-sufficiency of Jesus.—*"Testimonies for the Church," Vol. VI, page 117.*

A WISE DISTRIBUTION OF MEANS

Church-members are to contribute cheerfully toward the support of the ministry. They should practice self-denial and economy, that they may come behind in no good gift. We are pilgrims and strangers, seeking a better country, and every soul should make a covenant with God by sacrifice. The time for saving souls is short, and whatever is not needed in supplying positive necessities, should be brought as a thank-offering to God.

And it is the duty of those who labor in word and doctrine to show an equal self-sacrifice. A solemn responsibility rests upon those who receive the liberal donations of the church, and administer the means in God's treasury. They are to study carefully the providences of God, that they may discern where there is the greatest necessity. They are to be co-laborers with Christ in establishing His kingdom on the earth, in harmony with the prayer of the Saviour, "Thy kingdom come. Thy will be done in earth, as it is in heaven." [1]

The work all over the world is to receive consideration. New fields are to be entered. Let our brethren remember that much means and much hard labor are required to carry forward the work in new fields.

In planning for the cause in foreign countries, the difficulties to be met there are to be considered, and willing support must be given to the workers. Those at the heart of the cause are to examine closely into

[1] Matt. 6 : 10.

the needs of the different fields; for they are God's stewards, set for the extension of the truth in all parts of the world. They are inexcusable if they remain in ignorance regarding the needs of the work. They are to know the advantages and difficulties of each field, and then with a spirit of unselfish interest they are to work for the advancement of the cause as a whole.

When those who are to appropriate to the needs of the Lord's work the means in His treasury, have unselfishly tried to gain a right understanding of the situation, they should come to the mercy-seat, asking for clear intuition and heavenly wisdom, that they may see the necessities of the far-off countries, as well as of those nearer by. Never will they seek the Lord in vain. As they ask Him to help them to advance the work in regions beyond, they will receive grace from on high.

An unselfish equality is to be shown in dealing with the working forces in home and foreign lands. More and more we must realize that the means which is brought to the Lord's treasury in the tithes and gifts of our people, should be used for the support of the work, not only at home, but in foreign fields. Those living in places where the work has long been established, should bind about their supposed wants, so that the work in new fields may go forward. In the institutions that have been long established there is sometimes a desire to grasp more and still more advantages. But the Lord declares that this should not be. The money in His treasury is to be used in building up the work all over the world.

Those places in the Lord's vineyard where but little or nothing has been done, call upon the places in which institutions are already established, to understand the situation. Let the men in those fields which by God's appointment have already been largely worked, and where the cause is strongly established, curtail their ambition to branch out. Let them not think of the great things they would like to do, and continue to add to their facilities, while other parts of the vineyard are destitute. It is selfish ambition that leads men to call for more for a field already possessing ample facilities, while missionary fields are in need.

If the Lord favors the work in some countries above that in other countries, it is that there may be revealed a spirit of true liberality, a desire to assist those who greatly need help in order to find a standing-place, and to give character to the work. The Lord is no respecter of persons or of places. His work is one great whole. His truth is to be proclaimed to every nation, kindred, tongue, and people; and as new fields are entered and people accept the truth, houses of worship and schoolhouses are to be erected, and other needed facilities supplied. Printing-presses are to be set in operation in many parts of the world.

The Lord's work in new territories is to be carried forward to a successful accomplishment. And God's plans must be followed, not the inclinations of those who would gather into the section over which they have supervision, every possible advantage, while the utter destitution of other parts of the Lord's vineyard is forgotten.

In some conferences it has been considered commendable to save up means, and to show a large surplus in the treasury. But in this God has not been honored. It would have been better if the money thus laid by had been wisely expended in supporting diligent, efficient laborers in needy fields.

In their efforts to economize, our brethren should be careful lest they restrict the investment of means where wise investment is needed. In establishing schools and sanitariums, enough land should be purchased to provide for the carrying out of the plans that the Lord has outlined for these institutions. Provision should be made for the raising of fruit and vegetables, and, wherever possible, sufficient land should be secured so that others may not erect, near the institution, buildings of an objectionable character.

Sometimes, when a work has been brought to a certain stage of development, and those who have labored earnestly in its behalf have called for further needed help, they have been repulsed, and have not been given the advantages that would have made their work effective. This has brought discouragement to their hearts, and has hindered the cause of God. Those who have been fearful of undertaking work in the great cities, because it means earnest labor and the investment of means, need to understand the magnitude of the gift that the Lord made in giving His Son to save the world. Our cities may be worked if men will trust in God, and labor earnestly and unselfishly.

ECONOMY IN MISSION WORK

Laborers for God must work with intelligence, frugality, and humility. There are those who undertake too much, and by so doing accomplish little. Our efforts must be more concentrated. Every stroke must tell. The mind must be active to discern the best ways and means of reaching the people near us. In an effort to do a work at a distance from us, we often let opportunities within our reach slip away. Thus time and means are lost in both places.

Our missionary workers must learn to economize. The largest reservoir, though fed by abundant and living springs, will fail to supply the demand if there are leakages which drain off the supply. It must not be left for one man to decide whether a certain field will warrant large efforts. If the workers in one field so fashion the work as to incur large expenses, they are barring the way so that other important fields —fields which perhaps would better warrant the outlay—cannot be entered.

Our younger laborers must be content to work their way among the people slowly and surely, under the advice of those who have had more experience. The ideas of many are too high. A more humble manner of working would show good results. It is encouraging to see the young enter the missionary field, enlisting all their ardor and zeal in the work; but they must not be left to manage for themselves, and keep the cause of God weighed down with debt. All should strive by wise management and earnest labor to gather enough to pay their own expenses. They should labor to make the cause self-sustaining, and should teach the people to rely upon themselves.

Our ministers should not feel at liberty to pay large sums for halls in which to hold meetings, when they do not feel the burden of following up the interest by personal labor. The results are too uncertain to warrant the using of means so rapidly. If churches and halls are opened to any of the laborers, and there is a desire to hear, they should embrace the opportunity, and do the best they can; but it is not wisdom for a single individual to strike out as if he had some great talent, as if he were a Moody or a Sankey, and make a lavish outlay of means.

In sending missionaries to foreign countries, we should select those who know how to economize, who have not large families, and who, realizing the shortness of time and the great work to be accomplished, will keep themselves as free as possible from everything that would divert their minds from the one great work. The wife, if devoted and left free to do so, can, by standing by the side of her husband, accomplish as much as he. We want missionaries who are missionaries in the fullest sense of the word, who will put aside selfish considerations, and let the cause of God come first; and who, working with an eye single to His glory, will keep themselves as minutemen, ready to go where He bids, and to work in any capacity to spread the knowledge of the truth. Men who have wives who love and fear God, and who can help their husbands in the work, are needed in the work, are needed in the missionary field.

Our laborers must learn to exercise economy, not only in their efforts to advance the cause of truth, but in their home expenses. They should place their families where they can be cared for at as little expense as possible. Donations and bequests do not come to our work as they do to other denominations; and those who have not educated themselves to live within their means, will surely have to do this, or else engage in some other employment. Habits of self-indulgence, or a want of tact and skill on the part of the wife and mother, may be a constant drain upon the treasury; and yet that mother may think she is doing her best, because she has never been taught to restrict her wants or the wants of her children, and has never acquired skill and tact in household matters. Hence one family may require for its support twice the amount that would suffice for another family of the same size.

All should learn how to keep accounts. Some neglect this work as non-essential; but this is wrong. All expenses should be accurately stated. This is something that many of our laborers will have to learn.

The Lord is not pleased with the present lack of order and accuracy among those who do business in connection with His work. Even in the business meetings of the conference, much time could be saved and many mistakes avoided, by a little more study and punctuality. Everything that bears any relation to the work of God should be as nearly perfect as human brains and hands can make it.

As laborers together with God, you should come close to one another. Lessons of love, confidence, respect for one another, must be given, both in and out of the desk. You must live that which you teach. Remember that new converts look to you for an example.

Some for whom you labor will wish to have the work done in their own way, thinking that their way is best; but if you have the spirit and the meekness of Christ, if you show respect and love for one another, God will enable you to perfect the work in a manner that will please Him. Work for your own souls until self is subdued, until Christ recognizes His image in you. This will be the most impressive lesson that you can give to those whom you educate.

In foreign fields, especially, the work cannot be accomplished except by well-considered plans. While you should endeavor to labor in harmony with the instructions of those at the head of the work, many unforeseen circumstances will arise for which they could make no provision. There must be something ventured, some risks taken, by those on the field of battle. There will be crises in which prompt action is necessary.

When missions are opened in foreign lands, it is of special importance that the work be started right. The laborers should be careful that they do not restrict it by narrow plans. While the state of the treasury demands that economy be exercised, there is danger of an economy which results in loss rather than gain. This has actually been the case in some of our missions, where the workers have bent their powers almost wholly to planning how to get along in the least expensive manner. With different management, far more might have been accomplished;

and on the whole less means would have been taken from the treasury.

In new fields our growth has been slow, because the special truths which we present are not popular with the world. The observance of the seventh-day Sabbath is a heavy cross for every one who accepts the truth. Many who can see that our doctrines are sustained by the Scriptures, shrink from accepting them, because they do not wish to be peculiar, or because by obedience to the truth they would be cut off from their means of support. Because of these things, much wisdom is needed in planning how to bring the truth before the people.

In some places the work must begin in a small way, and advance slowly. This is all that the laborers can do. But in many cases a wider and more decided effort might be made at the outset, with good results. The work in England might now be much farther advanced than it is if our brethren, at the beginning of the work there, had not tried to work in so cheap a way. If they had hired good halls, and carried forward the work as though we had great truths, which would surely be victorious, they would have had greater success. God would have the work started in such a way that the first impressions given shall be, as far as they go, the very best that can be made.

Be careful to maintain the elevated character of the missionary work. Let all connected with our missions, both men and women, be constantly inquiring, "What am I? and what ought I to be and to do?" Let all remember that they cannot give to others what they themselves do not possess; therefore they should not settle down content with their natural ways and habits, seeking to make no change for the better. Paul says, "I press toward the mark." [1] There must be constant reformation, unceasing advancement, if we would perfect a symmetrical character.

———◆———

The Lord wants men who see the work in its greatness, and who understand the principles that have been interwoven with it from its rise. He will not have a worldly order of things come in to fashion the work in altogether different lines from those He has marked out for His people. The work must bear the character of its Originator.—"*Testimonies for the Church," Vol. VII, page 209.*

———◆———

In establishing the work in new places, economize in every possible way. Gather up the fragments; let nothing be lost. The work of soul-saving must be carried on in the way that Christ has marked out. He declares, "If any man will come after Me, let him deny himself, and take up his cross, and follow Me." [2] Only by obeying this word can we be His disciples. We are nearing the end of this earth's history, and the different lines of God's work are to be carried forward with much more self-sacrifice than has yet been manifested.— *Idem, pages 239, 240.*

[1] Phil. 3 : 14.   [2] Matt. 16 : 24.

THE REGIONS BEYOND

The church of Christ was organized for missionary purposes. Christian missionary work furnishes
the church with a sure foundation, a foundation having this seal, "The Lord knoweth them that are His." [1]
By it the members are inspired with zeal to deny self,
to put forth self-sacrificing efforts to send the truth
to the regions beyond. It has a salutary influence
upon unbelievers; for as the workers labor under divine supervision, worldlings are led to see the greatness of the resources that God has provided for those
who serve Him. We are laid under a most solemn
obligation to furnish, in Christian missions, an illustration of the principles of the kingdom of God. The
church is to work actively, as an organized body, to
spread abroad the influence of the cross of Christ.

God is calling for men who are willing to leave all
to become missionaries for Him. And the call will
be answered. In every age since the advent of Christ,
the gospel commission has impelled men and women
to go to the ends of the earth to carry the good news
of salvation to those in darkness. Stirred by the love
of Christ and the needs of the lost, men have left the
comforts of home and the society of friends, even that
of wife and children, to go to foreign lands, among
idolaters and savages, to proclaim the message of
mercy. Many in the attempt have lost their lives,
but others have been raised up to carry on the work.
Thus step by step the cause of Christ has progressed,
and the seed sown in sorrow has yielded a bountiful

[1] 2 Tim. 2 : 19.

harvest. The knowledge of God has been extended, and the banner of the cross planted in heathen lands.

There is nothing more precious in the sight of God than His ministers, who go forth into the waste places of the earth to sow the seeds of truth, looking forward to the harvest. None but Christ can measure the solicitude of His servants, as they seek for the lost. He imparts His Spirit to them, and by their efforts souls are led to turn from sin to righteousness.

For the conversion of one sinner, the minister should tax his resources to the utmost. The soul that God has created and Christ has redeemed is of great value, because of the possibilities before it, the spiritual advantages that have been granted it, the capabilities that it may possess if vitalized by the word of God, and the immortality that it may gain through the hope presented in the gospel. And if Christ left the ninety and nine that He might seek and save one lost sheep, can we be justified in doing less? Is not a neglect to work as Christ worked, to sacrifice as He sacrificed, a betrayal of sacred trust?

I feel intensely over the needs of foreign countries, as they have been presented before me. In all parts of the world angels of God are opening doors that a little while ago were closed to the message of truth. From India, from Africa, from China, and from many other places is heard the cry, "Come over and help us."

To show a liberal, self-denying spirit for the success of foreign missions is a sure way to advance home missionary work; for the prosperity of the home work depends largely, under God, upon the reflex influence of the evangelical work done in countries afar off. It is in working to supply the necessities of others that we bring our souls into touch with the Source of all power. The Lord has marked every phase of missionary zeal that has been shown by His people in behalf of foreign fields. He designs that in every home, in every church, and at all the centers of the work, a spirit of liberality shall be shown in sending help to foreign fields, where the workers are struggling against great odds to give the light to those who sit in darkness.

That which is given to start the work in one field will result in strengthening the work in other places. As the laborers are freed from financial embarrassment, their efforts can be extended; and as people are brought into the truth and churches are established, there will be increasing financial strength. As these churches grow stronger, they will be able not only to carry on the work in their own borders, but to send help to other fields.

HOME CHURCHES TO HELP

The members of our churches in the home field should carry on their hearts the burden for the work in regions beyond. An American business man, who was an earnest Christian, in conversation with a fellow-worker, remarked that he himself worked for Christ twenty-four hours of the day. "In all my business relations," he said, "I try to represent my Master. As I have opportunity, I try to win others to Him. All day I am working for Christ. And at night, while I sleep, I have a man working for Him in China."

Why should not the members of a church, or of several small churches, unite to sustain a missionary in foreign fields? If they will deny themselves, they can do this. My brethren and sisters, will you not help in this great work? I beseech you to do something for Christ, and do it now. Through the teacher whom your money shall sustain in a foreign field, souls may be saved to shine as stars in the Redeemer's crown. However small your offering, do not hesitate to bring it to the Lord. If given from a heart filled with love to the Saviour, the smallest offering becomes a priceless gift, which God smiles upon and blesses.

When Jesus said of the widow, She "hath cast in more than they all," [2] His words were true, not only of the motives of the giver, but of the results of the gift. The "two mites, which make a farthing," [3] have brought to God's treasury an amount of money far greater than the contributions of the rich Jews. Like a stream small at its beginning, but widening and deepening as it flows toward the ocean, the influence of that little gift has widened and deepened as it has flowed through the ages. The example of self-sacrifice shown by the poor widow has acted and reacted upon thousands of hearts in every land and in every age. It has brought to the treasury of God gifts from the high and the low, the rich and the poor. It has helped to sustain missions, to establish hospitals, to feed the hungry, and to preach the gospel to the poor. Multitudes have been blessed through her unselfish deed. And in like manner every gift bestowed, every act performed, with a sincere desire for God's glory, is linked with the purposes of Omnipotence. Its results for good no man can measure.

[2] Luke 21:3.   [3] Mark 12:42.

METHODS OF LABOR IN FOREIGN FIELDS

As soon as a new field is entered, educational work should begin, and instruction should be given line upon line, precept upon precept, here a little and there a little. It is not preaching that is the most important; it is house-to-house work, reasoning from the Word, explaining the Word. It is those workers who follow the methods that Christ followed who will win souls for their hire. Over and over again the same truths must be repeated, and the worker must place his entire dependence on God. And what rich experiences the teacher obtains when instructing those in darkness! He too is a learner, and as he explains the Scriptures to others, the Holy Spirit is working in his mind and heart, giving him the bread of life for hungry souls.

The worker in foreign fields will come in contact with all classes of people and all varieties of minds, and he will find that different methods of labor are required to meet the needs of the people. A sense of his own inefficiency will drive him to God and to the Bible for light and strength and knowledge.

The methods and means by which we reach certain ends are not always the same. The missionary must use reason and judgment. Experience will indicate the wisest course to follow under existing circumstances. It is often the case that the customs and climate of a country make a condition of things that would not be tolerated in another country. Changes for the better must be made, but it is best not to be too abrupt.

Let not controversy arise over trifles. The spirit of love and the grace of Christ will bind heart to heart, if men will open the windows of the soul heavenward and close them earthward. By the power of the truth many difficulties might be adjusted, and controversies hoary with age find quietude in the admission of better ways. The great, grand principle, "Peace on earth, good will toward men," will be far better practiced when those who believe in Christ are indeed laborers together with God.

HELP FROM HEAVEN

The worker in a foreign field must carry in his heart the peace and love of heaven; for this is his only safety. Amid perplexity and trial, discouragement and suffering, with the devotion of a martyr and the courage of a hero, he is to hold fast to the hand that never lets go, saying, "I will not fail nor be discouraged." He must be a close Bible student, and should be often in prayer. If, before talking with others, he will seek help from above, he may be assured that angels of heaven will be with him. At times he may yearn for human sympathy, but in his loneliness he may find comfort and encouragement through communion with God. Let him be cheered by the words of the Saviour, "Lo, I am with you alway, even unto the end of the world." [4] From this divine Companion he will receive instruction in the science of soul-saving.

Energy and self-sacrifice are needed in the missionary field. God calls for men who will push the triumphs of the cross; men who will persevere under discouragements and privations; men who have the zeal and resolution and faith that are indispensable in the missionary field. By persevering toil and a firm

[4] Matt. 28 : 20.

trust in the God of Israel, resolute, courageous men will accomplish wonders. There is scarcely a limit to what may be achieved if the efforts made are governed by enlightened judgment and backed by earnest endeavor.

Let us rejoice that work which God can approve has been done in foreign fields. Let us lift our voices in praise and thanksgiving for the results of the work abroad. And still our General, who never makes a mistake, says to us, "Advance; enter new territory; lift the standard in every land. 'Arise, shine; for thy light is come, and the glory of the Lord is risen upon thee.' [5] "

The time has come when through God's messengers the scroll is being unrolled to the world. The truth contained in the first, second, and third angels' messages must go to every nation, kindred, tongue, and people; it must lighten the darkness of every continent, and extend to the islands of the sea. There must be no delay in this work.

Our watchword is to be, Onward, ever onward! Angels of heaven will go before us to prepare the way. Our burden for the regions beyond can never be laid down till the whole earth is lightened with the glory of the Lord.

[5] Isa. 60 : 1.

FOR FURTHER STUDY

In Relation with One Another

" Be ye kind one to another, tender-hearted, forgiving one another, even as God for Christ's sake hath forgiven you."

IN CONTACT WITH OTHERS

Every association of life calls for the exercise of self-control, forbearance, and sympathy. We differ so widely in disposition, habits, education, that our ways of looking at things vary. We judge differently. Our understanding of truth, our ideas in regard to the conduct of life, are not in all respects the same. There are no two whose experience is alike in every particular. The trials of one are not the trials of another. The duties that one finds light, are to another most difficult and perplexing.

So frail, so ignorant, so liable to misconception is human nature, that each should be careful in the estimate he places upon another. We little know the bearing of our acts upon the experience of others. What we do or say may seem to us of little moment, when, could our eyes be opened, we should see that upon it depended the most important results for good or for evil.

CONSIDERATION FOR BURDEN-BEARERS

Many have borne so few burdens, their hearts have known so little real anguish, they have felt so little perplexity and distress in behalf of others, that they cannot understand the work of the true burden-bearer. No more capable are they of appreciating his burdens than is the child of understanding the care and toil of his burdened father. The child may wonder at his father's fears and perplexities. These appear needless to him. But when years of experience shall have been added to his life, when he himself comes to bear its burdens, he will look back upon his father's life, and understand that which was once so incomprehensible. Bitter experience has given him knowledge.

The work of many a burden-bearer is not understood, his labors are not appreciated, until death lays him low. When others take up the burdens he has laid down, and meet the difficulties he encountered, they can understand how his faith and courage were tested. Often then the mistakes they were so quick to censure are lost sight of. Experience teaches them sympathy. God permits men to be placed in positions of responsibility. When they err, He has power to correct or to remove them. We should be careful not to take into our hands the work of judging that belongs to God. . . .

The Saviour bids us, "Judge not, that ye be not judged. For with what judgment ye judge, ye shall be judged: and with what measure ye mete, it shall be measured to you again." [1] Remember that soon your life record will pass in review before God. Remember, too, that He has said, "Thou art inexcusable, O man, whosoever thou art that judgest: . . . for thou that judgest doest the same things." [2]

[1] Matt. 7 : 1, 2.   [2] Rom. 2 : 1.

FORBEARANCE UNDER WRONG

We cannot afford to let our spirits chafe over any real or supposed wrong done to ourselves. Self is the enemy we most need to fear. No form of vice has a more baleful effect upon the character than has human passion not under the control of the Holy Spirit. No other victory we can gain will be so precious as the victory gained over self.

We should not allow our feelings to be easily wounded. We are to live, not to guard our feelings or our reputation, but to save souls. As we become interested in the salvation of souls, we cease to mind the little differences that so often arise in our association with one another. Whatever others may think of us, it need not disturb our oneness with Christ, the fellowship of the Spirit. "What glory is it, if, when ye be buffeted for your faults, ye shall take it patiently? but if, when ye do well, and suffer for it, ye take it patiently, this is acceptable with God." [3]

Do not retaliate. So far as you can do so, remove all cause for misapprehension. Avoid the appearance of evil. Do all that lies in your power, without the sacrifice of principle, to conciliate others. "If thou bring thy gift to the altar, and there rememberest that thy brother hath aught against thee; leave there thy gift before the altar, and go thy way; first be reconciled to thy brother, and then come and offer thy gift." [4]

If impatient words are spoken to you, never reply in the same spirit. Remember that "a soft answer turneth away wrath." [5] And there is wonderful power in silence. Words spoken in reply to one who is angry

[3] 1 Peter 2 : 20.   [4] Matt. 5 : 23, 24.   [5] Prov. 15 : 1.

sometimes serve only to exasperate; but anger met with silence, in a tender, forbearing spirit, quickly dies away.

Under a storm of stinging faultfinding words, keep the mind stayed upon the word of God. Let mind and heart be stored with God's promises. If you are. ill-treated or wrongfully accused, instead of returning an angry answer, repeat to yourself the precious promises:

"Be not overcome of evil, but overcome evil with good." [6]

"Commit thy way unto the Lord: trust also in Him; and He shall bring it to pass. And He shall bring forth thy righteousness as the light, and thy judgment as the noon-day." [7]

"There is nothing covered, that shall not be revealed; neither hid, that shall not be known." [8]

"Thou hast caused men to ride over our heads; we went through fire and through water: but Thou broughtest us out into a wealthy place." [9]

We are prone to look to our fellow-men for sympathy and uplifting, instead of looking to Jesus. In His mercy and faithfulness, God often permits those in whom we place confidence to fail us, in order that we may learn the folly of trusting in man, and making flesh our arm. Let us trust fully, humbly, unselfishly, in God. He knows the sorrows that we feel to the depths of our being, but which we cannot express. When all things seem dark and unexplainable, remember the words of Christ, "What I do thou knowest not now; but thou shalt know hereafter." [10]

[6] Rom. 12 : 21. [7] Ps. 37 : 5, 6. [8] Luke 12 : 2.
[9] Ps. 66 : 12. [10] John 13 : 7.

Study the history of Joseph and of Daniel. The Lord did not prevent the plottings of men who sought to do them harm; but He caused all these devices to work for good to His servants, who amid trial and conflict preserved their faith and loyalty.

So long as we are in the world, we shall meet with adverse influences. There will be provocations to test the temper; and it is by meeting these in a right spirit that the Christian graces are developed. If Christ dwells in us, we shall be patient, kind, and forbearing, cheerful amid frets and irritations. Day by day and year by year we shall conquer self, and grow into a noble heroism. This is our allotted task; but it cannot be accomplished without help from Jesus, resolute decision, unwavering purpose, continual watchfulness, and unceasing prayer. Each one has a personal battle to fight. Not even God can make our characters noble or our lives useful, unless we become co-workers with Him. Those who decline the struggle lose the strength and joy of victory.

We need not keep our own record of trials and difficulties, griefs, and sorrows. All these things are written in the books, and heaven will take care of them. While we are counting up the disagreeable things, many things that are pleasing to reflect upon are passing from memory; such as the merciful kindness of God surrounding us every moment, and the love over which angels marvel, that God gave His Son to die for us. If as workers for Christ you feel that you have had greater cares and trials than have fallen to the lot of others, remember that for you there is a peace unknown to those who shun these burdens.

There is comfort and joy in the service of Christ. Let the world see that life with Him is no failure.

If you do not feel light-hearted and joyous, do not talk of your feelings. Cast no shadow upon the lives of others. A cold, sunless religion never draws souls to Christ. It drives them away from Him, into the nets that Satan has spread for the feet of the straying. Instead of thinking of your discouragements, think of the power you can claim in Christ's name. Let your imagination take hold upon things unseen. Let your thoughts be directed to the evidences of the great love of God for you. Faith can endure trial, resist temptation, bear up under disappointment. Jesus lives as our advocate. All is ours that His mediation secures.

Think you not that Christ values those who live wholly for Him? Think you not that He visits those who, like the beloved John in exile, are for His sake in hard and trying places? God will not suffer one of His true-hearted workers to be left alone, to struggle against great odds and be overcome. He preserves as a precious jewel every one whose life is hid with Christ in Him. Of every such one He says: "I . . . will make thee as a signet: for I have chosen thee." [11]

Then talk of the promises; talk of Jesus' willingness to bless. He does not forget us for one brief moment. When, notwithstanding disagreeable circumstances, we rest confidingly in His love and shut ourselves in with Him, the sense of His presence will inspire a deep, tranquil joy. Of Himself Christ said: "I do nothing of Myself; but as My Father hath taught Me, I speak these things. And He that sent Me is with Me: the Father hath not left Me alone; for I do always those things that please Him." [12] . . .

[11] Haggai 2 : 23.   [12] John 8 : 28, 29.

Cultivate the habit of speaking well of others. Dwell upon the good qualities of those with whom you associate, and see as little as possible of their errors and failings. When tempted to complain of what some one has said or done, praise something in that person's life or character. Cultivate thankfulness. Praise God for His wonderful love in giving Christ to die for us. It never pays to think of our grievances. God calls upon us to think of His mercy and His matchless love, that we may be inspired with praise.

Earnest workers have no time for dwelling upon the faults of others. We cannot afford to live on the husks of others' faults or failings. Evil-speaking is a twofold curse, falling more heavily upon the speaker than upon the hearer. He who scatters the seeds of dissension and strife, reaps in his own soul the deadly fruits. The very act of looking for evil in others develops evil in those who look. By dwelling upon the faults of others, we are changed into the same image. But by beholding Jesus, talking of His love and perfection of character, we become changed into His image. By contemplating the lofty ideal He has placed before us, we shall be uplifted into a pure and holy atmosphere, even the presence of God. When we abide here, there goes forth from us a light that irradiates all who are connected with us.

Instead of criticizing and condemning others, say, "I must work out my own salvation. If I co-operate with Him who desires to save my soul, I must watch myself diligently. I must put away every evil from my life. I must overcome every fault. I must become a new creature in Christ. Then, instead of weakening those who are striving against evil, I can strengthen them by encouraging words.''

We are too indifferent in regard to one another. Too often we forget that our fellow-laborers are in need of strength and cheer. Take care to assure them of your interest and sympathy. Help them by your prayers, and let them know that you do it.—*"Ministry of Healing," pages 483-493.*

———◆———

All who profess to be children of God should bear in mind that as missionaries they will be brought into contact with all classes of minds. There are the refined and the coarse, the humble and the proud, the religious and the skeptical, the educated and the ignorant, the rich and the poor. These varied minds cannot be treated alike; yet all need kindness and sympathy. By mutual contact our minds should receive polish and refinement. We are dependent upon one another, closely bound together by the ties of human brotherhood. . . .

It is through the social relations that Christianity comes in contact with the world. Every man or woman who has received the divine illumination is to shed light on the dark pathway of those who are unacquainted with the better way. Social power, sanctified by the Spirit of Christ, must be improved in bringing souls to the Saviour. Christ is not to be hid away in the heart as a coveted treasure, sacred and sweet, to be enjoyed solely by the possessor. We are to have Christ in us as a well of water, springing up into everlasting life, refreshing all who come in contact with us.— *"Ministry of Healing," pages 495, 496.*

VARIED GIFTS

The Lord does not apportion to any one man some special territory in which he alone is to labor. This is contrary to His plan. He designs that in every place where the truth is introduced, different minds, different gifts, shall be brought in to exert an influence upon the work. No one man has sufficient wisdom to manage an interest without helpers, and no one should think himself competent to do so. The fact that a person has ability in one direction, is no evidence that his judgment on all other subjects is perfect, and that the wisdom of some other mind does not need to be united with his.

Those who do labor together should seek to be in perfect harmony. And yet no one should feel that he cannot labor with those who do not see just as he sees, and who do not in their labors follow just his plans. If all manifest a humble, teachable spirit, there need be no difficulty. God has set in the church different gifts. These are precious in their proper places, and all may act a part in the work of preparing a people for Christ's soon coming.

Our ministers in responsible places are men whom God has accepted. No matter what their origin, no matter what their former position, whether they followed the plow, worked at the carpenter's trade, or enjoyed the discipline of a college; if God has accepted them, let every man beware of casting the slightest reflection upon them. Never speak disparagingly of any man; for he may be great in the sight of the Lord, while those who feel great may be lightly esteemed of God because of the perversity of their hearts. . . .

Not one moment of our precious time should be devoted to bringing others to conform to our personal ideas and opinions. God would educate men engaged as co-laborers in this great work, to the highest exercise of faith, and the development of a harmonious character.

Men have varied gifts, and some are better adapted to one branch of the work than another. What one man would fail to do, his brother minister may be strong to accomplish. The work of each in his position is important. One man's mind is not to control that of another. If one man stands up, feeling that no one shall influence him, that he has judgment and ability to comprehend every branch of the work, that man will fail of the grace of God.—"*Testimonies for the Church,*" *Vol. IV, pages 608, 609.*

———◆———

It is the faithfulness, the loyalty to God, the loving service, that wins the divine approval. Every impulse of the Holy Spirit leading men to goodness and to God, is noted in the books of heaven, and in the day of God the workers through whom He has wrought will be commended. They will enter into the joy of the Lord as they see in His kingdom those who have been redeemed through their instrumentality. And they are privileged to participate in His work there, because they have gained a fitness for it by participation in His work here. What we shall be in heaven is the reflection of what we are now in character and holy service.—"*Christ's Object Lessons,*" *page 361.*

UNITY IN DIVERSITY

God has different ways of working, and He has different workmen to whom He entrusts varied gifts. One worker may be a ready speaker; another a ready writer; another may have the gift of sincere, earnest, fervent prayer; another the gift of singing; another may have special power to explain the word of God with clearness. And each gift is to become a power for God, because He works with the laborer. To one God gives the word of wisdom, to another knowledge, to another faith; but all are to work under the same Head. The diversity of gifts leads to a diversity of operations; but "it is the same God which worketh all in all." [1]

The Lord desires His chosen servants to learn how to unite in harmonious effort. It may seem to some that the contrast between their gifts and the gifts of a fellow-laborer is too great to allow them to unite in harmonious effort; but when they remember that there are varied minds to be reached, and that some will reject the truth as it is presented by one laborer, only to open their hearts to God's truth as it is presented in a different manner by another laborer, they will hopefully endeavor to labor together in unity. Their talents, however diverse, may all be under the control of the same Spirit. In every word and act, kindness and love will be revealed; and as each worker fills his appointed place faithfully, the prayer of Christ for the unity of His followers will be answered, and the world will know that these are His disciples.

[1] 1 Cor. 12 : 6.

In loving sympathy and confidence God's workers are to unite with one another. He who says or does anything that tends to separate the members of Christ's church, is counterworking the Lord's purpose. Wrangling and dissension in the church, the encouragement of suspicion and unbelief, are dishonoring to Christ. God desires His servants to cultivate Christian affection for one another. True religion unites hearts, not only with Christ, but with one another, in a most tender union. When we know what it means to be thus united with Christ, and with our brethren, a fragrant influence will attend our work wherever we go.

The workers in the large cities must act their several parts, making every effort to bring about the best results. They are to talk faith and to act in such a way as to impress the people. They are not to narrow the work down to their own particular ideas. In the past too much of this has been done by us as a people, and it has been a drawback to the success of the work. . . .

No human being is to seek to bind other human beings to himself, as if he were to control them, telling them to do this, and forbidding them to do that, commanding, dictating, acting like an officer over a company of soldiers. This is the way the priests and rulers did in Christ's day, but it is not the right way. After the truth has made the impression upon hearts, and men and women have accepted its teachings, they are to be treated as the property of Christ, not as the property of man. In fastening minds to yourself, you lead them to disconnect from the Source of their wisdom and sufficiency. Their dependence must be wholly in God; only thus can they grow in grace.

However large may be a man's claim to knowledge and wisdom, unless he is under the teaching of the Holy Spirit, he is exceedingly ignorant of spiritual things. He needs to realize his danger and his inefficiency, and to place entire dependence upon the One who alone is able to keep the souls committed to His trust, able to imbue them with His Spirit, and to fill them with unselfish love for one another, thus enabling them to bear witness that God has sent His Son into the world to save sinners. Those who are truly converted will press together in Christian unity. Let there be no division in the church of God, no unwise authority exercised over those who accept the truth. The meekness of Christ is to appear in all that is said and done.

Christ is the foundation of every true church. We have His unalterable promise that His presence and protection will be given to His faithful ones who walk in His counsel. To the end of time Christ is to be first. He is the source of life and strength, of righteousness and holiness. And He is all this to those who wear His yoke and learn of Him how to be meek and lowly.

The duty and delight of all service is to uplift Christ before the people. This is the end of all true labor. Let Christ appear; let self be hidden behind Him. This is self-sacrifice that is of worth.—*"Testimonies for the Church," Vol. IX, pages 144-147.*

THE SPIRIT OF INDEPENDENCE

Before leaving Australia, and since coming to this country, I have been instructed that there is a great work to be done in America. Those who were in the work at the beginning are passing away. Only a few of the pioneers of the cause now remain among us. Many of the heavy burdens formerly borne by men of long experience, are now falling upon younger men.

This transfer of responsibilities to laborers whose experience is more or less limited, is attended with some dangers against which we need to guard. The world is filled with strife for the supremacy. The spirit of pulling away from fellow-laborers, the spirit of disorganization, is in the very air we breathe. By some, all efforts to establish order are regarded as dangerous,— as a restriction of personal liberty, and hence to be feared as popery. These deceived souls regard it a virtue to boast of their freedom to think and act independently. They declare that they will not take any man's say-so; that they are amenable to no man. I have been instructed that it is Satan's special effort to lead men to feel that God is pleased to have them choose their own course, independent of the counsel of their brethren.

Herein lies a grave danger to the prosperity of our work. We must move discreetly, sensibly, in harmony with the judgment of God-fearing counselors; for in this course alone lies our safety and strength. Otherwise God cannot work with us and by us and for us.

O how Satan would rejoice if he could succeed in his efforts to get in among this people, and disorganize the work at a time when thorough organization is essential, and will be the greatest power to keep out spurious uprisings, and to refute claims not endorsed by the word of God! We want to hold the lines evenly, that there shall be no breaking down of the system of organization and order that has been built up by wise, careful labor. License must not be given to disorderly elements that desire to control the work at this time.

Some have advanced the thought that as we near the close of time, every child of God will act independently of any religious organization. But I have been instructed by the Lord that in this work there is no such thing as every man's being independent. The stars of heaven are all under law, each influencing the other to do the will of God, yielding their common obedience to the law that controls their action. And, in order that the Lord's work may advance healthfully and solidly, His people must draw together.

The spasmodic, fitful movements of some who claim to be Christians are well represented by the work of strong but untrained horses. When one pulls forward, another pulls back; at the voice of their master one plunges ahead, and the other stands immovable. If men will not move in concert in the great and grand work for this time, there will be confusion. It is not a good sign when men refuse to unite with their brethren, and prefer to act alone. Let laborers take into their confidence the brethren who are free to point out every departure from right principles.

If men wear the yoke of Christ, they cannot pull apart; they will draw with Christ.

Some workers pull with all the power that God has given them, but they have not yet learned that they should not pull alone. Instead of isolating themselves, let them draw in harmony with their fellow-laborers. Unless they do this, their activity will work at the wrong time and in the wrong way. They will often work counter to that which God would have done, and thus their work is worse than wasted.

On the other hand, the leaders among God's people are to guard against the danger of condemning the methods of individual workers who are led by the Lord to do a special work that but few are fitted to do. Let brethren in responsibility be slow to criticize movements that are not in perfect harmony with their methods of labor. Let them never suppose that every plan should reflect their own personality. Let them not fear to trust another's methods; for by withholding their confidence from a brother laborer who, with humility and consecrated zeal, is doing a special work in God's appointed way, they are retarding the advancement of the Lord's cause.

God can and will use those who have not had a thorough education in the schools of men. A doubt of His power to do this, is manifest unbelief; it is limiting the omnipotent power of the One with whom nothing is impossible. O for less of this uncalled-for, distrustful caution! It leaves so many forces of the church unused; it closes up the way, so that the Holy Spirit cannot use men; it keeps in idleness those who are willing and anxious to labor in Christ's lines; it discourages from entering the work many who would become efficient laborers together with God, if they were given a fair chance.

To the prophet, the wheel within a wheel, the appearance of living creatures connected with them, all seemed intricate and unexplainable. But the hand of Infinite Widsom is seen among the wheels, and perfect order is the result of its work. Every wheel, directed by the hand of God, works in perfect harmony with every other wheel. I have been shown that human instrumentalities are liable to seek after too much power, and try to control the work themselves. They leave the Lord God, the mighty Worker, too much out of their methods and plans, and do not trust to Him everything in regard to the advancement of the work. No one should for a moment fancy that he is able to manage those things that belong to the great I AM. God in His providence is preparing a way so that the work may be done by human agents. Then let every man stand at his post of duty, to act his part for this time, and know that God is his instructor.

THE GENERAL CONFERENCE

I have often been instructed by the Lord that no man's judgment should be surrendered to the judgment of any other one man. Never should the mind of one man or the minds of a few men be regarded as sufficient in wisdom and power to control the work, and to say what plans shall be followed. But when, in a General Conference, the judgment of the brethren assembled from all parts of the field, is exercised, private independence and private judgment must not be stubbornly maintained, but surrendered. Never should a laborer regard as a virtue the persistent maintenance of his position of independence, contrary to the decision of the general body.

At times, when a small group of men entrusted with the general management of the work have, in the name of the General Conference, sought to carry out unwise plans and to restrict God's work, I have said that I could no longer regard the voice of the General Conference, represented by these few men, as the voice of God. But this is not saying that the decisions of a General Conference composed of an assembly of duly appointed, representative men from all parts of the field, should not be respected. God has ordained that the representatives of His church from all parts of the earth, when assembled in a General Conference, shall have authority. The error that some are in danger of committing, is in giving to the mind and judgment of one man, or of a small group of men, the full measure of authority and influence that God has vested in His church, in the judgment and voice of the General Conference assembled to plan for the prosperity and advancement of His work.

When this power, which God has placed in the church, is accredited wholly to one man, and he is invested with the authority to be judgment for other minds, then the true Bible order is changed. Satan's efforts upon such a man's mind would be most subtle, and sometimes well-nigh overpowering; for the enemy would hope that through his mind he could affect many others. Let us give to the highest organized authority in the church that which we are prone to give to one man or to a small group of men.—*"Testimonies for the Church," Vol. IX, pages 257-261.*

CONSIDERATION FOR THOSE STRUGGLING WITH DIFFICULTIES

For years a lack of wisdom has been shown in dealing with men who take up and carry forward the Lord's work in difficult places. Often these men labor far beyond their strength. They have little money to invest for the advancement of the work, and they are obliged to sacrifice in order to carry the work forward. They work for small wages, and practice the strictest economy. They make appeals to the people for means, and they themselves set an example of liberality. They give God the praise for what is done, realizing that He is the author and the finisher of their faith, and that it is by His power that they are enabled to make progress.

Sometimes, after these workers have borne the burden and the heat of the day, and by patient, persevering effort have established a school or a sanitarium, or some other interest for the advancement of the work, the decision is made by their brethren that some other man might do better, and therefore that he is to take charge of the work they have been doing. In some cases the decision is made without giving due consideration and due credit to those who have borne the disagreeable part of the work, who have labored, and prayed, and striven, putting into their efforts all their strength and energy.

God is not pleased with this way of dealing with His workers. He calls upon His people to hold up the hands of those who build up the work in new and difficult places, speaking to them words of cheer and encouragement.

In their ardor, their zeal for the advancement of the cause, these workers may make mistakes. They may, in their desire to get means for the support of needy enterprises, enter into projects that are not for the best good of the work. The Lord, seeing that these projects would divert them from what He desires them to do, permits disappointment to come upon them, crushing their hopes. Money is sacrificed, and this is a great grief to those who had fondly hoped to gain means for the support of the cause.

While the workers were straining every nerve to raise means to help them over an emergency, some of their brethren were standing by, criticizing and surmising evil, putting a prejudicial construction on the motives of the heavily burdened laborers, and making their work more difficult. Blinded by selfishness, these faultfinders did not discern that their brethren were sufficiently afflicted without the censure of men who had not borne heavy burdens and responsibilities. Disappointment is a great trial, but Christian love can turn the defeat into victory. Reverses will teach caution. We learn by the things we suffer. Thus we gain experience.

Let care and wisdom be shown in dealing with workers who, though they have made mistakes, have manifested an earnest, self-sacrificing interest in the work. Let their brethren say, "We will not make matters worse by putting another in your place, without giving you opportunity to retrieve your mistake, and to stand on vantage-ground, free from the burden of unjust criticism." Let them be given time to adjust themselves, to overcome the difficulties surrounding them, and to stand before angels and men as worthy workers. They have made mistakes, but would those who have questioned and criticized have done better? To the accusing Pharisees Christ said, "He that is without sin among you, let him first cast a stone." [1]

There are those who are premature in their desire to reform things that to them appear faulty. They think that they should be chosen to take the place of those who have made mistakes. They undervalue what these workers have done while others were looking on and criticizing. By their actions they say: "I can do great things. I can carry the work forward successfully." To those who think they know so well how to avoid mistakes, I am instructed to say, "Judge not, that ye be not judged." [2] You might avoid mistakes on some points, but on other things you are liable to make grave blunders, which would be very difficult to remedy, and which would bring confusion into the work. These mistakes might do more harm than those your brethren have made.

The instruction given me is that the men who lay the foundation of a work, and who, in the face of prejudice, fight their way forward, are not to be placed in an unfavorable light, in order that others may take their places. There are earnest workers who, in spite of the criticisms of some of their brethren, have moved forward in the work that God said should be done. Should they now be removed from their position of responsibility, an impression would be made that would be unjust to them, and unfavorable to the work, be-

[1] John 8 : 7.　　　　　　　　　　[2] Matt. 7 : 1.

cause the changes made would be looked upon as a justification of the unjust criticisms made and the prejudice existing. The Lord desires that no move shall be made which would do injustice to those who have labored long and earnestly to build up the work given them.

Many changes are made that might better never be made. Often, when workers become discontented, instead of being encouraged to stay where they are and make a success of their work, they are sent to another place. But they take with them the same traits of character that in the past have marred their work. They will manifest the same unchristlike spirit; for they have not learned the lesson of patient, humble service.

I plead for a different order of things. Changes must be made in the groups of workers in our conferences and institutions. Men of efficiency and consecration must be sought for and encouraged to connect with the burden-bearers as helpers and co-laborers. Let there be a harmonious union of the new and the old, in the spirit of brotherly love. But let not changes of management be made abruptly, in such a way as to bring discouragement to those who have labored earnestly and successfully to bring the work to a degree of progress. God will not sanction anything done to discourage His faithful servants. Let the principles of justice be followed by those whose duty it is to secure the most efficient management for our publishing houses, our sanitariums, and our schools.

God calls for workers. The cause needs men who are self-made, who, placing themselves in the hands of the Lord as humble learners, have proved them-

selves workers together with Him. These are the
men that are needed in the ministry and in the school
work. Let those who have shown themselves to be
men move out, and do what they can in the Master's service. Let them step into the ranks of workers,
and by patient, continuous effort prove their worth.
It is in the water, not on the land, that we learn to
swim. Let them fill with fidelity the place to which
they are called, that they may become qualified to
bear still higher responsibilities. God gives all opportunity to perfect themselves in His service. . . .

God has endowed some of His servants with special talents, and no one is called upon to disparage
their excellence. But let none use their talents to
exalt self. Let them not regard themselves as favored
above their fellow-men, nor exalt themselves above
other sincere, earnest workers. The Lord looks upon
the heart. He who is most devoted to God's service
is most highly esteemed by the heavenly universe.

Heaven is watching to see how those occupying
positions of influence fulfil their stewardship. The
demands upon them as stewards are measured by the
extent of their influence. In their treatment of their
fellow-men, they should be as fathers,— just, tender,
true. They should be Christlike in character, uniting
with their brethren in the closest bonds of unity and
fellowship.—*"Testimonies for the Church," Vol. VII,*
pages 277-282.

"CONSIDER ONE ANOTHER"

You will often meet with souls that are under the stress of temptation. You know not how severely Satan may be wrestling with them. Beware lest you discourage such souls, and thus give the tempter an advantage.

Whenever you see or hear something that needs to be corrected, seek the Lord for wisdom and grace, that in trying to be faithful you may not be severe. It is always humiliating to have one's errors pointed out. Do not make the experience more bitter by needless censure. Unkind criticism brings discouragement, making life sunless and unhappy.

My brethren, prevail by love rather than by severity. When one at fault becomes conscious of his error, be careful not to destroy his self-respect. Do not seek to bruise and wound, but rather to bind up and heal.

———————

No human being possesses sensibilities so acute or a nature so refined as does our Saviour. And what patience He manifests toward us! Year after year He bears with our weakness and ignorance, with our ingratitude and waywardness. Notwithstanding all our wanderings, our hardness of heart, our neglect of His holy words, His hand is stretched out still. And He bids us, "Love one another as I have loved you." [1]

Brethren, regard yourselves as missionaries, not among heathen, but among your fellow-workers. It requires a vast amount of time and labor to convince

[1] John 13: 34.

one soul in regard to the special truths for this time. And when souls are turned from sin to righteousness, there is joy in the presence of the angels. Think you that the ministering spirits who watch over these souls are pleased to see how indifferently they are treated by many who claim to be Christians? Man's preferences rule. Partiality is manifested. One is favored, while another is treated harshly.

The angels look with awe and amazement upon the mission of Christ to the world. They marvel at the love that moved Him to give Himself a sacrifice for the sins of men. But how lightly human beings regard the purchase of His blood!

We need not begin by *trying* to love one another. The love of Christ in the heart is what is needed. When self is submerged in Christ, true love springs forth spontaneously.

In patient forbearance we shall conquer. It is patience in service that brings rest to the soul. It is through humble, diligent, faithful toilers that the welfare of Israel is promoted. A word of love and encouragement will do more to subdue the hasty temper and wilful disposition than all the faultfinding and censure that you can heap upon the erring one.

The Master's message must be declared in the Master's spirit. Our only safety is in keeping our thoughts and impulses under the control of the great Teacher. Angels of God will give to every true worker a rich experience in doing this. The grace of humility will mould our words into expressions of Christlike tenderness.—*"Testimonies for the Church," Vol. VII, pages 265, 266.*

CHURCH DISCIPLINE

In dealing with erring church-members, God's people are carefully to follow the instruction given by the Saviour in the eighteenth chapter of Matthew.[1]

Human beings are Christ's property, purchased by Him at an infinite price, bound to Him by the love that He and His Father have manifested for them. How careful, then, we should be in our dealing with one another! Men have no right to surmise evil in regard to their fellow-men. Church-members have no right to follow their own impulses and inclinations in dealing with fellow-members who have erred. They should not even express their prejudices regarding the erring; for thus they place in other minds the leaven of evil. Reports unfavorable to a brother or sister in the church are communicated from one to another of the church-members. Mistakes are made and injustice is done because of an unwillingness on the part of some one to follow the directions given by the Lord Jesus.

"If thy brother shall trespass against thee," Christ declared, "go and tell him his fault between thee and him alone." Do not tell others of the wrong. One person is told, then another, and still another; and continually the report grows, and the evil increases, till the whole church is made to suffer. Settle the matter "between thee and him alone." This is God's plan.

"Go not forth hastily to strive, lest thou know not what to do in the end thereof, when thy neighbor hath

[1] See Matt. 18 : 15-18.

put thee to shame. Debate thy cause with thy neighbor himself; and discover not a secret to another." [2] Do not suffer sin upon your brother; but do not expose him, and thus increase the difficulty, making the reproof seem like a revenge. Correct him in the way outlined in the word of God.

Do not suffer resentment to ripen into malice. Do not allow the wound to fester and break out in poisoned words, which taint the minds of those who hear. Do not allow bitter thoughts to continue to fill your mind and his. Go to your brother, and in humility and sincerity talk with him about the matter.

Whatever the character of the offense, this does not change the plan that God has made for the settlement of misunderstandings and personal injuries. Speaking alone and in the spirit of Christ to the one who is in fault, will often remove the difficulty. Go to the erring one, with a heart filled with Christ's love and sympathy, and seek to adjust the matter. Reason with him calmly and quietly. Let no angry words escape your lips. Speak in a way that will appeal to his better judgment. Remember the words, "He which converteth the sinner from the error of his way shall save a soul from death, and shall hide a multitude of sins." [3]

Take to your brother the remedy that will cure the disease of disaffection. Do your part to help him. For the sake of the peace and unity of the church, feel it a privilege as well as a duty to do this. If he will hear you, you have gained him as a friend.

All heaven is interested in the interview between the one who has been injured and the one who is in

[2] Prov. 25 : 8, 9.　　　　　　　[3] James 5 : 20.

error. As the erring one accepts the reproof offered in the love of Christ, and acknowledges his wrong, asking forgiveness from God and from his brother, the sunshine of heaven fills his heart. The controversy is ended; friendship and confidence are restored. The oil of love removes the soreness caused by the wrong; the Spirit of God binds heart to heart; and there is music in heaven over the union brought about.

As those thus united in Christian fellowship offer prayer to God, and pledge themselves to deal justly, to love mercy, and to walk humbly with God, great blessing comes to them. If they have wronged others, they continue the work of repentance, confession, and restitution, fully set to do good to one another. This is the fulfilling of the law of Christ.

"But if he will not hear thee, then take with thee one or two more, that in the mouth of two or three witnesses every word may be established." Take with you those who are spiritually minded, and talk with the one in error in regard to the wrong. He may yield to the united appeals of his brethren. As he sees their agreement in the matter, his mind may be enlightened.

"And if he shall neglect to hear them," what then shall be done? Shall a few persons in a board meeting take upon themselves the responsibility of disfellowshiping the erring one? "If he shall neglect to hear them, tell it unto *the church*." Let the church take action in regard to its members.

"But if he neglect to hear the church, let him be unto thee as a heathen man and a publican." If he will not heed the voice of the church, if he refuses all the efforts made to reclaim him, upon the church rests the responsibility of separating him from fellowship. His name should then be stricken from the books.

No church officer should advise, no committee should recommend, nor should any church vote, that the name of a wrong-doer shall be removed from the church books, until the instruction given by Christ has been faithfully followed. When this has been done, the church has cleared herself before God. The evil must then be made to appear as it is, and must be removed, that it may not become more and more widespread. The health and purity of the church must be preserved, that she may stand before God unsullied, clad in the robes of Christ's righteousness.

If the erring one repents and submits to Christ's discipline, he is to be given another trial. And even if he does not repent, even if he stands outside the church, God's servants still have a work to do for him. They are to seek earnestly to win him to repentance. And however aggravated may have been his offense, if he yields to the striving of the Holy Spirit, and by confessing and forsaking his sin gives evidence of repentance, he is to be forgiven and welcomed to the fold again. His brethren are to encourage him in the right way, treating him as they would wish to be treated were they in his place, considering themselves, lest they also be tempted.

"Verily I say unto you," Christ continued, "Whatsoever ye shall bind on earth shall be bound in heaven: and whatsoever ye shall loose on earth shall be loosed in heaven."

This statement holds its force in all ages. On the church has been conferred the power to act in Christ's stead. It is God's instrumentality for the preservation of order and discipline among His people. To it the Lord has delegated the power to settle all questions respecting its prosperity, purity, and order. Upon it rests the responsibility of excluding from its fellowship those who are unworthy, who by their unchristlike conduct would bring dishonor on the truth. Whatever the church does that is in accordance with the directions given in God's word, will be ratified in heaven.

REMISSION OF SINS

"Whosoever sins ye remit," said Christ, "they are remitted; . . . and whosoever sins ye retain, they are retained." [4] Christ here gives no liberty for any man to pass judgment upon others. In the sermon on the mount He forbade this. It is the prerogative of God. But on the church in its organized capacity He places a responsibility for the individual members. Toward those who fall into sin, the church has a duty, to warn, to instruct, and if possible to restore. "Reprove, rebuke, exhort," the Lord says, "with all long-suffering and doctrine." [5]

Deal faithfully with wrong-doing. Warn every soul that is in danger. Leave none to deceive themselves. Call sin by its right name. Declare what God has said in regard to lying, Sabbath-breaking, stealing, idolatry, and every other evil. "They which do such things shall not inherit the kingdom of God." [6] If they persist in sin, the judgment you have declared from God's word is pronounced upon them in heaven. In choosing to sin, they disown Christ; the church

[4] John 20 : 23.   [5] 2 Tim. 4 : 2.   [6] Gal. 5 : 21.

must show that she does not sanction their deeds, or she herself dishonors her Lord. She must say about sin what God says about it. She must deal with it as God directs, and her action is ratified in heaven. He who despises the authority of the church, despises the authority of Christ Himself.

But there is a brighter side to the picture. "Whosoever sins ye remit, they are remitted." Let this thought be kept uppermost. In labor for the erring, let every eye be directed to Christ. Let the shepherds have a tender care for the flock of the Lord's pasture. Let them speak to the erring of the forgiving mercy of the Saviour. Let them encourage the sinner to repent, and believe in Him who can pardon. Let them declare, on the authority of God's word, "If we confess our sins, He is faithful and just to forgive us our sins, and to cleanse us from all unrighteousness." [7] All who repent have the assurance, "He will have compassion upon us; He will subdue our iniquities; and Thou wilt cast all their sins into the depths of the sea." [8]

Let the repentance of the sinner be accepted by the church with grateful hearts. Let the repenting one be led out from the darkness of unbelief into the light of faith and righteousness. Let his trembling hand be placed in the loving hand of Jesus. Such a remission is ratified in heaven.—*"The Desire of Ages," pages 805, 806.*

[7] 1 John 1 : 9.   [8] Micah 7 : 19.

FOR FURTHER STUDY

VARIED GIFTS   Acts, pp. 269-280.

UNITY IN DIVERSITY   Test. Vol. I, pp. 323, 324.
                                      Test. Vol. V, pp. 722-726.
                                      Test. Vol. VIII, pp. 174, 175.
                                      Test. Vol. IX, pp. 179-194, 195-
                                          198.
                                      Acts, pp. 273-280, 399-406.

THE SPIRIT OF INDEPENDENCE   Test. Vol. I, p. 207.
                                      Test. Vol. III, pp. 66, 414-424.
                                      Test. Vol. V, p. 238.
                                      Test. Vol. IX, pp. 270-284.
                                      Acts, pp. 163-165, 188-200, 399-
                                          406.

CONSIDERATION FOR THOSE   Test. Vol. IV, p. 238.
  STRUGGLING WITH DIF-   Test. Vol. V, pp. 298-302.
  FICULTIES   Patriarchs, p. 386.

"CONSIDER ONE ANOTHER"   Test. Vol. I, p. 383.
                                      Test. Vol. III, pp. 93, 94.
                                      Test. Vol. IV, pp. 66, 485-489.
                                      Test. Vol. V, pp. 341-348.
                                      Test. Vol. IX, pp. 223, 224.
                                      M. of H., pp. 493-496.
                                      C. O. L., pp. 185-197, 385-389.

CHURCH DISCIPLINE   Test. Vol. I, pp. 164-168, 214-
                                          216.
                                      Test. Vol. III, pp. 99-109, 113-
                                          116, 186-188, 196, 265-269.
                                      Test. Vol. IV, pp. 268, 269, 515-
                                          517.
                                      Test. Vol. V, pp. 147, 241, 615-
                                          617.
                                      Test. Vol. VII, pp. 260-264.
                                      Ed., pp. 88-92.
                                      M. of H., pp. 161-170, 493-496.
                                      C. O. L., pp. 70-75, 243-251.
                                      Desire, pp. 437-442, 652-661,
                                          807-817.
                                      Acts, pp. 515, 516.

Closing Words

" Finally, my brethren, be strong in the Lord, and in the power of His might."

POWER FOR SERVICE

What the church needs in these days of peril is an army of workers who, like Paul, have educated themselves for usefulness, who have a deep experience in the things of God, and who are filled with earnestness and zeal. Sanctified, self-sacrificing men are needed, — men who will not shun trial and responsibility; men who are brave and true; men in whose hearts Christ is formed "the hope of glory," and who, with lips touched with holy fire, will "preach the word." For want of such workers the cause of God languishes, and fatal errors, like a deadly poison, taint the morals and blight the hopes of a large part of the human race. —*"The Acts of the Apostles," page 507.*

Those who are men in the sight of God, and who are thus recorded in the books of heaven, are those who, like Daniel, cultivate every faculty in such a way as best represents the kingdom of God to a world lying in wickedness. Progress in knowledge is essential; for when employed in the cause of God, knowledge is a power for good. The world needs men of thought, men of principle, men who are constantly growing in understanding and discernment. The press is in need of men to use it to the best advantage, that the truth may be given wings to speed it to every nation, and tongue, and people.

———————

"Go out into the highways and hedges, and compel them to come in," Christ bids us, "that My house may be filled." [1] In obedience to this word we must go to the heathen who are near us, and to those who are afar off. The "publicans and the harlots" must hear the Saviour's invitation. Through the kindness and long-suffering of His messengers, the invitation becomes a compelling power to uplift those who are sunken in the lowest depths of sin.

Christian motives demand that we work with a steady purpose, an undying interest, an ever-increasing importunity, for the souls whom Satan is seeking to destroy. Nothing is to chill the earnest, yearning energy for the salvation of the lost.

Mark how all through the word of God there is manifest the spirit of urgency, of imploring men and women to come to Christ. We must seize upon every opportunity, in private and in public, presenting every argument, urging every motive of infinite weight, to draw men to the Saviour. With all our power we must urge them to look unto Jesus, and to accept His life of self-denial and sacrifice. We must show that we expect them to give joy to the heart of Christ by using every one of His gifts in honoring His name.— *"Ministry of Healing," pages 164, 165.*

———————

It is not the length of time we labor, but our willingness and fidelity in the work, that makes it acceptable to God. In all our service a full surrender of self

[1] Luke 14 : 23.

is demanded. The smallest duty done in sincerity and self-forgetfulness, is more pleasing to God than the greatest work when marred with self-seeking. He looks to see how much of the spirit of Christ we cherish, and how much of the likeness of Christ our work reveals. He regards more the love and faithfulness with which we work than the amount we do.

Only when selfishness is dead, when strife for the supremacy is banished, when gratitude fills the heart, and love makes fragrant the life,— it is only then that Christ is abiding in the soul, and we are recognized as laborers together with God.—*"Christ's Object Lessons,"* *page 402.*

Of all people in the world, reformers should be the most unselfish, the most kind, the most courteous. In their lives should be seen the true goodness of unselfish deeds. The worker who manifests a lack of courtesy, who shows impatience at the ignorance or waywardness of others, who speaks hastily or acts thoughtlessly, may close the door to hearts so that he can never reach them.

As the dew and the still showers fall upon the withering plants, so let words fall gently when seeking to win men from error. God's plan is first to reach the heart. We are to speak the truth in love, trusting in Him to give it power for the reforming of the life. The Holy Spirit will apply to the soul the word that is spoken in love.

Naturally we are self-centered and opinionated. But when we learn the lessons that Christ desires to teach us, we become partakers of His nature; henceforth we live His life. The wonderful example of

Christ, the matchless tenderness with which He entered into the feelings of others, weeping with those who wept, rejoicing with those who rejoiced, must have a deep influence upon the character of all who follow Him in sincerity. By kindly words and acts they will try to make the path easy for weary feet.— *"Ministry of Healing," pages 157, 158.*

It is not the highest work of education to communicate knowledge merely, but to impart that vitalizing energy which is received through the contact of mind with mind and soul with soul. It is only life that can beget life. What privilege, then, was theirs who for three years were in daily contact with that divine life from which has flowed every life-giving impulse that has blessed the world! Above all His companions, John the beloved disciple yielded himself to the power of that wondrous life. He says, "The life was manifested, and we have seen it, and bear witness, and show unto you that eternal life, which was with the Father, and was manifested unto us." "Of His fulness have all we received, and grace for grace." [2]

In the apostles of our Lord there was nothing to bring glory to themselves. It was evident that the success of their labors was due only to God. The lives of these men, the characters they developed, and the mighty work that God wrought through them, are a testimony to what He will do for all who are teachable and obedient.—*"The Desire of Ages," page 250.*

Before honor is humility. To fill a high place before men, Heaven chooses the worker who, like John

[2] 1 John 1 : 2; John 1 : 16.

the Baptist, takes a lowly place before God. The most childlike disciple is the most efficient in labor for God. The heavenly intelligences can co-operate with him who is seeking, not to exalt self, but to save souls. He who feels most deeply his need of divine aid will plead for it, and the Holy Spirit will give unto him glimpses of Jesus that will strengthen and uplift the soul. From communion with Christ he will go forth to work for those who are perishing in their sins. He is anointed for his mission; and he succeeds where many of the learned and intellectually wise would fail. —*"The Desire of Ages," page 436.*

He who calls men to repentance must commune with God in prayer. He must cling to the Mighty One, saying, "I will not let Thee go, except Thou bless me. Give me power to win souls to Christ."

Paul says, "When I am weak, then am I strong." [3] When we have a realization of our weakness, we learn to depend upon a power not inherent. Nothing can take so strong a hold on the heart as the abiding sense of our responsibility to God. Nothing reaches so fully down to the deepest motives of conduct as a sense of the pardoning love of Christ. We are to come in touch with God, then we shall be imbued with His Holy Spirit, that enables us to come in touch with our fellow-men.

Then rejoice that through Christ you have become connected with God, members of the heavenly family. While you look higher than yourself, you will have a

[3] 2 Cor. 12 : 10.

continual sense of the weakness of humanity. The less you cherish self, the more distinct and full will be your comprehension of the excellence of your Saviour. The more closely you connect yourself with the Source of light and power, the greater light will be shed upon you, and the greater power will be yours to work for God.—"*The Desire of Ages,*" *page 493.*

———

Nothing is more needed in our work than the practical results of communion with God. We should show by our daily lives that we have peace and rest in the Saviour. His peace in the heart will shine forth in the countenance. It will give to the voice a persuasive power. Communion with God will ennoble the character and the life. Men will take knowledge of us, as of the first disciples, that we have been with Jesus. This will impart to the worker a power that nothing else can give. Of this power he must not allow himself to be deprived.

We must live a twofold life,— a life of thought and action, of silent prayer and earnest work. The strength received through communion with God, united with earnest effort in training the mind to thoughtfulness and care-taking, prepares one for daily duties, and keeps the spirit in peace under all circumstances, however trying.—"*Ministry of Healing,*" *page 512.*

———

To the consecrated worker there is wonderful consolation in the knowledge that even Christ during His life on earth sought His Father daily for fresh supplies of needed grace; and from this communion with God He went forth to strengthen and bless others.

Behold the Son of God bowed in prayer to His Father! Though He is the Son of God, He strengthens His faith by prayer, and by communion with Heaven gathers to Himself power to resist evil and to minister to the needs of men. As the Elder Brother of our race, He knows the necessities of those who, compassed with infirmity and living in a world of sin and temptation, still desire to serve Him. He knows that the messengers whom He sees fit to send are weak, erring men; but to all who give themselves wholly to His service He promises divine aid. His own example is an assurance that earnest, persevering supplication to God in faith — faith that leads to entire dependence upon God, and unreserved consecration to His work — will avail to bring to men the Holy Spirit's aid in the battle against sin.

Every worker who follows the example of Christ will be prepared to receive and use the power that God has promised to His church for the ripening of earth's harvest. Morning by morning, as the heralds of the gospel kneel before the Lord and renew their vows of consecration to Him, He will grant them the presence of His Spirit, with its reviving, sanctifying power. As they go forth to the day's duties, they have the assurance that the unseen agency of the Holy Spirit enables them to be "laborers together with God." [4] —*"The Acts of the Apostles," page 56*.

[4] 1 Cor. 3 : 9.

THE REWARD OF SERVICE

"When thou makest a dinner or a supper," said Christ, "call not thy friends, nor thy brethren, neither thy kinsmen, nor thy rich neighbors; lest they also bid thee again, and a recompense be made thee. But when thou makest a feast, call the poor, the maimed, the lame, the blind: and thou shalt be blessed; for they cannot recompense thee: for thou shalt be recompensed at the resurrection of the just."[1]

In these words Christ draws a contrast between the self-seeking practices of the world, and the unselfish ministry of which He has given an example in His own life. For such ministry He offers no reward of worldly gain or recognition. "Thou shalt be recompensed," He says, "at the resurrection of the just." Then the results of every life will be made manifest, and every one will reap that which he has sown.

To every worker for God this thought should be a stimulus and an encouragement. In this life our work for God often seems to be almost fruitless. Our efforts to do good may be earnest and persevering, yet we may not be permitted to witness their results. To us the effort may seem to be lost. But the Saviour assures us that our work is noted in heaven, and that the recompense cannot fail. The apostle Paul, writing by the Holy Spirit, says, "Let us not be weary in well doing: for in due season we shall reap, if we faint not."[2] And in the words of the psalmist we read, "He that goeth forth and weepeth, bearing precious

[1] Luke 14 : 12-14.　　　　　　　[2] Gal. 6 : 9.

seed, shall doubtless come again with rejoicing, bringing his sheaves with him." [3]

While the great final reward is given at Christ's coming, true-hearted service for God brings a reward, even in this life. Obstacles, opposition, and bitter, heart-breaking discouragements, the worker will have to meet. He may not see the fruit of his toil. But in face of all this he finds in his labor a blessed recompense. All who surrender themselves to God in unselfish service for humanity are in co-operation with the Lord of glory. This thought sweetens all toil, it braces the will, it nerves the spirit for whatever may befall. Working with unselfish heart, ennobled by being partakers of Christ's sufferings, sharing His sympathies, they help to swell the tide of His joy, and bring honor and praise to His exalted name. In fellowship with God, with Christ, and with holy angels, they are surrounded with a heavenly atmosphere, an atmosphere that brings health to the body, vigor to the intellect, and joy to the soul.

All who consecrate body, soul, and spirit to God's service will be constantly receiving a new endowment of physical, mental, and spiritual power. The inexhaustible supplies of heaven are at their command. Christ gives them the breath of His own spirit, the life of His own life. The Holy Spirit puts forth His highest energies to work in heart and mind.

"Then shall thy light break forth as the morning, and thine health shall spring forth speedily." Thou shalt "call, and the Lord shall answer; thou shalt cry, and He shall say, Here I am." "Thy light" shall "rise in obscurity, and thy darkness be as the noonday: and the Lord shall guide thee continually, and

[3] Ps. 126 : 6.

17

satisfy thy soul in drought, and make fat thy bones: and thou shalt be like a watered garden, and like a spring of water, whose waters fail not." [4]

Many are God's promises to those who minister to His afflicted ones. He says: "Blessed is he that considereth the poor: the Lord will deliver him in time of trouble. The Lord will preserve him, and keep him alive; and he shall be blessed upon the earth: and Thou wilt not deliver him unto the will of his enemies. The Lord will strengthen him upon the bed of languishing: Thou wilt make all his bed in his sickness." "Trust in the Lord, and do good; so shalt thou dwell in the land, and verily thou shalt be fed." [5] "Honor the Lord with thy substance, and with the first-fruits of all thine increase: so shall thy barns be filled with plenty, and thy presses shall burst out with new wine." "There is that scattereth, and yet increaseth; and there is that withholdeth more than is meet, but it tendeth to poverty." "He that hath pity upon the poor lendeth unto the Lord; and that which he hath given will He pay him again." "The liberal soul shall be made fat: and he that watereth shall be watered also himself." [6]

While much of the fruit of their labor is not apparent in this life, God's workers have His sure promise of ultimate success. As the world's Redeemer, Christ was constantly confronted with apparent failure. He seemed to do little of the work which He longed to do in uplifting and saving. Satanic agencies were constantly working to obstruct His way. But He would not be discouraged. Ever before Him

[4] Isa. 58 : 8-11. [5] Ps. 41 : 1-3 ; 37 : 3.
[6] Prov. 3 : 9, 10 ; 11 : 24 ; 19 : 17 ; 11 : 25.

He saw the result of His mission. He knew that truth would finally triumph in the contest with evil, and to His disciples He said: "These things I have spoken unto you, that in Me ye might have peace. In the world ye shall have tribulation: but be of good cheer; I have overcome the world." [7] The life of Christ's disciples is to be like His, a series of uninterrupted victories — not seen to be such here, but recognized as such in the great hereafter.

Those who labor for the good of others are working in union with the heavenly angels. They have their constant companionship, their unceasing ministry. Angels of light and power are ever near to protect, to comfort, to heal, to instruct, to inspire. The highest education, the truest culture, the most exalted service possible to human beings in this world, are theirs.

Often our merciful Father encourages His children and strengthens their faith by permitting them here to see evidence of the power of His grace upon the hearts and lives of those for whom they labor. "My thoughts are not your thoughts, neither are your ways My ways, saith the Lord. For as the heavens are higher than the earth, so are My ways higher than your ways, and My thoughts than your thoughts. For as the rain cometh down, and the snow from heaven, and returneth not thither, but watereth the earth, and maketh it bring forth and bud, that it may give seed to the sower, and bread to the eater: so shall My word be that goeth forth out of My mouth: it shall not return unto Me void, but it shall accomplish that which I please, and it shall prosper in the thing whereto I sent it. For ye shall go out with

[7] John 16: 33.

joy, and be led forth with peace: the mountains and the hills shall break forth before you into singing, and all the trees of the field shall clap their hands. Instead of the thorn shall come up the fir-tree, and instead of the brier shall come up the myrtle-tree: and it shall be to the Lord for a name, for an everlasting sign that shall not be cut off." [8]

In the transformation of character, the casting out of evil passions, the development of the sweet graces of God's Holy Spirit, we see the fulfilment of the promise, "Instead of the thorn shall come up the fir-tree, and instead of the brier shall come up the myrtle-tree." We behold life's desert "rejoice, and blossom as the rose." [9]

Christ delights to take apparently hopeless material, those whom Satan has debased and through whom he has worked, and make them the subjects of His grace. He rejoices to deliver them from suffering, and from the wrath that is to fall upon the disobedient. He makes His children His agents in the accomplishment of this work, and in its success, even in this life, they find a precious reward.

But what is this compared with the joy that will be theirs in the great day of final revealing? "Now we see through a glass, darkly; but then face to face;" now we know in part, but then we shall know even as also we are known. [10]

It is the reward of Christ's workers to enter into His joy. That joy, to which Christ Himself looks forward with eager desire, is presented in His request to His Father, "I will that they also, whom Thou hast given Me, be with Me where I am." [11]

[8] Isa. 55:8-13.   [9] Isa. 35:1.   [10] See 1 Cor. 13:12.
[11] John 17:24.

The angels were waiting to welcome Jesus, as He ascended after His resurrection. The heavenly host longed to greet again their loved Commander, returned to them from the prison-house of death. Eagerly they pressed about Him as He entered the gates of heaven. But He waved them back. His heart was with the lonely, sorrowing band of disciples whom He had left upon Olivet. It is still with His struggling children on earth, who have the battle with the destroyer yet to wage. "Father," He says, "I will that they also, whom Thou hast given Me, be with Me where I am."

Christ's redeemed ones are His jewels, His precious and peculiar treasure. "They shall be as the stones of a crown,"—"the riches of the glory of His inheritance in the saints." [12] In them "He shall see of the travail of His soul, and shall be satisfied." [13]

And will not His workers rejoice when they, too, behold the fruit of their labors? The apostle Paul, writing to the Thessalonian converts, says: "What is our hope, or joy, or crown of rejoicing? Are not even ye in the presence of our Lord Jesus Christ at His coming? for ye are our glory and joy." [14] And he exhorts the Philippian brethren to be "blameless and harmless," to "shine as lights in the world; holding forth the word of life; that I may rejoice in the day of Christ, that I have not run in vain, neither labored in vain." [15]

Every impulse of the Holy Spirit leading men to goodness and to God, is noted in the books of heaven, and in the day of God every one who has given him-

[12] Zech. 9 : 16 ; Eph. 1 : 18. [13] Isa. 53 : 11.
[14] 1 Thess. 2 : 19, 20. [15] Phil. 2 : 15, 16.

self as an instrument for the Holy Spirit's working, will be permitted to behold what his life has wrought. . . .

Wonderful will be the revealing as the lines of holy influence, with their precious results, are brought to view. What will be the gratitude of souls that will meet us in the heavenly courts, as they understand the sympathetic, loving interest which has been taken in their salvation! All praise, honor, and glory will be given to God and to the Lamb for our redemption; but it will not detract from the glory of God to express gratitude to the instrumentality He has employed in the salvation of souls ready to perish.

The redeemed will meet and recognize those whose attention they have directed to the uplifted Saviour. What blessed converse they will have with these souls! "I was a sinner," it will be said, "without God and without hope in the world; and you came to me, and drew my attention to the precious Saviour as my only hope. And I believed in Him. I repented of my sins, and was made to sit together with His saints in heavenly places in Christ Jesus." Others will say: "I was a heathen in heathen lands. You left your friends and comfortable home, and came to teach me how to find Jesus, and believe in Him as the only true God. I demolished my idols, and worshiped God, and now I see Him face to face. I am saved, eternally saved, ever to behold Him whom I love. I then saw Him only with the eye of faith, but now I see Him as He is. I can now express my gratitude for His redeeming mercy to Him who loved me, and washed me from my sins in His own blood."

Others will express their gratitude to those who fed the hungry and clothed the naked. "When despair bound my soul in unbelief, the Lord sent you to me," they say, "to speak words of hope and comfort. You brought me food for my physical necessities, and you opened to me the word of God, awakening me to my spiritual needs. You treated me as a brother. You sympathized with me in my sorrows, and restored my bruised and wounded soul, so that I could grasp the hand of Christ that was reached out to save me. In my ignorance you taught me patiently that I had a Father in heaven who cared for me. You read to me the precious promises of God's word. You inspired in me faith that He would save me. My heart was softened, subdued, broken, as I contemplated the sacrifice which Christ had made for me. I became hungry for the bread of life, and the truth was precious to my soul. I am here, saved, eternally saved, ever to live in His presence, and to praise Him who gave His life for me."

What rejoicing there will be as these redeemed ones meet and greet those who have had a burden in their behalf! And those who have lived, not to please themselves, but to be a blessing to the unfortunate who have so few blessings,— how their hearts will thrill with satisfaction! They will realize the promise, "Thou shalt be blessed; for they cannot recompense thee: for thou shalt be recompensed at the resurrection of the just." [16]

"Thou shalt delight thyself in the Lord; and I will cause thee to ride upon the high places of the earth, and feed thee with the heritage of Jacob thy father: for the mouth of the Lord hath spoken it." [17] —"*Testimonies for the Church*," *Vol. VI, pages 305-312.*

[16] Luke 14 : 14.   [17] Isa. 58 : 14.

FOR FURTHER STUDY

Power for Service

Test. Vol. VI, pp. 443, 444.
Test. Vol. IX, pp. 28, 29, 40, 141-143.
Ed., pp. 51-70.
Desire, pp. 249-251, 416, 417.
M. of H., pp. 58, 139-160, 503-516.
C. O. L., pp. 36-43, 336, 337.
Acts, pp. 205, 241, 242, 464, 465, 478, 484, 514-528, 539-556, 564-567.
Counsels, pp. 409, 410, 509, 510, 513.

The Reward of Service

Ed., pp. 305-309.
Desire, pp. 223-225, 312, 328-332, 369-371, 623, 624, 827, 828.
C. O. L., pp. 58-61, 397-404.
Acts, pp. 601, 602.

Index of Scripture References

GENERAL INDEX

Disease, how caused, 215.

Disorganization, evil of, 486, 487.

Disunion, dishonoring to God, 484.

Doctrine, sound, 311-315.
  speculative, 305-310, 311-315.
  see also Fanaticism ; Foundation of faith.

Dream, " gathering the fruit," 136-139.

Dress, of ministers, 145, 172-174.
  of priests of Israel, 173.

Earnestness, in prayer, 177, 178.
  in service, illustrations of, 31-34.
  need of, 144, 151, 152, 506.
  not seen as it should be, 65.
  Paul's example of, 59-61.

Economy, in mission work, 458-463.

Education, the essential, 334.
  see also Training ; Workers ; Youth.

Elisha, 116, 333.

Eloquence, not to be minister's highest aim, 153-155.

Enoch, 51-54.

Erring, dealing with the, 498-503.

Ethiopia, 85.

Etiquette, danger of attaching undue importance to, 333, 334.

Evangelists, *see* City work ; Ministers ; Workers.

Evil, *see* Sin.

Evil-doing, duty of church toward, 501, 502.

Evil-speaking, results of, 479.

Exclusiveness, Christ's example a rebuke to, 334, 335.
  warning against, 330-332, 334-336.

Extremes, Christ's example regarding, 317.
  workers to guard against, 317.

Faith, in contrast with presumption, 260.
  foundations of Seventh-day Adventist faith, 307, 321, 322.
  meaning of, 259, 260, 262.
  need of, 161, 215, 259-263, 274.
  not feeling, 260.
  power of true, 259, 261.

Family of minister to be an example, 204, 205.

Fanaticism, 170.
  warning against, 316, 317.
  see also Dangers.

Feeling not a safe guide, 382.

Finances of cause, management of, 423-425.

Foreign fields, economy in, 458-463.
  instruction to workers in, 461-463.
  methods of work in, 461-463, 468-470.
  needs of, 465.
  result of helping, 465-467.
  support of workers in, 454, 455, 465, 466.
  workers needed in, 459, 469, 470.

Foreign languages, 82, 83.

Foundation of faith, how laid, 148, 307, 321, 322.

General Conference, position of, 489, 490.
  president of, 415, 416.

Gideon, 333.

God, care of, for his people, 265.
  greatness and power of, 21-23, 178, 179, 263, 267.
  ideal of, 95.
  love of, for sinners, 140, 157, 181-184.
  love of, revealed to Enoch, 51.

Godliness, power of, 59, 60.

Good Shepherd, parable of, 211.

Gospel, and medical missionary work, 232.
  no place in, for caste, 333.
  support of, 224-228.

Gospel ministry, examination for, 437-440.
  how regarded by God, 63.
  preparation for, essential, 70-72.
  young men to enter, 63, 65.

Gospel work, helps in, 249-294.

Government, civil, recognition of, 389, 390.

Health, importance of, 242.
  preservation of, 239-242, 244, 422, 423.

Health food business, the, 363.

Health reform, extremes in, to be avoided, 233.
  God's purpose in, 242, 348.
  how to present, 233.
  ministers to teach, 231, 232, 347, 348.

Helps in gospel work, 249-294.

Heresies, 299, 305-310.
  see also Dangers ; Fanaticism.

Hezekiah, healing of, 220.

Higher classes, Christ's work for, 45-47.
  efforts to be put forth for, 361.

Holy Spirit, an aid in study of Bible, 100, 253.
  given to strengthen and encourage, 66.

Message of truth — *Continued.*
  presentation of, 66, 88, 325-329, 470.
  result of proclamation of, 27-29.
  to be given to rich and poor, 436.
Methods, 345-410.
  defective, 381-383.
  house-to-house, 181-191.
  in city missions, 364-366.
  in cities, 345-363.
  in mission fields, 458-463, 468-470.
  in new fields, 119, 120, 191, 192.
  less preaching, more teaching, 76.
  Paul's, a lesson for us, 102, 118.
  sowing and reaping, 409, 410.
Ministers, and business matters, 271, 422-425.
  and commercial work, 271, 339-342.
  and manual work, 234-238, 240.
  as under-shepherds, 181-248.
  as watchmen, 13-15.
  attitude of, toward opposers of truth, 372-376, 380.
  care to be shown in choosing, 438, 439.
  causes of failure in work of, 249-251, 271, 272, 290-292, 319-321, 337, 338, 367-371, 381-383, 425, 437, 438.
  Christ's ambassadors, 13.
  Christ their efficiency, 14, 16, 19, 36-39, 57, 65, 80, 108, 166, 263, 336, 416-419.
  compared to stars, 13, 14.
  dangers of, 124-132, 153-155, 297-342.
  deportment of, 17, 20, 60, 91, 124-132, 145, 172-174.
  dress of, 172-174.
  duty of, to children, 204-206, 271 ; to youth, 207-212 ; to unworked cities, 353.
  examination of, for the ministry, 71, 72, 437-439.
  financial burdens of, 449, 450.
  God's purpose for, 124.
  greatness of work of, 18, 19, 95, 172, 173.
  home life of, 204-206.
  how regarded by God, 481, 482.
  ideal for, 108, 109.
  illustrations of true, 51-62.
  illustration of work of, 197.
  in centers of travel, 352.
  in discouragement, to look to Christ, 49.

Ministers — *Continued.*
  in meeting opposition, to keep to the affirmative, 358, 359, 373-376, 379, 380.
  in the pulpit, 147-179.
  objects of Satan's special attacks, 124.
  older, to educate younger, 75, 101-103.
  preparation of, for service, 22, 23, 69-109.
  public prayer, 175, 176.
  pulpit deportment, 172-174.
  qualifications needed by, 111, 437-439 ; consecration, 111-116, 254-258 ; courtesy, 121-123 ; decision, 133-135 ; humility, 143, 144 ; propriety, 124-132 ; tact, 117-120 ; thoroughness, 367-371.
  remuneration of, 271, 449-452.
  responsibility of, 13-17, 20-23, 30-35, 64, 76, 124-128, 150-152, 186, 187, 253, 315, 342, 396.
  reward of, 18, 85, 267, 482.
  secret of power of, 60.
  speech of, to be guarded, 163, 164.
  taxing labors of, 450-452.
  to be Bible students, 249, 251-253.
  to cultivate the talent of speech, 87-91.
  to give evidence of true conversion, 79, 80.
  to give much time to prayer, 76, 254-258.
  to preach Christ and His word, 147-152, 158-160.
  to set church-members at work, 196-200, 351, 352.
  to show increased love for souls, 65
  to show self-sacrifice, 16, 56.
  to teach church-members regarding the tithe, 224-228.
  to train helpers, 76, 210, 211.
  what to preach, 147-160, 162.
  words of counsel to, 307-310.
  work of, compared to that of physicians, 338.
Ministers, young, 63-72, 81-85, 101-109.
  association of, with older ministers, 101-103.
  guarding against indolence, 106, 107, 237, 238.
  not to forfeit individuality, 102, 103.
  repaying hospitality, 106.
  to be close Bible students, 98-100, 105, 106.